CW01653934

THE SHAAR PRESS

THE JUDAICA IMPRINT
FOR THOUGHTFUL PEOPLE

From The Bronx to Bnei Brak: The amazing true story of Rabbi Yossi Wallis

THE SHAAR PRESS

INCREDIBLE!

RABBI NACHMAN SELTZER

First edition – First impression / July 2016

Published by **SHAAR PRESS**
Distributed by MESORAH PUBLICATIONS, LTD.
4401 Second Avenue / Brooklyn, N.Y 11232 / (718) 921-9000

Distributed in Israel by SIFRIATI / A. GITLER
Moshav Magshimim / Israel

Distributed in Europe by LEHMANNS
Unit E, Viking Business Park, Rolling Mill Road / Jarrow, Tyne and Wear, NE32 3DP/ England

Distributed in Australia and New Zealand by GOLDS WORLD OF JUDAICA
3-13 William Street / Balaclava, Melbourne 3183 / Victoria Australia

Distributed in South Africa by KOLLEL BOOKSHOP
Northfield Centre / 17 Northfield Avenue / Glenhazel 2192, Johannesburg, South Africa

ISBN 10: 1-4226-1775-0 / ISBN 13: 978-1-4226-1775-5

Printed in the United States of America by Noble Book Press

TABLE OF CONTENTS

BOOK FOUR: Reunions

THANK YOU

The most important thank-you goes to the Master of the World for all His kindness to us, His children.

I would like to take this special moment to thank my father and mother, my wife, Sandy, my sons and daughters, my sons-in-law and daughters-in-law. Thank you for all the amazing years. I cannot tell you how much your support means to me.

A big thank-you goes to Rabbi Berel Wein and Rabbi Ashley Lazarus for all the creative work we have done together and for introducing me to Rabbi Nachman Seltzer, who wrote my story with enthusiasm, attention to detail, devotion to the project, and with a graceful turn of phrase that resonates throughout. Our collaboration led to an unlikely yet powerful friendship, for which we are both grateful.

The publication of this book grants me the opportunity to publicly thank my good friends Rabbis Shalom Srebrenik, Zvi Inbal, and Yehuda Rubin—the pioneers of Arachim, who invested so much effort to return me to the proper path.

Above all, I must thank my rebbe, Rav Chaim Greineman *zt"l*—and his family—who guided the Arachim organization and the Wallis family for decades with his insightful advice and words of wisdom and compassion.

I miss you with all my heart.

Rabbi Yossi Wallis

INTRODUCTION

For many years I kept my family's stories bottled up inside myself and didn't share them with anyone. They were too extraordinary, too improbable, and I feared that no one would believe I was telling the truth. But at the end of his life, my father made a request of me, asking me to please share the stories—especially those that happened to him during the war years—with the world. I was torn when it came to fulfilling his mandate, since his stories seemed incredible even to me, who had heard them so many times.

I am not a historian, but I knew one thing beyond a shadow of a doubt: If I were to finally share my father's stories, and my own personal history, with the world, I needed witnesses who could testify to their truth, credible witnesses who could stand up and back up my claims. Without their testimony, the stories would seem fanciful and outlandish. So I prayed.

"I want to fulfill my father's request," I told Hashem, "but I can't do it without proof. If the people reading the stories find contradictions or details that don't make sense, the Wallis family credibility will be destroyed, as will our claims of accuracy. Please send me witnesses!"

And Hashem, in His infinite wisdom, sent me witnesses. Not one or two, but many, who corroborated what I had been told by my father. They came forth from different cities around the world and found me, each on his own, through numerous individual paths. When pieced together, their testimony was conclusive and my father's claims irrefutable.

You, the reader, can rest assured that everything you are about to read actually happened. You will come to love the characters and identify with the heroes. And the most amazing thing about all of this is that this book is not a work of fiction, but rather a truthful narrative of events that really happened, all documented and thoroughly researched.

Together, we will embark on an epic saga through hundreds of years and some of the saddest and most dramatic epochs in both Jewish history and my family's personal history. As we journey through time and space I hope you emerge inspired to do your part in the battle for the soul of the Jewish people.

Rabbi Yossi Wallis
March 2016

PROLOGUE

There are statistics, and they are impressive. Since its founding in 1979, over 500,000 people have attended Arachim seminars on Jewish thought and observance, given in five continents and in seven languages. In the year 2014, 30,000 people participated in more than 200 seminars, with programming by Arachim's more than 700 staff members and thousands of volunteers.

There are statistics—and there are stories. Countless stories of Jews finding their way back to their heritage through Arachim—army generals and men selling vegetables in Yerushalayim's Machaneh Yehudah market; scientists and lawyers and journalists and business czars and cab drivers and prisoners sitting in their cells; Jews who thought of themselves as traditional but knew little of Torah, and Jews who hated anything to do with their religion—every one of these Arachim "returnees" has a story.

Yes, there are statistics and there are stories. And behind those statistics and those stories stands the towering figure of Rabbi Yossi Wallis.

This book tells his story.

Rabbi Nachman Seltzer
Ramat Beit Shemesh
March 2016

BOOK ONE

THE POWER OF ROOTS

CHAPTER ONE

The story of Rabbi Yossi Wallis and of Arachim starts long before 1979, when the organization was first formed.

Perhaps it begins a few hundred years ago, with one Rafael Vallis, the last Jew to be put to death at a public auto-da-fé in Spain. Rafael Vallis was a Jew of iron will, a Jew who would not bend, a Jew who stubbornly resisted the Catholic Church until the last breath had left his tortured body.

Every person is partially a product of his DNA and Rabbi Wallis is no exception. In order to understand who Rabbi Yossi Wallis is and how he developed into the person he became, one has to go back to that evil time when Jews were targeted by the Catholic Church for conversion or death.

♦ ♦ ♦

Having grown up without the luxury of grandparents—his had been murdered in the Holocaust—Yossi Wallis's sole connection to the past was through his parents. As he got older and felt the need to fill in the blanks in his family history, he naturally turned to his father for assistance.

"Abba," Yossi said, "I would like your help in sketching a family tree. Tell me about your father and your grandfather."

"I remember, as a child back in Poland, a *Chumash* that occupied a prominent place of honor in our home," his father replied. "It was ancient, passed down from father to son for generations. When you opened the cover you'd find a list of all the people who had owned this *Chumash*. Every father inscribed his name on the inside cover, and also wrote down what country the family was living in at that time. When the owner passed away and the *Chumash* was handed down to the next in line, his first task would be to inscribe how many years his father had lived and when he had passed away. This *Chumash* was a precious family artifact that was to be preserved at any cost. It would have been my greatest pleasure and honor to preserve this link to our history, but our entire family was sent to the camps and, as you know, there were no personal libraries there for the inmates' use. The *Chumash* and most of the information contained on the front cover were lost forever. But there are a number of details that I remember, such as the name of the first person on the list and some of the countries that our ancestors passed through on their improbable journey through Europe to Poland.

"The first name on the list was Rafael Vallis from Majorca in Spain."

"What happened to him?" Yossi, intrigued, asked his father.

"Rafael Vallis was put to death—burned at the stake in an auto-da-fé at the hands of the Inquisition, but I don't recall the dates."

"What else do you remember from the *Chumash*?"

"I remember that we passed through Holland and Italy, and that our family made a stop in Vienna, Austria, before moving to Poland, where we remained until the war."

His father reflected for a moment before continuing.

"The fact that the Wallis family owned such a *Chumash* wasn't really so remarkable. There were many families who recorded similar lists in a favored prayer book or *Chumash*, which they handed down from father to son just as we did."

"Why was this such a common tradition?"

"Take my family for example," his father replied. "When they were exiled from Spain they had no idea where they were heading or what awaited them when they got there. All they knew was that life was filled with challenges and the world was a difficult place for a Jew. So they wrote down the barest details—just enough information to make sure they never forgot their roots—where they were from and why they had to leave."

Yossi listened with rapt interest. This was the first time he was hearing any of this and it was fascinating. To think that the Wallis family had its origins in Spain of all places! But though it was interesting information, he didn't see what relevance it had for the Wallis family in this day and age.

♦ ♦ ♦

The years flew by. Having organized seminars in South America, Arachim had a team of lecturers on staff who were proficient in Spanish. With the idea of organizing a seminar for Spanish Jews germinating in his brain, Rabbi Wallis invited Yisroel Friedman, editor of the Israeli daily newspaper *Yated Ne'eman*, to travel to Spain with him to investigate the Jewish situation in cities like Madrid and Toledo. He explained to Rabbi Friedman that the Wallis family was able to trace its roots back to Majorca and that he was curious what a trip to Spain would uncover about his own family history.

"Let's see what we come up with. Who knows, maybe there's a story buried amid the ancient buildings and artifacts of a long-ago world."

As a journalist, Rabbi Friedman was intrigued. As the CEO of Arachim, so was Rabbi Wallis. The pair traveled to Spain, did some groundwork, and considered possible locations for seminars. It was a fascinating trip, but as he returned to Eretz Yisrael Rabbi Wallis wasn't sure what kind of future (if any) Arachim had in Spain.

One afternoon sometime later, Rabbi Wallis's son Asaf traveled to visit a friend in a Haifa hospital. While sitting in the waiting room, he happened to pick up a copy of the newspaper *Mekor Rishon*. An article immediately caught his attention.

The government of Spain consented to allow a team of researchers to enter the official archives of the Inquisition for historical research purposes.

The investigative team uncovered the name of the last Jews to be burned at the stake, in 1691. They were Rafael Vallis, his student Rafael Benito Terongi, and Terongi's sister, Catalina Terongi. They lived in Majorca and theirs was the last official auto-da-fé carried out by the Inquisition on Spanish soil.

Asaf called his father on the spot. "Abba, remember when Saba told you about his family's *Chumash* with the names inside the cover and how the name Rafael Vallis from Majorca, Spain, was the first name on the list?"

"Yes?"

"A team of researchers from Eretz Yisrael just returned from a trip to the Inquisition's archives in Madrid and they discovered that not only was Rafael Vallis burned by the Inquisition, he was one of the last Jews to be killed in that way in Spain."

The article had been written by an Israeli journalist named Birnbaum, who had been part of the team that had gone through the Inquisition records. Originally from Argentina, Birnbaum spoke Spanish fluently and was apparently quite an expert on Spanish-Jewish history. Rabbi Wallis called him, introduced himself, and asked the journalist to come meet with him at Arachim headquarters. Mr. Birnbaum accepted the invitation and, sitting with Rabbi Wallis in his office, related the epic story of Rafael Vallis and the Inquisition.

"In all probability," Birnbaum told the Arachim CEO, "this Rafael Vallis was your great-great-great-great-grandfather. The fact that he was from Majorca is in itself proof of this, because the name Vallis, which means 'valley' in Spanish, was bestowed upon the family by the Church when they originally converted. The Vallis name was only given to one Jewish Marrano family—and that family resided in Majorca."

"You have gotten us off to a very good start," Rabbi Wallis told the journalist, "but I need more information. This is my family history we're talking about and you've whetted my appetite for more. I want to know what happened to the family after the auto-da-fé. I want to know if there are any members of the Vallis family still living in Majorca or any other part of Spain. I want to get to the bottom of this."

"I'll be very happy to help you out," Birnbaum offered.

With the Spanish-speaking journalist on board, Rabbi Wallis was ready to return to Spain. He picked up the phone, dialed Yisroel Friedman from *Yated Ne'eman*, and told him that things were moving.

"Yisroel, I think we're standing on the cusp of a tremendous story. Let's return to Spain and check this whole thing out."

Rabbi Friedman didn't need to be asked twice. Any journalist would have jumped at the opportunity. A few days later, they were boarding a plane. Destination: Madrid, Spain—Inquisition headquarters.

Team Wallis was allowed into the archives—a seemingly endless array of documents describing the thousands of cases handled by the Inquisition over its years of operation. Mr. Birnbaum knew in which section to look, and it wasn't long before they were holding the case file of Rafael Vallis in their hands. It was over 1,000 pages long, filled with the densely flowing script of the Inquisition scribe who covered the trial and the dramatic events that transpired in the Inquisition dungeons and torture chambers in copious—and horrific—detail.

Historically, the Inquisition's official job was to investigate any Spanish citizen who had accepted the Church's offer to convert, making sure that they had not reverted to their original religion. When King Ferdinand and Queen Isabella first instituted the Inquisition, many Spanish Jews sold their businesses, converted their savings into gold and diamonds, and abandoned Spain for friendlier shores. Unfortunately this was not financially viable for people who made their money from the leasing of property. Selling was not an option, since they would have received a fraction of the value. They were trapped. It was those Jews who often ended up converting to Christianity, Marranos* living secret lives as Jews.

---

* There are several terms for the Jews forced to convert to Christianity in Spain. *Anusim*, literally "coerced," is a halachic term for any Jew forced to convert to another religion. *Conversos*, literally "converts," was coined by the Christian

Secret Jews who were found to be derelict in their relationship to their adopted faith were arrested, their property confiscated and divided between the Church and the Spanish government. Of course, avarice being what it is, this meant that the Inquisition focused on the wealthier Jews, and an entire network of spies were soon operating within the *converso* neighborhoods.

The Vallis file was an eye-opener. Since the majority of the family's wealth had been in property and buildings, the Church had been keen to find a reason to arrest them. But the extent of the family wealth ended up being detrimental to both church and state, since the lawyers for the government and the Church weren't able to arrive at a mutually satisfactory agreement. According to the case files, the warring factions never managed to come to terms and the property had never been divided, remaining embroiled in legal holdups until this very day! This meant that the Vallis family fortune was still theoretically available to be reclaimed from the Spanish government, and it also meant that the file had never been closed and remained active despite having been left to gather dust in the archives for a few hundred years.

There was one gigantic question running through Rabbi Wallis's brain: Why did the Inquisition arrest Rafael Vallis? What crime had his ancestor been accused of?

After reading through a few hundred pages of Spanish script, they eventually uncovered the answer. The Vallis family lived in Majorca, an island off the coast of Spain. It made sense for them to use the adjacent ocean for commerce. Rafael had been a successful businessman, specializing in import/export. His line of work had put him in touch with sailors and ship captains on a regular basis, and made him the de facto liaison between his community of *anusim* and the Jewish world that existed outside Spain. Vallis had been placed under scrutiny by the Holy Office of the Inquisition and their network of spies had been given strict

---

Church. *Marrano* literally means "swine" in Spanish, and was a derogatory term for the Jews in Spain who chose to convert. In this book I have tried to use whichever terms seems the most appropriate.

orders to keep him under close surveillance. No one doubted that Vallis was breaking the law; the only question was how.

With an entire team of Inquisition spies working full-time on the Vallis operation, it wasn't long before the order was given for his arrest.

◆ ◆ ◆

Ten o'clock in the morning. Palma de Majorca. The palm fronds were swaying silently in the crisp ocean breeze as the powerful Spanish sun began its inevitable climb to the center of the sky. The city streets were serene and undisturbed. All was silent save for the sound of a child laughing in a neighboring courtyard.

Suddenly the tranquil atmosphere was replaced by terror as a black coach pulled by two powerful horses turned the corner, coming to a halt outside the Vallis home. A squat monk in a black cloak emerged from the coach, a rolled-up scroll of parchment clutched tightly in his hand. If the street had been previously silent, now it had acquired the feeling of a tomb.

The monk strode nimbly around the coach and up to the front door. He knocked three times. The door was opened by a maid in uniform, who stared at the visitor, her face chalky white.

"Please call your master," said the monk.

It wasn't a request.

"Yes, Father," she replied, and scurried off to do his bidding.

Rafael Vallis presented himself to the monk within minutes.

"Good morning, Father, how can I help you?"

"You are ordered to accompany me to the headquarters of the Inquisition."

"On what charges?"

"You know your crimes. Pack a bag and come with me."

Vallis returned a few minutes later, satchel in hand, a grave expression on his face. His weeping wife stood in the doorway as he was ordered into the dreaded black coach with the Inquisition crest on its doors. With a casual flick of his whip, the coachman sent the horses down the peaceful street in the direction of the Inquisition headquarters of Palma de Majorca. On arrival, Rafael Vallis was tortured and interrogated ceaselessly and mercilessly, as the agents of the Inquisition attempted to learn everything they could about his sins.

♦ ♦ ♦

The Vallis file, now in his Israeli descendant's hands, cited some of the instructions that Rafael, under torture, admitted having received from rabbinical authorities abroad.

"We recommend that you instruct your coreligionists in one particular mitzvah which should be carried out, come what may."

The team was very curious. Which mitzvah had the rabbis from abroad chosen for the Jews of Spain to perform no matter what?

"We suggest that Spanish Jews keep the Fast of Esther to the best of their abilities. This is the most vital mitzvah for your community to keep right now."

The Inquisition files detailed the interrogations to which Rafael was subjected as they attempted to uncover the extent of his crimes.

Inquisitor: "Why did you specifically instruct your fellow Marranos to keep the Fast of Esther? What is so special about that particular commandment?"

Rafael Vallis: "I was given to understand by the rabbis from abroad that the reason it is so important that the Jews of Spain fast on that day is because through this action, they will never forget who they are and where they come from."

Inquisitor: "How so?"

Rafael Vallis: "Queen Esther was the first Marrano in Jewish history. On the surface she pretended to be like everyone else, but on the inside, she never ceased keeping the commandments and acting like a daughter of Israel. Remembering the Fast of Esther, which commemorates her bravery, will also remind us who we are and the life we used to lead. Another additional reason for choosing a fast day for our commandment is because it is a very easy commandment to keep from a practical point of view, since nobody has to know if a person is choosing not to eat."

The files stated that Rafael Vallis was charged with spreading the awareness of this commandment to his male coreligionists, including his student and relative, Rafael Benito Terongi, who was also being held by the Inquisition. Terongi's sister, Catalina Terongi, was arrested for doing the same among the community of female conversos. After being subjected to unspeakable tortures on the dreaded rack and wheel, the Inquisition obtained Vallis's confession and he was put on trial, where an Inquisition judge, face covered with a cowl, read out his sentence in flat tones.

"You have been sentenced by the Holy Office of the Inquisition to be burned at the stake for what you've done. If you would have contented yourselves with performing a commandment or two in the privacy of your own home, that would have been one thing. But you didn't stop there. You were determined to instigate rebellion, while promulgating unrest within the newly converted members of our faith. By spreading the edicts of the rabbinical authority from abroad, you have overstepped all boundaries.

"And so, by order of the Church, all of you have been sentenced to be burned at the stake. Before you are taken to the pyre, however, you will be tortured in the Inquisitional dungeons for an additional two years in punishment for your heinous crimes against the church."

♦ ♦ ♦

There were many ways to kill a Marrano. It all depended on the severity of his crimes and whether or not he had officially repented for his sins. Neither Rafael Vallis nor Rafael Benito Terongi or his sister Catalina Terongi had expressed any desire to repent and it was therefore decided to punish them in the worst way possible. Instead of binding them to the wood that would then be set on fire, the three were to be placed in close proximity to the flames—close enough for the flames to burn them, far enough for it to take an awfully long time. The Church, in its mercy, had their priestly representative standing by, cross in hand, waiting for the prisoner to express a desire for repentance. The moment this occurred, the priest would approach the burning Marrano, wait for him to express a sincere desire to repent, and then the man would be removed from the fire. (Generally, he would still be killed, but in a less painful way.) Rafael Vallis and the Terongis had been provided with ample opportunities to do "*teshuvah*" throughout their incarceration, but had never once shown any interest in returning to the life of a Spanish Christian. The Church was very angry with them and intent on punishing them to the fullest extent of the law.

The handwritten files uncovered in the Inquisitional archives were fascinating to read: the tight, flowing script bearing testimony to the utmost seriousness with which the case had been treated. Yossi Wallis and his comrades read and read, assimilating every detail of the investigation, interrogation, subsequent years of punishment and torture, and the eventual execution.

Mr. Birnbaum translated further.

"On the day of the auto-da-fé," he told them, "30,000 citizens of Palma de Majorca gathered to watch the spectacle in the grand square situated directly in front of the local municipal seat of government. In a complex religious ceremony that lasted half the day, the prisoners were eventually removed from the Palace of the Inquisition and led through the streets of the town for about a kilometer, until they reached the square where the auto-da-fé was to take place. A giant wooden cross was planted in the ground every 20 feet or so along the route to the pyre, and as they walked, the crowd accompanied them singing religious songs. Every religious symbol meant another chance for the prisoners to stop, to bow down, kiss the cross, and apologize for their misdeeds. The three prisoners did not utilize any of these opportunities.

"When they reached the square, they were manhandled onto the stage, the pyre was made ready for kindling, and they were tied to pillars just adjacent to the pyre. Close enough to feel the awful heat, far enough that death would be yearned for.

"The mayor of Majorca was honored with lighting the pyre.

"After some time tied near the stake, the heat grew so powerful that it was impossible to stand in close proximity to the stage...their skin blistering and singed...color a fiery red. They were being burned slowly...roasted alive...as the populace of Majorca watched in silent glee and the priests waited to see if they'd repent before the life was literally sucked out of them...

"At one point, Rafael Vallis tried to lift his hand. The heat must have become unbearable and he couldn't stand it anymore. The merciful priest—crucifix in hand—had been waiting for the signal and came rushing over, intent on saving Rafael's soul...

"Catalina was tied to a neighboring pillar. Upon seeing Vallis raising his hand, she screamed with her final bit of strength, 'Don't give in. They are only able to burn our clothing, they won't be able to touch our souls!'

"The moment he heard those words, Rafael Vallis motioned for the priest to leave him alone. The disappointed priest retreated and the three were burned at the stake, dying in full view of the people they had known their entire lives."

So concluded the Inquisition's 1,000-page description of the Vallis case. Rabbi Wallis photocopied every single page of his ancestor's story for his personal archives and left the Inquisition headquarters ready to investigate further. Somehow, he had a feeling that the story of Rafael Vallis was just beginning.

♦ ♦ ♦

Team Wallis had been in the Palace of the Inquisition for hours. When they finally emerged from within, blinking and squinting from the rays of the powerful Spanish sun, Rabbi Wallis knew that while his journey may have begun in Madrid, it wouldn't be over until he visited Palma de Majorca. He needed to stand in the same cobblestoned square where they'd burned his ancestor hundreds of years earlier and to walk the route where they had led him from the Inquisition building to the pyre. Most importantly, he had to meet the people of Majorca.

They hailed a cab and made the return drive to the airport, where he booked three tickets on the next flight leaving Madrid for Palma de Majorca, a magnificent vacation island on the coast of the Mediterranean. It was time to revisit the Wallis family history. Rafael Vallis was his great-(several times over) grandfather, and Rabbi Wallis owed it to him to uncover as much of his life and story as he could.

After all, this was his *zeide* they were talking about.

♦ ♦ ♦

Waiting for their flight to take off from the Madrid airport, the rabbi contacted a man on his list of Spanish experts to ask for advice.

"What should I be searching for in Majorca?"

"You are looking for people who share your family name. You are also searching for people with a Marrano past. That shouldn't be difficult to find since vast numbers of Majorca inhabitants have a past that involves the Marranos and the Inquisition, on one level or another."

"Any particular area we should be searching in?"

"Check out the ancient marketplace in Majorca. One corner of the market is devoted to fine crafts: the silversmiths and goldsmiths. That might be a good place to begin. Traditionally those were Jewish businesses. Oh, and one more thing."

"Yes?"

"Tell the townspeople you're looking for the *Chueta*."

"The what?"

"*Chueta*. It means 'pig' in the local dialect. That's the derogatory term the local Christians used when referring to the Marrano converts. Around these parts of Europe, people have long memories. Some families converted 500 years ago and the Catholics still call them pigs."

He thanked the expert and ran to catch his plane.

As the jet winged its way through fluffy white clouds in the bluest of Spanish skies, the splendid island of Majorca became visible through the cabin windows. The plane began its descent and Rabbi Wallis said to himself, *It may have taken a few hundred years, but a Wallis is back now—here to right a wrong. Majorca—I have come home.*

♦ ♦ ♦

One might have assumed that after hundreds of years of living the Catholic life of Spanish gentiles, the Jews of Majorca would have completely assimilated and would all be married to non-Jews. In an interesting turn of events, however, the Catholics had been unanimous in their decision to keep the two communities as separate as possible. They did this by assigning the Marranos special names and by forcing them to obtain permission from the Church anytime one of them wanted to get married. Despite their having officially converted, the Church would only allow the Marranos to marry one another.

The Marranos were also forbidden to leave the island, weren't allowed to attend university, and were unable to rise to the rank of officer in the military. Jewish blood was filled with impurity—even after they converted—and the Spanish made sure that the Jews never forgot who they really were. The Marranos weren't even allowed to attend the regular churches of their countrymen. Instead, their synagogues were turned into churches and that's where they were forced to pray—ensuring yet another level of separation from the locals.

♦ ♦ ♦

Majorca was beautiful. People use the word "beautiful" a lot, but in this case, the term was absolutely justified. The island was simply breathtaking. Lush vegetation grew in heavy abundance, the beaches were resplendent with millions of grains of the whitest sand, and the ocean was a shade of blue just short of sapphire. A popular tourist destination, one heard a hodgepodge of languages while walking the streets, and the sound of Spanish music was never far away. But they hadn't come to Majorca to examine ancient castles or to watch a bullfight. They were there to right a wrong, and to do that the team needed to meet some Jews.

They had been advised to go to the marketplace, and they followed their instructions. Leaving behind the glittery world of modern hotels and restaurants, the three of them, Wallis, Birnbaum, and Friedman, plunged into the ancient section of Majorca, in the direction of the marketplace, where commerce took on a simpler feel. Gone were the tall buildings and sense of newness. It was as if they were entering a time warp—traveling back a few hundred years into an ancient world. Pots boasting tangled swaths of flowers emitted a delicious aroma. Faded wooden signs attached to nearby stone walls swung high above them, advertising assorted business establishments. Rough workmen strode past the little group, their hands swinging back and forth. The alleyways were narrow and tight, the stores cramped, the lighting dim.

Rabbi Wallis stopped a passerby.

"Silversmith?"

He saw the confusion on the man's face and realized that he didn't know what he was talking about.

"Marranos?"

Now the other smiled, nodding his swarthy head in vague recognition.

"*Chueta*?"

The man pointed toward the other side of the marketplace.

How fascinating it was. The Catholics had so wanted their Jewish neighbors to convert, had been willing to burn them at the stake to achieve that aim—but when the Jews had finally become their coreligionists, theirs to befriend, the non-Jews were unable to truly welcome them. They were still referring to them by the ancient epithet of *Chueta*—piglet. Even now. After so very, very long.

"Vallis," Rabbi Wallis asked the man, trying to pronounce the name like a Spaniard would.

The stranger pointed at a group of stores.

The Vallis craftsmen of Majorca owned a factory and store that sold all manner of gold and silver jewelry. Entering the establishment, the team couldn't help but feel a sense of excitement. There was a man standing behind the counter. He was slightly older than the rabbi, with a serious demeanor and the air of a successful businessman.

"Excuse me?"

"Yes?"

"Is your name Vallis?"

He nodded.

"The Vallis family that were secret Jews?"

Another nod, perhaps a shade reluctant.

"Tell me, are you a descendant of Rafael Vallis?"

"Yes."

"How do you know?"

"Because of the Church."

"What do you mean?"

"Every time one of us gets married, the Church keeps a record of it. They've been doing this for hundreds of years. They have a family tree for every *converso* family, which documents the name of every family member, going back generations. We possess a copy of our family tree. In fact, it's right here in the basement of the store. If you'll excuse me for a minute, I'll run downstairs and bring it up to show you."

"Please do that."

He returned with the family tree in his hand. A long, parchment-type document. A simple perusal of the writing showed that he was a direct descendant of Rafael Vallis.

Rabbi Wallis looked him in the eye.

"You're the great-great-great-great-grandson of Rafael Vallis and I'm the great-great-great-great-grandson of Rafael Vallis—that means that both of us are family. Hello, cousin. Bet you didn't know that you have relatives who look like me."

"So we're cousins," the man replied. "So what?"

The rabbi wasn't really sure.

"I don't know yet," he admitted. "Right now, I'm just enjoying the most unlikely reunion ever—between the Orthodox Jew from Israel and his Marrano cousin from Majorca!"

They shared a laugh.

"Tell me something."

"For you, cousin, anything."

"How many people like you live here in Majorca—descendants of the Marranos, kept track of by the Church?"

"About 20,000 people."

Rabbi Wallis could have whistled in disbelief.

"Twenty thousand people descended from Jews, who never intermarried with the local population?"

"They wouldn't let us. It was always *Chueta* marrying *Chueta*."

"But if that's the case and everything is written down with such exact record-taking, then that means all of you are still Jews!"

His cousin gave him a dubious look.

"No, really," Rabbi Wallis insisted. "Think about it. None of you ever married non-Jews. You weren't allowed to. You married Jews, your parents were Jews, you prayed with Jews, you were kept separate by the Church, you have your own family trees... I have to tell you, cousin, for all practical purposes, all 20,000 of you are as Jewish as I am!"

The man stared at his unexpected visitor for a long time in silence.

"How can you possibly claim that I'm a Jew," he finally burst out. "I've lived my entire life as a Catholic!"

"The Torah, the bible of the Jewish people, considers you a Jew."

"But I don't live my life according to the laws of the Torah! I've never even heard of the Torah!! We might be cousins, but you can't seriously expect me to accept what you're saying!"

He was right. How on earth was Rabbi Wallis going to convince this man that he was supposed to live his life according to the dictates of a Torah he'd never heard of?

"Are there other members of the Vallis family living here?"

"Are you kidding? Majorca is crawling with your cousins!"

The next thing Rabbi Wallis knew, the message had gone out that a long-lost Israeli cousin had just surfaced at the jewelry store in the marketplace. Vallis cousins began streaming en masse toward the store, all jabbering in Spanish and all excited to meet him. It was collectively decided to take the three Israelis on a tour of the Jewish ghetto of Majorca, whose weather-beaten facades had been in existence for over 1,500 years. They were shown a church called Shaarei Tzion, which had been a synagogue before it became a church, and whose name had been retained. The "church" was decorated with a wide assortment of beautifully crafted menorahs and silver pointers that had been used when reading from the Torah. Unwelcome by the Catholics and unable to join the regular prayer services at the local churches, the *anusim* of Majorca had remained in their houses of worship, amid the religious artifacts they knew so well.

Rabbi Wallis turned to his host.

"I understand that you couldn't intermarry for the last few hundred years. What about now, have things changed? Are the non-Jews more open to marrying *Chueta* now?"

The craftsman shook his head.

"Most consider us low-class merchandise even now, hundreds of years after the Inquisition has shut down. Both groups stay far away from each other. Even now."

The entrance to Shaarei Tzion

Moving through the ghetto's narrow streets, they passed some of the *Chueta* homes.

"Look here," one of the excited group said, catching their attention. "See that doorway?"

Rabbi Wallis gave the doorway a closer inspection, and noticed that a cross had been engraved in the spot where there had once been a mezuzah.

"The Church forced the Jews to put crosses up in every doorway. Any house sporting a cross in the doorway belongs to a Jew."

Ironically, the Catholics had never been forced to hang crosses in the doorway, so the sight of a cross in the doorway was a clear giveaway whose house it was.

Meanwhile, their visit was causing a commotion in the city. Everyone was talking about the visitor who had arrived from Israel accompanied by a few journalists: how he was claiming to be a descendant of the Marranos and that he seemed to be related to half the town. The news reached the local municipality offices and Rabbi Wallis and his friends were invited down to city hall to meet

An underground oven used by Marranos to bake matzah for Pesach

the authorities. They gathered in the mayor's office, surrounded by a cadre of local politicians smiling for all they were worth. The atmosphere was all light and goodwill, and handshakes were exchanged, along with pictures taken for the local newspapers.

"Mr. Wallis," said the mayor of Majorca, "we are so pleased to make your acquaintance! We consider you an honored guest of our city and want to offer you honorary Spanish citizenship."

The mayor was beaming, the vice mayor was beaming. Friendship and love extraordinaire!

Until the guest of honor spoke. "An honorary citizen of Spain? No, thank you. In fact, I would be embarrassed to be the holder of Spanish citizenship—even if it was only honorary!"

Their faces fell.

"Why do you feel this way?" they asked him in their careful English, a look of deep pain on their faces. "You're a native son of Spain; you should be excited to be given such an opportunity!"

Rabbi Wallis had his answer ready. "Your great-grandfather burned my great-grandfather at the stake. A short walk from where we are standing is the Palace of the Inquisition, where they tortured him first. Your ancestors turned your Jewish citizens' houses of prayer into churches, and you never once felt the need to put up a sign or a monument commemorating the evil that was done here in Majorca! It's a disgrace, a disgrace!! You ignored all the infamy that happened here, acting as if nothing evil ever occurred! You've treated the Marranos as third-class citizens for hundreds of years. Now you want to offer me the chance to become an honorary citizen and you're surprised that I'm not interested in accepting your offer?!"

"So what do you want?" the mayor asked him.

"One," the rabbi replied, ticking details off on his fingers, "put up signs explaining what happened here—the history—the atrocities—so that the citizens of Spain and the tourists know the real story of Majorca's Jews. Second, now that we know exactly what happened to my great-grandfather—how he was burned at the stake before some 30,000 cheering Catholics standing right here—I would like to return to Majorca on the Jewish anniversary of the day that he died, on the day we Jews call a *yahrtzeit*. I want to return here with a quorum of 10 Jews and I want to say the Kaddish prayer for Rafael Vallis on the day he died, in the place where he died. That's what I want!"

Their faces were grave with concern and disappointment.

"Mr. Wallis," said the mayor, "I'm afraid that you are requesting the impossible."

"Why's that?"

"Because Majorca is a major tourism hub. People travel to enjoy our beautiful beaches, luxurious hotels, and historical relics from around the world. Many of the tourists who support our local economy are Muslims from North Africa. We like to keep things peaceful and nonreligious. The kind of plaques you are suggesting we put up would offend these visitors. Conducting a ceremony with 10 Jews and the recital of Jewish prayers would offend these visitors. We're not looking for trouble here. I hope you can understand me. All we want is peace and prosperity."

"I hear you loud and clear," Rabbi Wallis responded, "and here's what I suggest. Forward my request to the government in

Madrid and ask them to make the decision. That way it's out of your hands and you won't get in trouble."

They parted on good terms, handshakes all around.

"Our offer for honorary Spanish citizenship still stands," they told the rabbi.

"First let me know what the prime minister decides about saying Kaddish for Rafael Vallis and then I'll see about becoming a citizen."

Rabbi Wallis, Rabbi Friedman, and Mr. Birnbaum left the municipality, took a taxi to the airport, and retraced their steps back to Madrid and then on to Eretz Yisrael. It had been a fascinating journey back in time. And now Rabbi Wallis faced halachic questions requiring broader shoulders than his own. He needed to go to Bnei Brak: to the *beis din*, the Jewish court of law of Rav Nissim Karelitz.

♦ ♦ ♦

Standing before Rav Nissim Karelitz, Rabbi Wallis laid out his problem.

Rabbi Wallis and Rav Nissim Karelitz *shlita*

"Rebbe," he began, "if what I saw with my own eyes in Majorca is accurate—and I see no reason to doubt this information—then we have 20,000 men, women, and children who are Jewish and very possibly do not even need to convert! The maternal line was Jewish straight down through the generations. This is all backed up by their family trees and by records kept by the Church, which we were given access to. I'm not a *rav* and I'm not qualified to make a halachic ruling on such a complicated and sensitive question. This is a job for a *beis din*. Please send a *dayan* down to Spain and tell us what is incumbent upon Arachim to do in this situation. Arachim's mission is to teach Jews their heritage. Do we reach out and teach the Marranos of Majorca? Are these people Jewish or not? If they are Jewish, we will fly in our lecturers and teach them what it means to be a Jew. If not, not. We're not looking to convert anyone."

In the end, the *beis din* decided to send a team of rabbinic judges over to Spain to formulate an official halachic ruling on the matter. The team of expert *dayanim*, including the *av beis din*, Rav Yisroel Weisel, flew to Spain to investigate the situation. This meant revisiting the Inquisition archives, meeting some of the 20,000 descendants of the Marranos, and carrying out a painstaking examination of the records that had been scrupulously kept by everyone involved. The team concluded its task and returned to Bnei Brak with all the relevant information. It was on the day before Shavuos—the holiday that marks the giving of the Torah—when the rabbinic court finalized its verdict, issued in Bnei Brak and stamped by Rav Nissim Karelitz.

It stated as follows: "All descendants of Marranos who reside in Majorca, Spain, and possess the necessary documents attesting to their family tree and lineage, are Jewish in every way and need to be dealt with accordingly."

The *psak* of Rav Nissim's *beis din* was revolutionary in the sense that it provided the possibility to change the lives of 20,000 people, because now that his suspicions had been confirmed, Rabbi Wallis began sending his Arachim outreach workers to give seminars to people who were "pigs" no longer; they were Jews.

CHAPTER TWO

A surprise awaited Rabbi Yossi Wallis in the office one morning. A thick vellum envelope, rich in texture and exuding the sense of wealth, rested in the inbox on the polished conference table. The return address identified the sender as the Spanish parliament, Madrid. Rabbi Wallis removed the expensive paper from the envelope, glanced at the crest of arms prominently displayed on top of the page, and read the somewhat brief message informing him that his extraordinary request to say Kaddish at the municipal hall in Majorca had been approved, and that he was being officially invited by the Spanish government to do just that.

Not only was he to be granted the opportunity to say Kaddish for Rafael Vallis in the town square of Majorca, there would be a formal ceremony to which the Spanish government was planning to invite the ambassadors of all their major allies and friends: the United States, Britain, France, and more. The ceremony would be attended by many of the top echelon of the Spanish government, and many major newspapers including *The New York Times* would be invited to attend.

Not content to stop there, the mayor of Majorca would deliver a major address at which he would read an official Spanish letter of apology for the atrocities that had been visited onto the Jewish citizens of Spain hundreds of years earlier at the hands of the Church and the Inquisition. This was to be the first time Spain would be making a public apology for the crimes of the Inquisition. The mayor of Majorca had been chosen to give the address, since it had been the mayor of Majorca who had lit the fire that had burned Rafael Vallis and two other Jews at the final auto-da-fé on Spanish soil. Everything was coming full circle.

"Please recite the Kaddish," they wrote in the letter, "and when you finish with the prayer, the government of Spain would appreciate if you would say a few brief words."

With that, the ceremony would conclude.

Of course Rabbi Wallis asked his rabbinic advisers before giving his secretary the go-ahead to book the ticket. He was advised to attend. There was one additional detail that he needed to make sure of before boarding the plane for Majorca.

"Don't bother inviting all the VIPs," he wrote back to his government contact. "The main thing is that the government of Spain makes sure to invite every single descendant of Marranos living in Majorca. Again, I don't care about anyone else—invite them or don't invite them—but I want to make certain the 20,000 Marrano children are there to hear the public apology from the mayor."

Rabbi Wallis was hoping that hearing the apology would stir something long dormant within their souls and help them realize that they were not ordinary Spaniards, and certainly not Catholics like everyone else.

◆ ◆ ◆

The Spanish government went all out for the big day. There was a bright-red carpet leading up the stairs to the dais and a flock of pure white doves was released into the sky in the middle of the ceremony. Rabbi Wallis does not consider himself to be much of a musical connoisseur, but the full orchestra in black tuxedo and white tie seemed formal and professional in every sense of the

(l to r): Michael Freund, Director of Shavei Israel;
the mayor of Palma; Rabbi Wallis; Rabbi Nissan ben Avraham

word. The Spanish government apparently knew how to throw a party.

Taking his seat on the dais, the rabbi found himself in close proximity to the mayor, who shook his hand and leaned over to whisper a few words into his ear in accented English.

"You should know that I'm up for reelection in a few weeks' time," he said, "and the speech that I'm about to give today will ensure that I am going to lose the election."

"So what are you going to do?"

"I'm going to apologize. It's worth it and it's time."

(He did lose the election.)

"At this time," said the master of ceremonies, after a few high-ranking politicians gave their speeches, "we would like to invite Rabbi Joseph Wallis to rise and recite the Kaddish for his ancestor Rafael Vallis, who was burned at the stake at the hands of the Inquisition."

Rabbi Wallis said the Kaddish—every single word of that age-old prayer recited with great concentration and emotion—and when he finished, he explained to the assembled what the Kaddish meant and its significance. He was then invited to speak.

He had purposely not prepared a speech, understanding that an occasion such as this would demand something really special that mere written words would find difficult to convey. Since he hadn't been sure who would be attending the ceremony until he actually saw them face-to-face, Rabbi Wallis had decided to allow his heart to speak, and that's exactly what he did.

"I would like to share two things with you," he began. "First, I never, ever thought, even in my wildest dreams, that one day I'd be standing up here in front of the municipality of Majorca, Spain, to accept an official apology on behalf of my ancestor Rafael Vallis. I want you all to look at me. I'm a Jew, authentic, original, the real thing. Black skullcap on my head, beard and sidelocks. Unashamed. Unapologetic.

"It was people like me whom the Inquisition wanted to destroy. They burned my great-grandfather and thought they had taken care of the problem: everyone converted, no more Jews.

"But no. Here I am, as Jewish as Rafael Vallis was!

"I'm back on the island. The Jews are back on the island and the Jewish religion is still very much a part of millions of lives around the world. This can be summed up in one statement: '*Am Yisrael chai*.' The Jewish nation lives on and will never be destroyed, no matter what anyone says or tries.

"That is why I flew here today, so that all of you should see a real Jew and understand that the Jewish nation is alive and well. There was an Inquisition, there were pogroms, there were Cossacks, there was even a Holocaust, and still we are back. That's point number one.

"But there's something else," he continued. "I didn't have to fly on a plane to Madrid and Majorca just to tell you what I just said. I could have sent a telegram, a fax, an e-mail—even a video. So why did I travel all the way here to stand before you on this momentous occasion?

"We, the Jewish nation, have a rule: '*Kol Yisrael areivim zeh lazeh*—Every Jew is responsible for his fellow Jew.' You, the Jews of Majorca, are our brothers and sisters forever, no matter what happens. As long as you remain Jews, we will follow you to the ends of the earth, to show you the path that will lead you back to who you really are. This is the reason why I made sure to come and physically stand here in front of you today, and why I would travel anywhere in the world to visit my fellow Jews. Because we, your Jewish family, care about you and are responsible for you."

The Marranos of Majorca, who had been seated in the front half of the audience, hardly knew how to react. No one had ever spoken to them like this before. They had always been treated like second-class citizens, and here was a rabbi, of all people, informing them that there were people around the world who loved them like family, despite the fact that they had never even met them!

Suddenly the aisles were packed with people crashing the stage, all of them asking, begging the Israeli rabbi, "Tell us what we are supposed to do."

Rabbi Wallis looked at them—at his cousins, and at so many more who weren't related by blood, but who were connected to him by ties going back to Mount Sinai—and said, "You have a lot of work ahead of you. You have to come back to the Torah."

In the months and years that followed, Arachim organized seminars for the Jews of Majorca with the organization's Spanish-speaking lecturers. Slowly, slowly, they made inroads, to the point that some of the Marranos of Majorca have flown to Eretz Yisrael and have undergone *giyur lechumrah*. Among them were twin sisters who went by the double last name Vallis Vallis, being descended from the Vallis family both paternally and maternally.

Rabbi Wallis sums up his encounter with Majorca, and with his martyred ancestor, with the following words:

"Every time that I think about the story of Rafael Vallis, I picture him bound to the wooden beams, the fire scorching his skin, the pain unbearable. I see him raising his hand, calling the priest, wanting, needing, to make it stop. To make the pain stop. And then I remember how a Jewish woman screamed out with her last vestige of strength, 'They are only able to burn our clothing, but they can't touch our souls!' and I tell myself that words like those are the backbone that have kept our nation intact from time immemorial. How it was the power of the Jewish women that kept us strong: from Queen Esther in Achashveirosh's palace, to Catalina Terongi being burned at the stake in a square in Majorca, Spain, in 1691."

♦ ♦ ♦

There's another element to the story that is not absolutely connected but which deserves to be included here, since it occurred on Rabbi Wallis's flight to Spain for the ceremony. The flight took him through Barcelona, where he was slated to catch a connecting flight to Majorca. While settling into his seat prior to takeoff, Rabbi Wallis looked around and noticed that every person in the immediate vicinity was abnormally tall and well built. It was like he was suddenly surrounded by giants. Feeling like Gulliver in the land of the big people, he turned to the closest giant and asked who the group was.

"We are Maccabi Tel Aviv."

That explained it. He was sitting with Israel's top basketball team.

"What are you doing here?"

"We're traveling to Barcelona to play Spain for the European championship. The championship takes place once every four years. It's a very big deal."

It certainly sounded like a very big deal to Rabbi Wallis, though he had stopped following basketball decades earlier. One topic led to the next and the rabbi and the basketball player found themselves enjoying a very interesting conversation, when they suddenly noticed a middle-aged man leading his adolescent son down the aisle of the plane and over to their seats.

"Sorry to interrupt your conversation," the man said to the basketball player, "but my son and I are on the way to Barcelona to watch the championship game, and he would really like your autograph."

"It will be my pleasure," said the player. He signed the boy's card and smiled warmly at him, but the father wasn't finished yet.

"My son just turned 13—bar mitzvah. I asked him what he wanted for a present and together we decided that the best bar mitzvah present in the world would be for me to fly with him to Barcelona for the championship game."

"What a father you've got," said the player to the bar mitzvah boy.

"My son really admires the whole team and you in particular," the father told the basketball star. "Would you be able to give him a *berachah*, a blessing, in honor of his bar mitzvah?"

"Of course I'll give him a blessing," he said, standing up from his business-class recliner. "Come here."

The kid shyly walked over.

The player placed his gigantic hands on the bar mitzvah boy's head and said, "You should grow up to become a first-class basketball player and join Maccabi Tel Aviv."

Needless to say, the CEO of Arachim was not enamored with his choice of *berachah*.

"Excuse me," Rabbi Wallis said to his new friend, "is that the way to bless a bar mitzvah boy?"

Father and son turned to stare at the bearded, previously docile rabbi, both of them unsure what to make of this new development.

The player gave him a puzzled look. "What should I have told him?"

"Come here, son," Rabbi Wallis said to the boy. The rabbi tousled the boy's hair and gripped his hand tightly in both of his.

"You have just celebrated your bar mitzvah, right?"

He gave a nod.

"Then let me give you a real *berachah*. I bless you *shetizkeh lemitzvot*—that you should merit to do lots of mitzvot and accomplish many good deeds over the course of your life! That," he said to the basketball player, "is the kind of blessing that a bar mitzvah boy needs to hear, not that he should grow up to play ball!"

The boy was smiling from ear to ear, the father shook the rabbi's hand and thanked him for his kind words, and all was well in the plane. Five minutes later, the aisle leading up to Rabbi Wallis's seat was suddenly full of fathers and sons, all searching for the "Rabbi of Maccabi Tel Aviv"! Apparently, the father and son had returned to their seats full of stories about being blessed by the "rabbi" of Maccabi Tel Aviv, who was accompanying the team on their way to Barcelona for the big game.

Rabbi Wallis now realized that the plane was full of fathers and their bar mitzvah–aged sons, all traveling together to watch the game: a collective, modern-day bar mitzvah present.

He didn't know who organized the group, but they were all fans of Maccabi, all heading overseas for the game, and all clamoring to be blessed by Maccabi's "rabbi." He utilized the unique opportunity to give each bar mitzvah boy a warm *berachah* full of Jewish concepts and hopes for the future, and watched, satisfied, as one by one they thanked him and returned to their seats.

Things quieted down and the rabbi turned to his basketball-star friend and asked, "So when's the game?"

The man squirmed uncomfortably in his seat and Rabbi Wallis suddenly comprehended that there was something happening that he wasn't particularly keen on Rabbi Wallis finding out.

"The game's on Friday, Rabbi."

"On Friday? Really? What time on Friday?"

Lowering his eyes, the athlete tried to justify himself. "Listen, Rabbi, we told the Spanish team that we didn't want to play on Shabbat. But they didn't understand that Shabbat starts at night, and ended up scheduling the game for 10 o'clock Friday night."

"Are you serious? You're really going to play basketball on Friday night? I can't believe this!"

"What are we supposed to do?"

"Look here, friend, what does it say on the back of your jersey?"

"Maccabi."

"That's right, it says Maccabi. Do you know what Maccabi stands for? It stands for '*Mi chamochah ba'eilim Hashem*—Who is like You, Hashem?' The battle cry of the Maccabees of old. Those are the words scrawled across your backs. Along with a Star of David. You're flying in from Israel with a planeload of bar mitzvah boys and by participating in such a game, you will be educating these children that it's okay to desecrate Shabbat for an important basketball game! Do you know why I'm flying to Spain right now? I'm heading to Spain to say Kaddish for my ancestor Rafael Vallis, who wanted to keep Shabbat and was caught by the Church and burned at the stake! And now, a Jewish team with the Maccabi slogan scrawled across its back is going to get on the court on Friday night and play ball without a second thought! You should all be mortified for even considering such a thing!"

The other team members, who'd been following the conversation closely, all had something to say. Everyone had his own excuse.

"Rabbi, please, it's not my fault... I try to keep Shabbat whenever I can... I return home every Friday night to listen to my father recite the Kiddush... At home I go to *beit knesset* with my father... My great-grandfather was a rabbi... I respect the religion very much, but what can I do, that's the game!"

Even the team captain got involved. "Please don't be angry, Rabbi, please bless us that we should win the game."

That was too much.

"You want me to bless you?"

The captain nodded.

"I'll bless you," the rabbi replied. "I'll bless you all that you should lose the game." (They did.)

The remainder of the flight passed in an uneasy silence.

♦ ♦ ♦

There was a posse of journalists waiting to greet Maccabi Tel Aviv on their arrival to Spain. Having sat beside the team throughout the flight, the rabbi was swept along with them through the airport and immigration, the players towering above him like trees surrounding a flower. Through it all, they heard people buzzing about how the "Rabbi of Maccabi Tel Aviv" had been on board. Eventually they parted ways: the basketball players to an impromptu press conference and then onto their chartered bus, and the rabbi to board a flight to Majorca to say Kaddish for Rafael Vallis.

It was a funny thing, but in the months after the trip to Spain, Rabbi Wallis was contacted numerous times by an assortment of schools who were celebrating collective bar mitzvah parties for their 13-year-old students. They wanted a speaker and chose to call the "Rabbi of Maccabi Tel Aviv" to come address their boys. Of course he accepted their invitations.

At his very first encounter with these boys, Rabbi Wallis came to speak, but even more important to him, he wanted to ask them a question.

In all honesty he had to admit that the basketball players he had met on the plane were nice guys...gentle guys...well meaning...and he had been really tough with them. Now he couldn't help castigating himself for having been so aggressive. Maybe he should have been nicer, more understanding. He wasn't sure. Now, in this junior high school, he was going to allow the audience to be the judge.

Rabbi Wallis entered an auditorium filled with children and their parents—none of them observant. Sweet Jewish faces stared at the "Rabbi of Maccabi Tel Aviv" as he walked up to the stage and took his place behind the podium.

"I want to tell you boys a story," he began. "Listen well, and when we're finished I'm going to have a few questions for all of you."

They were fascinated from the get-go. Rabbi Wallis told them how he'd been invited back to Spain for the Kaddish ceremony and how he'd found himself surrounded by basketball players.

How the father had asked a member of the team for a blessing, and how Rabbi Wallis had corrected him and given the boy a much better blessing: a blessing truly appropriate for a bar mitzvah boy. How he'd ended up dispensing blessings to all the bar mitzvah boys on the flight and been handed the sobriquet "Rabbi of Maccabi Tel Aviv" at the same time.

"Boys, here's the thing," said Rabbi Wallis in conclusion. "When the team captain asked me to bless Maccabi to win the game, I told him off. I gave it to him. I told him that I blessed them with a loss and not a win! I told them I was heading to Majorca to say Kaddish for the last Jew who was burned at the stake hundreds of years before and how it was unacceptable that a Jewish team should prance around the court on a Friday night while representing the State of Israel.

"I really gave it to them. And that's what I want to ask you boys. You decide. Was I wrong for being so tough with them? Be honest with me, tell me the truth. Part of me feels that I was too aggressive with those players. What do you think? Was I right for telling them off or should I call them up and apologize?"

Hands were raised in every corner of the auditorium.

Rabbi Wallis chose one of the boys.

"Yes?"

"You were right, Rabbi. Maccabi Tel Aviv had no business playing a championship game on a Friday night. You were right for giving it to them! They are a Jewish team and should never play on Shabbat! Maybe next time such a situation comes up, they'll remember your reaction from the plane and what you told them about playing on Shabbat and they won't do it!!"

The CEO of Arachim looked at those beautiful Jewish children: not religious, but so special despite the lack of faith in their lives. Then he turned to their parents and said, "Do you hear what your children just told me? Were you listening to the words coming out of their mouths? Your kids have the spark of Torah in their souls Embrace it—cultivate it—help it flourish!"

When he parted from the group of bar mitzvah boys and their parents, the rabbi couldn't help thinking to himself that, religious or not, the spark of Rafael Vallis was alive and well within these kids—and alive and well in so many of the nonreligious Jews whom we meet—and how sometimes all it takes is a tiny match to turn that dormant spark into a fiery blaze.

CHAPTER THREE

His insistence on his right to mark his forebear's tragic murder, his demand for an apology for a centuries-old wrong, and, most of all, his feeling of responsibility for his fellow Jews—whether they were basketball stars, bar mitzvah boys, or Jews so hidden they didn't know themselves that they were Jews—is classic Yossi Wallis behavior.

Where did that core of inner toughness, unflinching determination, and strength of character come from? Perhaps the actions of his ancestor, Rafael Vallis, provided his descendant with a DNA double helix of courage and caring that would serve him well in the future.

You surely would not have known it from Yossi's childhood.

Early life would prove extremely daunting for Yossi Wallis, and if one examines his childhood in detail, it is almost impossible to believe that a young boy from the wild, tough streets of the Bronx would one day stand at the helm of a global, huge, and respected Jewish outreach organization.

That, however, is exactly what happened.

♦ ♦ ♦

Yossi Wallis was born in Petach Tikvah and grew up in Eretz Yisrael in the 1950's. No one had any money worth speaking of and everyone was more or less content and satisfied with what they had because there were no expectations of getting anything more. Everyone was in the same boat and just relieved to be living on friendly soil, away from the killing grounds of Europe. The State of Israel had come into being just a few years earlier and the citizens of the newly created country were preoccupied with rebuilding their families, which had been decimated in the concentration camps of Nazi Germany.

Israel needed people to fill the country and was determined to accept as many refugees as possible. This policy was the catalyst for the large numbers of Sefardic Jews who were brought to Israel from across the Middle East. There were also the families who had been living in Israel from before the war, and who were generally wealthier and better connected than everyone else. The Wallis family belonged to a different class of people: those who had survived the Holocaust. They kept to themselves and didn't communicate much with those around them for one simple reason. It was impossible for anyone who hadn't been there to understand.

The majority of little Yossi's neighbors were families like his own, comprised of men and women who were, in many cases, the sole survivors of what had been large and prominent European families. Desperate to fill the gap within their lives, they created a society of people who were unrelated by blood, but who considered themselves family by virtue of their shared experiences. Most of the neighboring families were traditional Jews. Their connection to Judaism was tenuous after what they had gone through, yet they still attended shul (synagogue) on the *yahrtzeits* of their parents. Since everyone was saying Kaddish for countless family members, shul played a minor yet still integral role in their lives—as did the *yahrtzeit* candles, which were constantly being lit for one person's or another's *yahrzeit*.

The neighborhood children grew up in the shadow of the Holocaust. Yossi's father claimed Yossi was the spitting image of his brother. His mother fondly said that he looked exactly like

Yossi's parents

her brother. Everywhere he went, Yossi reminded people of those they had lost. Occasionally he felt like a walking *yahrtzeit* candle!

Daytime was one thing, but night was when the Holocaust really came to life. While his parents were able to conquer their fears and memories during the day, the demons of the past took control of them while under the influence of sleep. His father tossed and turned in his bed, the ravages of the past etched on his face, pathetic screams erupting from his mouth, as he yelled "No!!" or "Don't take them!!" Yossi heard the shrieks but had no idea what was wrong and why the nightmares came. His father was so loud at times that some of the neighbors would complain. Yossi and his mother would try to wake him up, but calming him was an arduous process. Even once he woke up it usually took him about half an hour to realize that he wasn't in the camps anymore, that he was safe. This scene repeated itself on a nightly basis.

Sometimes it was Yossi's mother who suffered from the nightmares and they had to rouse her from the terror of the past. In the morning, his parents would apologize and try to explain how and why it occurred, but it was impossible and the words would just dry up.

Yossi had no grandparents and to compensate, Mr. and Mrs. Wallis adopted third and fourth cousins; this one became his "grandfather" and that one was an "uncle." This was their way of creating an artificial family situation. Part of Yossi knew that it was a sham, but he was content with his life and enjoyed his relatives despite their not being the real thing. In retrospect, he realized that their life was not a normal one—parents who trembled and went into shock when they heard a siren, the absence of an extended family structure—but this was the only life he knew.

Yossi's father told stories about the Holocaust, what he went through, how they suffered, but his mother never said a word. His father couldn't say enough and his mother couldn't say a thing. It was a bone of contention between them. At the dinner table his father would begin relating a story that happened to him during the war, but it wouldn't be long before his mother would interject and tell him to stop.

"They don't need to hear about this," she'd say, and his father would cease his storytelling while turning to her with the rawest of pain in his eyes.

"Why not, let them know what happened!"

"No, they're just kids. They don't have to know all those terrible things!"

He wanted the children to know, felt it was imperative that they grasp what had occurred just a few short years earlier, while she was trying her hardest to protect herself and her children. It was an ongoing contradiction, but that was their life. Yossi found himself having to decide in which direction to go. On the one hand he was a very curious child and desperately wanted to know what they had experienced. On the other hand, the pain was so great that it hurt him to hear about it and to see their agony in the retelling. He wanted to help them and make them feel better, but there was nothing he could do for them, and that hurt most of all.

♦ ♦ ♦

School was another problem. The prevailing attitude among students and teachers alike was to look down at the Holocaust survivors. Instead of treating them with the compassion they deserved after going through hell on earth, people compared them to sheep going docilely to their slaughter, disparaged them as "ghetto Jews," made them feel guilty for not having fought back. Instead of offering them respect, they educated their children to disconnect themselves from the Holocaust survivors who, they claimed, were nothing like the new Jews of Israel who stood up for themselves and fought for their lives. How those holy survivors suffered! Here they had gone through the worst tribulations in the world and finally made it to Israeli shores, only to be looked down on and ordered to never share their suffering and memories with others! For some, it was almost like being sentenced to die all over again.

Many times Yossi couldn't help questioning his father. "Abba," he'd say, "why did you allow the Germans to take you to your deaths? Why didn't you rebel?"

He really wanted to understand how so many strong, smart people had turned into cowering shadows. "Why didn't you fight?!"

His father couldn't explain.

"Yossi," he'd reply, the pain in his eyes filling the entire room, "you won't be able to understand. Nobody can, unless they were there."

Not wanting to disagree with what they were teaching his son in school, and knowing that he was being viewed as a coward (for lack of a better word), Yossi's father found himself admitting that all those back in Europe had gone to their deaths like sheep and were different from the new Israeli Jew... He even found himself agreeing that they should disassociate themselves from the ghetto Jew of the past. Yossi's father, his brave father, did his best to find the right balance in this strange new world: doing whatever it took to find the peace that should exist between a father and his only son, trying to ensure that his son should feel comfortable within the system. But his son understands today that his father was living through another secret Holocaust, each and every day. Because he lived in a country where he was looked down upon and where he was forced to raise his only son to view him, and his martyred family, as cowards.

There were additional challenges as well.

In the early days of the Jewish State, David Ben-Gurion and his colleagues from the Mapai party were at the helm of every government agency. Anyone who identified with the Mapai stood a chance at being offered a job with decent pay. But if you were an individual who supported Menachem Begin and his Herut party, there was almost no opportunity for advancing a career of any sort. The environment was so polarized and based on political considerations that it affected everything in the country, down to the medical clinic to which you belonged. All this meant that Mr. Wallis couldn't get a decent job. He had to make do with working two shifts in a factory as a weaver—and his son remembers this well, because he was the one who brought him sandwiches and fruit for lunch and supper.

They were so poor that whenever his mother purchased a pair of shoes for Yossi, she bought them a few sizes too big, so they would last longer. The first year, she filled the extra space with crumpled-up newspaper. The second year, they were usually close to his size, but were more than a little worn out. By the time the third year rolled around, his mother had to cut the front off the shoes and Yossi's toes peeked out from within. He owned a grand total of two pairs of pants, one for Shabbos and another (which was basically a pair of shorts held up by a string) for the rest of the week. Shoes with socks were for Shabbos; the rest of the time, he wore sandals.

Yet with all this he was a happy-go-lucky, good-natured child.

♦ ♦ ♦

The kids in the neighborhood loved playing games, but who had money for games? Out of sheer necessity, they became inventors, architects, and engineers, turning useless articles they discovered lying around into complicated items of amusement. The positive side of poverty: The neighborhood kids were constantly together, busy developing their minds to think outside the box, because they had to if they wanted to have fun. The kids grew up together and eventually left to the army, where they looked after each other like brothers, able to read each other's minds due to years growing up on the streets together. One big, happy family.

Back then nobody had keys. The doors were left open because there was nothing to steal. Children felt comfortable enough to just walk into a neighbor's home, and everyone grew up in everyone else's house. It was that kind of life. The atmosphere on the street was that of a prevailing sense of brotherhood. It was a beautiful thing to see and a delightful way to grow up, but it wasn't easy. Yossi's father was working from early morning until late in the evening, and he barely had time to talk to his wife or just to take a breath. Not that he'd anticipated living the easy life in Eretz Yisrael, but at some point, life became too difficult even for a man who'd gone through so much, and he raised his hands in defeat.

♦ ♦ ♦

In what little spare time he had, Yossi's father enjoyed telling stories about the exciting life he'd led once he'd come to Palestine. Though many of the incidents were frightening for a young boy to hear, Mr. Wallis felt that his son needed to know what he and so many others had experienced just a few short years before he was born. Usually Yossi's mother made him stop. But there were times when the story wasn't about the war and then she'd sit and listen along with the rest of the family, pride in her husband's remarkable achievements filling her eyes with an adoring gaze. He was an excellent raconteur and knew how to describe a scene and spin a tale until you literally felt that you were there walking alongside him.

There was one story in particular that his son loved to hear.

"Your mother and I were finally beginning to settle into our new lives," he'd begin, "but there something bothering me, something niggling at me—and I knew that I wouldn't feel at ease until I took care of it."

"What, Abba, what was on your mind?"

"Here I was, a Holocaust survivor, a person who had cheated death at the hands of the Nazis for six endless years. Your mother and I had made it to Eretz Yisrael, incredible, obvious miracles happening every step of the way, and I felt like I needed to say thank you to Hashem. I could have said thank you anywhere, but I wanted to express myself in a special place. To me it seemed obvious where I should go, but anytime I raised my idea, people told me that I was crazy."

"Where did you want to go?"

"I wanted to thank G-d at the Western Wall, the Kotel HaMaaravi, but it wasn't safe for Jews to walk through the Old City of Yerushalayim during those days and everyone advised me to forget my idea. Officially Jews were allowed to visit the Kotel, but the British were very lax about Jewish security and it was extremely dangerous. I tried to convince myself to give up the idea but found that I couldn't. The more I tried to put the idea out of my mind, the more it crept right back in. Besides, I had been dreaming of visiting the Kotel since I was a child. Was I going to give up my lifelong dream because of a little danger? The answer obviously was no.

"Your mother and a few of our friends accompanied me through the deserted streets near one of the entrances leading into the Old City. My plan was to slip inside, make my way through the labyrinth of Old City alleyways to the Kotel, stay there a few minutes, and then return to your mother.

"That was the plan. Of course things didn't exactly go according to plan.

"Entering the Old City wasn't difficult. I had chosen a relatively quiet gate and once inside, I walked quickly through the narrow streets, my boots making clicking sounds on the cobblestones. I passed the shuttered stalls and stores of the Arab marketplace and was pleased to see that the *shuk* was deserted, with the residents already home eating dinner and chatting with their families after a long day. From time to time I caught sight of a British patrol, but it was usually at a distance and they never saw me. I pressed against the sides of the buildings, the shadows protecting me within their dark embrace. I didn't really know where I was going, so I allowed my innate sense of direction to guide me through the unfamiliar and somewhat sinister streets.

"It wasn't long before I emerged from the claustrophobic alleyways into an area that had been overtaken by Arab homes and garbage. I stared at the wall before me and was filled with a certain elusive peace I had never felt before. Here it was. The Western Wall. The place where it all began thousands of years earlier. Having just emerged from the destruction of European Jewry, I was able to relate and empathize with the tragic events that had taken place in this exact spot so many centuries before.

"I approached the last vestige of the Beit HaMikdash (Temple) on earth and ran my fingers over its fissures, cracks, and crevices. I felt the wild, untamed vegetation growing outward to the plaza and inexplicable warmth washed over me.

"'Thank You for saving my life,' I whispered upward at a sky filled with millions of stars. 'Thank You for taking my hand and for standing by my side through fire and water... For saving me even after I'd already given up hope.'

"I could have remained there for hours, but it was too dangerous and besides, Ima and our friends were waiting for me, no doubt growing more and more anxious as the minutes ticked by without my return.

"I turned to leave, feeling nervous by the utter solitude. I was the only person in sight now and certainly the sole Jew walking through the Arab Quarter. I began retracing my earlier steps, but the streets were dark and poorly lit and it was almost impossible to recognize the twists and turns of 45 minutes before. I could hear the sounds of Middle Eastern music from the windows of the shuttered homes and I was suddenly filled with dread at how this might turn out. Bored youths had scrawled Arabic graffiti on the shutters of many stores and you didn't need to be a linguist to discern the anger. I remained in the shadows of the storefronts and stayed away from open spaces, but then as I turned into another alleyway, I found myself face-to-face with a gang of Arab teenagers. We stared at each other for what must have been seconds, but felt like an eternity: the enmity of rival cultures spanning history.

"I turned and ran for my life, the gang running after me, the sound of their shoes pounding the cobblestones echoing through the Arab Quarter. I knew what they would do to me if they caught me; slowing down wasn't an option. As I ran, I berated myself for having voluntarily entered Mufti-controlled territory and for the risks I had taken.

"But I knew why I did it, and the reasons made sense.

"I took a nearby set of stairs three at a time, my breath coming in ragged gasps, spasms of pain making me cough, as sweat broke out all across my forehead. I felt my legs cramping from the unaccustomed and strenuous exercise. I ran from one alleyway into the next, up staircases and over roofs, the Arabs in hot pursuit, no doubt imagining what they were going to do with their prize catch. Behind a mosque and through a courtyard, a line of laundry falling down onto the floor, all tangled up, the sounds of the Arabs too close for comfort. I entered a long, shadowy area of storefronts, all closed, nowhere to hide, and ran through it faster than I'd run in years. I arrived at the final store and turned a corner, finding myself in an empty courtyard with nowhere to hide.

"Suddenly a boy stood in front of me.

"'Come,' he said, motioning with his arms, the language universal, the message clear.

"For some reason, maybe because I had no choice and was clear out of options, I followed him. As we stepped through a blue-painted door into a small living area the sounds of the gang followed me, their cries vicious, their disappointment at my evident escape almost palpable. The boy led me through his house and up another curving flight of stairs that led us to the rooftop. I followed him from roof to roof, until we reached yet another staircase, this one leading downward.

"'Go,' he said to me in halting Hebrew, when we stood on the ground once more. 'Turn the corner, you will be safe...'

"I thanked him for saving my life. Patted his cheek. Tried to convey my gratitude. He seemed to understand, as he turned around and disappeared into the inky blackness of the night. I followed his directions and found myself standing at the entranceway into Jewish Yerushalayim and safety. I walked 500 yards and found a bench on which to rest and catch my breath. My heart was still thumping mightily after my near brush with death and my feet wouldn't hold me. But at least I'd merited to lay my hand on the Kotel and to say thank you to Hashem for the fact that I was still alive."

When his father told him stories like these, Yossi found himself filled with pride at his bravery and fearlessness. But deep within his heart he couldn't help returning to the questions he'd heard in school a million times before.

"Where did all your bravery and resourcefulness go when the Nazis came? Why didn't you fight back?"

Yossi couldn't reconcile these two fathers: the father who feared nobody and nothing, and the other father, who had obeyed the Nazis and had gone everywhere he was sent without a fight.

He wanted answers from him: answers his father wasn't capable of providing. And so Yossi was left filled with mixed feelings. So proud of him on one hand, so ashamed on the other.

The day would come when his father would relate his story in its entirety, never all at once, but eventually Yossi would hear all the bits and pieces. In the end every question would be answered and every doubt addressed, but that would only happen many years later. Meanwhile, he was left to wonder and probe and stare with silent scorn at those who could have fought back but chose not to.

The typical life of the second-generation Holocaust survivor in Eretz Yisrael of the '50's.

♦ ♦ ♦

When Yossi looked at his parents he saw people who were active role models for *chesed*. They were people who despite possessing close to nothing in the way of material possessions never allowed themselves to stop helping their fellow Jews.

Between June 1949 and September 1950, the State of Israel airlifted 49,000 Jews from Yemen to Eretz Yisrael, in an operation known as "Operation on the Wings of Eagles" (colloquially it was called "Operation Magic Carpet"). Unfortunately, in many cases the Israeli government mistreated the Yemenites, who by and large were pious, Torah-observant Jews, and tried their best to convince them that religion was not needed in the Holy Land. They sent their children to virulently antireligious kibbutzim, where bareheaded counselors mocked them for davening, cut off their *pei'os*, and fed them nonkosher food. Impressionable children watched as their counselors smoked cigarettes on Shabbos, dressed immodestly, and explained to them that the mitzvah of living in Eretz Yisrael essentially replaced every other commandment in the Torah.

The Yemenite families were transported by bus to the *maabarot*—the refugee absorption camps—where they lived in crowded tents, disease and squalor their constant companions, caught in the poverty of the lowest echelon of society. Entire families left the *maabarot* searching for work, for any type of labor, no matter how demeaning or difficult. Anything to get out of the refugee camp, with its profusion of rats and open sewers, and into a normal home with windows and warmth.

Mr. Wallis was hard at work in the textile factory where he labored for 12 hours every day when a Yemenite family showed up begging for jobs, amid the clatter of the machines and the workers yelling to be heard over the awesome racket. A worker ran to call the boss, an older man who had arrived in the country years before the war, a man with a corpulent capitalist belly and a distrust of foreigners. He sized up the family—the wizened, elderly father with coal-black eyes and tightly coiled sidelocks, his wife, dressed in unique Yemenite garb, and their assorted children all eyeing him solemnly back—and waved a disparaging hand in the air.

"There's nothing here for you to do." He turned on his heel and disappeared back into his office.

Mr. Wallis looked at the family, his gaze sympathetic.

"If I learned any one lesson while surviving under German rule, it was that a Jew is a Jew, no matter what he looks like or how he dresses," he'd tell his son years later.

The family of dark-skinned Jews turned to leave, disappointed at once again being turned away, but Yossi's father caught up with them.

"Wait outside until I finish my shift," he said. At the end of the day he led the entire family to his house. The apartment near Jabotinsky Street was a tiny two-room apartment typical of those early years in Eretz Yisrael. There was a kitchen with barely enough space for three people to move around, a living room, and a bedroom. Yossi and his sister slept in the bedroom, while their parents used the living room for their bedroom, come nighttime.

It was early evening when Mr. Wallis led the Yemenite family into their lives. There was a father, mother, and about seven or eight children. Yossi's father welcomed them into his home with the air of someone being reunited with long-lost family.

He then addressed his son.

"Yossi, you and your sister will move out of your bedroom and into our room. You will sleep in the wooden box under the sofa where we store the extra pillows and blankets. We'll find the perfect bed for your sister too, don't worry. You see this family? They have no place to go. They have no money, no work, and no home. That's why they will be staying with us until they find their own way."

The family had a 15-year-old daughter and Mr. Wallis strongly felt that she needed her own space. He was a man of action and wasted no time. Leaving the house, he knocked on the neighbor's door and explained to the flabbergasted Ashkenazic family that he had taken in an entire Yemenite family into one of his two rooms and that he expected them to join the cause and provide some space for the young girl.

"They're Jews like us," Mr. Wallis told the neighbor, his eyes beseeching the man to understand and acquiesce, in a way that wouldn't belittle the family or make them feel more ashamed than they already did. It was almost impossible to say no to Mr. Wallis and within minutes the family was settled in their home, warm, fed, and cheerful, as they enjoyed the security of a real roof over their heads for the first time since their arrival in the country.

Yossi's father never gave him a speech about doing *chesed*. He didn't have to. He lived and breathed it. He gave up what little privacy he had for a family that would remain in their home for the next three months. His behavior would serve as the very best, most admirable lesson that a son could possibly receive from his father, a lesson that sank into Yossi's very marrow and blood: the lesson that all Jews were responsible for each other.

♦ ♦ ♦

It is impossible to know exactly when Mr. and Mrs. Wallis came to the conclusion that there was no future for them in the land of the Jews, but one day Yossi and his sister were informed that they were moving to the United States of America, where there were plenty of jobs and opportunities for advancement. The realization that they were never going to get ahead in this land of the "new" Israeli, coupled with the intense disregard for everything the Holocaust survivors had suffered, pushed his parents into the difficult decision. With the hope of making a new life for themselves—once again—they sailed across the ocean to the land of the free.

Mr. Wallis had entered World War II with six siblings. By the time the war came to an end, two of his brothers and two of his sisters had been murdered. His brother Dovid had been forced to escape to Russia and his sister Basha had made it to America. Mr. Wallis turned to Basha for assistance and she came through with tickets for him on a ship that would take him there. At home the family waited anxiously for a letter from him, telling them that he'd arrived safely, and one fine day a postcard showed up on their doorstep with a picture of the Empire State Building towering above the New York skyline. Looking at that picture of New York, their eyes grew wide and their excitement became almost palpable. What a land! What a city! What a future awaited them across the ocean!

Yossi's father sent a message that America was a beautiful country and that he was currently living with his sister and her family in the Bronx.

"I will send for you as soon as I am able to raise the necessary funds to pay for all your tickets," he wrote.

The children had mixed feelings about moving to America. On the one hand they were excited about the move, while another part of them was extremely sad to be leaving all their "extended family" in Eretz Yisrael. These were the people they had grown up with, the boys Yossi had played with for hours, the neighbors they had known and loved. All Eretz Yisrael was one big family and now they were about to say good-bye to all of that. It was not a good feeling.

And then one day their tickets arrived in the mail and it was time to leave. Yossi, his mother, and his sister, Leah, said good-bye to everyone on the block and didn't bother locking the front door when they crossed the threshold for the final time. There was nothing to steal and besides, no doubt they had lost the key long, long before. They flew to Switzerland, where they transferred onto another plane for the longer flight across the Atlantic.

America was calling.

CHAPTER FOUR

Yossi's father met them at the airport, his eyes gleaming with the happiness of reunion. Suitcases in hand, the family boarded one of the ubiquitous New York yellow cabs for the trip to their new home in the Bronx. As they drove, Yossi craned his neck to try and catch his first glimpse of the gorgeous New York skyline he'd seen in postcards.

"Abba," he asked, "where's the Empire State Building?"

"Manhattan," his father replied tersely.

It took Yossi a few minutes to process the fact that America was not going to be the glamorous world he had fondly imagined, first from his tiny bedroom in Eretz Yisrael and then as they were winging their way through the clouds. And it wasn't just the buildings that were disappointing. Driving deeper and deeper into the tenement sprawl, he took in the people loitering on the street corners. The Puerto Ricans and Irish teenagers were as menacing as anyone he'd ever seen. He shrank back into the cab's seat, refusing to look out the window anymore. If this was his new world, he wanted no part of it.

His aunt welcomed them into her apartment. Yossi met his cousins and saw a television set for the first time ever. Cowboys and Indians fighting each other in full Western glory! Mickey

Mouse, winking and smiling at him... He sat, transfixed, until his father pulled him away from the couch, announcing that they were going to get something to eat. His father escorted all the youngsters to the neighborhood candy store, where they found a brand-new world. A slowly revolving ceiling fan cast all sorts of delightful aromas through the air. There was a counter at the front of the store and beneath the glass Yossi caught a glimpse of the most astounding array of candies he had ever seen. His eyes grew big and round.

This is what it feels like to dream, he told himself.

"Yossi," said his father, "I am going to buy you the most delicious drink in the world."

He approached the man behind the counter, said a few words, handed him some money, and five seconds later Yossi was sipping a frosty cold cherry soda. He had never tasted anything quite so refreshing, and the bubbles tickled his nose. *Welcome to America,* the soda whispered, as it slid smoothly down his throat.

After they'd finished their drinks, his father led them down the street to an old-fashioned deli, for a first taste of real American hot dogs. A corpulent man in a tight-fitting apron sporting a ready smile handed the boy a thick hot dog sitting cozily in its bun, topped by ketchup, mustard, and sauerkraut. Yossi was sold from the first ecstatic bite. American hot dogs. So much better than falafel!

By the time he was ready to go to sleep that night, Yossi had experienced an entire gamut of emotions.

"Yossi," said his father as he got into bed.

"Yes, Abba?"

"Tomorrow you'll be starting junior high school at the local public school down the block. I'm sure you will make me proud."

He turned off the light and left the room, and Yossi pulled the blanket up to his chin and contemplated the idea of attending school without being able to communicate properly with the rest of the students.

What if they fight with you? a tiny voice whispered in his brain.

It's going to be just fine, he answered the voice, but he couldn't help but recall the teenagers he had seen on the street corners that afternoon. If looks were any indication, there were some dangerous times ahead in his quest to fit into a brand-new world.

♦ ♦ ♦

Walking up to the school building on his first day of school was an exercise in anxiety. Yossi was 12 years old and his English was poor. He was being thrown into the deep end of the pool with no clue how to swim. On the outside he put on a show of confidence, but his heart was beating rapidly and his palms were sweaty. He was smart enough to know that he was entering what could easily turn into a war zone.

He was at a huge disadvantage even before opening his mouth. The average American student of those days wore a dress shirt, long pants, and even a tie, while he was still wearing the same pair of shorts that he'd worn back in Petach Tikvah. Everyone stared at the bizarre creature who had dropped into their lives from another planet, and who could blame them?

Yossi stood at the front of the classroom, staring self-consciously at the floor as the teacher introduced him to the class.

"Children," she said, "this is Joseph. Joseph's family has just moved here from Israel. Please be nice to him and show him how to play baseball and all the rest of the games you play during recess because he doesn't know English very well and he needs to make new friends."

Since the students sat in alphabetical order and Wallis begins with a *W*, he was shown to a seat at the back of the room, from which he studied the goings-on in the class. Things were calm and orderly until the bell rang for recess. Following the crowds of kids rushing outside he couldn't help noticing that although there might have been a few Jewish kids in the school, they were helplessly outnumbered. Yossi saw Irish kids, Italian kids, and Puerto Rican kids, but almost nobody that he'd be able to count on in a moment of truth, and this realization filled him with stark terror.

As he stood on the asphalt alone and off to the side, a group of ninth graders approached, malice on their faces. Exchanging barely a word, the gang began marching in his direction, hate emanating out of them like heat from a furnace. The scene that followed could have been transported from the streets of Berlin circa 1937. The Irish and Italians had become Hitler Youth and Yossi Wallis was the helpless Jewish kid. Standing in a semicircle around the new boy from Israel, every one of them raised his right hand and vocally yelled out "*Heil Hitler*" as loud as he could—as the Stars and Stripes swayed high above them in the breeze.

It was a far cry from "Give me your tired, your poor, your huddled masses yearning to breathe free..."

Yossi was a skinny child—not a fighter. He looked around, and all he saw was hatred. These children were his enemies. Later on, he'd replay that moment over and over, but right then, all he felt was shock. He had no idea what to do or how to react. Tears came to his eyes but he blinked them away. Pushing past the group of laughing boys he retreated to the relative safety of the classroom, where he would able to cry in peace.

The teacher looked at him, pity on her face, and said, "Joseph, why are you crying?"

He showed her what the boys had done; he copied the terrible gesture they'd made to welcome him into their world.

She sighed.

"Joseph, this is America. It's a great country. A wonderful land. The opportunities are endless. At the same time, America is a melting pot. Every nation, nationality, religion, and country has contributed some of their own to create this land. It's not going to be an easy process, but don't let these children break you along the way. You have to understand; unfortunately, this is also part of life in America and especially in New York."

He understood her speech more or less, but he couldn't even respond. The hurt was way too fresh. Instead of encouraging him, her speech made him feel even worse.

If this is what America is all about, who needs it? he thought to himself.

At that moment he was more depressed than he'd ever been before.

When the bell rang that afternoon and school was out for the day, he began walking home on the Grand Concourse, one of the major thoroughfares in his new neighborhood. As he was approaching his home on Mount Eden Avenue, a bunch of black kids converged on him from behind and began cursing and yelling as they trapped him in a circle. With clenched fists they approached the new boy. This was too much. It was a rainy day and using his umbrella as a weapon, he slammed one of them in the stomach before turning and running away. They tried to catch up with him but he was too quick for them and he managed to get away—the sounds of thumping footsteps and cursing voices following him for what seemed like forever.

The sunny skies of Petach Tikvah had never seemed farther away.

◆ ◆ ◆

The lobby was rundown and forlorn, with a sad look of decay. It was seedy and dirty and screamed of decades of neglect, and it was the last thing Yossi wanted to see so soon after running for his life. But as much as he hated to admit it, for the time being the tiny vestibule leading to a cramped, darkened apartment was home.

"Welcome to America."

He made up his mind not tell his parents about his day. There was nothing they could do about it and it would just make them sad. Over the next few days Yossi took stock of his situation and realized that he was in trouble. The neighborhood was predominantly Irish and Italian, and he couldn't leave the apartment because every time he tried to walk down the street he was beaten up for having the temerity to show his face on "their" sidewalk. He was forced to hide out in the apartment, forced to sit and watch television all afternoon, and if he ever needed to go down to the street, he had to check from the window first to make sure that the gangs weren't waiting for him. The inactivity was driving him insane. He had been an active kid his entire life, a kid who spent hours outside the house every day playing ball and just having fun, and here he couldn't walk down the street for fear of being beaten mercilessly.

"Yossi," his father said to him one day.

"Yes, Abba?"

"Would you be willing to help contribute to the family income a little bit and get an after-school job?"

This type of a request was normal back then. Most people were struggling and every bit of cash was vital. Yossi asked around at school and a few people recommended that he try to get a job delivering newspapers for *The New York Post*. And so Yossi Wallis became a paperboy. He had a delivery route through a few of the local high-rise buildings, with collection day once a week. Being an energetic boy he decided to challenge himself by taking on two routes. He'd ride the elevator up to the top floor of the building, then run down floor by floor, tossing newspapers onto the doormats, constantly commanding himself to do his route in shorter amounts of time.

One day he came up with what he considered to be an idea that was nothing short of genius. Instead of taking the elevator to the top of the building and working his way down, he worked his way upward from the ground floor to the roof, ran across the wide-open space, threw his bag of papers over to the next roof, and then jumped across the divide to the adjacent building, flying through the air six stories above ground. His newfound methods were so time efficient that he managed to finish two routes in the time that the other boys were doing one. His boss at the paper was impressed on the one hand, but was exasperated with him on the other. Yossi was doing the work of two people, but the paper was getting calls and complaints about the "flying paperboy." In the end, the paper eventually found him more trouble than he was worth and he was fired.

Thus ended Yossi Wallis's short-lived career in journalism.

♦ ♦ ♦

Things on the streets were becoming progressively worse. The gangs were always on the lookout for anyone who didn't belong and Yossi was constantly finding himself on the receiving end of the stick. One day, after he'd crawled back home with yet another black-and-blue eye, he looked at himself in the mirror and said, *Yossi, if you can't beat them, join them.*

There was one problem with a statement like that. He was a Jew and there was no place for a Jew in the street gangs of the Bronx. He had no in, no friends to get him accepted. But he knew that if he didn't find a way of protecting himself, sooner or later he was going to be seriously harmed by their attention. He needed a plan.

One day he arrived home from school to find an Italian man standing in the living room, repairing one of their windows. He was a glazier and one look at him told Yossi that here stood the answer to his problems. The man was a bodybuilder; that was obvious. Yossi had never seen anyone quite like him before. His arms were the sizes of small tree trunks. His physique was simply outstanding.

"Mister," he said to the workman, "how'd you become so strong?"

He looked at him. "You want to be as strong as I am?"

Yossi nodded, mesmerized.

"Start drinking five or six eggnogs every day. When you're full, force yourself to drink another one. That will set you on the right path. Then go down to the store and buy yourself some weights. Drink eggnog and lift weights. Do this every day and you'll begin to see a difference. Before you know it, you're going to start looking like me."

"Ima," Yossi told his mother, "please start preparing pitchers of eggnog."

He purchased a bunch of weights and began working out. Standing in his room on the first official workout day, filled with eggnog and excitement, he measured his bicep with a tape measure and told himself that as soon as his arm had grown and he had reached the goal he had set for himself, he was going to fight the neighborhood gangs, come what may. He was not a fighter by nature and had no desire to be part of a gang, but Hashem had put him into a very challenging situation and Yossi Wallis would do whatever it took to stand up for himself.

In retrospect, the years of hardship and toughness would prepare him for the arduous road that lay ahead, teaching him that he was capable of handling any challenge or accomplishing any goal: whether in the world of business or later on, while turning Arachim into the international outreach organization it would become. But right then, all he felt was fear. Fear and determination.

♦ ♦ ♦

Time waits for no man, and without even thinking about it, Yossi had gone from being 12 years old to becoming bar mitzvah.

"Yossi," his father said to him one day, "you're going to be bar mitzvah next week."

Yossi had no idea what that meant or even that turning 13 was something to be excited about. They celebrated his special day at one of the local synagogues with some cake and soda, and he received a plastic Kodak camera as a present from his parents. Later on that day his father took him over to meet one of the members of the synagogue.

"Yossi," his father said, "introducing you to this man is my real present to you for your 13th birthday."

"What's so special about this man?"

"This man owns the wedding hall a few blocks down and I've arranged a job for you at his hall."

That evening Yossi arrived at the hall eager to begin his new job. He was outfitted with a red jacket and bow tie, and was given detailed instructions as to what he was supposed to do.

"When the fancy people come walking up to the hall," the manager explained, "you open the front door for them. It's simple and easy and you can make nice tips. When it rains, you run over to the parking lot and escort the guests from their cars over to the hall, holding an umbrella over their heads to keep them dry."

"Anything else?"

"Yes, during the actual wedding or party, you circle the hall with a broom and dustpan, sweeping up any litter or cigarette butts that the guests drop on the floor. When the party is over, you'll help clean up and set up the ballroom for the next evening's affair."

It was a good, clean job and Yossi made lots of tips. People would flip a coin in his direction and he became adept at sweeping it out of the air. He'd open the door and they'd flip him a coin. He'd hold the umbrella over their heads and they'd flip him a coin. The rich guests loved watching the busboys and waiters scrambling for their tips and Yossi became a master at efficient tip recovery. When he arrived home after a night's work, his father would be waiting. He'd count the money and say, "Okay, Yossi, this is what you made. How much money do you need for yourself and how much can we put aside so that I'll be able to buy a candy store and open up a real business?"

Mr. and Mrs. Wallis were still working at menial labor in those years, his father working endless hours at a factory, his mother as a cook, and Yossi desperately wanted them to succeed. His father could have demanded that he give him everything he was making, but instead he put Yossi in charge of deciding what to do with the money. Usually they divided up the money four ways: for his father's future candy store, money so his sister could buy what she needed, money so his mother could purchase household supplies, and money for him. Dividing up the money gave him a sense of responsibility and he was happy to be able to help out.

One evening he arrived at the hall, donned his uniform, and began the nightly schedule. As he was circling the hall making sure that everyone had what they needed, the bride approached.

"Joseph," she said to him, "what a surprise! What are you here in that uniform? Is this where you spend your evenings?"

He was taken aback. The bride was his schoolteacher and from her tone of voice it was obvious that she was less than impressed with her student's nightly schedule. Cheeks flaming red with embarrassment, Yossi exchanged a few more words and wished her well.

When he arrived home that evening, he informed his father that he wanted nothing more to do with that job anymore.

"What happened?"

Yossi told him about meeting his teacher and how ashamed he'd been when he realized she was looking down at him for what he was forced to do to make money.

Mr. Wallis didn't usually get angry. He was laid back and unflappable. But that night he gave it to his son.

"Yossi," he said, "don't ever let me hear you say that you are ashamed at having to work for a living or for having to help your father raise the funds to purchase a business! There is nothing wrong with having to do work, be it menial labor or any other kind and I never, ever, want to hear you suggest such a thing again. You will return to school tomorrow morning and to your job at the hall in the evening and you will be proud that you can help your parents make it here in America! Do you understand?"

Yossi nodded meekly.

"Be proud of yourself."

His father's words penetrated his heart as they always did.

In the end he kept the job and learned a lesson that remained with him forever. There's no shame in having to work. On the contrary, that's the way a person succeeds in life: by rolling up one's sleeves and doing what needs to be done.

◆ ◆ ◆

Throughout the days and months following the eggnog resolution, Yossi never forgot his goal, measuring his bicep from time to time to update himself on his progress. One morning he measured his bicep and to his surprise found that he had finally reached his target.

That's it, Yossi, he said to himself, *now you stand up for yourself.*

It wouldn't be long before his resolve was tested. In fact, the first battle would occur the very next day. It was midmorning and he was walking down the street when he noticed three members of the Scorpions, a gang comprised of Irish and Italian kids who'd banded together, strolling down the center of the pavement as if they owned it.

Yossi Wallis prepared himself mentally for the upcoming confrontation. Then he did something he had never done before: He continued walking right down the center of the pavement on a course that would lead him into a head-on collision with the three Scorpions.

This time you are not going to run, he told himself.

The three gang members were heading directly toward him. Either they would move over a little bit and he would move over a little bit and their shoulders would graze with a few rough words exchanged, or they would carry on without giving an inch and there would be a fight.

The distance between them narrowed. The gang members noticed that instead of running and crossing the street as the Jewboy always did, Yossi was heading right toward them. They were slightly confused and weren't sure what to make of this development.

Suddenly they were standing face-to-face. A "rumble" was inevitable. Yossi had crossed the line of no return.

"Hey, kid," one of them finally said, "you want to start a fight?"

"Yes," he replied, staring the other in the eye, "I want to fight."

"Then it will be three of us against the one of you."

"Okay with me."

The next thing he knew all three of them had their hands in their pockets. It didn't take a lot of brains to know they were going for their switchblades. He knew he didn't have much time before those knives would emerge, their sharp blades gleaming wickedly.

Yossi looked around, searching for inspiration. He was standing beside a car that sported a large metal antenna built into its hood. There it stood, tall and proud, waving languidly in the wind. Instantly he knew his next move. Reaching over, he snapped the antenna off the car and extended it to its fullest length. His three opponents stood with their blades out, while he stood opposite them, antenna in hand. Both sides waited to see who would make the first move.

Then, cursing, the Scorpions jumped toward him. Yossi stoutly defended himself with the antenna, even though it was three against one and the others had knives. They hadn't been fighting for long before they heard the sound of police sirens rapidly drawing near. Without wasting a second, Yossi headed for the nearest alley, chucked the antenna into a garbage dumpster, and headed home, thrilled that he had finally stood up for himself.

You were lucky this time, Yossi, a little voice whispered in his brain, *but they're going to tell their friends what happened and soon you're going to have to face them all.*

He drifted off to sleep that night with mixed feelings. On the one hand he was proud that he had stood up for himself. On the other hand, he feared the Scorpions' deadly sting.

♦ ♦ ♦

Over the next few days Yossi Wallis learned the meaning of real fear. He had become a marked man in the Bronx. Every member of the Scorpions had been commanded to keep a sharp lookout for him and he couldn't show his face in the street. The situation was extremely volatile.

He was in Taft High by this time and had a few friends whom he was able to count on: a few other Israeli Jews, some kids from his class. There was one boy in particular, by the name of David, with whom he was very close. David's family was originally from Russia and had traveled to the United States via Israel. David was a few years older than Yossi and much stronger. They hit it off the moment the two of them were introduced. Neither one had any close friends and both of them had lived in Israel for part of their lives, and that gave them enough common ground to feel a connection. David had grown up fighting on the streets of his hometown back in Russia and was no stranger to violence. More important, he possessed the type of loyalty Yossi could depend on in any situation, and that meant more than the most powerful bicep.

One afternoon, not long after Yossi's encounter with the gang members, the two of them were walking home from school when Yossi caught sight of a whole group of Scorpions heading their way.

"Dave," he said, "let's get out of here, there's 20 of them!"

David was the most stubborn person he knew.

"No, Joe," he replied, "I'm not going anywhere."

"They're searching for me! C'mon, we can still get away!"

David shook his head.

"They're going to kill me and you as well just for standing here. Please run for it!"

By this time, the gang had seen them. Yossi never forgot the next few words that came out of David's mouth, words replete with the wisdom of the streets.

"Joe," his friend said, "if you run now, you're going to run for the rest of your life!"

"Dave," he replied, arguing with him desperately, "it's not even your fight! Why are you doing this?"

"Joe, you're going to get out of here and so will I. We're going to survive the moment."

"But there are 20 of them!!"

"Never run away."

David wouldn't back down no matter how much his friend begged him to leave. There were a bunch of metal garbage cans sitting on the curb awaiting pickup. Reaching down, David grabbed the cover off one of the cans, handed it to Yossi, and took another cover for himself. Twenty members of the Scorpions were about to attack and they were protecting themselves with garbage-can covers.

The distance between them lessened until the gang members were standing a few feet away. Yossi's heart was beating so loudly he was sure that everyone standing in their vicinity could hear it.

"This is our last chance," he whispered to David. "Let's turn into the alleyway and run for our lives!"

"We're not running anywhere."

The chief of the Scorpions took a step forward. He was a huge Irish teenager with bright-red hair and a red face. He had a hulking, bruising body that had seen years of fighting on the streets of New York.

"You are going to pay for what you did."

The next few minutes passed as if in a dream. All Yossi and David had were the garbage-can covers, but they held on to them for dear life, swiping and smashing against their opponents. Twenty against two, but they gave as good as they got. Five minutes later they heard the welcome sounds of the police sirens heading their way, and 10 seconds later everyone had disappeared.

By some miracle the two of them had managed to survive with their lives, but they had been beaten badly.

"David," Yossi said, "what are we going to do? Now both of us are marked! They are never going to stop until they destroy us both!!"

David remained unfazed.

"Joe," he said, repeating his earlier sentiments, "if you run, you always end up running! You have to stand your ground and protect your people."

As impossibly challenging as all this was for a young man who had no interest in living a life of violence, Yossi's time on the streets would teach him some important lessons that would remain with him throughout his life. It taught him what it meant to believe in yourself, and that a person should never be afraid to fight for the important things in life. In his early years, that meant survival on the streets. In the years to come, Rabbi Yossi Wallis would transfer those lessons, learned on the battlefields of the Bronx, to the challenge of returning his fellow Jews back to the Master of the World.

At that moment, however, his work for Arachim and Klal Yisrael lay shrouded in an improbable future, and all young Joe Wallis felt was fear.

♦ ♦ ♦

An anxious week passed. The word on the street was there was going to be a rumble down at the school yard of Taft High, which was situated right on the border that separated the Irish/Italian and Puerto Rican neighborhoods from each other. The Scorpions were planning a fight with a Puerto Rican gang that wanted to break into the neighborhood. If the Puerto Ricans won, they'd take that as a sign that they could begin moving into the area en masse, and the Irish and Italians were determined to prevent this by any means possible. In an ironic turn of events, the street fights between the teenagers usually gave a pretty good indication of what their parents could expect in the future. Both sides were equally determined to fight it out to the bitter end, since in the event of a win by the Puerto Ricans, the Irish and Italians would be faced by an invasion on their own street corners.

Every kid in the neighborhood was talking about the upcoming fight as if it were the sporting event of the year. Truthfully, it wasn't difficult to understand why everyone was taking the matter so seriously, considering that this fight would help determine the future social makeup of the neighborhood.

The night of the fight found Yossi Wallis hiding in a tenement in one of the adjacent alleyways, watching the proceedings from a street-level window that gave him a decent view of the situation. He watched as more and more Scorpions converged on the outside of the school yard. It was a chilling sight. Suddenly, he heard the sound of a souped-up '56 Chevy convertible screeching to a stop right beside the gang. The heads of the Scorpions were sitting in the car.

The atmosphere was intense. The rest of the gang took up positions on the car's outer perimeter, like some ancient battle formation. The car began to slowly roll in the direction of the school yard, and the gang members ran alongside it like infantry surrounding a tank.

As the Scorpion "tank" made its approach to Taft High, Yossi Wallis jumped out of his hiding place, ran over to the gang, and said, "You guys want some help?"

He had known from his first day walking the streets of the Bronx that the only real way to survive in the urban jungle was to join one of the gangs. This was his ticket back to life, the only way to avoid a death sentence.

The moment of truth had arrived. He waited breathlessly to hear the answer.

They were both surprised and impressed by his offer.

"Come with us," one of the leaders said, after a moment's hesitation, and Yossi joined the outer phalanx of guys defending the Scorpion vehicle from attack. Approaching Taft High they could see the Puerto Rican gang walking toward them from the opposite direction. The Scorpions reached the school yard, climbed the fence. The Puerto Ricans did the same on the other side of the yard.

There were no winners or losers that night. A few minutes of mayhem, of brute violence, and then the sound of sirens filled the bloody night. Everyone ran for his life, dispersing in every direction. Yossi scaled the fence and threw himself down a flight of stairs into one of the basements lining the street. After he caught his breath, he looked around and noticed that he wasn't the only person to have taken refuge there. He was surrounded by Scorpions nursing their wounds.

He looked at them. They looked at him. Finally one of them spoke up.

"Joe," he said, "you fought pretty good out there."

Yossi nodded at him.

On vacation from the Bronx. Yossi is sitting on the car.

The Italian stared the Jewish boy in the eye.

"You want to be part of our gang?"

Yossi pretended to think about it for a few seconds, but the truth was, this was all he really wanted. Being part of the gang would mean that the Jewish boy from the Bronx could finally walk down the Grand Concourse without fear of being attacked or challenged.

"Yes, I want to join."

"Okay, you're in," the kid said. And just like that, Yossi "Joe" Wallis became the very first Jewish Scorpion.

CHAPTER FIVE

Bloodied by the abbreviated rumble, his initiation complete, Yossi bought himself a black leather jacket and walked the streets with newfound confidence. He could navigate the Bronx sidewalks now without fear of attack. Instead of threats, there were greetings.

"Hiya, Joe."

"How's it going, Joe?"

"Nice to see you, Joe."

Life had changed into something remarkably less stressful and he appreciated every moment. Some nights the gang had nothing to do. Then they would stand at one of the street corners and sing together a cappella. It was funny and kind of ironic seeing the toughest Italian guys singing their hearts out, before getting drunk and breaking the windows of passing cars.

Life in the Bronx.

♦ ♦ ♦

David and Yossi were still the best of friends. David was happy that his friend had been accepted to the Scorpions; this meant that no one dared look at David the wrong way, since everyone knew that the two of them were like brothers. But after the first feelings of relief, Yossi found he'd traded one difficult life for another that was even tougher. He didn't like the way the gang members ran their lives. He hated the fact that they preyed on the weak and bothered people just because they could. More than once, he wished that he had never moved to the Bronx and been forced to associate with low-lifes like these.

"Joe"

After some months, with gang life palling on him, he decided to leave the Scorpions come what may.

A few days after his momentous decision he got together with David for a drink and some conversation.

"I'm leaving the Scorpions."

"What are you going to do now?"

"It's we—what are we going to do. We are going to open up our own gang."

"We're what?"

"You heard me. We're opening the first all-Jewish gang in the Bronx. Our goal will be to provide protection for the Jews in our neighborhood who are unable to protect themselves. Are you in?"

David was in.

They called their gang "the Louie Louies." David's last name was Lewis and he was the strongest, toughest young Jew his age in the Bronx. There was also a popular song called "Louie Louie" that people were singing everywhere. Before they knew it, they had more recruits than they could handle, many of them Israelis who were sick of being bullied, and they were in business.

Yossi removed the Scorpion from his leather jacket and for the first time ever, the Jews of the Bronx were under the protection of young Jewish kids whose priority was to ensure that no one harmed or harassed their brethren.

Wallis's group of tough young Jews was not even slightly affiliated with religion. The only reason they identified with Jewish people was because their parents were Jewish. But they had made up their minds to stand behind their people, fully intending to live up to their promise.

And they did.

♦ ♦ ♦

The next part of the story was almost inevitable.

It began when the Italian Mafia began showing a more than casual interest in Yossi Wallis.

By now, he was running his own Jewish gang and building up a reputation as quite the tough guy. It was only a matter of time until they came for David and Joe: to make them an offer they couldn't refuse.

Back then, if you were a teen in the Bronx, the main thing was to make it in life. Looking around the run-down neighborhood, at the hardworking men in their dirty undershirts, old before their time, all they knew was that they wanted something different. Something better. The only question was how to get out of the quicksand and onto the beach.

From time to time one of the big boys would come down to their part of town. Those guys wore suits and ties, sunglasses shielded their eyes, their fedoras were rakishly tilted to the side. They smelled like money. They were made men. When one of those guys walked down the street, everyone's eyes followed their every move. They were the ticket out of a no-future life.

What no one knew, however, was that once you tested the water, there was no way out. You became part of them, part of the Cosa Nostra for life.

It didn't happen all at once. They drew you in with their bait, until you hung there like a fish at the end of their rod, squirming and struggling, wanting to throw yourself off the hook, but not knowing how.

That's the way it went with the young Jew from the Bronx.

Future rabbi.

Future outreach professional.

Future warrior for the Jewish nation.

Back then, however, he was just a kid, finding his way.

♦ ♦ ♦

One day, Yossi was hanging out at the corner with a few of the boys when everything changed. It happened so quickly, from one second to the next. It was all because of the man. The man wore a dark blue suit and a matching tie. His hat was white and it shone in the sun. He looked like a heavy. And that's exactly how he wanted to look.

"Come here, kid," he said to Yossi.

Yossi glanced at his friends. They met his gaze wide eyed. Why was this "made" man calling their friend over for a conversation?

"Don't worry, kid, nothing to be afraid of. Just come over here. I want to ask you something."

Yossi "Joe" Wallis was intimidated by the newcomer, no question about it, but there was no way he was going to admit that to the neighborhood boys. Casually, with his heart pounding in his chest, he sauntered over to the man with the suspenders and starched white shirt.

"Let's take a walk."

"See you later," Yossi said to one and all. He turned to the stranger. "Where do you want to go, Mr.—?"

"Why don't you show me around the neighborhood?"

"Okay."

"Tell me something, kid, how old are you?"

"I'm 17."

"Best years of your life, enjoy them, enjoy them."

"I am."

"Okay, here's what I want you to do. See that car over there across the street?"

"The red Cadillac?"

"Yes."

Joe and the gang

"I see it."

"When I come back here tomorrow morning, I want to see it minus the wheels and up on blocks. Do you understand?"

As mischief went, it was pretty tame for the Bronx.

"What's in it for me?"

"You'll get a hundred dollars up front and another hundred when I see that the job was done."

They shook on it.

That night Yossi returned to the Caddy with a bunch of guys from the Louie Louies. They had that car up and off the ground in no time and five minutes later, the deal was done. The tires had disappeared and the car was up on blocks. The next morning Yossi met the guy in the suit, who praised his work and handed him another hundred dollar bill.

"Thanks, mister," he said to the man when they parted. "If you need me for anything else, don't hesitate to ask."

"Don't worry, I won't."

♦ ♦ ♦

He didn't. Over the next few months, they ran into each other a little too often for comfort. There was always another mission for Yossi to carry out. Though he didn't know it at the time, he was being graded on the jobs that he did. People were watching him, deciding whether they wanted to groom him for a future life in the Mob. He carried out the jobs they assigned him faithfully and more importantly, never bragged about the work he did. That element, more than anything else, was what impressed the leadership. They needed people they could trust and Joe Wallis fit the bill.

Things were moving along beautifully, when the man in the suit sent the young man on another mission. This time the job they had him do involved actual violence, and his conscience protested.

"It boiled down to the Jewish element," Rabbi Wallis explained so many decades later. "It was my *neshamah* talking to me, trying to save me from myself."

"How was it?" the man asked him the next day.

"I don't want to do anything like that ever again," he told the man emphatically. The man didn't respond, but nodded thoughtfully. The following afternoon as Yossi was walking down the street, a fancy car suddenly pulled up beside him. Two guys jumped out. They grabbed his arms and proceeded to give him a beating. The handsome man in the suit and white hat stood by and watched the entire spectacle. When Yossi appealed for mercy, he said, "You don't say no to us. You don't tell us what you are willing to do or what your morals are. We tell you what to do, not the other way around."

They were trying to teach Joe Wallis a lesson. He was not to question orders. He was not to even consider disobeying their commands. It was a tough beating, leaving his body bruised and sore, but it was probably the best thing that had ever happened to this kid from the Bronx. Every blow helped him understand that he had to escape their net before it was too late.

But how? A young man couldn't just decide to leave the Mob. If he moved somewhere else, they'd find him. They weren't afraid of anyone or anything, and they had informants everywhere. Yossi knew that he couldn't live life this way, but as he fell onto his bed, black and blue and aching, he couldn't think of any way to escape them.

There's nothing like a good beating to get the brain moving; when he woke up the next day he had an idea.

Near his high school, there was a series of recruitment booths for the Army, Navy, and Air Force. This was the answer. He was going to enlist. He knew that the one place he'd be safe from the Mob was in the military.

He wasted no time and didn't ask anyone for advice. Before the day was up, Joe Wallis had already enlisted.

He never spoke to the man in the suit again.

Though he had managed to escape the Cosa Nostra connections, his friend David did not. He remained in the Mafia for life. And although Yossi took another path—one completely removed from the slightest taint of organized crime—he still kept in touch with David. Once you serve in the trenches with someone, your friendship is for life. They'd become close when they were young, and there are no friends like the friends of your youth. Yossi Wallis loved David like a brother. David had been there for him, bled for him. Acted like a brother in every way. And brothers do not cut one another out of their lives.

Yet though they went their separate ways, their paths would cross again in the future. That, however, would occur only many years later.

Meanwhile, Yossi Wallis continued living according to the signposts and directions that Hashem sent his way. His life was being choreographed with extreme care because there was a mission waiting for him. A mission so powerful that it would literally change the world. One Jew at a time.

He just didn't know it yet.

CHAPTER SIX

Once Yossi Wallis had made up his mind to join the military, he moved full speed ahead. The Vietnam War was in full swing and the military was actively recruiting. Whereas most young men had the choice to enlist or wait until they were drafted, Yossi Wallis was straight out of options. The Mafia wanted him in their ranks and he couldn't think of any other way of avoiding them.

The Navy, Air Force, and Marines all had their own booths. The Marines in particular drew him with their catchy slogans and promises about job training and the ability to change the world. At that point in time joining the military was not something most people aspired to do. America was against the war. University students were turning their campuses into bastions of radical antimilitary rebellion. The country was in turmoil, with an incredibly wide divide separating the political leadership and the younger generation. Flying off to 'Nam was not a popular move since a majority of Americans couldn't figure out why they were sending their troops to the other side of the world to fight in the first place. When the Vietnam vets came back to the States, they'd remove their uniforms before going out to the street, rather than face the nation's disdain.

On the other hand, Yossi had seen many pictures of the Marines fighting in World War II, and if he was going to join any particular branch within the military, that was the one in which he wanted to serve. He presented himself at the Marine recruitment booth the morning after the assault and told the officer sitting behind the desk that he wanted to sign up.

The man looked him up and down.

"You're going to have to go through the admission process," he said. "There will be quite a few tests, both mental and physical, before you can join the Marines."

"What do you mean by physical tests?"

"We need to determine whether you're strong enough."

Yossi had no problem with that. Next thing he knew they were taking him out to the playground to see how many push-ups, chin-ups, and sit-ups he could do.

"Okay," the Marine instructor said. "You definitely have the physical stamina needed, but we still have to test your mental acumen."

Yossi had never given much credence to the importance of schoolwork up until then—not being able to imagine why he should care where Napoleon Bonaparte was born or why the

Joseph Wallis's certificate from the U.S. Marines

French people had had him exiled—but the Marines had him tested with an eye to his overall capabilities. They were appreciative of the intuitive grasp he showed toward mathematics and sciences. Within a short time, he had been accepted to what many considered the most elite branch of the military.

The Louie Louies were very proud of him. Being accepted to the Marines meant that he was taking a step up in life. A few days later, one of his friends joined the Air Force, while another joined the Coast Guard. The word flew around the Bronx: Joe Wallis, ex-member of the Scorpions, had been accepted to the Marines. Big news! Everyone was excited about his accomplishment and proud of the fact that he'd taken such a courageous step.

There was just one person who was opposed to the news: Yossi's father.

"There is no way in the world I am going to allow my son to become a marine," he yelled at Yossi. "You think I want to see you come home in a casket?"

"But I want to become a helicopter pilot!"

"Not for all the money in the world!"

His father—the meek, ineffectual immigrant—suddenly showed his true strength. He hired a firm of top-class lawyers and slapped an injunction against the Marines for having accepted Yossi illegally, based on the fact that Yossi was the only son of a Holocaust survivor. The military was convinced and gave him a deferment on one condition: his agreement to attend night-school courses in engineering at City College.

"If you manage to maintain a B average over the next two semesters, you'll receive a permanent deferral from the military," he was told. "But if you fail, you'll be drafted and sent off to war."

Though his exit strategy hadn't panned out, the Mafia, it seemed, chose to ignore Yossi, realizing that he'd chosen a different path, and he never heard from them again.

Yossi Wallis was suddenly filled with a newfound ambition to succeed in life, though he was still not completely sure how to succeed or even what success really was.

♦ ♦ ♦

It was during this exciting time of life that he met his wife.

Sandy and Yossi hit it off immediately and it wasn't long before they decided to get married. Like most things in Yossi Wallis's life, though, the courtship wasn't simple. Sandy was Jewish, upper class, a gentle girl with perfect manners and style. Lots of style. Yossi Wallis was a child of the Bronx, a former gang member, proud wearer of a leather jacket, tough guy, and, if he was being honest, not upper class at all. Yet despite all the differences, they knew it was right and that they were meant for each other.

Sandy's parents, Mr. and Mrs. Milstein, didn't quite see it that way.

They took one look at the man she had chosen and knew where he was coming from. They wondered how he'd ever be able to take care of their daughter. They were not in favor of the match.

Vociferously not in favor.

Sandy's friends, too, were against the match. At times it seemed like everyone was against them getting married. Yet they stuck it out and made it through the engagement period intact. Sandy knew the real person hiding beneath the tough exterior. She saw Yossi's inner core, a combination of gentleness and strength, and recognized his capabilities. Much like Rachel the wife of Rabbi

Sandy and Joe

Yossi's mother with the bride and groom.

Akiva (whom neither of them had ever heard of!), Sandy was able to look past his rough exterior to what was inside, and see the future and the potential. Once she recognized the truth of who he was, she made her decision and didn't allow anyone to change her mind.

The Wallis wedding was a classic example of two worlds meeting. On one side of the room guests saw Sandy and her bridesmaids: gentle and genteel, the upper-class progeny of established homes. People who had grown up with money and pride. They had gone to the right schools and camps, had done all the right things. Yossi's friends, on the other hand… They were street kids, tough guys, boys who thought leather jackets were the height of fashion and had never learned what it meant to be polite.

It all came together at the wedding, the two worlds colliding with terrific force. His friends couldn't get over who Sandy was and what she represented. As for Sandy's parents, friends, and relatives, the less said the better.

Suffice it to say, there were quite a few people at that wedding who weren't as happy as they might have been. But it didn't matter to the young Mr. and Mrs. Wallis, because they knew it was going to be okay. When you know, you know, and they knew. Sure, on the outside, the two of them couldn't have been more different, but on the inside where it counted, they were perfect for each other.

With marriage came a new focus and different priorities, with Yossi starting to truly understand that he didn't have to remain in the same quagmire he'd been in since moving to the States. Life was filled with opportunity and it was time to begin developing himself into the person Sandy had seen hidden beneath the leather.

It's incredible what the right wife can do for a person.

♦ ♦ ♦

From the moment he came to the realization that he wanted more out of life and that his dreams were obtainable and not fairy tales, everything began to change. Yossi stopped hanging out with his old friends and closeted himself in his home from morning until evening, passionately studying for his tests. When report cards were handed out at the end of the semester, he discovered to his surprise and delight that he had achieved close to a perfect A average in the science courses he'd taken.

The military grew excited now.

"There's no reason for you to content yourself with a night-school education," he was told. "We want you to become a full-time university student."

So he did.

He majored in engineering—an extremely tough field—and passed his tests. For the first time in his life he was actually doing something worthwhile and feeling good about himself for it. People couldn't believe what he had managed to accomplish in so short a time. He hadn't changed his personality completely, still insisting on wearing his trademark black leather jacket wherever he went. But on the inside his ambitions had been critically altered. If just half a year earlier his greatest ambition had been to enter the field of construction, now he was dreaming of a career at the highest level.

The little boy from the Bronx was finally starting to grow up.

♦ ♦ ♦

The military kept its word and gave him a deferment, just as they had promised. But not wanting to let go completely, they conditioned the deferment on his accepting job offers with specific defense contractors. This meant that he was being offered highly classified work while still a student. It was a far, far cry from his days working as a paperboy. One summer the military sent him to work as an intern at Brookhaven National Laboratory in Long Island. Brookhaven was a gigantic institute dealing exclusively with the field of nuclear development and instrumentation. Some of Yossi's fellow employees at Brookhaven had been part of the original team on the Manhattan Project, which developed the atom bombs that were dropped on Hiroshima and Nagasaki during World War II.

Sometimes he looked around and couldn't believe that the kid from the Bronx who'd spent most of his early years in the States running away from Irish and Italian kids was now a member of a government team consisting of some of the smartest minds in the country. The U.S. military assigned him to different firms for various short-term projects. One firm in particular did a lot of business with Arab countries. The fact that Yossi was taken on by this particular company was a story in itself, because the firm never hired Jews. Many of their clients hated Jews and wanted nothing to do with them, and a majority of the influential people working there identified with these beliefs and did their best to keep the atmosphere "Jew-free." The company had contracts with countries that didn't allow Jews entrance and since the employees had to travel to those countries, there were no Jews.

Being that this was the United States of America, a company (especially one that worked directly on military defense contracts) couldn't very well refuse to hire Jews as part of their charter.

But the company could make their hiring calls based on the last names of the people that were sent to them by the military. If your name was Berkowitz, Goldstein, or Jacobowitz, there was no chance of your being selected. But Yossi's name was J. C. Wallis, and there was nothing intrinsically or overtly Jewish in the name. Without even intending to do so, the son of Holocaust survivors slipped through the corporate cracks into the world of the surprisingly virulent American anti-Semites.

J. C. Wallis had been accepted for the job and reported for work, unsuspectingly entering the den of the demons.

♦ ♦ ♦

On his first day on the job he looked around and noticed that he had entered a world without Jews. Everyone was white, tall, and Waspy. The atmosphere was cold, genteel, and tasted like hate. Worse, there were many Germans employed at this company: scientists whose knowledge had been deemed too commercially valuable by the United States government to punish them or send them into exile for their work with the Nazis. Instead of being exposed for their past crimes, they were employed by the government and paid lavish salaries to share their know-how, experience, and training with the United States.

Yossi's immediate superior, and the man tasked with his training, was named Mr. Eckhart. The moment he opened his mouth and introduced himself, Yossi recognized the hated accent.

"Are you a German?"

His boss nodded proudly.

"Indeed I am."

"Where were you during the war?"

"I served my country in the German military."

He must have seen the look on Yossi's face, because he quickly clarified, "But I was sent to Finland."

(Millions of Nazi soldiers, and every one of them served in Finland. What an incredible coincidence!)

So his boss was a former Nazi, candidly remarking that he had served as an engineer during World War II.

Yossi set about doing his job while ignoring the comments he heard at the water cooler from time to time. He couldn't, however, control the thoughts constantly running through his mind, unstoppable, like runaway freight trains careening off the tracks.

The old man working at the computer console, what had he done for the Nazis at Dachau?

The brilliant scientist who seemed so involved in his work, had he been an engineer at Treblinka?

What about that rugged-looking man, with the coiled muscles under his tweed jacket? Might he not have been an SS officer stationed at Birkenau?

I can't believe that I'm working for a bunch of Nazis, he thought to himself. *Me, Yossi Wallis of all people! These people killed every single one of my grandparents and I'm working for them!!*

Still he held his peace. At least temporarily.

One day the company threw a party for the workers, as a way for everyone to get to know the newest members of staff. Attendance, while not mandatory, was certainly expected. One of the conference rooms was set up for the party, with fancy napkins and china cups for coffee and tea. When the working day drew to a close, all the employees straggled into the conference room, where the newest workers were asked to stand up, introduce themselves, and say a few words about where they came from, their education, and previous work experience in their respective fields.

They went around the room. Employee after employee introduced himself, making no waves and drawing no undue attention. Then it was Yossi's turn.

Now it was time. Finally.

"Honored colleagues," he began. "I'm so happy to be a member of such a prestigious company and I hope that together we will achieve an even greater level of success. I certainly intend to carry out my job to the best of my potential."

The bosses were smiling, mentally patting themselves on the back at the sight of their wonderful new protégé.

"That said," he continued, "and having been here already for a few weeks, I can't help feeling that a mistake has been made regarding hiring me."

That caught the attention of everyone sitting in the room. The heads of the department managers snapped up and they fixed their eyes on him. He focused his gaze on the older members of the company: the ones that cut the deals with the Arab countries and the ones who hired the Nazis walking their corridors.

"You're probably asking yourselves why on earth I'm telling you all this, right? Well, I'm a real honest person and since we're all supposed to give a little background about ourselves, I guess that means that I should probably be coming clean with all of you."

They were really nervous now, trying to figure out what they could possibly have missed when they went over his profile.

"Here's the thing. Because my name is Joe Wallis you were under the erroneous impression that I am just as much a WASP or an Aryan (as the case may be) as you are. The truth, however, is that I am and have always been a Jewish boy—and the initials J. C. happen to stand for the name *Joseph Chaim Wallis*."

Their mouths had dropped open somewhere along the way. He could see the consternation in their eyes.

"You probably had no idea," he carried on mercilessly, "that both my father and mother are graduates of one of Germany's finest institutions, a middle-size correctional facility named Auschwitz. I believe you've all heard of it..."

An extremely awkward silence descended on the room.

As he spoke, Yossi studied their faces, witnessing a host of emotions fluttering across every face. They'd made terrible comments about Jews numerous times in his presence and even worse, his own boss was a Nazi! He looked at them and saw panic.

"My dear colleagues," he said to them, "you don't have to worry about what I'm going to say or who I'm going to tell, because I'm quitting right now, effective immediately!"

It took them a couple of minutes before their mouths finally closed, while Yossi went to his cubicle, retrieved his belongings, and exited the premises. He took the subway home, replaying the dramatic scene over and over in his mind the entire journey. Then he walked through the door and found his wife.

"Sandy," he said. "I quit my job today."

She looked at him.

"I don't want us to live in America anymore."

He paused for a moment before continuing.

"On my second day in America, I was welcomed to the school yard by a platoon of teenagers screaming '*Heil Hitler*' while delivering the Nazi salute, and my latest job for the United States military means working with former Nazis and their protégés. I don't want to be a part of this anymore. I want us to move to Israel."

It didn't happen overnight, but recognizing the truth in what he was saying, his wife agreed to give Israel a try. And so the Wallis family, then consisting of two, flew to Europe and backpacked their way across the continent. With very little in the way of possessions, travel was easy and decisions were made on the spur of the moment according to how they felt on any given day. The next few months passed in a haze of adventure and the freedom of youth. Neither of them had ever really been on their own before and the feeling of finally being able to make their own decisions was heady and liberating.

They traveled by train, plane, and automobile, and eventually one day they crossed the border into Israel. When the customs officer stamped their passports and waved them into the country, they looked at each other with broad smiles and walked with confident steps into their new lives. As the palm trees waved in the tepid breeze and a *chamsin* wind blew gritty sand across the far-off reddish mountains of Moav, Yossi and Sandy Wallis gazed through the window of the Egged bus, listened to the words of Hebrew coming out of the radio, and felt that they had just come home.

CHAPTER SEVEN

Yossi's parents owned an apartment in Petach Tikvah that the couple used as a temporary base. It was rent-free, centrally located, and perfect as a starting point. It was also small, shabby, and more than a little rundown, but they were young, idealistic, and happy to be in Israel, and they made the best of it. Being that army service in Israel was compulsory, Yossi figured he might as well get it over with as soon as possible so he could start a business and get on with life. He went down to the local army induction center to offer his services, and was informed that he would most likely be drafted within the next three months. This meant that he was temporarily unoccupied and unemployed and in need of a job with which to fill his time.

The first job he found was in construction. With no experience in this particular field, he was assigned the worst parts of the job to do. The construction company he worked for had been awarded the job of refurbishing the Great Synagogue of Tel Aviv on Allenby Street, and it was his job to transport wheelbarrows filled with cement up to the uppermost floor. Muscles straining, he carted the heavy loads up the steep, unfinished ramps from morning till night. Having just left a job where he'd been using his brain in a top-level capacity, it was very difficult for him to reconcile the person he'd been and the work he'd been involved in with the man he'd become, doing menial labor with Arab workers from the lowest echelons of society. He did this for about a month, detesting every minute.

Then one day during his lunch break, he happened to pick up a newspaper and saw an ad that seemed to be tailor made for him.

The ORT Naval Academy in Ashdod is seeking a mathematics teacher for one month. To apply, please call the following number...

He called the number, applied for the job, and was hired immediately.

He had no teaching experience, had never heard of the school in question, and was accepted without an interview. Their immediate acceptance should have raised a few red flags of warning—or at least given him an indication of what he was getting himself into—but being optimistic by nature, Yossi merely thanked Heaven for getting him off the construction site and into a classroom where he could use his head and years of academic knowledge to inspire Israeli youth to reach the stars. He did not dream that he had just been accepted for a teaching post at what was arguably the worst high school in the country.

♦ ♦ ♦

The class Yossi was assigned were boys in their final year of high school. This was a navy feeder school—Ashdod being located on the Mediterranean —and 95 percent of the class intended to join what was then the Israeli military's weakest link. The bus dropped him off a 10-minute walk from the school, which was located just adjacent to the Ashdod beach, the sand dunes literally beginning where the sports facilities came to an end. The grounds were impressive if slightly rundown, and he entered the school building and found the principal's office with no trouble. He introduced himself, was handed a stack of math textbooks, and led down the hall to the classroom. The closer they got to the classroom, the more noise he heard. Kids were screaming and singing and banging on the tables and walls, and they could hear the sound of desks being slammed into the floor. It sounded like a carnival in there. With no idea what to expect, he was stunned when the principal opened the door of the classroom and, with no word of explanation or introduction to the class, proceeded to shove his newest recruit into the room and run away—almost as if he had just offered him up as a lamb to the hungry wolves.

Yossi knew nothing about education aside from his natural instincts. But it didn't seem as if anybody cared whether he was qualified to teach or not, because the students couldn't even be bothered to take note of the fact that a newcomer had just been shoved into their universe. Nobody looked, nobody cared. They went on banging, thumping, throwing things at one another, and singing American rock and roll music at the top of their lungs.

What on earth am I supposed to do with this bunch of kids? Yossi asked himself. He felt as if he'd walked right back into his distant past, back into the Bronx, and he was once again staring into the faces of the neighborhood thugs who were daring him to take a stand.

It didn't take him long to make up his mind.

Walking over to the teacher's desk at the front of the room, he slammed his palm down on the wooden surface with his every ounce of strength. The sound of that slap reverberated through the room and echoed down the hallway. It sounded like someone had fired a gun in close quarters and it quieted them down for a few seconds, as they finally looked at the person who had just been thrown into their lair.

"It's time to learn some math," he said to them.

"We don't want to learn any math," they yelled back. "We don't want to learn anything. In this school, we don't learn! What are you going to do about it?"

Ignoring their protests, he began attempting to teach them, while they remained true to their word and paid him no heed. None of them listened at all, except for one bespectacled, red-headed kid sitting in the front row, who listened carefully and took notes. The bell rang a few minutes later and the class jumped out of their seats as if choreographed and rushed out to the yard.

On the way out of the room, the toughest, most vocal boy in the class detoured over to the red-haired kid's side.

"You cooperated with the teacher and listened to him," he whispered, in a voice he made certain was loud enough for his teacher to hear. "If you walk outside to the yard, we're going to make sure you regret being such a goody-goody!"

Maybe the tough kid wanted Yossi to appreciate his power. But he had underestimated his newest opponent.

"Are you threatening this boy?" Yossi asked the student. "Because if you want to threaten anyone, why not start with me?"

Perhaps for the first time since he'd entered a classroom, the bully showed a bit of common sense.

"You're the teacher," he said. "I never hit teachers."

"So what if I'm the teacher," Yossi replied. "If you're so anxious to fight someone, you might as well fight someone who can actually defend himself!"

Yossi Wallis wanted to teach this class. That's what the school was paying him to do. It was obvious to him that no teacher would ever be successful with the class as long as this bully was allowed free rein, and he was determined to vanquish him as soon as possible so he could get down to the real reason he was there. This situation was no different from what he'd faced growing up; the same rules of attack, divide and conquer applied just as much here as they had among the tenement projects surrounding Taft High.

The kid looked at his teacher, taking in his build and fine athletic form. On the one hand he was scared to fight someone with such obvious confidence. On the other hand, his pride was at stake, as was his position of class leader. He didn't know what to do.

"Okay," he said at last, "let's fight."

"Done," Yossi told him.

"When?"

"Today at 4 o'clock when all the teachers leave, we go over to the beach and fight it out. Starting up with the weak kids in the class means starting with me. This afternoon, we'll see how tough you really are."

News of the upcoming fight spread like wildfire through the class, as everyone waited anxiously for 4 o'clock to arrive. When the bell rang and the class was dismissed, all the students—and their math teacher—made their way down the hallway, out to the playground. From there they stood in a large, ragged circle on the beach, waiting, waiting, waiting, until every teacher's car had left the parking lot and the coast was clear.

The two of them stood in the middle of the circle and started to box. Being that the kid had grown up on the streets of Ashdod, he'd imagined that he could handle himself in any given situation, but he was no match for someone who had fought with the Scorpions and Louie Louies in the Bronx, and who had been recruited by the Mafia.

The kid didn't stand a chance. A minute after they'd begun, he was on the floor and the class was cheering on the teacher who'd become their new hero. Apparently, leader or no leader, there was a lot of pent-up hostility toward the bully for the way he abused his position in the classroom hierarchy. Nobody was too sad to see him on the floor, receiving a taste of his own medicine for once.

"I hope you learned your lesson about starting up with weaker students," Yossi told the boy. "I don't want to see it happening again."

The entire class was quiet now, respect for their new teacher clearly evident in their eyes.

But the bully hadn't yet learned his lesson. Wiping the sand from his face and hands, he said, "I'm going to teach you a lesson. Tomorrow morning my father and brothers will be here with me and then we'll see if you're so tough."

"School starts at 8 o'clock tomorrow," Yossi replied. "I'll be here waiting for you at 7:30."

He was waiting on the beach bright and early the next morning. He wasn't alone; the entire class, it seemed, had risen at the crack of dawn and were waiting with anticipation to see the outcome of the match. At 7:30 on the dot, the bully arrived at the beach—three men accompanying him, all bearing a marked resemblance to one another. It was clear that his father and brothers had indeed arrived, determined to salvage the family's honor. They swaggered over toward the young teacher, and the father stepped into his face and asked with righteous bravado, "What did you do to my son yesterday?"

Yossi Wallis looked the man in the eye.

"Your son starts up with the weakest kids in the class," he told the man. "Kids like this," he added, pointing to the red-haired student. "He threatens them, beats them up. I told him, if he's such a brave guy, let him start up with me and win a fair fight, man to man. That's what happened yesterday... Ask him yourself."

The father turned to his son.

"Tell me the truth, did you start up with the *gingi* kid yesterday or not?"

"Yes, so what?"

"Did you have a fair fight with the teacher—one on one?"

The boy grudgingly admitted that it had been completely fair. The father and brothers shook the teacher's hand, wished him a good day, and left their son and brother on the beach to fight his own battles.

"Okay, boys," Yossi told them, "the action is over. Now it's time to go into class and learn some math."

They entered the school like the quietest of well-behaved lambs and Yossi Wallis surveyed them with affection. Round one was his. Now it was time to see if he could teach them anything. He told them to open their books. They obeyed. Five minutes later, they were involved in the day's lesson and, oddly enough, it soon became obvious that they were enjoying themselves. He challenged them to ask questions and to work things out for themselves.

The principal arrived 20 minutes after class officially began for the day. Curious as to how things were going with his bunch of tough guys, he made his way down the hall, intent on finding out how Yossi was handling the situation. To his immense surprise, there was no noise emanating through the walls. All was quiet.

He stood outside the door trying to figure out what was going on.

As he told Yossi later on, "I thought to myself, either they killed him, or they scared him off yesterday and he quit and never showed up today."

Barging into the classroom, the principal came skidding to a stop at the desk, faced with a sight he'd never seen in that classroom before. Every student was facing frontward. They were focused and attentive and some even had their hands in the air, and were waiting for their teacher to acknowledge them. Just yesterday, the principal had pushed Yossi through the door like a sacrifice to angry animals, yet somehow the animals had been tamed and he couldn't quite grasp what had occurred.

"What's going on here?" he asked.

"Everything's just fine," the teacher replied. "Is there anything in particular that I can help you with? I'm teaching them high-level mathematics and they're catching on like a house on fire. Some real sharp kids you have here."

Not knowing what to make of the situation but instinctively comprehending that he was missing part of the story, the principal told them to carry on and left the room.

And Yossi Wallis went back to teaching his students math—which was why he was being paid. The school tested his class two weeks later. The results were amazing, even better than he'd hoped, thereby proving the ancient adage once again that there is no such thing as dumb children.

In the short time that he served as their teacher, they came to love one another, in a way that only a teacher who possesses the respect of his students can manage to do. Yossi knew that they were all about to be inducted into the navy, and when he shared with them the fact that he was about to begin army service himself, they begged him to join the navy along with them and to serve as their officer.

"We'll follow you anywhere," they pleaded. "Please join us in the navy."

But it wasn't meant to be. He had studied radar technologies at the community college back when he joined the Marines and he had his eye on the air force. Much as he respected the navy, it wasn't for him.

"I'm enlisting in the air force," he explained to his students. "But no matter what we do or where we all end up, we're still going to keep in touch with one another."

And they did, for a good few years.

The month flew by, and his short-lived but rewarding teaching career came to an end. Yossi Wallis had learned a lot about teaching and teenagers and even about math, while reinforcing the lessons he had known all along—that every child is worth teaching—and that with the right education, every teenager can become a winner.

CHAPTER EIGHT

From the earliest days of his induction into the IDF at the Tel HaShomer army base, Yossi Wallis knew that despite being married and legally exempt from combat duty, he wanted to be in a unit that actually made a difference. He intended to become an officer in the IDF, and for that he needed to experience basic training and then go through pre-officer training courses, where he learned how to handle light and heavy weapons, machine guns, and pistols, and to use hand-to-hand combat in tight situations, along with important leadership techniques. Upon graduating the pre-officer courses, he was sent on to officer school at Mitzpeh Ramon for an additional half year of grueling work. When the course finally came to an end he was a fully commissioned officer in the Israeli army, assigned to the air force as a second lieutenant. Now he had to learn how airplanes work and techniques for air combat. He also gained familiarity with the various radar systems on different planes and helicopters.

Yossi was eventually assigned to a unit that dealt with electronic countermeasures, which essentially meant that he'd be focusing on countering the enemy's radar systems in real time. While the enemy attempted to use their sophisticated electronic systems (generously provided by what was then called the USSR) to figure out where the Israeli planes were flying, it was Yossi's job to jam their systems and to change frequencies so that they didn't know where to program their missiles to hit. He had to detect their radar systems before they detected his. It was extremely nerve-racking and painstaking work and the worst part about it was the fact that the margin of error was so very slim. One mistake could mean death for the pilot of a jet, plane, or helicopter.

Those were dangerous days in Israel's history, a few years before the Yom Kippur War, during what was known as the War of Attrition. Israeli soldiers were dug in deep on the Israeli side of the Suez Canal, while Egyptian forces were dug in equally as deep on their side. The Egyptians had batteries of missiles and were just waiting for the opportunity to use them. When Israeli jets flew over the border and into Egyptian territory, it was the job of officers like Yossi Wallis to jam the enemy radar frequencies so they remained unaware that the Israeli pilots were busy taking pictures of their military installments from high up above the Sinai.

Because the moment the Egyptians figured it out, a missile would be sent straight toward the Israeli jet.

♦ ♦ ♦

Near the Suez Canal stood a pole that reached into the sky like a militarized caricature of the Eiffel Tower. At its very tip was a radar-detection system that assisted the army to relay crucial information. Head in the clouds, the tower was exposed to the elements and needed maintenance on a regular basis. This meant climbing up an unending ladder of steel bars, no protection around the bars, nothing to catch a soldier if he slipped and fell. The higher you climbed, the scarier it became and you knew that the worst thing you could do was look down at the view, because the ground was so far below that you'd become dizzy and your hands would start to sweat, and then the challenge became three times as difficult.

And that was the easy part.

Because once you managed to climb all the way up to the top of the tower and were now in close proximity to the radar systems, you had to fix whatever was broken while hovering above the ground like a bird in flight. After attaching yourself to the tower, which incidentally swayed back and forth in the strong breeze blowing off the canal, you went about your work feeling like the whole thing was going to collapse at any second, throwing you to your death in the process. It was a difficult and nerve-racking experience.

One morning Yossi's commanding officer called him into his office and told him to climb the tower to fix a problem with the system. Yossi slowly climbed the rungs, hands feeling like they were slipping, brain protesting every step of the way. When he finally reached the top of the tower, he fastened himself to the pole and began the repair. Suddenly he heard a whoosh and felt an extraordinary rush of air enveloping him on every side. Glancing upward, he saw three Egyptian MIGs screaming toward him, flying at incredible speeds and rushing across the canal to bomb their positions! He had never felt as exposed in his life as he felt the moment those jets roared over his head, so close he imagined he could reach up and touch their wings.

It would have been the easiest thing in the world for one of the pilots to flip the strafing button on his machine gun from off to on, sending a stream of death to knock him off his perch. Yossi held on desperately for life as the tower rocked from side to side, caught in the undertow of air as much as he was. He held his breath as the jets passed overhead, envisioning in those seconds his wife, Sandy, his parents, his future, not knowing if those were his final moments on earth or if he'd been granted a reprieve.

He would never be able to fully describe the feeling of relief he experienced when he was finally back on the ground. It was one of those moments when the difference between life and death was no more than the thinnest line.

♦ ♦ ♦

One day Yossi's unit was ordered to cross the Suez Canal and to infiltrate the nearest army base, where they would make off with an entire radar system and bring it back to Israel—giving them the unique opportunity to study the newest Russian radar frequencies and technology. Such information was invaluable and the army needed it desperately. The brass toyed with sending in a combination of commando forces on the ground along with helicopters for the actual removal of the system, which was the size of a large room, but in the end decided to carry out the surprise mission from the air without sending in the ground troops. Intelligence informed them that they suspected the presence of Russian radar experts at the actual site, whose job was to train the Egyptians in how to use the equipment. No one was overly excited about the prospect of having to neutralize (translate: kill) Russian forces, which would further intensify the Soviet animosity toward Israel.

The new air force officer
with his wife and mother

The mission was scheduled for the middle of the night, but no one could foretell if the Egyptians would stand and fight or give up and run for cover. In a scenario where the enemy began shooting at the soldiers, it would not be possible to remove the entire system and therefore someone would have to decide which were the most important elements and dismantle those, all the while under fire.

Yossi Wallis was that someone.

The radar system was cased in an outside shell that sat on wheels and could be moved using heavy machinery. There were antennae on its roof and there was no question of mis-

Graduating from Officer Training
(Yossi is wearing sunglasses)

taking it for something else. It would be Yossi's job to enter the shell, decide which electronic systems to remove in case of an attack, and then to physically dismantle those units the old-fashioned way, using a screwdriver and manual tools. This type of mission—which necessitated remaining absolutely cool and controlled under enemy fire—was something he had been trained for at length. Now it was time to put that training to the test.

♦ ♦ ♦

They took off from their base in a CH53, a huge military helicopter built by Sikorsky, which was capable of lifting the entire radar system and carrying it back to Israel across the canal. It was 3 a.m., the dead of night, and there were 10 soldiers sitting in the back of that swaying machine. The canal lay beneath them, black, watery, deep. Water and sky blended together in one endless mélange of dark shapes that gave nothing away. They looked around at their fellow soldiers and wondered if all of them would be returning or...

The mission was extremely dangerous. It is easy for the radar officers to miss a clue or lose focus for even two seconds—and then, bam!!—because sometimes, two seconds is all it takes to lose a helicopter and its contingent of the finest, best-trained officers in the army.

Normally it was Yossi who was on the ground or in a nearby aircraft manning the radar controls, but he'd been assigned another job to do that night and now someone else was doing the job he knew so well. He could only hope the officer knew what he was doing, because one split second of indecision could spell the end for all of them.

♦ ♦ ♦

It took just a few minutes to cross the Suez Canal—a few gripping minutes spent feeling like sitting ducks ripe for attack by a Russian missile. But the Hand of Hashem guided them across the canal and they descended onto the Egyptian side without mishap—the stunned troops and Russian consultants fleeing in disarray at the sight of the Israeli Sikorsky unabashedly coming in for a landing right in the center of their base.

The soldiers spilled out of the helicopter and surrounded the radar-control system. Minutes later, they had attached multiple chains from the roof of the radar system to the underside of the helicopter, thereby allowing the helicopter to pluck the entire system off the ground like a piece of ripe fruit off a low-hanging branch. The carefully trained troops then raced back to the safety of the Sikorsky, which, with an ear-splitting roar, lifted off the ground, the entire Soviet-built-and-operated radar-control system swinging over the canal.

They flew back toward their base, jubilant. It had been the best, most successful of nights. Most importantly, no one had been harmed in the course of the mission. And that made everyone aboard the chopper happiest of all.

♦ ♦ ♦

On October 6, 1973, Syria and Egypt attacked Israel on Yom Kippur, the holiest day of the year. With almost everyone in the country praying in shul, the enemy forces took the IDF by surprise and achieved tactical supremacy far outweighing anything previously attributed to them by IDF intelligence. The war would last from the sixth of the month to the 25th and would end with nearly 2,800 dead on the Israeli side and 8,000 wounded. Though a military catastrophe in comparison to the lightning-quick victory of the Six Day War, the Yom Kippur War would eventually conclude with the IDF halting a mere 100 kilometers from Cairo and 40 kilometers from Damascus.

It would throw the entire Israeli economy into shambles as thousands of Israeli troops were declared prisoners of war and eventually swapped for their enemy counterparts, and it would severely harm the young country's morale. It would also lead to a reshuffling in both the military, as top commanders lost their post, and in the political arena, where Prime Minister Golda Meir was forced to resign.

During the Yom Kippur War, Yossi Wallis was stationed at the Syrian front, where his life was put in danger time and time again. Russia was supplying Syria with massive amounts of weaponry: surface-to-air missiles with names like SA2, SA3, SA4, and SA6. The fact that they were being flooded with weapons by the Russians meant that there was no sense of accountability or wastefulness on the Syrian end, and they simply bombarded the Israeli side with thousands of missiles, which took down hundreds of planes. The IAF was losing so many pilots that the air force eventually made the controversial decision to ground every one of their jets until they came up with a solution on how to deal with the Syrian missile threat to their skies.

It was a frightening time for the young officer who was repeatedly sent up into the sky to defend the Israeli jets from the Syrians, who were doing their utmost to get through the Israeli radar defenses. Sometimes they succeeded and sent missiles directly at the jets, while officers like Yossi Wallis had to sit calmly and continue to work the frequency systems, knowing that a missile might come screaming out of the sky at any moment and blow up the entire plane leaving no trace.

Sometimes, Yossi was assigned to sit in the jet alongside the pilot and engage in radar countermeasures while the pilot dropped his payload of bombs or engaged in dogfights with the Syrians. The pilot could be rolling over upside down in the sky while evading a Syrian jet, but Yossi couldn't afford to pay any attention to the skillful maneuvers; a moment's inattention might have spelled death for them all. Yossi would emerge from the jets at the end of the mission sweating and white faced, knowing that he'd never forget his daredevil rides through the Middle Eastern skies.

♦ ♦ ♦

Morning on the Ramat David air force base. Yossi Wallis wasn't on call that day and in consequence was able to enjoy a more leisurely breakfast than usual. Four young pilots, fresh out of training, took a seat at his table. They were high on life: extremely excited to be at Ramat David, excited to be flying sorties over enemy territory, excited to be doing their part for their country. There were four of them going out that morning; in general, the air force sent out planes in squadrons of four. Their mission was relatively simple. They were to fly over Syria, drop their load of bombs, and return to Ramat David. The entire mission was supposed to take no longer than half an hour. Yossi had been ordered to go over basic missile jamming and evasion tactics with them before they took off into the deep blue sky.

After their conversation, he walked them out to their jets. Before leaving the building, they stopped at the row of pay phones and called their mothers.

"Ima, just wanted to tell you that I'm leaving the base now on a mission and will be back in half an hour..."

"No, not nervous at all..."

"Yes, I'll call you as soon as I land..."

Then they left the building and strolled out to the runways. There was the normal joking around of soldiers going into battle: the backslapping, the special sense of camaraderie that a civilian can never understand. Yossi looked at those four boys in their smartly pressed pilot uniforms, full heads of hair framing youthful, handsome faces beaming with boyish pride and enthusiasm. He watched them climb into their jets, fuel tanks topped up for the journey, and listened as they warmed up the engines, rolled down the runway, picked up speed, and lifted up into the empty sky.

That was it. Once a pilot left on a mission, it was radio silence from that moment on until they returned. Communication between planes or the base could be picked up by the enemy and compromise a mission. This was meant to be a short mission—fly in, bomb, turn around, and fly back—so he waited for them. He wanted to be there when they landed. He wanted to pat them on the back and to see them reveling in the completion of a successful mission.

Sometimes a plane was shot down and the three remaining jets limped back into the base. Sometimes two planes were shot down. Every mission was dangerous and every mission was different. It was impossible to know how a mission was going to end. On that particular day Yossi waited at the side of the runway for half an hour. The minutes passed slowly. He could feel the tension on the base. They should have been back already! By the time another half-hour had passed, he knew that they weren't coming back: that it would be impossible for them to return even if they hadn't been bombed to pieces by the Syrians, because they didn't have sufficient fuel in their tanks to fly for that long.

No one returned that day. All four were shot down over enemy territory; not even one of the four survived to tell how or when it occurred. Within an hour the air force had lost four incredibly talented pilots who had spent years training for missions such as these. It was a tragedy beyond belief. In its aftermath, Yossi felt a depression such as he'd never experienced. Four young boys gone just like that, when they had been joking around a few minutes before. He couldn't conceive of such a loss. In a short time, though, he had to get over it; there was a war going on, he had a vital job to do, and this was no time to fall apart.

♦ ♦ ♦

When his enlistment ended, Yossi gave some thought to making a career out of the military, but ultimately he decided against it. He had made lots of friends during his years in the air force, and now that he was back in civilian life, it was time to begin networking. One lead led to another and before he knew it, he had an appointment to meet with a company that imported military aircrafts parts, and he was offered a job. He enjoyed the work, but found the business environment and culture in Israel somewhat stifling. He needed to spread his wings—maybe open his own company—and swing the kind of business deals that would allow him to play ball with the big boys in the aviation industry. There was a whole world outside of tiny Israel and he was anxious to find out whether he had what it took to make his mark on it.

The young businessman

It didn't take him very long to make up his mind. Having spent his formative years in the States, and feeling comfortable in the American corporate environment, it made sense to both Sandy and Yossi to relocate their growing family back to the States temporarily, so that he could focus on building an independent, successful business from the ground up. Having developed connections with some serious business people in Los Angeles, Yossi was offered a partnership in an import/export business dealing with military surplus and used equipment. He flew over to LA to check things out. It didn't take him long to see the potential in their business model, and three months later, the Wallis family were on their way to LA.

As much as they enjoyed living in Israel and were proud of what the Jewish nation had accomplished in so short a time, there was a growing family to support. They assured everyone who asked that they planned on returning as soon as possible, and they really meant it.

Their business model worked as follows. The company purchased surplus United States military aircraft, cleaned them up and fixed any parts that needed fixing, then sold them to foreign military forces who weren't as advanced as the United States Air Force, and who were willing to spend their cash on upgraded used equipment. The company went out of its way to develop connections with subcontractors who developed components for major weapons distributors, and eventually they began doing business with them as well. Because they were so friendly with the subcontractors, who were happy to sell them a wide range of aircraft parts and military equipment, Yossi's company was able to offer clients the opportunity of purchasing many of their military needs—which until that point had only been available from larger companies for a huge outlay—from them instead, for a significantly lower price.

The Wallis family's life at that point seemed to epitomize the perfect existence. They were living in the San Fernando Valley, in the suburbs near LA. It was a place where people grew up with major expectations when it came to materialism and were able to fulfill those expectations. It was a far cry from their cramped apartment in central Israel and Yossi's dangerous years in the army. Now they lived in a beautiful, sprawling home, surrounded by lush gardens and a delightful pool filled with sparkling clear water. He'd get dressed, eat something, and drive to work in the latest luxury vehicle. Yossi and Sandy had three cute boys whom they loved very much, and they were a happy family living the life of their dreams. Lots of barbecuing with the kids, lots of walks along the beaches. Sometimes getting dressed up for a show in the city. Good weather all year round. The most exquisite restaurants on the West Coast to choose from whenever Sandy wasn't in the mood to cook supper. Easy style, easy living.

Their lives were the polar opposite of the way he'd grown up, so different from the crowded streets of the Bronx where armed gang members roamed freely, terrorizing the neighborhood. Here they were relaxed. The streets were wide and green, leafy trees providing them with a country feel. LA meant palm trees swaying gently in the breeze, and cruising in a convertible down Sunset Boulevard. It meant taking the kids horseback riding through the Napa Valley vineyards. It meant going for drives through the winding windswept canyons outside the city, where you could see a million lights flickering at you from across the mountains, as the wind ruffled your hair and the expensive car responded to your every move.

On Shabbat morning, they'd sometimes attend one of the local Reform synagogues, where the rabbi played guitar and there was a nice gathering in the social hall afterward—and Yossi imagined that this was real Orthodox business and that he was taking his religion up to the highest level.

His office was located a mere 10-minute drive from the house, at the Van Nuys Airport. He'd finish work at 5 or 6 in the afternoon, get in the car, and a few minutes later he was home, relaxing with a cold drink in his hand and the boys jumping on his shoulders. His life was a far, far cry from those days and nights up in the sky over Syrian territory, bombing the enemy while attempting to evade all manner of missiles heading his way. Here he was finally able to try and forget the incredible sadness of the friends he'd lost in action and the wives and children they had left behind.

A few years passed. The business was thriving. The kids were growing up and doing well in school.

Despite their outward success, Yossi knew that it was only a matter of time before they'd be packing their bags once again to return to Israel for good. Things were different now. They had managed to save money. They were returning from a position of power. No low-level construction jobs for him anymore. It wouldn't be a big deal to open a branch of his LA-based company in Tel Aviv. It had been nice to decompress and relax for a couple of years out in LA, but Yossi Wallis had never been built for the easy life and he wasn't satisfied.

One day he turned to his wife and said, "Sandy, let's move back to Israel. That's where we really belong. We came to LA to make a living, and we succeeded beyond our wildest dreams. Now it's time to return."

Living in Israel didn't mean giving up a comfortable life. He wanted his wife to be happy and had the financial means to make her dreams come true.

"Here's an idea," he said. "I'll buy you a ticket to Israel for 10 days. Go house shopping. Choose a place wherever you want—any city, moshav, or village. I trust that you'll find us the perfect home. Don't worry about the money. The minute you find a house that you feel is right for us, give me a call and I'll wire you the cash."

She liked the idea of being able to pick any house she wanted and flew off to Israel shortly after (what a good wife!). The one thing he insisted on was that the front of the house should have a modest appearance, though he gave her carte blanche regarding the inside, kitchen, number of rooms, etc.

She called him up from Raanana a few days later.

"Yossi, I found a brand-new, perfect house."

"You like it?"

"Very much!"

"Is it finished?"

"Virtually."

"Good neighborhood?"

"Great neighborhood. The kids are going to love it!"

"Well then, I'll need the bank-account number so I can wire the funds to the contractor."

The house was finished within the next few months, and they loaded up a shipping container with furniture and appliances to take back with them to their new home. Not wanting to stand out from the Israelis around him and knowing that the type of cars he had been driving in LA for the last few years would cause everyone to stare, he opted to purchase the typical Subaru station wagon that most Israelis drove and had it shipped to Israel. Though it cost much more in the States, the American version of the Subaru was built to much higher standards and included features that were unavailable in Israel.

Everyone Yossi talked to about their upcoming return to Israel asked him what kind of car he was importing.

"What do you think I should bring with me?"

"At least a Caddy."

"I'm bringing a Subaru."

"You're crazy! Who on earth brings a Subaru with them all the way from LA!"

But he wasn't crazy. He had no interest in making a splash or becoming a topic of conversation. And indeed, he was driving that very unassuming, nondescript Subaru when the Wallis family pulled up to the seminar that would change their lives.

CHAPTER NINE

It was the end of a busy day and Yossi Wallis was on the road, heading home to his family for dinner. He was a successful businessman in his 30's, making lots of money. He was still working in the field he'd been in while living in LA: importing and exporting aircraft parts for companies and governments around the world. The company, headquartered in Tel Aviv, was respected in the industry and had lots of business thrown its way. The three boys were doing well in school, Sandy had made friends and was happy in her brand-new house, and things were fine all around.

Sandy called him half an hour before he left the office.

"Yossi?"

"Yes?"

"Do you mind picking up some takeout on the way home?"

"No problem."

Sandy had had no idea that her simple request was going to completely turn their lives around. Neither did Yossi. He was just being a good father and devoted husband and picking up some food for supper.

It was a hot summer day, and he was feeling somewhat lethargic in the steamy Tel Aviv atmosphere. Evening was approaching, but the heat had not yet dissipated and you could have fried an egg on the pavement. He got into his Subaru and five minutes later was driving down the highway in the direction of Raanana and home. As he drove, he considered dinner options. There were quite a few solid places to choose from on the side of the highway. Falafel. Schwarma. Steakhouses. Where to go?

Without giving the matter too much thought, he'd chosen a route that took him home via the junction at Kfar HaYarok. On the side of the highway was a famous restaurant called The Elephant Steakhouse. The restaurant boasted a comfortable sit-down area where families could relax and enjoy one another's company, and a takeout counter as well. It was a popular restaurant, like many side-of-the-road grill houses. Unlike many others, however, The Elephant Steakhouse provided the ultimate nonkosher culinary experience.

Yossi exited the highway and pulled into the parking lot that skirted the restaurant. The lot was full of cars. Daylight was fading as he parked and walked inside. About 10 or 12 customers waited at the take-out counter to place their orders. He could hear the sizzle of grilling meat and frying onions. From where he stood, it seemed like everything in the world was roasting on that grill. Standing in the line, he glanced upward at the backlit pictures of artfully arranged food displayed above the counter. Steak sandwiches? Lamb chops? What should he buy?

The alluring picture in the middle caught his eye.

"Pork in pita," it said in brightly colored letters. "Free salad bar and drinks."

The picture of the white meat looked enticing. Pork. Beef. Veal. What difference did it make? Yossi Wallis, the businessman from Tel Aviv, made up his mind. Pork in pita. The kids were going to love it.

He waited on line to place his order, and as he stood in the grill house surrounded by laughing people, all having a good time and enjoying their pork and chumus, he began to daydream. Disturbing pictures filled his mind, and he was transported a few decades back into the past. The steakhouse seemed to fade and finally disappeared, and all he could think about was a story he'd been told when he was young.

It was a story about his grandfather. His mother's father, Rav Shraga Feivel Winkler, a genuine *tzaddik*.

When the Nazis came to Debrecen and took the family away, his grandfather was the only one sent to a labor camp instead of Auschwitz. Separated from his family and the world he knew, Yossi Wallis's *zeide* was condemned to backbreaking labor. But whatever torments he faced, nothing in the world could break his love for Hashem and His Torah.

Slave laborers were given starvation rations, and although almost everyone around him ate whatever they could lay their malnourished hands on, Yossi's grandfather never defiled his mouth with impurity. He subsisted, it seemed, on air. No *tereifah* food for him.

Was he hungry? All the time. But his life as a Jew was too important to him to risk what he'd gained since entering the world on the momentary pleasures of the stomach.

The Jewish people never hold elections for their Torah leaders. It's a grassroots process that seems to happen by itself. You can't fool the people, they always know. So it was with Yossi's grandfather. Everyone in the labor camp knew that here was one special Jew. They looked at him with admiration, overcome by the chutzpah of a man who dared to go hungry for his beliefs, when everyone around him was succumbing to their ravenous hunger and eating whatever they could.

Months passed, and the inmates and their jailers knew that the Russians were on their way and that the German defeat was imminent. The only question was when. With the sounds of battle ever closer, every day seemed to harbor the chance that it might be the day of liberation.

One morning, the inmates were gathered in a giant circle on the assembly grounds for morning roll call when the SS officer in charge of the camp stood up and began to speak.

"Germany has lost the war," he began.

His face was paler than usual, his eyes red and bloodshot. His boots, normally polished to a mirrorlike sheen, were dusty and scuffed. You could see that this was a different man from the one they had known, loathed, and feared.

"The Russians will be here momentarily. No longer will we be able to carry out our mandate honorably. It has become clear that now it is time for us to remove our uniforms and run for our lives. The war is over. You are about to become free men again. You will leave this place, go home, and be reunited with your wives and children."

A pause.

"Before we let you go," he continued, "before we unlock the gates and allow you unrestricted access to the outside world, we want to do one last thing. One final test."

The inmates looked warily at one another. What was he threatening them with now, only seconds before liberation? The Nazi looked at all of them, enjoying the tension and drama even in these final moments.

"Before you all leave, we are going to test your rabbi. The Rabbiner Winkler. We have heard that he's a special man. Now we want to find out the truth. Is he really as special as you make him out to be? There's no time to waste anymore, we need to find out now. Right now."

The Nazi grabbed Rav Shraga Feivel Winkler and maneuvered him forcibly to the center of the circle.

"Rabbiner," the Nazi addressed his prisoner, "you want to go home like everybody else, don't you?"

The Nazi motioned to one of the officers, who walked over carrying a plate on which sat a solitary piece of pork.

"Rabbiner, if you want to go home, and I'm sure that you do, all you need to do is eat this delicious piece of pork. The moment you take a bite, you'll be freed. You'll be able to walk through the gate and go home. One bite, Rabbiner, one bite is all it takes."

No one breathed as they waited to see what Rav Shraga Feivel was going to do. What a terrible dilemma! A bite of pork suddenly equaled life. Every face turned to their beloved spiritual leader, waiting to see what decision he'd make. What was the *tzaddik* going to do now?

The German's voice echoed through the camp—and into every heart.

"If you eat this, you'll go home with everyone else, but if you refuse, Rabbiner, you will be the last one to be killed in this camp. Do you understand? The choice is yours."

The German pulled out his service revolver and held it against the rabbi's temple.

"Decide now, Rabbiner."

No one breathed.

Then he turned to the inmates. "Let's see what choice your rabbi makes."

The Nazi turned back to Yossi's grandfather. "Did you make up your mind yet?"

Rabbi Wallis in Feldish, near the city of Debrecen, where his maternal grandparents lived before the war. Today, there is not a single Jew living there.

"Yes."

"And?"

"And I will not eat this pork."

The German shot Yossi's grandfather and he crumpled to the ground, dying on the spot, the final Jew to perish at his camp. That's how he died, refusing to relinquish the holiness that made him so unique, refusing to compromise on the highest ideals of what it means to be a Jew.

♦ ♦ ♦

Yossi Wallis returned to The Elephant Steakhouse with a thud.

What on earth am I doing here? he asked himself, the image of his grandfather being shot by the Nazi flashing through his mind with savage power.

Your grandfather died at the moment of liberation, after longing for that day to come for so long, and though he knew it would cost him his life, he chose to die rather than eat even the tiniest sliver of pork.

You live in Eretz Yisrael, he continued the silent internal conversation, *and you're standing on line with your fellow Jews, ready to pay for the "privilege" of buying the meat that your grandfather would rather die than eat. And you want to feed this meat to your wife and children, when you could buy any type of food you could possibly desire?*

Yossi stood in the middle of that busy, noisy, cheerful—and very *tereifah*—restaurant, unaware of anything but the incredible argument taking place within him.

It wasn't so long ago. A few decades. Something is wrong and I don't know what it is. Either I am out of my mind or my grandfather was out of his. And I refuse to believe that my grandfather was insane—which must mean...

Yossi Wallis turned and walked out of The Elephant Steakhouse with empty hands.

♦ ♦ ♦

Something changed in Yossi Wallis on that humid summer evening. He began to question everything he knew and believed as he attempted to understand why his grandfather was willing to give up his life to avoid tasting a small piece of pork.

Yossi had three little boys at home who were still young enough to have to listen to their father. *What am I going to teach my boys?* he wondered. *That they can eat whatever they want? That nothing makes a difference?*

As long as no one was asking him why he did the things he did, life was easy. But he knew that one day his boys were going to look him in the eye and ask him to explain why they lived life the way they did, thought what they thought, ate what they ate.

Then what? What was he going say on the day that they asked? That nothing mattered? That every person should do whatever it is that makes him happy? Did he believe that was the truth?

You love telling stories. One day, you're going to tell your kids to take a seat on the couch and you'll share with them the story of your grandfather and how he gave up his life rather than defile his soul by touching pork—and then your kids will look at you and they won't be able to figure out why you fed them the very meat that their great-grandfather had given up his life to avoid.

And what would he tell them then? How would he justify himself and the decisions that he'd made?

He'd have no answer and no justification.

♦ ♦ ♦

Yossi's grandfather could have told himself that eating the pork was *pikuach nefesh* and therefore permitted. But it wasn't just about him anymore. The Nazi was trying to make a mockery of the Jewish people, a mockery of the Torah. With the stakes so high, there was no way the "*rabbiner*" would have considered taking a bite of pork, even to save his life.

Decades later, the decision made by Yossi Wallis's grandfather on the last day of the war—to give up his life rather than eat even one bite of forbidden food—would serve as the catalyst to bring his entire family back to the *Ribbono shel Olam*, the Master of the World. It was the moment when he passed the torch of belief in the Torah and fear of Heaven to his descendants, for eternity.

At the time, Yossi couldn't understand the reasoning behind his *zeide's* sacrifice. But he was soon to find out.

♦ ♦ ♦

Rafael Vallis's stubborn refusal to bend to the will of the Church back in Spain. Rabbiner Shraga Feivel Winkler's willingness to die rather than taste a bite of pork. These were pieces of the spiritual legacy of unyielding self-sacrifice for Torah bequeathed to Yossi Wallis by his ancestors.

There was still one more who would add to that spiritual inheritance: Rabbi Yossi Wallis's father.

Because more than anything else, it was his father's story and *mesiras nefesh* that would help shape Rabbi Wallis's destiny and teach him to never, ever give up the fight—to never, ever, give up on any Jew—no matter what.

BOOK TWO

ABBA'S STORY

CHAPTER TEN

Over the years, Rabbi Wallis's father told him many stories about his parents and ancestors, and about his own miraculous survival during the dark and deadly days of World War II. Though the stories were not told in the order in which they occurred, eventually Yossi was able to piece together the entire fascinating narrative of the distant events that took place across the ocean, in a world and time where the Jew had almost no chance of survival or hope for the future.

And yet his *abba* survived. One day at a time.

♦ ♦ ♦

Rabbi Yossi Wallis's paternal grandfather, Chaim Yosef Wallis, grew up in the Lomza province of Poland. He considered the Chofetz Chaim his rebbe and would consult with him on a regular basis. The Chofetz Chaim directed Yossi's grandfather to establish a Talmud Torah in the city of Lomza, which had a strong Chassidic presence, for children whose families wanted a Lithuanian style of learning.

Yossi's father, Yehuda (Yeedle) Wallis, was born in Konin, Poland; from there, the family moved to Pavenitz. Most of the

Chaim Yosef Wallis

town's inhabitants were either Gerrer Chassidim or Alexander Chassidim, and he came of age in the Chassidishe *shtieblach* of yesteryear.

As an adult, Yeedle Wallis possessed remarkable oratory skills, and he knew how to draw in his listeners. The stories he told came alive for his son, Yossi, who fell under his spell. Listening to his father, Yossi could visualize the little boy living in a sleepy Polish town.

♦ ♦ ♦

Thick clouds drift over the village during the early hours of the morning, dropping their heavy loads of white snow over the silent homes. Yossi pictures his father's house surrounded by snowbanks: an island of warmth in a freezing sea. He can almost feel the snowflakes descending on top of him as he tries to peer through the window. No use: The glass is frosted over with ice. Scraping some of the ice off the windowpane, he looks into the ramshackle room. He can make out a bed standing against the wall, where a young boy sleeps, the heavy goosefeather blankets pulled up around his chin to protect him from the intense Polish winter.

Suddenly the door of the room opens up and a woman enters. Yossi watches as the woman, his grandmother, prods the inert form lying under the covers.

"Yeedle, Yeedle," he hears her say through the thin walls, as she pats his cheek, gently singing out his name until he opens eyes heavy with sleep. He is only 6 years old and it is still very early in the morning.

He watches little Yeedle putting on his clothing, his every movement conveying how much he'd rather remain under the warm blankets and how reluctant he is to start his day. Slipping into a thick coat, he leaves

Rabbi Wallis's grandfather, Chaim Yosef Wallis, with his bride-to-be, Rabbi Wallis's grandmother Hadassah Denbinsky. Seated is Shraga Feivel Denbinsky, Rabbi Wallis's great-grandfather.

the house, his mother's eyes following him from the doorway, where she stands, waving.

In the center of the town stands a well, the source of the townspeople's water. Yeedle places three buckets on the ground and begins pumping water out of the well and into the buckets. It is hard work, but the family needs the money and there is no choice. Because he is so short and can barely reach the pump, he has to jump, and, using all his weight, he brings the pump handle up and down until he's filled his pails with water. It takes him many tries until they are all full.

Fascinated, Yossi sees Yeedle attach a pail to each side of a bar, which he then somehow manages to shift onto his thin shoulders, staggering beneath their weight. He doesn't stop there. With superhuman determination, Yeedle bends over the third pail and lifts it up with his teeth. Then, with two pails on his shoulders and one held in his mouth, the 6-year-old begins delivering water to the town's inhabitants. Yeedle's father is a melamed, and the few zlotys that Yeedle makes every morning keep the family from starvation.

Yossi zeroes in on his father's childish face, searching for a trace of sadness or resentment, but he cannot find any. Little Yeedle seems happy and good-natured—as if life is meant to be lived and he is enjoying himself despite the early-morning backbreaking labor.

♦ ♦ ♦

Perhaps it was that early-morning toil that gave Yeedle Wallis the strength, many years later, to spend long hours reminiscing with his son after a long day at work, when most men would want nothing more than to eat and drop down in front of a television.

"When I was 12 years old, my parents sent me away to yeshivah. It was located in another city and since they were so poor, I was only able to return home twice a year."

"Did you go home for your bar mitzvah?" Yossi asked his father.

"No, my parents couldn't afford the train fare."

"So you didn't have a party or anything?"

"Nothing. My parents sent me my *tefillin* and that was it. My father was not there to help wrap them on my arm for the first time. For all practical purposes I was on my own."

"Sounds like you had a hard life."

"It was certainly character building. Nobody took care of us. Our food was provided by the local homeowners, and more often than not, this meant that we received one meal a day—barely. At night we slept in a local warehouse and believe me, it was scary being there all by ourselves. We filled our stomachs with pages of Gemara and comforted ourselves in lonely times with a complicated *Tosafos*. But I was a happy child, much the same as you were when you were young. Carefree. Relaxed. Taking things one day at a time."

♦ ♦ ♦

When Yeedle Wallis turned 18, his father told him it was time for him to learn a trade and help support the family. Since Lodz was home to Poland's textile industry, it was a natural choice for a young, bright, ambitious boy. He divided his days between learning in the local *shtiebel* and making a living. Life was simple and satisfying.

The war broke out in September 1939, and from the first moment Poland didn't have a chance. The Germans attacked with Panzer tanks, while the Poles raced to the battlefield on horseback and were obliterated in a cloud of exploding horseflesh. Within one month, the entire country was under German control, with the utter collapse of the Polish military. The once-proud Polish officers in their opulent uniforms and arrogant complacency belonged to the past.

Their military conquest complete, the Germans were free to turn their attention to the Jewish problem. The first order of business was to set up a ghetto in every city in Poland, and Pavenitz, where Yeedle had returned when war broke out, was no exception. The Germans worked with alacrity to carry out their orders, enthusiastically assisted every step of the way by their Polish counterparts, who couldn't resist helping their conquerors deal with their Jewish neighbors.

Within a few days signs were plastered on every wall of the Pavenitz Ghetto, demanding that 500 Jews report to the local German military headquarters for resettlement at labor camps. The Jews in the ghetto searched for the best possible hiding places, but Yeedle's hideaway outdid them all; he chose to hide in the jaws of the devil. In retrospect, his choice epitomized his unique talent of thinking outside the box—a talent, which, along with a healthy dose of *siyatta diShmaya*, Heavenly assistance, would help him survive the upcoming six years—through the camps, death marches, and backbreaking labor all across Poland and Germany.

While the Jews scurried frantically through the streets searching for holes to crawl into, Yeedle concealed himself on the roof of police headquarters. This was a smart decision for a number of reasons. First, who would ever dream that someone would have such audacity. Second, the rooftop afforded him a perfect opportunity to witness anything of import that was happening in the ghetto.

This was how Yeedle Wallis came to see the long line of Jews who were snatched off the ghetto streets and lined up to await transport. Though temporarily safe, his heart went out to the hapless men shivering on the freezing street, unprotected by the elements and filled with the fear of an unknown future. He took in the rows of humiliated Jews: people he knew and loved, friends, neighbors…

Suddenly his blood ran cold. There, standing at the end of the line, was his brother-in-law. Married, with children. If he was sent away to places unknown, there was no way his family would be able to survive.

Yeedle had to do something. Saving his brother-in-law meant saving his sister and their children. Wasting no time, Yeedle climbed down from the roof and ran over to the end of the line, where his brother-in-law stood, silent and miserable.

"Go home," he told his brother-in-law.

The man looked at him, not comprehending.

"Go home now and take care of your family. I'm staying here in your place."

His brother-in-law turned to do as he was told. Suddenly a Nazi stood in his path.

"Who gave you permission to interfere?" he demanded of Yeedle. "How dare you tell him what to do?! Our quota has been reached, we have 500 men. You go home!"

Yeedle became desperate.

"But I am much stronger than he is," he argued with the Nazi. "I can be of much greater use to the military effort."

Something in his argument resonated with the Nazi and he relented; freeing the brother-in-law, and accepting Yeedle in his place.

His brother-in-law stared at him. He didn't know what to say.

"Go home to your family, they need you."

Yeedle watched as his brother-in-law turned and left the area, to go home to his family, never dreaming that they would never see each other again. Seconds later, Yeedle Wallis was marched out of his hometown.

He would remain under German rule for the next six years.

♦ ♦ ♦

His first labor camp was located on the Polish-German border. Not far from the camp was a battlefield that had been the scene of fierce Polish resistance. Testimony to this were the carcasses of thousands of horses that had been slaughtered in the carnage, and that had been abandoned by the Poles when they ran for their lives. The carcasses were surrounded by what seemed like millions of maggots and rats, and they lay on the ground, bloated and stench ridden. It was the slave laborers' job to clear the field and bury the horses. Burying the horses was both their job and food supply, because the Germans ordered them to eat the rotting horse meat for their sustenance. They were not provided with tools to carry out the job and were forced to use their bare hands to dig ditches large enough to accommodate what had been the Polish army's pride and joy.

While thousands of Jews had been sent by the Germans to deal with the health problem, only a tiny percentage survived their exposure to so much disease and death. Those who managed to avoid not getting sick eventually collapsed from the sheer burden of work that was demanded of them. Very few remained alive, but Yeedle Wallis was one of them.

♦ ♦ ♦

His next stop was at a labor camp, where he was assigned to a detail that was laying railroad tracks. The Germans had no intention of taking a rest and were already planning the total conquest of Eastern Europe and Russia. The Polish railroad system needed an overhaul and Yeedle was put on the job. Once again the Germans wasted no money outfitting their Jewish workers with tools, and the inmates had to use their bare hands while laying miles of track. It was backbreaking labor, and he watched the people around him dropping to the ground, dead of sheer exhaustion. The Jews of Poland were not cut out for this type of manual work, especially without tools. Very few of those sent to develop the railroad system remained alive, with Yeedle Wallis one of the lucky survivors. For the remainder of the six years that he spent under German domination, Yeedle would find himself being shunted over the railroad tracks of Poland, tracks which in many cases he had laid with his bare hands.

Decades later, Rabbi Yossi Wallis and his father journeyed together through Poland to revisit all the places where Yeedle had suffered during the war. They stopped in Lodz to visit the cemetery where Yeedle's father, Reb Chaim Yosef Wallis, is buried. Not far from the cemetery there is a train station set up to look just as it did when the Jews of Poland were forced to board the railway cars for their final journey to Auschwitz. A full-length cattle car waits eternally alongside the platform, the door open and awaiting passengers; it is an invitation to step inside the minds of our ancestors, an invitation to feel the pain of the past, an invitation to internalize the inhuman suffering that happened right where Yossi and his father were now standing.

Yeedle Wallis stood on the platform and refused to enter. In a voice ringing with strength of purpose he declared:

"I will never, for as long as I live, ever enter another one of those cattle cars. Not for all the money in the world. I'll escort you right up to the door, but something deep inside me will not allow me to step inside—to that world of misery.

"You have to understand the way it was. The SS troops sat on the roof of the car that you're walking into. They sat there, their guns anxiously waiting to be used on any passenger who attempted to saw through the bars covering the train's tiny window, who tried to jump from the speeding train to safety.

"When traveling on one of these cars it was imperative that a person find a spot right beside the window, because the putrid air inside was almost impossible to breathe. But if anyone tried to stick their head out of the window for a breath of fresh air, even for a second, the Germans shot them on the spot. No questions asked.

"If you had a child with you on the train and he was small enough, you threw him out the window to the Polish countryside. You did it

when the train was going around a bend and had to slow down. True, you knew that the child might die from the fall or from a German bullet. But he had a greater chance of surviving those odds, than whatever lay in wait for him at his destination. So many people threw their little children out the window of the trains. Many of them died, but some survived. Of course, you never threw the child out near a station, because a station meant a town and a town meant Germans and Poles only too happy to trade a Jew for a piece of bread. No, you threw the child out in the middle of a forsaken forest, where you prayed the partisans would find him and save his life.

"When you finally arrived at your destination, at least one-third of the passengers were dead. They had been weak when they boarded the train, and being stuffed into an airless compartment without water or food and no bathroom facilities killed them just as effectively as the German bullets.

"By this point, the people already knew where they were headed and what horrors awaited them the moment they'd step off the trains. Can you imagine the cries of agony and screams of fear that emanated from this very train as it rolled through the towns, cities, and countryside of Poland? It was the wails of the living dead. Off in the corners, you could find a tzaddik sitting and reciting Tehillim, but such pious behavior only served to infuriate the people who were angry at their fate. Arguments broke out through the train, the clash of miserable humans terrified that every moment was to be their last. Terrible arguments abounded between those who were no longer religious and those holding on to their faith by the edge of their fingernails.

"The decisions people had to make on these trains were heartbreaking in their intensity. To share your water with a child (even your own) or not? The chances of the child surviving were virtually nil, while an adult might survive. What to do?! What to do?

"And it got worse. You never knew how long you'd be on the train. For an hour, three hours, three days, or a week. And you didn't know where they were taking you and what awaited you when you got there. The idea of not having any control over your life and destiny is a special torture all its own and not comparable to anything else in the world.

"That's the way it was back then and that's why I cannot possibly enter this accursed space. No matter how long I live."

♦ ♦ ♦

From the wilderness of the Polish forests, the remaining Jews were sent to Auschwitz, the ultimate killing grounds. To survive Auschwitz, a person had to be powerful and healthy, both physically and mentally, and Yeedle Wallis, a boy used to the harshest of physical labor, never doubted himself or faltered in his quest to survive the war.

♦ ♦ ♦

"When Abba discussed his wartime memories," Rabbi Wallis says, "they were never in chronological order. Each memory was a piece from the gigantic jigsaw puzzle that made up his six years of life beneath the Nazis. The Holocaust was part and parcel of my father's very essence, branded into his body and soul. Consequently, the memories came to the fore at any given time, and we never knew what experience would trigger the recounting of yet another wartime episode. Traveling through Poland, my father accompanied us into ghettos and cemeteries, sharing the past with us every time. But when we reached the gates of Auschwitz, he stopped and wouldn't go one step further."

Outside looking in:
Rabbi Wallis on a trip to Auschwitz

"You will have to go into this accursed place without me," he said, "because I am never stepping through those gates again. But before you all go in, I want to

prepare you so you'll have a better understanding of what this place was really about.

"When I reached Auschwitz, it was after living under Nazi control for over three years. I was a shadow of my former self. While the Jews who were shipped here from Hungary and Greece had no idea what a hell they were about to enter, I knew only too well what Auschwitz meant. I was already starving and sick and wounded from the years of work I had put in and had no illusions remaining.

"I had been working for a long period of time laying the metal train tracks that carried thousands of trainloads of Jews across Europe and into camps such as this. In a twist of irony, I prepared the very tracks that would carry me through the gates of Auschwitz!

"Taking leave of our previous overseers, we were handed 'certificates of merit,' attesting to the fact that we had been model workers. We were instructed to show these documents to the officers in Auschwitz who decided the fate of every new arrival.

"'Show them these certificates and you will be sent to do other important work. This will serve as proof of how valuable you were.'

"We naively considered those 'passports' priceless and guarded them with our very lives. But when some of the people who arrived with me showed the SS officers their 'passports,' they laughed in their faces and shot them in the head. I never showed anyone my letter, but the duplicity felt like a poison-tipped arrow straight to the heart.

"Take a minute," he continued, pointing toward the gates, "and peer past the barbed wire. It's serene, quiet—almost pastoral in appearance. Pleasant air, lush greenery everywhere you look. But back then, the Nazi animals did their best to make sure that every single one of our senses underwent purgatory on some level.

"The gas chambers were situated near the end of the camp, with the ovens working overtime spewing a constant cloud of black pollution across the entire camp. The trains delivered millions of Jews through the camp, a few short minutes' walk from the steps leading to the gas chambers. Then clothing off—into the gas chambers, hundreds dead—bodies into the ovens for burning. It was a technically perfected process and it worked. The smell of smoke was constant, filtering through the air of Auschwitz until you couldn't breathe without tasting the rem-

nants of the ovens on your tongue. You breathed soot and smoke into your nose and the smell of charred flesh from millions of Jews from countries all over Europe. Our sense of smell was constantly assaulted by the terrible profanity of death. It landed on the inside of a person's nostrils and there was no way to get rid of death's intrusive stench. And you could never get used to it, because that meant coming to terms with the burning of your brothers and sisters, parents and friends.

"And then there was the sense of taste.

"We need to breathe. We're humans, and humans need to breathe. But when you opened your mouth to let in some air, the soot and the smoke entered as well and attached themselves to your lips and palate and between your teeth and you had no way of getting it off of you. And there was absolutely nothing to do about it, because what was the alternative: stopping to breathe?! But you tasted your brother's flesh in your mouth and it sent you over the edge of sanity.

"What about our sense of hearing?

"Look around you. Do you think we heard the peaceful sounds of the wind blowing across the freshly mown grass? We heard the trains rumbling through the gates twenty-four hours a day, and the inevitable crying that accompanied the screeching of the brakes on the metal as the giant wheels finally came to a halt with fresh cargo for the never-satisfied fires. The crying, the screams, the heart wrenching sounds of millions of children being separated from their parents. It didn't matter if you understood Yiddish or Greek or Polish or Hungarian; you heard the screams and they were universal and you felt it inside your gut and it pounded on your head like a kettledrum that never stopped. One train entered, the next one left. The doors were opened, the people jumped out, or fell out, or lay dead within the carriages, having died somewhere along the line. Two, three hundred people crammed into every car, children crying, Germans yelling, dogs barking, guns thundering randomly, the brutal sounds assailing you from every direction.

"What about our sense of sight?

"See the green grass. It looks so lush, so thick. Back then, the grass was eaten—snatched up by the starving prisoners. Outside the gates, the world was green. Inside, all was bare and arid, like a desert, except that this particular desert was carpeted with the endless rain of soot

from the belching chimneys, turning the grounds the mottled gray color of death. And you couldn't bring yourself to glance at the gates, because your fellow Jews threw themselves onto the electrified gates in an attempt to kill themselves, and then the electricity had to be shut off and the bodies peeled off the fence. And you saw your brothers and friends dying on every side, just collapsing and breathing their final breath and then easing themselves onto the ground and never rising again.

"How could we have looked at any of this? Yet on the other hand, could a person afford to close his eyes in Auschwitz for even a second? Not if he wanted to live.

"I recall the tiny toddlers who couldn't find their mothers and fathers, running through the crowds beside the train, yelling, "Mama! Tatte!" at the top of their lungs and crying, tears staining their little cheeks, their bewildered eyes searching and running and calling for the mother they loved so much. And you couldn't help the child, much as you so desired. There was nothing you could do for the tiny person helplessly roaming the corridors of hell on earth. And you had to watch this all the time..."

Yeedle Wallis turned away. He would not enter those gates.

CHAPTER ELEVEN

As a young boy growing up in Eretz Yisrael in the '50's, Yossi Wallis was constantly being confronted by the fact that people like his father hadn't fought the Nazis. Consequently, he would badger his father to tell him stories about people who *did* fight back.

One day his father told him a story that fit the bill perfectly. It was the story of the Greek boxer. Yossi listened, fascinated, as his father told the tale.

"As Jews trying to survive in the camps, we came to certain conclusions. One thing we learned was that it was much more effective to combine into groups, because there was a certain strength in numbers. An invisible strength, but a strength nonetheless. If one member of the group was sick, the rest of the group banded together to help him, breaking off a piece of the bread they so critically needed to save a friend's life.

"Every evening we were given a supply of bread to be divided between ourselves. It wasn't enough for us and we were never full, but that's what there was. In a camp like Auschwitz, bread meant a lot more than just bread. It took the place of money. Bread would buy a person cigarettes or medicine if he was sick. Bread was vital to a

person's survival. Unfortunately, the Ukrainian kapo in charge of our barracks considered our bread as his personal bank account, to use as he saw fit. Every evening when the bread was brought to the barracks, the kapo would cut off half the amount received and take it for himself, turning an already insufficient ration into a starvation diet. It was an untenable situation, even in an unfair world like Auschwitz, made all the worse because the kapo was a huge man with powerful fists who didn't hesitate to use them.

"One evening, we had enough. Making a decision that could have brought with it dire consequences, we decided to take a stand and revolt. It was either that, or dying very, very slowly from starvation. All at once, every Jew in the barracks began to bang his hands and feet against the walls, the floors, the doors. This was uncommon for Auschwitz, where nobody dared step out of line if they wanted to live another day. Yet here was an entire barracks making an absolute racket.

"It wasn't long before a patrolling soldier heard the noise and the officer in charge of our barracks turned up. Throwing the door open, he charged into the room, a look of utter fury in his eye.

"'What's going on here?!'

"One of the Jews spoke up.

"'We know that we have taken a huge risk making this kind of noise, but we don't see any alternative.'

"'What on earth are you talking about?' barked the German.

"'Our barrack is being run with complete injustice,' the Jew explained.

"'Meaning?'

"'Meaning that the Germans have set up the camp to work a specific way. Prisoners work during the day and are provided with bread. But in our case, our bread is being stolen every single day, and we know that if things continue this way, we will die from starvation.'

"'Who is stealing your food?'

"'Our kapo steals our food, taking half of the bread allocated us, every single day. We would like to obey German law, but the law is not respected in this barrack.'

"Remarkably, the Nazi didn't just shoot us all on the spot. Instead he called the kapo to appear before him.

"Reviewing the charges against him, the German made his decision. Here was a chance for a little fun to relieve the monotony of camp life.

"'You,' he said to the kapo, 'will fight one of the men from this barrack. It will be a fight to the death. Whoever is left alive at the end of the fight is the winner. If you win,' he said, turning to the Jews, 'you will never have to suffer this man again. If he wins, your gamble will have backfired.'

"Obviously, Yossi," continued his father, "the kapo was starting off with a huge advantage. He was well fed, in excellent physical condition, indignant that we had gotten him in trouble and belligerent at the best of times. We, on the other hand, were all weak and sick, in no condition at all to fight such a monster. But the Nazi had made his decision and one of us would have to volunteer. The question was who. As we all looked at one another, the feeling of fear grew stronger and more powerful, pervading the barracks until it felt like the very air was being sucked out of the room.

"Suddenly we heard a voice speaking.

"'I'll fight the kapo.'

"We looked at the speaker and weren't sure whether to laugh or cry. It was one of the Greek Jews who had been shipped into Auschwitz. He was a small, slight man and nothing about him inspired our confidence. Yet as he stood on the wooden floor, his body relaxed, a slight smile on his face, we tried to hope that there might yet be a miracle that night.

"And yes, there was a miracle, because that Greek Jew was a featherweight boxer. None of us knew it, but he had made a career for himself fighting, and when you know how to fight, it doesn't really matter how big your opponent is.

"The Ukrainian took his spot on one side of the long, narrow room, the Greek on the other. The Nazi stood against the wall, taking in the scene, a sadistic look of pleasure on his angular face. The kapo towered over the Jew, his huge palms almost the size of the Greek's arms. Despite his size he moved agilely from side to side, his big feet dancing with cagey rhythm. The Greek balanced on the balls of his feet, his lithe body swaying back and forth, his arms hanging loosely at his side.

"The Nazi ordered them to begin. The Ukrainian bridged the distance between them with two jumps, his hands positioned upward,

bunched up into fists, and then he was raising them high in the air, intent on bringing them down on the Greek Jew's head with all the considerable strength he possessed.

"He brought them down, but by the time those hands were on their downward journey, the Greek had already moved out of their way and the power had been spent on nothing. The Ukrainian howled with rage and turned to catch the clever Jew, who had danced out of his range just in time, but as he turned, the Greek's fist caught him solidly in the chest, and he lost his breath for a moment. The Greek pushed the advantage, following up the first punch with another few good ones: some to the gut, some to the solar plexus, some to the ribs, and then two perfect shots right to the face, cracking the Ukrainian's jaw and dislocating his nose.

"The kapo tried to fight back, but the blood was blinding him now and his large size was acting as a deterrent to his fighting abilities, while the Greek used his small size to dance in and out, in and out, punching his opponent rapidly three times and moving away, then back in and catching the Ukrainian in the face again.

"Eventually the Ukrainian tired from all the punishment and the Greek moved in and battered him with his fists, smashing him again and again, while the rest of us stood there, thunderstruck, and the German looked on in astonishment. And then the Jew pummeled our Ukrainian torturer to death because, you see, there could only be one winner in that particular game.

"From that day on the bread was divided equally.

"And after that, when the Germans were bored and wanted entertainment, they called on our Greek Jew to fight for them in boxing matches and tournaments that they set up inside the camp. Many was the time that our boxer was called to fight. And he fought and he won every time, and when he returned to us, he shared the bread he had won.

"We were on his team, and being part of a team was the most important thing."

The Greek Jew survived the war and remained friends with Yeedle Wallis for many years.

◆ ◆ ◆

It didn't take Yeedle Wallis long to figure out that the only way to outlive Auschwitz and the tall chimneys of death was to join one of the transports leaving Auschwitz for points unknown, and he waited for his opportunity. Every morning began with lineup at the *appelplatz*, where the Germans counted and recounted every inmate and tallied up their numbers with precisely written figures. A Jew who didn't make it to the morning assembly was a dead man.

One morning, the commanding officer made an announcement.

"All Jews of Greek origin take one step forward. You will be part of a transport leaving immediately."

Yeedle was not a Greek. He did not look Greek, nor could he speak a word of Greek. But he knew one thing. There was no way he could stay alive long if he remained in Auschwitz. If the Germans wanted Greek Jews, then a Greek Jew he would be. He took one step forward, as did every other Greek in the assembly. The officer began making his rounds through the lines, giving a close examination to every Jew who had stepped forward, and choosing the strongest among them for the transport.

He reached Yeedle Wallis. Took a good look at him.

"Jew," he noted with Aryan certainty, "you are not a Greek!"

Yeedle stared back defiantly.

"Yes I am," he stated with a confidence he did not feel. He was playing with fire, but willing to take the risk if it meant escaping Auschwitz.

"If you're a Greek, Jew," smiled the German, talking menacingly, dangerously, "then speak to me in Greek. Go ahead, talk to me. Prove it."

The Jews in the nearby rows stiffened. No one made a move. There was extreme danger in the air. You could almost taste it. The German stood in front of Yeedle Wallis waiting for him to open his mouth. The Nazi was going to kill him for lying.

Yeedle Wallis didn't know a word of Greek. But he knew something else. A language that was at least slightly similar. Aramaic, the language of the Gemara. Standing on the Auschwitz assembly grounds, Yeedle traveled back in time to the nights he had remained awake, *shteiging* over his *sefer*, his body draped over the *shtender*, his voice rising and falling with the melody of the Gemara.

He was a teenager once again and he and his fellow students were studying Gemara by the dim warehouse light. It was cold inside the warehouse and they felt vulnerable and unprotected. Their only comfort was the ancient words of the Gemara. And they repeated the sugya over and over again until they knew it by heart and were able to shout the Aramaic lines through the thin walls that divided them from the other bachurim in the adjoining warehouse.

Suddenly Yeedle knew exactly what to say.

He opened his mouth and began reciting a piece of Gemara that he knew by heart, a piece that he had studied so many times with his friends that he was able to repeat it even under the pressure of almost certain death. As he recited the Gemara, he unconsciously took on the image of a yeshivah student: the rise and fall of the study hall voice, the unique tune, the pace, and the *shuckel*, the unceasing movement every Jew does when he learns. Stranger still, as Yeedle moved toward the SS officer, the officer moved unconsciously toward him, mirroring the stance of his "*chavrusa*," his eyes never leaving Yeedle's face, almost as if they were study partners learning together and loving it. A lowly Jew and a mighty German. Prisoner and captor. Life and death. It was a classic case of the Torah saving and protecting a person.

The Jewish men in the vicinity stood watching, utterly captivated by the scene. It had been years since any of them had heard a genuine *kol Torah*. Yet now it was happening before their very eyes, not two minutes from the gas chambers. Miracles and wonders! The sound of Yeedle's voice wafted through the air, entering every heart, reviving the walking dead.

Yeedle finished. He had come to the end of the *daf*.

The German looked at Yeedle. Yeedle stared right back at him. No one breathed.

"It sounds like Greek to me," conceded the Nazi. And just like that Yeedle Wallis was on his way out of Auschwitz.

◆ ◆ ◆

They were headed for the Warsaw Ghetto, or more accurately, the remains of the Warsaw Ghetto. The Jews of the ghetto had risen up against the Nazis with the crudest of weapons and had managed to hold the German forces at bay from the 19th of April until the 16th of May 1943. Assisted by the ghetto Jews, the Jewish resistance attacked the Nazis and killed many German troops. Through Polish connections, the underground managed to obtain a few machine guns, rifles, revolvers, hand grenades, and even German uniforms to be used in confusing and misleading the enemy. Though the Polish underground was well armed and had been toying with the idea of rebelling against the Germans for years, they did not rise to the challenge at the moment of truth, leaving the Jews to mostly fend for themselves. The uprising, the largest of its kind carried out by Jews during the war, was finally dealt with from Berlin when the previous commanding officer was removed and replaced with one Jürgen Stroop, who had orders to destroy the resistance come what may, and was given whatever he needed to do the job.

He needed a lot.

The German force used to evacuate the Warsaw Ghetto was composed of over 2,000 men armed with mine throwers, artillery pieces, armored vehicles, and more than 200 submachine and machine guns. The Jews put up an incredible fight and sent the Germans retreating numerous times. Every alleyway, sewer, roof, and tunnel was utilized for the war effort. Guns were used down to their very last bullets, and it didn't take the Germans long to realize that they were facing a very determined, brave, and uncommonly savvy enemy.

In the end, the Germans were forced to raze the Warsaw Ghetto to the ground, blowing up street after street and turning the entire area into rubble, while losing many troops from the elite Waffen SS during the operation. In total, some 13,000 Jews were killed in the uprising, with the remaining 50,000 Jewish residents shipped to various concentration camps, most notably Treblinka. Thus ended a particularly bloody yet heroic chapter of World War II.

The site of the Warsaw Ghetto was also the destination of the Greek Jews from Auschwitz, Yeedle Wallis included.

♦ ♦ ♦

The Greek Jews of Auschwitz entered the site of the Warsaw Ghetto, where their mission was explained to them by the Nazis. The ghetto had been razed to the ground. Rubble littered every surface. The area needed to be cleared up. But before the rubble could be carted away, the Germans needed to make sure that everything of value had been recovered from the wreckage. Yeedle and the rest of the Jews were part of a task force whose job it was to go from bunker to bunker, enter the ruins, do a quick search, and then report their findings to the Germans waiting outside. They were supposed to search for leftover weapons, gold, and money. Once the team exited the bunker and gave the all clear, the bunker would be blown up from the inside and any remaining bricks would be shipped off to Germany for construction purposes.

The Germans didn't want to use Polish Jews for this operation for a variety of reasons. First of all, most Greek Jews had never been to Warsaw, had no idea what they were seeing, and were not emotionally connected to the area. Secondly, Polish Jews had the incentive and ability to connect with the underground and would not hesitate to undermine the Germans at every step, especially considering the fact that they were familiar with the area and knew all the hiding places. The Greeks, on the other hand, couldn't even communicate with the Poles and wouldn't know where to go if they decided to escape. A number of Hungarian Jews were also chosen for the mission, including Rav Yekusiel Yehuda Halberstam, the Klausenberger Rebbe.

"Don't think this job was a picnic," Yeedle told his son as he remembered those days. "The demolished Warsaw Ghetto was no country club."

The sights that he witnessed sifting through the ghetto would remain embedded on his psyche for the rest of his life. The ghetto was a ghost town of destroyed homes and memories. Charred wood and smoky mounds of earth were piled everywhere, and the stench of death permeated the abandoned streets.

"Abba had to clamber down into the sewer systems and into half-destroyed homes," Rabbi Wallis remembers. "The Germans were deathly afraid to enter the buildings themselves, rightly fearing an attack by the partisans and Jewish resistance fighters who had somehow remained alive against all odds. If searchers found something valuable they were rewarded by the Germans with extra rations as an incentive to tell the truth. As soon as they reported a bunker or home sterile, the Germans would toss a stick of dynamite into it and blow it up."

On one occasion Yeedle descended into a section of sewer that had been the site of major fighting and made his silent way through the underground passageways. Water dripped from above and the sounds of pattering rodent feet were everywhere. The Warsaw sewers had been teeming with people just a short while before, but were now devoid of human life. He was about to turn around and return to street level, when he heard muffled voices. Yeedle followed the sound, turned a corner, and saw them: A *Chassidishe Yid*, still clad in his *kapote*, straggly beard framing a gaunt face and piercing eyes, sitting on a low crate surrounded by a bunch of ghetto boys dressed in filthy rags, cloth caps perched on their heads. Open pipes hung from the ceiling, dripping sewer water ceaselessly. The Yid held a *Mishnayos* in his hands and was teaching the boys. From his demeanor and noble bearing, it seemed that Yeedle had stumbled on the scion of a Chassidic dynasty and his children. The Rebbe stared at the intruder for a second and went right on learning, his voice a singsong that never wavered.

Yeedle hesitated to interrupt him, but there was no choice.

"Rebbe?"

The *Yid* turned and looked at him questioningly.

"I was sent by the Germans to give them a report about anything that I find inside the sewer."

He didn't reply.

"You have to come out with me."

The *Yid* shook his head in the negative. Yeedle felt the tears come to his eyes and said, "Rebbe, please take your children and leave the sewer."

"Why?"

"Because the Germans are going to blow it up with dynamite the moment I return."

"We're not going anywhere."

"But Rebbe, you are all going to die! Please leave with me!!!"

"I begged him to leave, Yossi," Yeedle told his son, decades later. "I begged him with every fiber of my being!"

He refused.

"They will kill us no matter what we do. We are not leaving the sewer."

Yeedle left them sitting and learning in the tunnel, feeling his way back through the unyielding darkness, the sounds of their voices accompanying him through the rough, damp walls, gradually growing softer and softer the farther he went, until he barely heard them at all. Yet the picture of that holy man sitting and studying *Mishnayos* with his righteous children never left his mind. It took every bit of self-control that he had not to scream with desperation when the Germans blew the entire sewer up in a heap of concrete and blinding smoke. To Yeedle Wallis, that Rebbe and his holy children symbolized everything Klal Yisrael had lost.

On another occasion the Nazis ordered him to scale the frame of a five-story building whose insides had been demolished. He found a mother hiding on the uppermost balcony, her three starving children huddled beside her.

"Come down with me," he begged her.

She merely shook her head, unwilling to even meet his eyes.

"I will carry you all down on my back! Please don't remain here! The Nazis are going to dynamite the entire structure as soon as I give them the all-clear signal!"

How he pleaded with her. But nothing he said made any difference. She preferred being blown up along with the building to the alternative.

Yeedle Wallis was stationed at the Warsaw Ghetto for close to half a year, and carried out his particularly unpalatable job alongside the Klausenberger Rebbe under terrible duress and hellish conditions. The sights he witnessed would become the stuff of his future nightmares. Very few of the Greek Jews who had arrived with him at the Warsaw Ghetto remained alive at their mission's end, but once again, Rabbi Wallis's father was one of the blessed few who lived to tell the tale.

CHAPTER TWELVE

Yeedle's next wartime destination was the Dachau concentration camp, located across the border in the heart of Germany. By this point Yeedle had been under German rule for five years, somehow managing to cheat death time and again.

The journey from Warsaw to Dachau would take him across Poland on a death march in which thousands of his fellow Jews dropped to the sides of the road out of sheer exhaustion. At times they'd be ordered to board a train, which would transport them for a few hours, and then they would be ordered off the train to continue the journey without rhyme or reason.

"The worst part of the death march," he told his son, "was the thirst. The devastating thirst. There are many ways to torture people. I myself have been subjected to a wide range of tortures. But to deny a person water is by far the worst of the lot. The Germans made us walk for hours under the broiling hot sun, until we felt faint and dizzy and couldn't muster the energy to take another step. Polish summers are brutal, with a kind of sluggish heat that saps the energy out of everyone, until you just want to lie down on the floor and sleep forever. But if you stopped marching—stopped for even a second—you were shot."

The German officer in charge of the march must have been bored that day, because he decided to come up with a game that would provide him and his men with some amusement. Diverting a group of men from the rest of the march, Yeedle among them, they were taken to a nearby stream where they were ordered at gunpoint into the water. Initially they were overjoyed. The feel of the water was fantastic, the wetness, the coolness, the utter delight of a swim in summertime. But their delight rapidly turned to horror, when they realized the challenge they were facing.

The Germans were testing them, trying to determine how long it would take to push the prisoners over the brink of insanity. So close, yet so far away. So thirsty, yet denied drink while literally standing in the water! It was enough to drive the strongest person over the edge.

"You will march through the water in a circle," said the officer. "Your hands will remain at your sides. You will not drink any water. Any person caught drinking even one drop of water will be shot right where he is. I trust everyone understands how serious I am about this."

Thus began one of Yeedle's absolute worst moments in six years of war. The water was knee-high. There was a wooden bridge spanning the stream and the Germans stood above looking down at the Jews from their vantage point, guns poised for slaughter.

"Wade farther into the stream," the officer commanded the prisoners. "Circle the stream in a chain. We want to see how long you will be able to withstand the temptation of trying to take a drink. If you reach down to the stream and put water in your mouths, any water, we will shoot you on the spot. You've been warned. Now begin walking!"

It was an incredibly sadistic game. No one had an inkling how long they were going to be in the water. They hadn't had anything to drink in hours, and the feeling of the liquid lapping at their legs proved too much for many of the prisoners. One by one, they tried to surreptitiously slip their hands down into the stream and scoop up a little water, but the Germans kept a sharp lookout and no one succeeded. It wasn't long before the stream was filled with Jewish bodies sinking to the bottom and the water had turned a frothy red from their blood.

All the while, as the Germans shot the Jews and the agony of being denied a drink grew progressively worse, Yeedle Wallis and the few remaining Jews kept on circling in the stream, again and again, maneuvering past their dying brethren until they were finally ordered out onto dry land. They clambered out of the water and collapsed on the land, so insanely thirsty that they didn't know how they would ever be able to rise again.

"Rub the ground with this," someone lying beside Yeedle whispered in his ear, handing him a bent old spoon.

"What's that going to do?" he whispered back.

"Try it, you'll see."

Yeedle shrugged. He had no strength left to think. He accepted the sharp object and scraped at the ground, and water began shooting out from beneath the grass! The survivors of the march clawed at the ground and stared at the emerging water as if it were a mirage. They lapped at the water, desperately trying to quench a thirst that felt as if it would never be satisfied. The Klausenberger Rebbe himself would later testify about that miraculous moment: how it was as if the Well of Miriam suddenly appeared and they were able to drink their fill, while the Germans watched the water shooting out of the ground.

And the Germans allowed them to drink.

"When my father first related this story," Rabbi Wallis later related, speaking of the incident, "I didn't believe it. It seemed impossibly far-fetched, and I found myself doubting his words. But then I heard the same story from the mouth of the Klausenberger Rebbe and from others who witnessed the miracle, and I was forced to accept the fact that sometimes water may very well come shooting out of the ground when you need it most, if Hashem decrees that it should be so."

◆ ◆ ◆

Eventually, numbers severely depleted, the march was terminated at the Dachau concentration camp near Munich, Germany.

Dachau was a combined labor and death camp. The basic idea was to simply work people to death. The moment they ceased being productive to the German war machine, they were put to death. It was a branch of hell on earth.

One morning Yeedle Wallis witnessed a group of Jews being directed to their deaths. Having outlived their usefulness, they were being sent the way of the millions who had already been killed. One of the passing Jews, perhaps knowing that these were his final moments on earth, chose to do a courageous act. Catching Yeedle's eye, and communicating without speaking, the man removed a pouch containing a pair of *tefillin* from the sleeve of his striped pajamas and tossed it in Yeedle's general direction, beseeching him with his eyes to take good care of his legacy.

"When I caught the pouch," Rabbi Wallis's father told him later on, "my first thought was that it contained bread, or some other type of food."

Then he opened the pouch and saw what it contained. A pair of *tefillin*. Suddenly he was faced with a terrible choice. Hiding a pair of tefillin in the barracks or on one's person was an act of rebellion punishable by death. On the other hand, though he was no longer an observant Torah Jew (having lost more than just his family in the war years), Yeedle Wallis couldn't bring himself to throw out a pair of *tefillin*. Shoving the *tefillin* beneath his shirt, he pressed his arm against his chest so as to keep the *tefillin* as inconspicuous as possible and went about his work. That evening he hid the *tefillin* in the barracks.

When he rose the next morning, before going out to the morning assembly at the *appelplatz*, Yeedle made an impulsive decision to don the *tefillin* he had received so unexpectedly, a priceless gift. We can only imagine the feelings coursing through him when he wrapped that pair of *tefillin* around his arm and head for the first time since 1939.

There are moments in life and there are moments in life, and this was a moment he would forever remember.

As he stood in the Dachau barracks, black boxes on his bicep and head, the door opened and a German officer entered the cavernous room, catching sight of him before he had a chance to hide. Within moments he had summoned the ever-present guards to arrest him.

"Your act of rebellion will not go unanswered," the Nazi said as they dragged him out of the barracks, toward the *appelplatz*.

♦ ♦ ♦

Camp life began and ended with *appel*, or assembly. The Germans were obsessive when it came to matching numbers. Before the inmates retired to their bunks for the night they were counted. They were counted again come morning. The numbers had to match. The problem lay in the fact that many Jews passed away every night. Yet the numbers had to match. So the dead Jews would be dragged out of the barracks in the morning and carried over to the assembly grounds, where they "stood," propped up between live inmates, and were counted. With assembly over, the dead bodies would be dropped on the ground, to be collected, thrown onto a pile of corpses, and eventually burned, while life in Dachau went on.

Men were counted on one side of the grounds, women on the other. A barbed-wire fence separated the two sides.

In the *appelplatz*, Yeedle was surrounded by Nazi soldiers. All around him, his fellow Jews were rushed out of their barracks toward the assembly area. Men lined up. Women lined up. Everyone knew that something bad was about to happen. The Germans exuded a feeling of anticipation, the Jews of dread. Yeedle stood exposed in the center of the *appelplatz*, watched by every eye.

The officer in charge called out Yeedle's number and he stood at attention.

"Step up."

He stepped up.

"Approach."

Yeedle Wallis approached.

A table stood in the center of the assembly grounds.

"Get on the table."

He clambered up onto the table.

A bar hung above the table. There was a noose attached to the bar.

"Every inmate will look at the punishment. If you look away, you will be shot."

The men and women on both sides of the fence watched as the SS man slipped the noose around the Jew's neck. Every eye was on the prisoner. Eyes filled with sorrow, hearts filled with horror, everyone waited for the spectacle to come to an end. The German standing next to the table held the *tefillin* high up in the air so that everyone could get a good look.

"Do you see these boxes?" he asked the assembled. "This man used them, and that's why he's being put to death."

Across the grounds, not one person moved. The silence was intense. Not a sound. Not a word exchanged, nor the chirp of a bird.

"If anyone dares to use these items," he said, venom dripping from his mouth, "they will end up going the same way as this man. He's a spy. This is the equipment that he uses to contact the British and provide them with information for bombing purposes, and the punishment for spying and treason is death."

Everything slowed down now. With death only seconds away, Yeedle's every sense was heightened. He could feel the slight tremor of hundreds of people swaying on emaciated legs. He could smell the stench of death, waiting to welcome him over to the other side, and the fear that emanated from the people watching the macabre spectacle. He could see their sorrow, their bewilderment, and degradation. He tasted the utter despair in the air. Every person stood out in sharp relief against the bleak background.

Just a few seconds more, Yeedle told himself, *then it will be over*.

But the Nazi wasn't done just yet. As he spoke, he gripped the *tefillin* firmly in his hand. All watched them swinging slowly from side to side. Turning to Yeedle, *tefillin* still swinging in the air, the German barked, "*Jude*, dog, do you have a final request before you are hanged?"

He meant it as a joke. The officer laughed as he said the words, and the Germans standing around the table laughed with him. What could the stupid Jew possibly desire for a last request?

But Yeedle seized the unique opportunity that had been offered him on a silver platter.

"Yes, I have a request."

"And that is?" Mockery in the Aryan blue eyes.

"I want to wrap myself in the *tefillin* one last time."

"*Wunderbar*," the German exclaimed. "We'll allow you to put on those boxes, then we'll hang you wearing them, then we'll leave you hanging until tomorrow morning wearing the boxes and everyone will understand why you were punished. Very educational. Can there be a clearer message?!"

A moment later, rope draped around his neck, Yeedle prepared to don the *tefillin* for what would no doubt be his final time in this world, as the entire inmate population watched his every move. Not a sound was heard. Not from the Jews. Not from the Germans. Not even from the dogs. He wrapped the *tefillin* around his arm and head, and recited the words every Jew says when donning his *tefillin*.

"*Ve'eirastich li le'olam*—I will betroth you to Me forever. *Ve'eirastich li betzedek u'vemishpat u'vechesed u'verachamim*—And I will betroth you to Me with righteousness, justice, kindness, and mercy. *Ve'eirastich li be'emunah, veyadaat es Hashem*—I will betroth you to Me with fidelity, and you shall know Hashem."

He spoke the words slowly and deliberately, feeling every one of them more deeply than he had ever felt them before. The words reverberated and echoed through the grounds of Dachau, sending a chill up the collective spine of every prisoner as they heard the timeless sounds of a Jew at prayer, of a Jew connecting with his Creator even with the tip of the sword on his neck.

Yeedle looked at all of the Jews and they looked at him. Their eyes met and he saw something that he hadn't seen in many a month.

"What did you see, Abba?" Yossi Wallis asked his father, as he listened, spellbound, to his father's narrative.

"This was already near the end of the war. We were all cried out by then. There were no tears left. But during those moments I looked at my brothers and I saw the tears rolling down their emaciated cheeks. I knew that the Germans were going to kick the table out from under me at any second. But instead of feeling like a victim, I felt like I was standing on top of the world! Can you imagine what it's like to stand in the middle of a concentration camp with *tefillin* on your body and everybody, including the Germans and their dogs, watching you? Can you understand how it feels to know that putting on *tefillin* is the final act you are going to do before leaving this world? I didn't feel beaten down, I felt like I was flying. Like I had won the war all by myself!

"'*Yidden*,' I yelled out at them, knowing that noose was going to tighten around my neck at any second, 'why are you crying?! Don't you understand that I am the winner here!!! Can there be a greater revenge than this??'"

Those were Yeedle Wallis's final words in Dachau an instant before he was to be hanged.

Everyone watched. Everyone held their breath. This was it. The man who was no longer religious was going to die while wearing *tefillin* and was happier than he'd been in years.

Just then a Nazi officer by the name of Otto Tybet gave a scream.

"This man thinks he's the winner?!" He motioned to the other officers to join him. The Nazis huddled together, trying to decide how to handle such an unexpected situation.

"Get him down off the table," Tybet finally ordered, "and we'll beat him over the head until he dies." He turned to Yeedle. "Jew, get down off the table."

Yeedle obeyed the command.

"Come here, dog," said another Nazi officer. "I'll tell you how you're going to die. Not on top of a table. That's way too easy a death for a hero like you. And take off those boxes."

Yeedle removed the *tefillin* and listened to the man rant.

"Crouch down on the ground," Tybet ordered him. "Pick up those two rocks. You will hold them in your hands when we whip you. We're going to whip you over the head 25 times. If you drop one of the rocks anytime during the whipping, you will be shot immediately."

A German soldier went to stand opposite them, his rifle aimed straight at Yeedle's heart.

"This," said the SS officer, "is the way you are going to die. In pain. With suffering. Let me give you some good, free advice. Why don't you drop the stones now? You will die a painless death. What's the point of trying to stay alive, when there's no way for you to beat us? You've seen people getting lashed before. You know what happens to them. Don't even bother trying to survive, just drop the rocks now and die."

Needless to say, Yeedle Wallis didn't follow his advice, free or not.

"I will not drop the rocks. Not now and not later."

"They were hitting me, Yossi," his father told him years later. "Each whiplash made me feel like it was my last second on earth. I weighed 45 kilo. I was a shadow. But they were hitting me like I was an elephant. Dimly, as if from a very great distance, I could hear them counting the lashes. I was just skin and bones, I was exhausted, I was famished, but one thing I knew: there was no way I was going to drop those rocks. I was going to live!"

Yeedle Wallis survived the 25 lashes. Blood gushing from his head, unable to move, he was flung onto a pile of bodies slated to be burned.

He hadn't dropped the rocks.

And he wasn't dead. There was still an astounding amount of life left in the little Jew from Poland. But the Nazis didn't know that. They flung him onto the bodies like a sack of garbage and tossed the *tefillin* onto the pile beside him.

When he regained full consciousness and opened his eyes he realized that he had to get away from the dead bodies immediately if he didn't want to end up in a ditch and on fire. Using his very last vestiges of strength, he crawled off the pile of dead people and onto the ground. One of the inmates saw him crawling like a wounded animal. The man gave him some water, threw a rag over his head to stanch the bleeding, and carried him to a hiding place in the crawl space beneath the barracks.

There he lay, more dead than alive, unseeing, unfeeling. And there beneath the barracks he was nursed back to a semblance of health.

With the Allied forces rapidly approaching, the Germans cleared out Dachau, taking the Jews on one final, brutal death march. There was no reason for it: the remaining Jews were sick and weak and could only slow them down as the Germans ran for their lives. Yet winning the war had never been the Germans' true objective. It had always been of secondary importance, compared to the real goal of killing the Jews.

Yeedle Wallis survived this final march as well, even as the last of the survivors fell to the earth on his every side. And then one unbelievable day, the Germans were gone and the Americans had arrived.

They were free.

◆ ◆ ◆

"My father's story is the most miraculous Holocaust story I've ever heard in my life," Rabbi Wallis likes to say. "It's so unusual that sometimes even I find it difficult to believe that so many miracles happened to one person!"

One day, they were sitting together having a cup of coffee.

"Abba," Rabbi Wallis said, turning to his father, "there's something I've been meaning to ask you for a long time."

"What's that, Yossi?"

"How did you do it?"

"How did I do what?"

"How did you survive? You went through so much. All those camps. Digging graves for horses and laying train tracks with your bare hands! How were you able to survive when so many people around you gave up hope and died from sheer exhaustion and despair? What was your secret? Where did you get the willpower to remain alive? You're not a prophet, you had no idea when it was going to end. Why didn't you give up?"

"Do you remember my telling you how I jumped off the police-station roof to switch places with my brother-in-law?"

"Of course I remember, Abba. I remember every single detail of every single thing that you ever shared with me."

"When I joined that line of prisoners, I knew I was voluntarily subjecting myself to extreme danger, but I went willingly. This act of *chesed* that I did gave me something concrete to hold on to. When I'd wake up in the morning, I'd look Heavenward and say, 'Hashem, please give me today. I want to survive today. All I'm asking for is one day.' And then I'd say, 'Hashem, I risked my entire life to save another Jew, won't You give me one day?'

"And Hashem gave me that day. I did the exact same thing on the morrow. Made the exact same request, asked Hashem for the exact same thing. For one day. And He gave it to me. I did it the next day and the next day and the next day…for six years."

Yeedle Wallis leaned back in his chair and stared at his son with a piercing gaze.

"If you want something from G-d, you can always ask for it, but be modest. I only asked for one day. Make sure that you have merits; that you have the leverage you need to make the requests that you need. And then don't hesitate to ask. Don't ever be afraid to use the money in your Heavenly bank account. Now you know how I survived. I asked G-d to grant me every single day as a gift, and He did.

"Do you understand me, son?"

Yossi Wallis hugged his father hard and kissed his hand.

♦ ♦ ♦

Often, when people hear Rabbi Wallis tell the tale of how Yeedle Wallis stood up to the Nazis, and how he chose to die with the *tefillin* on and the noose around his neck, they ask a question: How is it possible that a man like this, who spoke with steadfast courage and certainty to the Jews of Dachau about dying to sanctify the Name of G-d, how is it possible that such a Jew stopped being religious after the war?

The truth is that Yeedle Wallis—like many survivors—never really stopped believing in G-d and His Torah. Angry at Him? Perhaps. Overwhelmed by his experiences and the difficulties of life even after the war's end? Certainly.

But not to believe in Hashem?

Never.

Yeedle Wallis never really left. The Jew who screamed that he was the real winner because he was about to die wearing his *tefillin* never lost his faith; he was just waiting for an opportunity to renew his connection.

How could it be otherwise? After all, Yeedle was the descendant of Rafael Vallis, the last Jew to be burned in Spain's auto-da-fé. His ancestors died sanctifying G-d's Name. The roots were there, buried deep within the soul of the Jewish people. And when the roots are in place, it's almost impossible to lose the connection.

And that is exactly what happened.

CHAPTER THIRTEEN

One Friday afternoon, as Rabbi Wallis walked into his shul, he glanced at the pile of weekly Torah newsletters offered for free to the congregants. On the front page of one of the more popular periodicals he saw the story of his father and the *tefillin* in Dachau. At the end of the story it said, "As heard from Rabbi Yossi Wallis, CEO of Arachim."

The problem was, Rabbi Wallis had never been interviewed by anyone on the staff of this periodical.

Instead of allowing his annoyance to fester within, after Shabbos he asked his secretary to please get the editor of the newsletter on the phone so they could discuss the matter. Minutes later, the editor was on the line.

"Hi, this is Yossi Wallis."

"*Shalom aleichem*, Rabbi Wallis."

"*Aleichem shalom*. I'm going to get right to the point. I'm upset by the fact that you published my story without asking me first, and that you wrote that you heard it from me, when in fact we have never spoken to each other."

"You're right," the editor said, "and I apologize. We should definitely have asked your permission before publishing the story. But I actually did hear the story from you."

"You did?"

"Yes, I heard a recording of you telling the story."

Rabbi Wallis was slightly mollified.

"Anyway, I hope you won't be too upset," the editor went on, "because I have good news for you. Something positive has already happened as a result of our publicizing your father's story."

"And that is...?"

"I was actually going to call you later today about this. I was just contacted by a Mr. Lasky from Ramat Aviv. He told me that he read the story this past Shabbat, and that he knew the man we wrote about, Yeedle Wallis.

"'I was with him in Dachau,' he told me. 'We were prisoners in the same barracks. I was there during the hanging incident. I witnessed the entire story. But the end of the story came as a surprise.'

"'Why is that?' I asked him, intrigued.

"'I always thought that Yeedle Wallis was killed. The last time I saw Yeedle, the Nazis had thrown him onto a pile of dead bodies. I never dreamed that he managed to crawl off and was nursed back to life! I want you to know something. Yeedle Wallis was a very great man! He saved my life. To hear that he has a son and a legacy and that he lived to tell the tale—I want you to introduce me to his son, I want to thank him and tell him all about his father. I want to share with him some details that he couldn't possibly know. I was there on the day that Yeedle was about to be hanged and I saw him laugh in the Germans' faces, and I want to share my memories with his family.'

"So, Rabbi Wallis, can I bring the two of you together?"

All resentment forgotten, Rabbi Wallis eagerly took the number and called Mr. Lasky, and they set up a meeting.

Mr. Lasky couldn't take his eyes off his guest.

"I can't believe that I'm sitting here talking to Yeedle Wallis's son. I saw the Germans whipping him. I saw him die and yet here you are!"

Rabbi Wallis nodded. It truly was an amazing turn of events.

"I want to tell you something about the day your father was 'killed.'" He stopped for a moment, lost in memories. "I was also supposed to die that day."

Rabbi Wallis's eyes opened wide in shock.

"I had typhus. I could barely move. My fever was so high on the morning they caught your father, I could no longer even stand. When I woke up that day, I knew it was my final day on earth, because there was no way in the world that I would be able to stand outside for morning assembly. I tried getting off my bunk, but my legs refused to obey. I pictured being reunited with my family, but even that didn't work. With no choice, I was prepared to die.

"It was at that crucial moment that your father came over to me.

"'Lasky.'

"He was talking to me, but I was too weak to acknowledge him.

"'Lasky, listen to me. I managed to get ahold of this pair of *tefillin*. I want you to put them on. Either they will give you the necessary strength to carry on, or this will be the final mitzvah you do before the end. Put them on, Lasky.'

"'I have nothing to cover my head with,' I whispered. 'I can't put on *tefillin* with a bare head.'

"Your father ripped a piece of paper off a cement bag that had been left in the barracks and covered my head with it. Then he helped me wrap the *tefillin* around my arm and head. I started to daven slowly, but your father told me to hurry up.

"'Finish up quickly, Lasky, many other people still have to put them on!'

"I obeyed him, finished davening, and he removed the *tefillin*.

"Yossi," Mr. Lasky said to his guest, "you're not going to believe this, but as I unwound the straps from my arm and from around my head, I literally felt my fever disappear. It was miraculous. I had been so, so sick just a few minutes before and suddenly I was all better—able to stand, able to walk. I felt like I had just been handed a new promise of life."

Rabbi Wallis stared at Mr. Lasky: at his living room, at the furniture, at the home of a man who, by all rights, should not have survived the war, yet who sat across from him telling him about his personal miracle, which was delicately intertwined with the Wallis family's own set of miracles.

"Yossi, you should know something. Your father put those *tefillin* on as many people as possible, rushing us so that everyone could have a chance, before finally wrapping them around his own arm and head. And then he got caught. Understand, Yossi—he didn't have to do this. He could have kept them for himself. Could have put them on quickly, taken them off, and gone outside safely for assembly. But that wasn't your father. He cared too much about the people around him. He literally saved my life that day, even while subjecting himself to unspeakable danger.

"When we stood outside on the *appelplatz* watching the Nazis slipping the noose around Yeedle Wallis's neck, we, the people who had no tears, couldn't help ourselves, and we cried like we hadn't cried in years. Because they were killing Yehuda Wallis, and he was one of the best people we had ever met! We saw him on the gallows, we saw them beat him mercilessly, we saw him fall, and we saw them throw him onto the pile of dead bodies. Was it any wonder that we imagined he was dead?!

"All my life I've been waiting to thank him for saving me, and now I've met his son and can finally give thanks for the miracle that your father brought about!"

He was completely overcome with emotion.

"There's something else you should know. I served as a witness to your father's story about five or six years ago, when I personally testified about what happened that day in Dachau for the archives of Yad Vashem."

Rabbi Wallis listened, visibly moved by what he was hearing. It wasn't just the story, although that was amazing. The ramifications of what Mr. Lasky was saying were going to change Rabbi Wallis's life. For years he had hesitated to share his stories with the wider public because they weren't documented and he wasn't sure how accurate they were. Maybe, in the course of time, they had been embellished. Maybe they weren't 100 percent true. After all, his father had gone through so much. Could he rely on his memory? But here was a man who was not only able to corroborate every detail of Yeedle Wallis's phenomenal story, but was also able to supply additional details that none of them had even known.

Rabbi Wallis had felt the need for witnesses and suddenly here was a witness of the finest caliber. His visit with Mr. Lasky was a breakthrough for him in every single way.

Mr. Lasky was witness number one.

♦ ♦ ♦

A short while later Rabbi Wallis received another phone call. The man on the other end of the line introduced himself, told him he was calling from LA, and then said that his father-in-law, the owner of a glatt-kosher butcher shop in LA, had been a participant in the same exact story. Dachau. The story of the *tefillin*. Every last detail.

"My father-in-law also thought that Yeedle Wallis had died. Now we finally know the whole story. And there's something else that I have to tell you. Something that you didn't know."

More information? Rabbi Wallis thought, his excitement rising. What else was he slated to learn about that fateful day in Dachau?

"After the Nazis threw Yeedle Wallis onto the pile of dead people, my father-in-law passed by the pile of bodies and managed to snatch the *tefillin shel yad* from where it had been oh-so-casually tossed by the Germans. From that day until the end of the war, the people in his barracks put on the *tefillin shel yad* before leaving for the *appelplatz* every morning."

Rabbi Yossi Wallis, CEO of Arachim International, sat in stunned silence. He had desired accuracy and proof so he could tell his father's story to the world, and his wish was coming true.

That was witness number two.

♦ ♦ ♦

Arachim sponsors many trips throughout the year. One very successful overseas trip is to Poland, where they tour the concentration camps and hear thought-provoking speeches from the Arachim team of lecturers, including, often, Rabbi Wallis himself. At one of the camps, a member of their group arose and requested permission to relate a personal story.

"This story occurred at the end of the war," he began, "and I heard it from my father who saw it happen with his own eyes."

The man then proceeded to tell the story of Yeedle Wallis and the *tefillin* and the way he stood up to the Nazis.

"My father never forgot what he witnessed at the assembly grounds that day," the man concluded. "He couldn't possibly forget what he saw, since it was his barracks that managed to retrieve the *tefillin* that had been discarded on the pile of bodies."

Witness number three had just testified. It was a *chazakah*—a three-pronged proof.

Where some people might have heard a fascinating Holocaust narrative, Rabbi Wallis heard something more. He heard the One Above instructing him to share his father's personal history with the world.

♦ ♦ ♦

But the story is not over yet.

There is another chapter that needs to be told, and that is the impossible tale of Otto Tybet.

The story of Otto Tybet is so far-fetched that there have been many times when Rabbi Wallis hesitated to relate it to an audience, for the simple fear that they wouldn't believe him. On one particularly memorable occasion, he was invited to address an audience of women in Kiryat Sefer, who asked him to relate his father's miraculous *tefillin* story in Dachau. He began the story, and in the middle of his speech a woman raised her hand and asked for permission to say something.

"Rabbi Wallis?" From her tone of voice, it was obvious that she was upset at him for something.

"Yes?"

"How come you left out such an important part of the story?"

He asked her to clarify which part of the story she was referring to.

"Why didn't you tell them the truth about Otto Tybet?!"

It was obvious that this woman knew who Otto was and the role he had played—and that she was majorly unhappy with Rabbi Wallis for leaving such an essential part of the story untold.

"You left out the part of the story where you found out Otto Tybet's real identity!"

Rabbi Wallis explained that the reason he had left that part out was because he didn't want people to think he had made up the entire story.

"It's too much," he said to her. "Sometimes, I myself have a difficult time believing that something so unbelievable happened!"

Still she wasn't mollified, insisting that either he tell the story or that she would tell it herself. In the end he gave in and told the audience the tale.

It's an incredible story, but it's the truth, and it's something that every single Jew in the world should know about. Because it proves beyond a shadow of a doubt that even in the darkest of places, the Hand of Hashem is alive and operating ceaselessly, at every moment of every day.

♦ ♦ ♦

About a decade ago, Rabbi Wallis received a phone call from Sarah Pachter. A well-known Israeli author and journalist, Mrs. Pachter introduced herself as someone who specializes in stories from the Holocaust. She wanted to know whether she'd be able to interview his father about his wartime experiences. After securing his father's agreement to be interviewed, Mrs. Pachter came to meet him. Yeedle Wallis was a master storyteller and he chose to lead off the story with his dramatic near-hanging in Dachau—the *tefillin* around his arm and head, the whisper of death on his neck—and how his declaration of victory beneath the gallows so enraged one of the SS officers, that he had decided to torture him to death by whip, rather than allowing him to die rapidly.

"I'll never forget that Nazi officer," he told Mrs. Pachter. "His name was Otto Tybet and he was the ultimate German. A head of blond hair that was so fair it was almost white; eyes so blue they were almost clear. Spoke a flawless German. The quintessential Nazi. How angry he was at me when I delivered that speech beneath the gallows. But in the end his plan backfired, because I didn't drop the rocks and managed to survive the beating."

"Hold on one second," she interrupted him. "What was the Nazi's name again?"

"Otto Tybet, why do you ask?"

"I'm not sure, but I seem to recall having come across that name before more than once."

"So what if you heard his name?"

"There's something going on here that we're missing."

"What do you mean?"

"I mean that I need to do some research into Otto Tybet."

"Why? What's so special about Tybet?"

"Well I could be wrong, but it seems to me that in every single instance where the name Tybet was mentioned, the bottom line time and again was that the Jew in the story managed to survive!"

Deciding to investigate this unexpected angle, Mrs. Pachter began by publicizing a request that any Holocaust survivor or family of survivors who had come across the name Otto Tybet during the war should please contact her immediately. The phone began ringing right away. Many people, it seemed, knew the name Otto Tybet. As before, in every story featuring his name, the final outcome was that a Jew was saved.

Stranger and stranger.

One morning she received a phone call that changed the entire picture.

A young woman was on the line. She wanted to meet Mrs. Pachter.

"How old are you?" the journalist asked her. "You don't sound old enough to have the kind of information that I'm looking for."

"You'd be right, except for one thing," the caller responded.

"What's that?"

"Otto Tybet was my uncle."

"But you are Israeli...Jewish."

"Yes, I am a Jew."

"And Otto Tybet was an SS officer?"

"That's true, he was an SS officer, but he was also a Jew."

"I think we have to meet."

"That's what I've been telling you from the beginning."

♦ ♦ ♦

The young woman was clearly eager to tell the story.

Her Uncle Otto was born to the Klar family of Yerushalayim. He came of age in the years preceding World War II. As a scion of an old, distinguished family from Vienna that had immigrated to Yerushalayim years before, the Yerushalmi youth grew up speaking a perfect German. When war broke out her uncle volunteered to go and fight—against the family's wishes—and presented himself at British headquarters determined to enlist, come what may. The British recruitment officer took one look at the blond-haired, blue-eyed youth who was able to converse in German like he'd just stepped off the Kurfürstendamm in Berlin, and shipped him off to spy school in England.

And so it came to be that the Yerushalmi boy with the golden hair and ocean-blue eyes was trained in the fine art of espionage, and finally dropped behind enemy lines, using the name Otto Tybet.

Tybet/Klar soon managed to join the Wehrmacht and began sending messages back to his handlers in Britain detailing German military secrets and any important information he was able to lay his hands on.

"So how did Otto Tybet become an SS officer?"

"It's like this," explained his niece. "My uncle was serving in the regular German military. At some point along the way, he realized what the Germans were doing to the Jewish population of Europe and decided that he couldn't possibly remain in the Wehrmacht as a British spy, when he could be doing a much more important job if he managed to join the SS. Without informing his superiors back in London, Otto Tybet used his innate resourcefulness to leave the German army and join the SS. The moment he donned the hated uniform with the death's head-skull-collar insignia, Tybet effectively ended his career as a spy and dropped off the grid as far as London was concerned."

Operating under the guise of an SS officer gave Otto many unique opportunities, which he utilized to the fullest. He saved numerous Jews, while never revealing, even to his brethren, that he was a Jew as well. He was the ultimate Nazi—at least on the outside. Vicious. Handsome. Well bred. Bloodthirsty. Culturally well informed. But beneath the disguise lay a Jewish heart beating with sympathy and empathy, a man who strolled among death on a daily basis, constantly dancing on the thinnest line between saving his brothers and acting like his fellow German officers. He was the consummate actor and no one ever suspected him of being anything other than the perfect Aryan.

After the war was over, Otto managed to make his way back to Israel. He told nobody about his wartime adventures and kept his past closed firmly shut. He feared the British, who would not have hesitated to court-martial him for deserting his post, and later on the Israelis, who may not have seen things the way they really were and might have considered him a traitor and a Nazi collaborator. And so Otto Tybet kept his past a secret.

"His neighbors never knew that the man who lived in the apartment next door had operated as an SS officer during the war. Humans being humans, however, Otto couldn't control himself completely, and he shared his secret with his brother—my father—after making him promise that he would never tell a soul while he remained alive. Uncle Otto passed away about two years ago," she concluded, "at which time my father shared his brother's fascinating past with me. One of the many stories Uncle Otto told my father was the story of Yehuda Yeedle Wallis and the *tefillin* in Dachau."

It was now time for Sarah Pachter to update the Wallis family with the rest of the story.

"There's something you should know," she told Rabbi Wallis. "Otto Tybet, the SS officer who decreed your father should be whipped, was a Jew from a Yerushalmi family originally from Vienna, posing as a Nazi."

He could hardly believe it. "Are you sure?"

"I have the proof in my hand and computer. All the stories involving Tybet—the supposedly bloodthirsty Nazi—end up with Jews who survived the war. Whipped, hurt—but alive."

Rabbi Wallis was absolutely stunned. This was the last thing he had been expecting to hear.

"Otto's family wants to meet your father. He has brothers and sisters. They all want to meet him."

"I'll ask him if he's up to it."

Rabbi Wallis didn't tell his father exactly who it was that wanted to come see him. He merely told him that a group of people wanted to come interview him about the *tefillin* story.

"I have no strength to tell the story again."

"Please, Abba, it's important that you share your stories with as many people as possible."

In the end, Yeedle acquiesced.

They arrived at the Wallis home, a whole group of people sitting on the couch. Cameras, pencils, and pads. They were in recording mode, to preserve the memory of this historic meeting for all posterity.

"Who are all these people?" his father wanted to know.

"From the newspaper."

"What, all of them?"

"Yes, they're all related and they all want to hear what you have to say."

After Yeedle retold the story, Otto's niece handed Rabbi Wallis a picture of her uncle.

"Please ask your father if he recognizes that man."

Before showing his father the picture, Rabbi Wallis said, "Abba, do you remember telling me about that Nazi, Otto Tybet?"

"Of course."

"Do you recall what he looked like?"

"Yes," his father replied. "He was a tall, skinny man with a pointy nose, blond hair, and eyes so blue they were almost colorless."

"If I showed you his picture, would you recognize him?"

Shrugging his shoulders, he said, "Show me his picture and I'll see."

He showed him the photograph. Yeedle Wallis stared at it for a few long minutes.

"That's him without a doubt, that's Otto Tybet. How did you get this picture?"

"Abba," Rabbi Wallis said to his father, "I know this is hard to believe, but Otto Tybet was a Jew named Klar. These people sitting across from you are members of his family."

His father sat silent, completely overwhelmed. When he finally opened his mouth, it was to say the following unexpected words.

"Now I understand everything. Everything just fell into place."

"What do you mean, everything just fell into place?"

"Yossi, do you know what I used to call Otto Tybet?"

"No, what?"

"I used to call him 'my Nazi.' You know why I called him that? Because he was different from all the other officers."

"How was he different?"

"I'll give you an example. Whenever it came to the High Holy Days season, the Nazis, being familiar with the Jewish calendar, made sure to work us much harder than they did on a regular day. One Rosh Hashanah, the Nazis took us out of the camp to go dig ditches in the fields. It was pointless work designed just to break us. At some point along the route, Otto Tybet separated a group of us from the main detail and commanded us to follow him behind a far-off hill.

"'I know you have a holiday today,' he told us when we were far from the rest of the prisoners, 'and I have something for you, a little gift.' Then he pulled out a *shofar* from beneath the outer layer of his coat. 'I'm going to go sit on top of the hill over there, and if I see a German patrol heading in our direction I'll blow my whistle. Meanwhile, go pray to your hearts' content. Have a good time. It's your day.'

"We managed to get through the entire Rosh Hashanah davening, including *shofar* blowing, with a Nazi officer keeping watch for us! Is it any wonder that I used to call him 'my Nazi' after that?"

The entire room was silent, overcome by Yeedle Wallis's memories.

"Tell me more," his son said.

"Everyone knew that the war was almost over and that it was only a matter of time until the Germans were defeated, but we didn't know details because of course there was no way to get our hands on any newspaper. But at times, Tybet used to take me with him to one of the local warehouses. I'd help him with carrying goods back to the camp, and he always made sure to wrap objects in pages of current newspapers, which would give us a picture of the war. This knowledge translated into hope for all the prisoners.

"That wasn't all.

"Sometimes, Otto commanded me to steal certain items from the warehouse—things which were off-limits to the German officers as well—and to smuggle them back into the camp for him. In return, he gave me medicine that brought down fever. Many Jews in the camp suffered from typhus, which caused high fever, and the medicine he gave me as 'payment' helped save Jewish lives. I never realized why he 'paid' me for my help with medicine instead of any other currency.

"When I stood on the table in Dachau with the noose around my neck, *tefillin* around my arm and head, yelling out that I was the winner, it was Otto who convinced the other Germans to make me suffer a much more painful death." His voice broke. "I realize now that he was trying to save my life with the only plan he could think of. He knew I was strong and figured there was a good chance I'd survive a beating. And I did. And it was all because of Otto Tybet, 'my Nazi.'"

It was all a little too much for everyone to take in.

And you know what? The story doesn't even end there.

♦ ♦ ♦

Rabbi Aharon Levy, senior lecturer for Arachim, was celebrating his son's bar mitzvah and invited Rabbi Wallis to attend. When he arrived, Reb Aharon placed him at the head table, diabolically preventing him from even making an attempt at an early escape. Ten minutes later, the door of the hall opened up and an entire posse of what appeared to be relatives trooped inside and were seated by the host at a nearby table. A few questions yielded the surprising information that they were members of the extended Klar family, close friends of Rabbi Levy and relatives of SS Officer Otto Tybet. Abandoning his spot at the head table, Rabbi Wallis took a seat among the Klars. They were soon joined by Reb Aharon, who abandoned the head table as well to sit with them.

During the course of that evening, Rabbi Levy heard the story of Otto Tybet and Yeedle Wallis. In the days following the bar mitzvah, Aharon Levy and Yossi Wallis decided to pay a visit to Otto Tybet's grave, to pay tribute to a great man who had committed anonymous acts of tremendous courage.

On the Yerushalayim hilltop where he was buried, the two Arachim rabbis recited *Tehillim* for Otto Tybet—Chaim Michel Klar—whose resourcefulness and ingenuity were virtually unknown. No doubt, the people who pass by his grave on Har HaMenuchos know nothing of his bravery and the mission he undertook without being asked.

Though he passed on to the next world without leaving progeny behind, Chaim Michel Klar did leave something eternal to remember him by. Having worked for Solel Boneh, one of Israel's most prestigious construction companies, for many years after his return to Israel, Klar was a man of means. When Rav Yehuda Ashlag, known as the Baal HaSulam on account of his monumental commentary, *Peirush HaSulam* on the *Zohar* (a work that took him 10 years to write and is held in the highest of esteem by serious scholars of Kabbalah), finished his magnum opus, the question was how to finance the printing. Clearly the job would be extremely expensive and would need a sponsor with deep pockets. It was at that point that Reb Moshe Boruch Klar, a student of the Baal HaSulam, approached his brother Chaim Michel and asked him to pay for the printing costs.

Chaim Michel Klar cashed in his pension fund and used the money that had been earmarked for his retirement to finance the first printing of the *Peirush HaSulam* on the *Zohar*. Despite not having been blessed with physical descendants, Chaim Michel was granted an abundant source of merit by the One Above. Every time that a Jew opens up the *Zohar* and studies it, using the illuminating explanations of the Baal HaSulam, reward is deposited in the Heavenly bank account of one "SS Officer Otto Tybet"—reward that will grow until the end of time.

May his memory be a blessing for the entire Jewish nation.

CHAPTER FOURTEEN

While his father was the product of a Jewish Polish family, Rabbi Wallis's maternal grandparents, the Winklers, were typically Hungarian in every way. Born in a town called Feldish, his mother was raised in the more well-known city of Debrecen. His mother's father was a teacher in the local *cheder*, as was his father's father in Poland. Whereas the Germans were fixtures of daily life in Poland from 1939, they only arrived in Hungary in 1944.

Ably assisted by the Hungarian Arrow Cross, the Nazi soldiers entered every tiny village and town and systematically shipped the Jews to the concentration camps. It was Friday evening when the Germans entered the Winklers' town. The dining-room table was covered with a pristine white tablecloth. A bouquet of fresh flowers sat regally in a crystal vase perched on the sideboard. The entire house gleamed with Shabbos cleanliness and purity.

Rabbi Wallis's mother, Yehudis, was the oldest child in the family, 16 years old on that dreadful night. With the davening over, Rav Winkler arrived home from shul and the entire family took their seats around the dining-room table. Faces scrubbed and clean. The girls in their pretty Shabbos finery. The boys in their white shirts. Her father lifted the silver *becher* to make Kiddush. At that moment the door was thrown open and the Germans entered their lives.

The family was given five minutes to gather whatever belongings they could put together before being forced to leave their home for the town square. From there, the entire Jewish population was marched on foot for a long distance before being crammed into the cattle cars that would transport them the rest of the way to Auschwitz. It was a brutal wake-up call from what had been a beautiful life.

In an ironic twist of fate, Yehudis and the rest of the Winkler family arrived at Auschwitz on the saddest day of the year.

Tishah B'Av. The 9th of Av.

Her father was sent to a labor camp, but everyone else—her mother, sisters, brothers, aunts, cousins, the entire family—was immediately directed to the infamous Dr. Mengele, who was waiting to decide their destiny. Dr. Mengele didn't waste too much time deliberating, immediately sending the entire group to the left.

Then he looked at Yehudis—blond, blue eyed, 16 years old—and said to her, "You must be the maid of this family, you can't possibly be Jewish! Go to the right."

Rabbi Wallis's mother, with no idea what the ramifications of being sent to the right or left meant, only knowing that she had just been separated from her entire family, began arguing with the demon of Auschwitz.

"You're mistaken," she said, trying to correct the man in the white gloves. "I'm just as Jewish as they are. That's my mother, my sisters... I want to go with them."

She was desperate.

"You don't tell me where you want to go," he replied. "You stay on the right and they will go to the left. You're the maid and you will go to the right."

Yehudis didn't give up and continued arguing with the Angel of Death, insisting that she didn't want to be separated from the rest of her family. Perhaps Mengele would have given in, but at that moment Yehudis's mother chose to sharply intervene. Realizing that being sent to the left was no good, Rabbi Wallis's grandmother ordered her to stay right where she was.

Choking over her tears, the teenager called out, "Mommy, I want to come with you and you are sending me away?!"

Unspoken were the sentiments, "How can a mother act this way to her oldest daughter?"

Ignoring her own emotions, Mrs. Winkler reiterated her earlier command. "Stay right where you are. I forbid you to come to me!"

The teenager was devastated. The entire family stood on the left while she remained by herself on the right, alone and friendless. As her family was marched away, Yehudis and her mother kept eye contact for as long as they could. Just before Rabbi Wallis's grandmother reached the turn which would take them out of sight forever, she raised her voice above the din of Auschwitz and screamed out to her daughter, "Yehudis, never forget that you are a Jewish girl!"

Those were the final words Rabbi Wallis's mother heard her mother say. They would reverberate within her for the rest of her life.

"Yehudis, never forget that you are a Jewish girl!"

♦ ♦ ♦

The Winkler family was dispatched to Heaven in a cloud of dark smoke, while Yehudis was directed to a barracks. Though the barbers cut the hair off every other girl, her head was left untouched, and her blond hair was the oddest of sights in a sea of shorn heads. Though every girl was hit by the block master when they walked through the barracks doors, for some unexplained reason, she never hit Yehudis Winkler. It was as if an angel had grabbed hold of the girl and was guiding her through Auschwitz so that she would stay alive. From the windows of the rectangular wooden shed that served as barracks, she had a vantage point and direct view of the gigantic towers that never ceased belching black smoke into the atmosphere. Turning to one of the veterans, she innocently inquired as to where the rest of her family had been taken.

"Look out the window," she was told. "See those chimneys with all the smoke?"

She nodded.

"That's your family."

She was a young, innocent Chassidic girl and she couldn't comprehend what they were telling her.

Later, seeing her uncle on the other side of the fence, she decided to give him her bowl of thin soup. She didn't like the taste and besides, she wasn't hungry. Instead of pouring it on the ground and wasting it, she elected to pass it beneath the fence and over to him. Using the same straightforward almost simpleminded approach with which she operated from her first moments in Auschwitz, Yehudis walked straight over to the barbed-wire fence—a fence sizzling with electricity, a fence that killed any inmate who threw himself on it. Standing beside the fence, she bent down, lifted up the bottom of the fence, and passed her soup through to her uncle.

Years later, she would tell her son, "I have no idea why the electricity coursing through that fence didn't electrocute me on the spot, or why the soldiers seated in the guard towers didn't shoot me for passing food to an inmate in a different section of the camp. Nothing happened to me, no matter what I did. For some reason, I was earmarked for survival and though everything I did by rights should have had the opposite effect, I managed to survive."

She remained in Auschwitz for sufficient time to experience multiple miracles. As the Allied forces closed in on Berlin, the Germans cleared out the camps and forced millions of emaciated, sickly Jews to accompany them toward Germany. Yehudis was taken along with thousands of other Jews on a death march, placing one foot after the next in a determined effort not to think, but just to exist. With thousands of Jews dying on her every side, she managed to make it all the way to Dachau, where she was "introduced" to Yeedle Wallis for the first time—as he stood on a table with a noose around his neck and *tefillin* around his arm and head.

Though all the witnesses thought he had died, he managed to survive.

And so did she.

With the Allied forces about to reach Dachau, Yeedle and Yehudis were taken on their final death march. Forced to endure for hours on end while shivering in the frigid wind, they ceased to think, ceased to feel. From morning till night they marched, marched for no reason, marched to no destination, while the sound of the German guns served as continuous accompaniment. That was where the Americans finally caught up with them. On the death march from Dachau.

Yeedle Wallis was among the first Jews to be taken prisoner by the Germans at the start of the war, and one of the last Jews to be freed.

Yehudis Winkler witnessed his magnificent behavior during what he imagined were his final moments on earth.

She saw the noose around his neck.

She heard him recite the words of "*ve'eirastich.*"

Yossi's parents on their wedding day

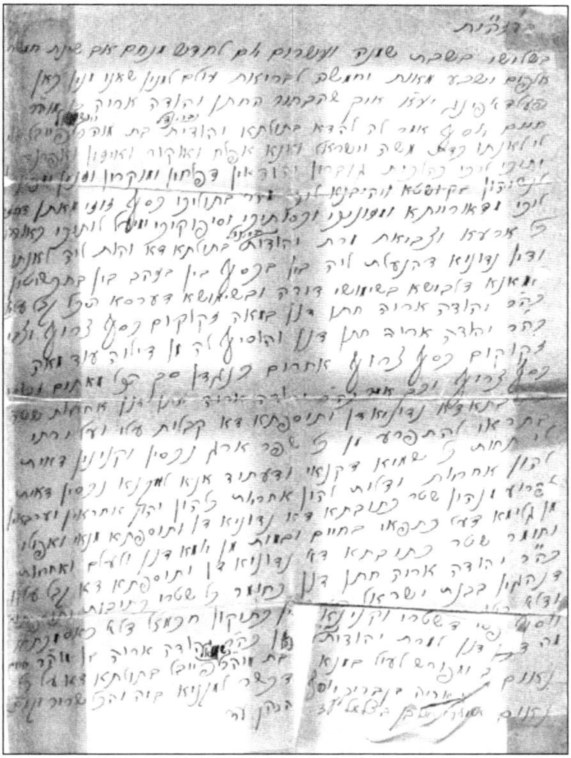

The handwritten *kesubah* of Yeedle and Yehudis Wallis

She heard him, a malnourished prisoner facing execution, declaring that he was the victor.

Now it was all over and Yehudis was left without any family. She was 17 years old. Almost invisible in a gigantic, friendless world. Approaching Yeedle Wallis, Yehudis spoke her heart.

"I'm all alone without a soul in the world," she told the man who had survived six years of Holocaust. "Will you marry me?"

"Yes," Yeedle replied simply, "I will."

The Klausenberger Rebbe officiated at their wedding, penning the words of their *kesubah* on a piece of paper, from memory. Their wedding was the first the Rebbe conducted after the war, the first of many. Decades later, the Rebbe's son, the Klausenberger Rebbe of Netanya, came over to Rabbi Wallis's house with a team of specialists to examine his parents' *kesubah* and to verify that it had indeed been written by his father. Needless to say, it was.

♦ ♦ ♦

From a purely statistical viewpoint, Yeedle Wallis was a walking miracle. If you estimate his chances of survival at 10 percent in every camp, there was really no way to explain the fact that he was still alive.

Ghetto.

Concentration camp.

Auschwitz.

Warsaw Ghetto.

Death march.

Dachau.

Death march.

Mathematically, there was no chance. The majority of those who survived the Holocaust were people who began their ordeal in the 1940's, or who joined the partisans in the European forest or managed to escape to the Russian tundra or who were given refuge by non-Jews. But Yeedle Wallis had done none of those things; his suffering began in 1939, and yet he was still alive in 1945. It defied all logic.

In those wild postwar days, many Nazis fell into the American net while trying to flee to South America with the help of a clandestine Nazi escape network. In many cases, the Americans wanted to put them on trial for their war crimes but needed witnesses to do so.

One day Yeedle Wallis was walking down the street in Germany when he saw a sign that had been posted by the American military. The sign stated tersely that the American military had caught Germans who were suspected of being Nazi officers, listed their names, and requested that anyone with knowledge of these men and their alleged crimes should please present themselves at the designated courthouse.

"Yossi," his father said to him, "you'll never believe whose name I saw on the list. It was the German officer who had devised the diabolical water test on the death march, the Angel of Death who had turned the water a bloody red with Jewish blood. He had been caught by the Allies. Satan himself was in their hands and they had no idea. Would I testify? What was the question! How could I ever forget the look of enjoyment on his face as he stood on that wooden bridge overlooking the stream, gun trained on the hapless Jews below, waiting in anticipation for a Jew to try and sneak some moisture onto his dry, cracked lips. Almost nobody remained alive who had witnessed his crimes. But I was there; I had seen everything and had remained alive to tell the world.

"Would I testify? You bet I would."

♦ ♦ ♦

He presented himself at the military camp early the next morning. A soldier stood in the guard booth checking the documentation of anyone seeking to enter.

"Papers?"

Yeedle showed him his papers.

"Purpose of visit?"

"To testify against one of the SS officers who is currently incarcerated here."

The guard checked his documents.

"You can go inside, sir."

"Thank you."

It was his first time in an official military courtroom and he was slightly overawed by it: the gleaming mahogany fittings, the judge's bench, the witness stand. He was struck by the irony of the situation. Just a few months before he had been a walking dead man who could be shot for no reason at all, and now he was being called to testify against one of the very villains who had controlled the lives of so many.

The SS officer was brought forth under guard from his cell and placed in the prisoners' dock. The judge, a United States military officer, took his place on the judge's platform. Yeedle Wallis was called up to the witness stand.

"Mr. Wallis," said the judge, "do you recognize this man?" He pointed to the Nazi as he spoke.

"I do, sir."

"Have you seen him committing crimes against humanity?"

"I have."

"Can you please describe those crimes for the court?"

Yeedle Wallis needed no second invitation. He described in precise language how the Jews had been marched halfway across Poland in the terrible summer heat without being given anything to drink. How anyone who had collapsed had been shot without a second glance. He described the sadism of the man on trial. Then he told the court about the day that was forever burned into his mind. About being forced into the stream and how the Nazi officer stood on the bridge and shot at the Jews who couldn't stop themselves from taking a drink. How he drove the Jews insane and shot them for the crime of taking a drink of water.

The room was utterly silent as he spilled his heart.

The judge turned to the German. "What do you have to say in your defense?"

The German stared Yeedle in the face, his jaw jutting forward pugnaciously.

"The Jew is lying. He's imagining things. It never happened."

The judge turned back to Yeedle. "Can you refute his words? Can you prove him wrong?"

The implications were clear. If the man wouldn't admit to the accusations, it would be Jew against German and the German would be released for lack of evidence.

"Your Honor, do you really think I am capable of dreaming up such a story?" Yeedle asked the judge. "Allow me to approach the witness box. I want this man to look into my eyes and tell me to my face that I am a liar. You decide which one of us is telling the truth. The Nazi officer or his Jewish prisoner. Can you do that for me?"

The judge agreed.

Rabbi Wallis's father crossed the courtroom. Stood before his erstwhile torturer. Met his gaze with a vengeful stare of his own.

"Are you going to look me in the eye and tell me that you did none of the things that I described here today?"

The German didn't even flinch.

"That's right, *Jude*. You're a liar! You're making it all up. Very creative. But all a lie. No truth to anything that you said."

That was when Yeedle Wallis lost his temper. Reaching over the railing, he grabbed the German by his two ears and pulled with all his considerable might. The courtroom erupted. Soldiers ran forward to try and release his grip on the Nazi. But Yeedle Wallis was both very powerful and fueled by anger so raw it made him lose control completely. Nobody could get his hands off the German's ears. The melee reached epic proportions. No one could recall witnessing such a brawl in an American courtroom before. Everything was way out of control.

"Leave go of him!" they yelled at the Polish Jew.

"Never," he screamed back, pulling even harder. "This man tortured my friends and shot them to death. And now he has the audacity to lie in my face!"

By the time the soldiers managed to subdue him and pull him away from the German, Yeedle was holding one of the Nazi's ears in his hand and blood was gushing down the side of the Nazi's face.

The military judge was decidedly not amused. "Take this man," he ordered the troops, pointing at Yeedle, "lock him up, and send the German to the hospital."

The German was rushed off to the hospital for an emergency operation, while Yeedle Wallis was locked up in the very cell that had been vacated by the now earless Nazi. Next to him on both sides were other cells filled with former Nazi officers, and Yeedle utilized the prime opportunity he had been given to tell the Nazis exactly what he thought of them.

They were very unhappy with him and told him so, vocally.

"Watch your step," he replied, "or I'll pull your ears off too."

In the prison's central courtyard there was a gallows that was used for hanging convicted criminals. Later on that same day, as Yeedle sat in his cell peering out at the world, he witnessed a few American troops returning from the hospital with the German—his head all bandaged—his spirit crushed. In a shocking turnaround, the guards stood him beneath the gallows and fastened the noose around his neck. Without ceremony or undue fuss, the German officer who had killed so many Jews was hanged in the courtyard—his death witnessed by his fellow officers and one of his former prisoners. Yeedle did not know if his testimony had been sufficient to cause the German's death or whether there had been other testimony that had come to light previously or afterward. He did not care. The only thing that mattered was that the Angel of Death should be fittingly punished.

"This was the best 'Purim' of my life," he would tell his son later on. "I saw 'Haman' hanging on the tree, and I held *oznei Haman* (the Hebrew word for hamantaschen, translated literally as 'Haman's ears') in my hands."

Later that day he asked the guards why they hung the Nazi.

"I guess the judge believed you," the soldier replied. "You were pretty convincing, all in all. Still we can't have prisoners pulling people's ears off all the time, can we?"

"I guess not, sir," Yeedle replied. Then they exchanged smiles, and in the soldier's smile he understood that the Americans were not really angry at him and that he would be released soon enough.

"How long did they keep you in the prison, Abba?"

"A few days. To be honest, I'm sure there were plenty of Americans in Munich and Dachau who would have been more than happy to do the same thing themselves. They understood that I was telling the truth and agreed with me that the German deserved everything he got."

"So they let you go?"

"They let me go."

CHAPTER FIFTEEN

Yeedle and Yehudit Wallis were living in a DP camp near Munich when events conspired to move them on to their next destination. Palestine was under British rule at that time and the British were the target of much criticism worldwide for their refusal to allow Jewish refugees into what would later become Israel. The British were simply following their gut feelings, which meant keeping young Jews away from Israeli shores and the ranks of Ben-Gurion's Haganah and Menachem Begin's Irgun. But with world pressure mounting on them to do something to help the thousands of refugees that had been left stranded after the Holocaust, the British came to a decision to change their policy, at least on the surface.

In a well-publicized act, the British called a press conference in a number of DP camps announcing that they would be granting certificates to a specific number of Jews, which would allow them entrance to Palestine. Big news indeed. Every press conference was covered by photographers and journalists, and the British made sure that everyone understood how magnanimous they were being. Of course it wasn't as simple as they made it out to be. The British weren't prepared to grant their precious certificates to every random Jew they saw.

Certificates were to be handed out to children, pregnant women, and elderly people—none of whom posed an imminent security threat to the British military presence in the mandate. Certificates were very definitely not to be given out to people like Yeedle Wallis, who was young, strong, and blessed with a powerful physique. There was no way the British were prepared to allow someone like him into Palestine.

By this time Rabbi Wallis's parents had been married for quite a few months and his mother was already expecting her first child, whom they would name Yossi. The British were consequently happy to offer her a certificate for entrance to Palestine. Unfortunately, their generous offer did not include a certificate for the unborn child's father.

"Thank you but no thank you," said his mother to the British official. "There is no way in the world that I am prepared to leave my husband and to travel on my own to another country while expecting a child, with the vague hope that we will be reunited one day. I am all alone in the world and have nobody other than my husband. I don't even speak Yiddish, let alone Ivrit. There is nothing to discuss. Give the certificate to someone else."

Yeedle disagreed.

"Take the certificate," he told her. "Travel to Palestine and don't worry about being alone for long, because I'll come join you before you know it!"

Yehudit remained unconvinced.

"How are you going to join me? The British aren't going to let you in!"

"Yehudit, I survived German rule for six years. Do you really imagine that I'm going to allow the British to keep me away from watching my child grow up?"

"Why are you so determined that I accept this certificate?"

"Because I do not want any child of mine, and certainly not my firstborn, growing up on the blood-drenched soil of Europe. Go to Palestine and I will get there too. You're asking me how? I don't know how right now, but one thing you can be sure of is that I will find a way."

Still she refused. Palestine was a dangerous place on the verge of war between the British, Jews, and Arabs. Yehudit had had enough war to last her a lifetime.

She refused to accept the certificate, while he insisted that she take it.

No. Yes. No. Yes.

In the end Yeedle prevailed, basically forcing Yehudit to accept the certificate. She gave in but couldn't stop the tears from leaking from her eyes and rolling down her face. It was a very sad woman who packed her bags and got ready to leave for Palestine.

♦ ♦ ♦

A stage, complete with podium, served as backdrop for the press conference celebrating the send-off of the Jewish refugees to Palestine. In the background a truck waited patiently, its exhaust pipe quivering gently, for the Jews of Europe to leave the DP camp on the initial stage of their journey. Phase one of the journey was the short drive to the local train station. From there, the Jews were to take the train to the French port city of Marseilles. A luxury liner would be waiting for them at the port to transport them across the ocean to Haifa, with a number of stopovers on the way. That was the plan and the British were making the most of this historic public relations coup.

When the speeches came to an end, the Jews were told to board the truck. Yehudit stepped up, tears rolling down her cheeks as she took a spot in the back. Her husband watched his expectant wife boarding the truck, wondering if he would ever see her again.

Suddenly Yeedle Wallis "heard" his father speaking to him.

Yehuda, his father said, *you survived the camps... Six years at the hands of the Nazis... And now you're just standing there as your wife boards a truck that will take her away from you! Are you going to watch your wife and unborn child drive out of your life without doing anything about it?*

Yeedle—jump on the truck!

Without stopping to think, Yeedle jumped onto the running board beside the driver's seat and, taking hold of the door handle, held on as the truck roared away.

The uproar was immense. The British authorities who had gathered to see the refugees off quickly motioned to the truck driver to halt and pulled the Jew roughly down to the ground.

"Do you have a certificate?" a British officer demanded.

Yeedle was forced to admit that he did not possess a certificate.

"Then why on earth did you jump onto the truck? This truck is only for people who have been granted certificates, and just to be very clear here, if anyone who doesn't possess a certificate succeeds in joining those who are rightfully making the trip, everyone will be punished and all of you will be sent right back to Europe without your certificates, with no chance of ever entering Palestine in the future! This transport will be legitimate and legal or it will not happen at all!"

So spoke the voice of British officialdom and authority.

All heads turned to look at the uninvited guest.

"I never wanted to smuggle myself onto the transport," he said. "All I wanted was to accompany my wife and unborn child to the train station. Is there anything wrong with that?"

His eyes shone with innocence and no one had a counterargument. Who really cared if the Jew accompanied his wife to the train station? What harm could come out of that? The man wanted to say good-bye to his wife, let him say good-bye.

"Very well," said the official in charge, softening. "You can go along for the ride."

Yeedle acknowledged their kindness and goodwill with profuse thanks. A minute later everything was settled. He boarded the truck and went over to sit beside his wife, who quickly wiped the tears off her face at the sight of her husband. The driver released the clutch and the truck rolled out of the DP camp toward the highway and the train station.

Round one was his, but he couldn't enjoy his victory, knowing that he was entering round two with no plan at all. On the other hand, he was sitting beside his wife on the truck, when by rights he should not have been allowed on at all.

Fifteen minutes later, the truck pulled up outside the train station and the passengers alighted.

Now what?

Yeedle joined his wife on the station platform and they waited for the train to arrive. Her joy at seeing him on the truck had dissipated, and the tears were beginning to fall once again. The train rolled into the station with typical German efficiency, and Yeedle watched helplessly as all certificate holders were told to board. He did his best to comfort his wife, but once again they parted in sorrow, she crying with fear, he filled with agony at the thought of letting her go. He stood beside her compartment and waved to her through the window as the train began to slowly leave the station.

And once again he heard his father's voice.

Yehuda, it said, *you survived six years of Nazi occupation! Are you going to just stand there as your wife and unborn child leave you on a train to France? Yeedle, do something! Jump onto the train!*

He broke into a run, leaped up, and hoisted himself onto the back of the train. From there he clambered up onto the roof of the train, praying it would not gain speed. He had no papers of any kind, no legal documents, no identification, no way on earth of crossing the German-French border. But he was listening to the beloved voice of his father; he was getting closer to his wife, and that was all that mattered.

He crawled his way on the roof until he spotted an open door between cars. He jumped down and walked inside, trying to look like he belonged there, and then he swiftly moved from car to car until he reached a storage area where the luggage had been piled. There, he crouched down among the suitcases and trunks.

After a few minutes in his makeshift shelter, knowing how worried his wife was about traveling alone, he decided to show her that he was still in her vicinity. He left the relative safety of the luggage compartment and raced from car to car, hoping no one would stop and ask for his papers. Finally, he reached the car where she sat crying silently.

He stayed long enough for her to see his face.

Then he disappeared back into the luggage compartment, where he hid behind a pile of suitcases until the train slid into the station right outside the port of Marseilles.

♦ ♦ ♦

At the port in Marseilles, things became even more complicated. The Jewish contingent was immediately moved into a separate area and there was no way for Yeedle to breach the security. The ship was a luxury liner and it was docked behind multiple gates, with access granted only to those with legitimate papers. Yeedle Wallis, needless to say, did not qualify. He watched what seemed like hundreds of soldiers in uniform approaching the ship with their gear. American, British, and French soldiers were all boarding—shipping out to their respective destinations at army bases around Europe. The fact that the ship was being used almost exclusively by the military was sure to complicate matters even more, since security was bound to be that much tighter.

Standing in the shadows, he watched the goings-on around him: the photographers and journalists sent to cover the send-off of the European refugees to Palestine, the sailors yelling to one another as they hoisted supplies onto the ship and pulled cords, cables, coils, and ropes every which way. The ship was going to slide away from shore with his wife and unborn child, and there didn't seem to be any way for him to sneak on board. The speeches came to an end, the photographers took their last pictures, and the Jews were led up the gangplank and on board, where they were taken to the bottom level. They may have been certificate holders, but there was no way that the British were paying for them to travel in first class. No, they were in steerage and grateful for the opportunity.

Meanwhile, Yeedle was left standing on the pier, helpless and beaten, knowing that there was no way for him to even get close to the ship. He began walking from side to side of the pier, using every ounce of his considerable ingenuity to find a way—any way—to get himself on board. But try as he might, nothing came to mind. The ship was too well guarded. There were too many policemen standing around, too many fences to climb, too many chances of getting caught and, while brave, he was not foolhardy.

What to do?

Suddenly he caught sight of an American officer. Yeedle looked at him, did a double take. The man was Jewish, he was sure of it.

"Yossi," he'd later explain, "there was no question in my mind that this man was a Jew. His nose, quite simply, gave him away."

Yeedle approached him. "*Bist a Yid?*" (Are you a Jew?)

The man nodded.

"I'm a Holocaust survivor and my wife just boarded that ship," Yeedle explained. "She has a certificate from the British to enter Palestine and I don't. My wife is expecting our first child and I'm about to see her floating away from me."

The officer listened to him with a sympathetic look on his face.

"Please help me get on this ship!!"

"I'm sorry to have to disappoint you," the officer replied, "but security is so tight on this ship that even an American officer like me will be subjected to five documentation checks before being allowed to board. I hate to say it, but I don't see how on earth you are going to be able to circumvent the security even with my assistance. I feel for you, but this is the situation."

The officer turned to leave and Yeedle watched as the American was repeatedly interrogated by security personnel before being allowed to board. He was right, they were taking no chances on stowaways here.

Meanwhile, the American officer entered the ship and climbed to the upper deck. He couldn't help but be impressed by the determined Jew he'd just met, and he waited curiously to see what would happen next.

Yeedle knew that sooner or later someone would realize that he didn't belong on the dock. He had to make a decision and a move. The trouble was, he was all played out. There were no moves to make. No rabbits to pull out of his sleeve.

Just then he saw the porters.

Carrying crates of luggage, suitcases, and heavy bags, a long line of porters, clad in the overalls of pier workers, were snaking their way across the pier, through the gates, past the security checkpoints and up onto the ship. No one was checking them for security clearances. No one was giving them a second glance.

As Yeedle stood watching, one of the porters left the line and headed over to the side of the pier, where he lowered the crates he was holding to the ground outside a nondescript, diminutive building. He then removed his overalls, hung them up on a nail that was protruding from the building's wall, and entered the doors. It took Yeedle a second to realize that the porter had just availed himself of the port facilities.

Without giving himself time to think, Yeedle fairly threw himself into the porter's overalls, zipped them up, and lifted the heavy crates in front of him to shield his face. Then he joined the long line of porters and walked past every security checkpoint leading up to the ship. No officer stopped him. No one asked to see his papers. He was a porter and had become invisible. Minutes later, he was climbing the gangplank, which was shaking in the wind, the crates balanced on his shoulders, confidence in his gait, a smile on his face. As he stepped onto the ship he thought of his wife, no doubt crying down below, and called out to her in a silent voice, *Don't worry, Yehudit, I'm here.*

The American officer was waiting for him on the uppermost deck.

"Well done," he complimented the young man, while separating him from the rest of the porters who were heading to the assorted storage facilities on board.

"I watched you from up here, saw what you did. Follow me."

Yeedle followed the American to the canteen—a small room on board where crew members, traveling military men, and lucky passengers with money in their pockets could buy food and alcoholic drinks. Directly adjacent to the canteen's entrance was a set of winding stairs, which led downward to another storage area—this one used by the canteen owner to store all the goods he would need for the long journey.

"Hide in this room," the officer told him. "One thing is certain, there's plenty of food here and you won't go hungry."

The dark room was filled with crates of all kinds and it was not difficult for Yeedle to hollow out a hiding place for himself behind a giant crate of potatoes, two cases of beer, and about twenty cartons of packaged foodstuffs. Then he settled down for the interminable wait until the ship left shore and headed out to the open sea, from where there would be no turning back.

A few hours later, the floor beneath him began to rock and he knew that they were casting off the ropes and beginning their journey. He hadn't eaten anything since early that morning, and he managed to pry open some of the cartons. He stared in wonder at the bounty within. Sardines...pickles...chocolate... He hadn't seen food like this since before the war, and now he was looking at unlimited quantities of the finest in gastronomical delights. Not knowing what else to do, he settled down on the floor, back perched against a crate, and began to quiet the rumbling in his stomach with a mouthful of heavenly chocolate.

The owner of the canteen was an Italian who made the trip down the stairs and into the storage room when he had to restock the shelves.

Eventually you are going to be caught, Yeedle told himself. *This is a long journey and as time goes on and the Italian empties more of the crates, there will be fewer and fewer places for you to hide.*

In the end, he saw no alternative but to come clean. Obviously, he did not dream of showing himself to the authorities on the ship, who would have thrown him off at the first port they made a stop in. But he decided to speak to the Italian at the earliest opportunity. Next time the Italian climbed down the stairs, Yeedle stepped out of the shadows.

"Don't be alarmed," he said, calming the very surprised canteen manager. "I'm a Jewish refugee from the camps who managed to sneak onto the ship. I have a wife down below deck who is carrying my unborn child. I need to reach Palestine. It's a matter of life and death! Do you understand?"

"Go on," the Italian said.

"I will work for you for no pay at all from now until we dock at the port in Haifa—just outfit me in the uniform of your staff. That's all I need from you."

The Italian took a liking to the Jew and his brash personality during their short interchange.

"You will be my man on board until we dock," he told the stowaway. And so it was. Yeedle was outfitted in an eye-catching uniform of white linen, with gold braid on the shoulders, beautifully pressed slacks, and a jaunty white cap. From one minute to the next he had gone from hiding with the rats behind the crates to being a free man with access to any place on board.

To get here, he'd jumped onto a truck, balanced himself on the roof of a train and passed himself off as a dock porter. And now, with unfettered access to every cabin, an exquisite uniform, and with as much fine food and drink as he could possibly desire, Yeedle Wallis was finally able to smile.

♦ ♦ ♦

The Jewish passengers were all locked down on the ship's lowest level. Knowing his wife was suffering by herself, lonely and forlorn, Yeedle decided to inform her that he had managed, against all odds, to board the "most tightly guarded ship" in France. He put together a delectable package of chocolate, fresh fruits, and all sorts of edibles that the Jews below had not seen in years and proceeded to descend to the lowest level of the ship. Removing a giant key from his belt, he unlocked the metal gate which separated the Jews from the rest of the passengers. At the sound of the door opening, the Jewish refugees took a look at the dashing sailor in his impeccably tailored uniform and gold buttons, carrying a carton filled with the best food that Europe had to offer—and then they did a double take and looked again.

Recognizing their old friend from the DP camp, their jaws simply dropped.

As soon as he told them his adventures, a ferocious argument broke out among the Jewish passengers. Some of them wanted to tell the authorities that an unauthorized passenger had managed to smuggle himself aboard.

"The British warned us that they will send every Jew on board back to Europe if even one illegal manages to infiltrate the boat," they said. "We have to give him up for the greater good."

The other side was unprepared to hand over a fellow Jew and was willing to live with the consequences.

"He made it this far," they argued, "let him go all the way and let's see what happens when we get to Haifa!"

The argument was bitter and acrimonious with everyone taking sides and everyone having something to say. Eventually they decided to take a vote. One by one, the passengers dropped a rolled-up piece of paper into a hat. Yes or no. Yeedle waited tensely for the verdict. In the end, though it was very close, the Jewish passengers decided not to say anything. Yeedle could stay!

Once they accepted the fact that he was free to roam the ship while they were locked up behind heavy steel gates, the Jews on the ship benefitted from Yeedle's position and largesse. He never visited his wife empty-handed, always coming bearing gifts, which his generous wife shared with everyone.

So it went as days turned into nights and the fierce Atlantic sun set over and over on the far edge of the ocean's horizon. And then one morning, as he was standing on the upper deck peering out into the distance, Yeedle spotted the barest outline of Haifa's magnificent Mount Carmel, and he knew that he was seeing Eretz Yisrael.

"You have to understand something, Yossi," he would tell his son many years later. "I was born in a small town in Poland. In my absolute wildest dreams I never imagined that I would one day set foot on the soil of Eretz Yisrael. You can't even imagine the feelings welling up inside my chest as I stared in silence at the beautiful homeland I had never seen. Growing up, we always chanted the words '*leshanah habaah beYerushalayim*,' but it was always an abstract concept that didn't translate into reality, and yet here I was, my family all gone into the chimneys of Auschwitz, and I, having defied the Nazis and the British while cheating death hundreds of times, was approaching Eretz Yisrael. And coming to the land with a wife, and a child on the way! I can't describe the awesome feelings coursing through my soul at that second. Eretz Yisrael before me, my family on the deck below—all my dreams were coming true."

CHAPTER SIXTEEN

The majestic luxury ocean liner swept into the Haifa pier, gently parting the cobalt waves with practiced ease. On the ground, reporters, journalists, and people from the Jewish Agency jockeyed for the best position to record the event. Down below, the Jews gathered their meager belongings, made sure they had not misplaced their precious certificates, and shuffled toward the gate locking them into third class.

Up on deck, Yeedle Wallis surveyed the scene with a glance of wry sadness as he prepared for phase four of his very dangerous game. He'd survived until now, but what would happen as they disembarked? He had no papers of any kind. How was he going to bluff his way into Eretz Yisrael?

On the dock, a stage had been built equipped with a lectern, a table, chairs, and a few bottles of lukewarm Tempo for the politicians and assorted dignitaries, while a large hall had been cordoned off directly adjacent to the dock to process the Jewish refugees. The British representative waited on the shore to welcome the Jews to Palestine and to show the world the humane face of Britain.

The captain of the ship had ordered his sailors to don their dress whites and to report to the bridge overlooking the harbor in an impressive display of naval authority. The sight of the white-coated sailors standing in formation served as the perfect backdrop for the official photograph of the day. The ship docked with a thunk. The gangplank was thrown down. An honor guard on the pier gave a crisp salute to a British officer as he stepped onto Haifa soil. What a day this was turning out to be. The ceremony. The pomp and splendor. What a welcome had been prepared for the penniless, destitute Jews of Poland! Yet Yeedle couldn't enjoy a second of it, knowing that he might be arrested at any minute.

The official British dignitary in charge of the proceedings boarded the ship and approached the captain.

The elegant Brit looked around. Not a Jew in sight.

"Where are the Jews?" he drawled in his Etonian public school accent. The Jews, after all, were the reason that everyone was there.

"I'll have the Jews out in a second," promised the captain.

Turning around, he bellowed at the line of sailors, "Where's the officer in charge of the Jews?"

There was no reply. Obviously the man was not at his post. But the British were waiting to see "their" Jews. There was tension in the air. This was no time for an officer to disappear.

It took Yeedle mere seconds to grasp the opportunity that had fallen into his lap. There was a temporary vacuum and he jumped right into it. It was a replay of the scene with the porter.

"You want the Jews," he yelled over to the captain, "I'll go get them, sir. They'll be up on deck momentarily!"

"Go, go," said the relieved captain.

Yeedle ran, deck softly rocking under his feet as he took the stairs three at a time, heart racing in reaction to the tension. This was it. Crunch time. If he didn't pull this off the British would arrest him or worse—send him back to accursed Poland without his wife and child. He raced through the corridors of the ship, past the endless line of cabins and portholes, feeling the internal hum and whir of the ship's engines settling down after their long journey. Out of breath he arrived at the entrance to third class, seeing the crowds of Jews milling about behind the gates, anxious to exit their claustrophobic confines.

"We have arrived. The ship has just docked at the Haifa pier."

A roar of triumph went up from the assembled.

"Everyone please line up right now."

The Jews took their place in the long line that snaked down the corridor.

"Please pass me your certificates now."

They removed the certificates bearing their names and passed them up to Yeedle Wallis, who cradled them in his hands.

"Follow me," he yelled, and the line of Jews, his wife included, followed Yeedle in his pristine white uniform up the curving flights of stairs and onto the upper deck, where they were temporarily blinded by the popping flashes of cameras and a blazing sun that shone down upon them from a cloudless Haifa sky. It was a glorious day, especially for people who had just been stuck in the bowels of a ship for the long journey.

Yeedle presented all the Jews to the captain, who wanted to know if everyone was accounted for.

"Yes, sir," he replied with crisp precision.

"Have you collected every certificate?"

"Yes, sir." *Other than my own, of course.*

"Did you count them yet?"

"I did, sir!"

"Then what are you waiting for?" bawled the captain. "Get them off the ship and let the press conference begin!"

"Yes, sir."

Moments later Yeedle began marching the entire group down the gangplank toward the authorities, certificates in hand, as if he were the official point man leading the entire operation. Yehudit Wallis couldn't help smiling proudly to herself as her husband led the pack. Down below the waters of the Haifa harbor swirled mightily in the breeze, circling and regrouping in little whirlpools.

Yeedle's heart was beating so quickly it was a miracle that no one could hear it through the fancy uniform. He was so close.

The short, husky, bespectacled Polish Jew, so incongruously clad in uniform, standing on the soil of Eretz Yisrael, but the fact remained that he didn't possess the necessary documents to enter.

What now?

As he led the group down onto the dock, his agile mind was racing, weighing and discarding options. Though he appeared to be completely in control, he was rapidly running out of options.

The ceremony commenced as soon as the refugees stepped onto dry land. Speeches, a musical tribute, a warm upper-class welcome, and the Jews were shepherded into a large shed, empty save for a wooden desk sitting squarely in the center of the huge space, windows on every wall of the room, and benches lining the sides. This was it: inspection time.

Yeedle motioned to the Jews to sit and presented himself to the British as the official go-between here to ease the refugees' entrance into Palestine. No one had any reason to doubt the veracity of his words and he was accepted as the de facto leader.

"Please put the certificates down on the desk."

He complied, standing beside the British. The Brit in charge—a career diplomat in his mid-50's with a pronounced limp and black-rimmed glasses—picked up the first certificate.

"Get this man, please," he told Yeedle in his Old Etonian tones.

Yeedle called the man, who came forward, had his certificate stamped, and was handed a brand-new identification card to be used from now on, granting him unrestricted access to Palestine. This repeated itself again and again: the British calling a name, the man or woman receiving an ID card, then exiting the room through the door at one side. The pile of certificates was diminishing rapidly, and Yeedle knew that very soon he would be the only one left in the room—and then what?

After his wife was safely out of the room, ID card stamped and a brand-new resident of Palestine, Yeedle snuck over to the far side of the room and, after making sure that the British were busy examining some documents, hoisted himself up on the windowsill, quickly opened the dusty window, and jumped out, landing on the ground below unharmed. Without stopping to catch his breath, he crossed the dusty Haifa street, made his way into a nearby alleyway, and broke into a run. The quaint homes and cheerful flower beds of the streets near the dock passed in a blur as the man from Poland ran for his life. His chest was heaving, his breath came in ragged gasps, but he was smiling as he inhaled the holy air of Eretz Yisrael for the first time in his life.

♦ ♦ ♦

At first no one even realized that he had gone. It was only when the final refugee had been processed and sent through the doors at the side of the room that the British registered that something nonkosher might have just taken place.

"Did you happen to notice where the man in the white uniform disappeared to?" one of them asked his friend.

"Jolly good lad that," the officer beside him concurred. "Did you catch his name?"

"I don't think he gave us a name."

"He needs to be processed as well. Boss or no boss, he can't enter the country without proper papers."

One of the officers called a guard. "See if you can find the man in the white uniform, so we can process his documents and be on our way."

"Yes, sir." The guard left the room, appearing a few minutes later with a look of anxiety on his pale face.

"I'm sorry to have to inform you, sir, that the man in the white uniform seems to have disappeared. He is not on the dock, not in this building, and the sailors are quite certain that he has not reboarded the ship."

"Well then, where could he possibly have gone off to?"

Slowly it dawned on them that they had been tricked and that the man in the white uniform had been a fraud.

"But how did he escape the building?"

One of the officers pointed at the open window. "Look over there. Gentlemen, I think that's the answer to our question."

"You mean he jumped out of the window?"

"That's exactly what I mean," he said, while fingering the certificates which were all piled neatly in an exact square in the center of the desk. "Please tell Lieutenant Davies that we might have a fugitive on our hands."

♦ ♦ ♦

The British began investigating. Immediately, two officers boarded the ship and began questioning the captain, who claimed to have no idea who the Jew was or what he was doing on the ship. As one sailor after another was interrogated and the pieces of the puzzle came together, the story began to emerge. The British quickly realized that the man had played them for fools, but though they longed for vengeance there was one problem: The Jew was gone out the window, and the passengers had all but disappeared from the port as well. There was nobody left to question or threaten.

Meanwhile, lonely, hungry Yeedle Wallis was running through the streets of Haifa, looking for a hiding place, knowing that the British would be searching for him with all the considerable resources at their disposal. While part of him was filled with anxiety at his predicament, another part of him was equally consumed with worry over his wife. He had no idea where she had been taken, and there was nothing he could do about it, since he was now on the run. Still, from time to time he paused for a second to glance back at the glorious ocean that had brought him to Eretz Yisrael and to grin Heavenward at the miracles which had brought him to this point.

He wandered through the *shuk*, past peddlers hawking every item under the sun and Arabs smoking nargilah at tiny tables. Everywhere he looked, people were drinking tiny china cups of powerfully aromatic black Turkish coffee and screaming at each other in guttural languages which he didn't understand. The lights went on in a nearby mosque and a loudspeaker on the minaret urged the faithful to prayer in undulating tones. And all the while, he knew that the British Tommies were searching for the runaway because they couldn't just let it go; his smuggling act would be taken as an act of defiance against the mighty British Empire and they couldn't afford to overlook such a thing.

When his breath started coming in ragged gasps, he realized that he couldn't run another step. The last thing he wanted was to reveal that he was a fugitive, but he was dealing with an emergency situation here and if he didn't find the right people, he'd be arrested. There was no time to lose. As the man who'd outsmarted the British every step of the way from Germany to France and straight into the Haifa bay, Yeedle knew his transgressions would never be forgiven. No, he needed help.

There was a group of merchants standing in front of him, organizing their wares at the end of a long day. One of them, a man with a brown face, thick eyebrows, and crooked teeth, appeared the friendliest of the bunch. More important, he was wearing a *kippah*.

Yeedle waited until the man locked up his stall and bade goodnight to all his friends. As he left the marketplace and entered the alleyways heading toward home, he fell into step beside him.

"I saw you watching me," the man said. "What do you want?"

It was time for full disclosure. "I need help. It's an emergency. The British are hot on my trail and if they catch me I go straight to jail, and I can't let that happen. My wife needs me. She's expecting our first child and I can't leave her helpless to fend for herself."

The old man just stared at him. Finally he spoke.

"Where on earth have you sprung from?"

"I just walked off the gangplank at the Haifa pier this afternoon."

"Where did you come from?"

"From France."

"Official British transport?"

"Every single person on board had certificates besides one: me. I smuggled myself on board back at Marseilles and walked around the ship like I owned it."

"And you got away with it." The man uttered the line as a statement.

"Yes."

A dawning look of respect crossed the old man's lined face.

"I'm going to put you in touch with some boys from the Irgun. They'll help you get away from here and provide you with assistance."

They walked side by side through the tangle of Haifa streets, into a sprawl of warehouses and factories. Eventually the old man brought Yeedle through the door of a shul, where they heard the final words of the evening Kaddish. A man lay in an insolent slouch on a couch in the shul courtyard, a burning cigarette held loosely between his fingers.

"Tell Dani I have someone for him."

The man merely grunted.

"They'll take care of you here," said the old man and left Yeedle without another word.

♦ ♦ ♦

Dani was a curly-haired youth of 21 who sized up the newcomer with one good look from beneath hooded lids.

"Come with me," he said tersely by way of introduction, and the two of them passed through the women's section and out the back door, using the warren of tiny roads that lined the neighborhood. It wasn't long before they arrived at what seemed to be an abandoned warehouse, surrounded by a junkyard secured with a chain-link fence, cars of every make and year lying in various stages of disrepair. The warehouse gave every impression of emptiness, but as soon as they stepped through the little door at the side of a giant, closed canvas awning, they stepped into a world of alert action. Irgun members came and went, all intent on their missions, everyone with a task to fulfill, no one with time to waste.

There was an office at the very back of the room, hidden behind rusty machinery and spare car parts. The local Irgun captain, a man of 24 (promotions came fast in those years), told Yeedle to sit down and had him repeat his entire story.

"So you want to work for the Irgun?"

Yeedle nodded.

The soldier looked him up and down.

"Somehow I don't see you running around with a Bren gun, shooting at the Tommies."

He put his finger to his head, and alternated between tapping against it and then the desk.

"I doubt that you'd make a worthwhile fighter, but there's no question you have what it takes to smuggle weapons wherever we need them."

His sharp eyes raked Yeedle's face.

"Can you handle such a job? Can you handle the pressure?"

Yeedle almost laughed. Here he'd just stepped off a ship he had no business being on where he'd lived like a king, and the man was asking him whether he could handle the pressure. He answered without rancor, with the weary patience of a person who has seen it all.

"Yes, I can do it."

"Good," said the other. "Welcome to the Irgun."

♦ ♦ ♦

The certificates had been divided between Israeli political parties, with every party receiving a share. Yossi's mother had arrived in Eretz Yisrael on a certificate that had been issued to her via the efforts of Agudath Israel, with whom Rabbi Wallis's grandfather had been affiliated before the war. Seeing her as their responsibility, Agudath Israel arranged to pick her up from the Haifa dock, driving her across the fledgling country to Kibbutz Chofetz Chaim, where, being all of 17, she was quartered with the 10- to 18-year-olds.

Knowing that there was no way for the two of them to be together at the moment, Yeedle contented himself with the knowledge that his wife was safe and well taken care of. Then he returned to the front lines of his brand-new battlefield and went about smuggling gun parts across the country. He had nerves of steel and nothing frightened him. After what he'd seen and experienced at the hands of the Nazis, it would be just about impossible to scare a man like Yeedle Wallis ever again.

The British, meanwhile, had not given up on his capture. They had made inquiries in Marseilles and had managed to trace his movements all the way back to the DP camp and the man who'd jumped on the truck to be with his expectant wife. Still smarting from having been taken advantage of, they plastered wanted posters with his face prominently displayed on trees and walls all over the country.

One evening, he left an Irgun hideaway to deliver a few guns to Irgun headquarters in another city. Making his way back home, he decided on a whim to visit his wife, who was staying in Tel Aviv, when he was suddenly blinded by the bright light of an army spotlight, and found to his chagrin that he'd wandered into the clutches of a British patrol, which had arbitrarily closed off the street and was checking the security documents of every passerby. The British officer in control looked determined, efficient, and extremely nasty, and Yeedle feared he'd finally met his match. The roadblock had been set up around the corner of a street, a calculated blind spot, in such a way that he'd been taken by surprise.

He considered turning around and retracing his steps, but he'd already been spotted, and turning tail would have looked suspicious.

What to do?

Glancing down at the bottle of water that he held in his hand, which he'd been using to quench his thirst, he was struck by a sudden brainstorm. He moved steadily forward toward the Tommies manning the roadblock, the glass bottle held loosely by its neck. Gently, he swung it back and forth. From the distance, the British soldiers grew concerned. Was that a bottle or a Molotov cocktail?

Using a megaphone, the commanding officer called out, "Lay the bottle down on the floor. Gently. Then back up five steps. Follow orders and nobody will get hurt."

Yeedle made as if to listen to them. After all, they had their machine-gun sights pointed straight at him. The last thing he wanted was to give them the impression that he was going to make a run for it.

He began to lower the bottle to the ground, and then, just before letting go completely, he straightened up and flung the bottle high in the air, right over the roadblock of the British troops! As he let it go, he turned and raced off into the night.

The sound of yelling troops assailed him from behind. Every soldier had thrown himself to the ground, taking cover behind any possible partition, protrusion, or wall, as they waited for the inevitable explosion. But the only sound they heard was that of shattering glass as the bottle hit the ground, and a moment later they realized they had been tricked. "After him!" roared the commander, and the troops fanned out through the city streets, intent on catching the man who'd made a fool of them.

Yeedle ran for his life. Through the brambles and underbrush of a public garden, down a long, secluded boulevard lined with tall, thick trees that provided shade for pedestrians in the heat of the day, and between buildings and stores. He ran with every ounce of strength he possessed, but the troops had stamina and were fresh from their barracks and they ran faster than he, and it wasn't long before they'd narrowed down the gap between them. Up the stairs of a fancy beachfront hotel and through the lobby, startling sitting guests, china cups of coffee balanced on their knees. Into a lower-class neighborhood filled with people sitting on lawn chairs shooting the breeze—all staring with surprise as he charged through their lives, British troops in hot pursuit.

Eventually he had to stop running. His chest burned like fire, his lungs cried out for a breath of air. It was too much. He couldn't run anymore. They threw him to the ground and handcuffed his arms behind his back. They hauled him over to a British military vehicle and threw him roughly into the back of the cab, where he landed on a spare tire. Locking the door behind him, the soldiers congratulated themselves on a job well done, and drove their prisoner away from Tel Aviv and in the general direction of the notorious Atlit Detainee Camp.

♦ ♦ ♦

Located 12 miles south of Haifa, the dusty, sandy Atlit Detainee Camp was surrounded by barbed wire and guard towers and was eerily reminiscent of the European concentration camps. One could almost smell the Mediterranean from within the barbed wire, so close was it to the coast. In the years following World War II, the British populated the camp almost exclusively with Holocaust survivors who, after surviving the war and clawing their way to Eretz Yisrael, found themselves incarcerated yet again and separated from those they loved.

The troops drove their armored vehicle through the detainee camp and over to the jail, which shared the premises. The doors of the vehicle were thrown open and two soldiers lifted Yeedle up and out. Setting him down on the ground, he was ordered to follow his captors into a nearby office. A solitary 20-watt lightbulb suspended over the desk, illuminating the scene with its meager rays. A tired-looking lieutenant, in a rumpled uniform and badly in need of a shave, conducted the interrogation.

Not knowing whom they held in their hands, Yeedle was asked a series of run-of-the-mill questions that he fielded with ease, giving nothing away. As they were wrapping things up, the officer asked him, "What's your profession?"

"I'm a cook."

As a Holocaust survivor, Yeedle Wallis attributed great prominence to the job of cook and jumped at any opportunity that granted him access to a kitchen. And so it came to be that while Yehudit Wallis was safely tucked away among the greenery of Kibbutz Chofetz Chaim, her husband spent his time peeling potatoes and onions in the industrial-size kitchen of the Atlit Prison, continually dreaming of the day he'd escape and be reunited with his wife and the child who was soon to be born.

Unknown to him, help was already on the way.

♦ ♦ ♦

Rav Yitzchak Meir Levin, known as Itche Meir, was a legend in his own time. One of the signatories to the Israeli Declaration of Independence, Rav Yitzchak Meir Levin achieved political prominence in prewar Poland as a member of the Sejm, the Polish parliament. He arrived in Palestine in 1940, became a leading member of Agudath Israel and served in Ben-Gurion's first and second governments as the minister of welfare. He remained in the Knesset until his passing in 1971. Rav Yitzchak Meir had been a close friend of Yeedle's father, who had been a respected and active member of the Agudas Yisrael branch in Pavenitz, Poland. Rav Itche Meir was a man who had his finger on the pulse of the entire country, and it wasn't long before he found out that Yeedle had been incarcerated in the Atlit jail.

Besides the fact that he wanted to help the son of his old friend, there was an additional consideration as well. If Yehudit Wallis gave birth while her husband was still in prison, the child would be given the legal name of the mother, not the father, and would consequently not be a Wallis. This did not sit well with Rav Levin, and he resolved to utilize the considerable power at his disposal to get Yeedle out of prison and to help him obtain the documents necessary to turn him into a legal citizen.

For that, he would first have to stage a prison breakout.

Yeedle was preparing breakfast when one of the dishwashers sidled up to him.

"I need to talk to you."

"Talk."

"Not here," the man insisted. "In a place where we can't be overheard."

"Okay," Yeedle agreed, "meet me in the supply closet in five minutes."

Surrounded by bottles of cleaning fluid and gigantic cans of olives, he was informed that Itche Meir Levin had taken his incarceration personally and had already taken measures to deal with it.

"There's a truck that comes to the prison every night."

Yeedle nodded.

"It delivers foods and other supplies that the prison needs on a daily basis. You are to find a way to get close to the truck. A special shelf will be built between the wheels. When nobody's around, roll under the truck and lie down on the shelf. It will take you to safety."

He saw the look of apprehension on Yeedle's face.

"What are you worried about, Itche Meir's on your side!"

Nighttime arrived. Yeedle was very nervous. Would everything go according to plan? The truck normally arrived at 2:30 a.m. By 1:30 he found himself looking out the window every five minutes with anticipation. At 2:30 the gate behind the kitchen area groaned open and the truck pulled inside. He left the kitchen and began unloading the truck, same as he did every night. Nothing unusual, nothing out of the ordinary. Just a regular night. He carried trays of bread from the back of the truck. Cheese and milk from Tnuva. A crate of pasta.

At 2:40 the yard was miraculously clear of people. Yeedle rolled agilely beneath the truck and swung his body onto the board. Then he waited silently for the truck to leave Atlit. He closed his eyes and thought happy thoughts. He imagined a sunlit reunion with his wife. He thought of the new baby that would soon be theirs to love. He dreamed of joy-filled days to come.

The truck started to move. It stopped at the first gate. He heard the sound of the soldiers joking with the driver. The gate opened with its trademark groan. They drove on through the main camp, coming to a halt at the outer gate. The soldiers threw open the back doors of the truck and examined it closely for stowaways. Next thing he knew, he heard the sound of the soldier's palm slamming itself roughly on the truck's outer wall, signaling the driver to move on. The bar lifted itself upward and the driver shifted into first and then second gear. Yeedle lay on the wooden shelf, mere inches from the ground, hearing the sounds of the wheels turning round and round, churning up the dusty, loamy earth and sending clods of dirt flying every which way.

The words "I will be free, I will be free, I will be free" were playing endlessly in his mind, a mantra signifying his fiercest desire and dream. A minute later, the truck was turning right onto the highway leading to the prearranged pickup spot, where Itche Meir's people were waiting to spirit him to freedom, presenting him with forged documents that would grant him the ability to walk into any government office after his child was born and register the baby under the Wallis name.

His troubles weren't over yet. He was still an escaped prisoner and the British Army would be searching for him. But for now, it would have to be enough.

♦ ♦ ♦

When Yehudit Wallis was ready to give birth, she was transported by ambulance from Kibbutz Chofetz Chaim to Beilinson Hospital in Petach Tikvah. Unfortunately her husband wasn't allowed the luxury of joining his wife in the waiting room, alongside his fellow soon-to-be-fathers. Instead of pacing the hospital corridors, cup of tepid coffee in hand, he was hiding in the orange orchard surrounding the hospital, anxiously waiting for one of the orderlies to sneak over to him with the good news.

Evening descended on Petach Tikvah. The British curfew took effect and Yeedle headed ever deeper into the orange groves, determined to stay far away from the British patrols. He wouldn't get caught. Not tonight. Not with his firstborn poised to enter the world. He'd arranged with one of the midwives to let him know as soon as his child was born. She was to give the message to the orderly, who was to hand it over to someone else who'd been told where he was hiding.

"Yossi," he said to his son years later, "there I was, hiding in an orchard, a fugitive from the law. My wife was in the hospital, but I couldn't stand by her bedside. In the middle of the night I heard the sound of footsteps squelching through the muddy ground and the half-rotten oranges that littered the ground between the trees. I peeked out from where I was hiding and saw an *ehrlicher Yid* heading in my direction, to give me the news of your birth. Stepping out from behind the tree, I probably frightened the man half to death.

"'Are you Yeedle Wallis?'

"I nodded.

"'Your wife just gave birth to a son.'

"Yossi, can you imagine how I felt when I heard the news? Here I was, a survivor of Dachau and Auschwitz and the Warsaw Ghetto. I had been through so much over the last six years. I had stared death in the face on countless occasions. I had been tortured. I had somehow managed to smuggle myself to Palestine. Avoided the British, been arrested by the British, successfully broken out of the Atlit jail. And now I stood among the orange trees hearing the greatest news in the world.

"I was a father. I had a son."

♦ ♦ ♦

Mrs. Ruth Lichtenstein is the editor-in-chief of *Hamodia*. Rabbi Wallis's path crossed hers the first time in her capacity as the director of Project Witness. He met her in *Hamodia's* corporate offices in New York and found himself impressed with what this woman had managed to accomplish for the cause of journalism in the Torah world.

At one point she contacted him and explained that she wanted to assign a reporter to write a feature detailing the revival of the postwar Jewish families: how the survivors rebuilt their lives after undergoing such horror. Would he be willing to share his story with the world? Wanting to follow his father's mandate to share his story with as wide an audience as possible, Rabbi Wallis told the reporter the entire story. She called him back a few days later. He could hear the embarrassment in her voice.

"Mrs. Lichtenstein feels that this story is just too much. We need proof if we want to publish it. Documentation. Could you please provide us with physical evidence, certificates, documents, pictures...that will back up what you're saying?"

"No problem," he told the writer. "I'll get back to you soon."

Rabbi Wallis drove over to his parents' home and asked his mother where she kept all the old documents they had saved from 50 years earlier.

She showed him the files, yellowed with age, brittle and cracking. He removed his father's witness pass, the one that allowed him into court and gave him access to the Nazi murderer's ears, his mother's official entry documents into the State of Israel, plus many additional documents that proved beyond a shadow of a doubt that the story he was telling the paper was accurate and reliable.

He was about to leave with the sheaf of papers in hand, when his mother mentioned a detail he had never heard before.

"I don't think you know this," she said offhandedly, "but your *sandak* was Itche Meir Levin."

This information blew Rabbi Wallis out of the water. He felt it especially appropriate that the man who had broken his father out of prison and provided him with false documentation had been honored to serve as *sandak* at Rabbi Wallis's own bris.

The best part, however, was still to come. Gathering all the information together, he brought it to the Israeli *Hamodia* office, to send it over to New York, mentioning the fact that Itche Meir Levin had served as *sandak* at his bris.

The next thing he knew Ruth Lichtenstein was on the phone.

"Itche Meir Levin was your *sandak*?"

"Yes."

"That's incredible!"

"Why?"

"Because Itche Meir Levin was my grandfather."

"In that case," he said to her, a smile in his voice, "now it's your turn to go searching for proof that this story happened. Go to your family archives and back me up!"

It wasn't long before they met in Mrs. Lichtenstein's office for a second time. He sat across from this powerhouse of Jewish journalism and history, taking in the roomful of awards.

"It's really true," she said, slightly overcome by this unexpected turn of events. "My grandfather, Itche Meir Levin, was your *sandak* and a good friend of your grandfather, Chaim Yosef Wallis from Poland."

"Look at the irony here," Rabbi Wallis said. "You asked for proof, and in finding that proof we learned that your grandfather was my *sandak*. It is said that a *sandak* is akin to the father of the baby. You and I are family now!"

◆ ◆ ◆

We are all a product of our roots.

Rabbi Yossi Wallis's roots included:

An ancestor choosing a fiery and fearful death in the Inquisition's flames—for the sake of his beliefs.

A grandfather on the cusp of liberation from the Nazis' remorseless grip giving up his life—so that those beliefs should not be made a mockery.

A father who walked to the scaffold—knowing that those beliefs were worth his very life.

When a father is willing to die *al kiddush Hashem*, then a son will be willing to live *al kiddush Hashem*.

And that is exactly what happened.

The power of roots.

BOOK THREE

TO CHANGE THE WORLD

CHAPTER SEVENTEEN

After his experience in The Elephant Steakhouse, Yossi Wallis found himself searching for meaning in his life. He couldn't get the picture of his grandfather's refusal to take a bite of pork out of his mind, and the more he considered the matter, the more he realized that it was time for him to begin investigating what being religious really meant. After asking many people where he could learn more about the questions that were puzzling him, he was advised to attend a private class in someone's home, where the lecturer was a man by the name of Dr. Shalom Srebrenik, one of the founders of Arachim, a relatively new organization dedicated to teaching Torah and renewing Jewish values.

During the class, Yossi felt comfortable enough to raise a number of key points that were bothering him. Eventually, he found himself embroiled in a fascinating discussion, which ended with Dr. Srebrenik recommending that he meet the founders of Arachim, who were about to host their first five-day seminar at a nearby hotel. Intrigued by what he had seen and heard, Yossi decided to sign up his family to attend. He figured that his wife and kids could go swimming while he attended the classes and that they would have a nice family vacation, no pressure, and no strings attached.

The very first Arachim seminar

Or at least, that was the plan.

To be honest, when he drove up to the hotel he had no intention of becoming religious. His only goal was to clarify a few things that were bothering him. He hoped to accomplish that and to return to his everyday routine, which all things considered was pretty enjoyable. Business was solid, his wife, Sandy, was happy, the kids were doing well in school, and life was just good. There was just the matter of getting rid of the pesky thoughts that kept on intruding.

As they drove into the parking lot of the hotel, Yossi stopped one of the rabbis that he saw and asked him where to park his car. The rabbi put down a box he was carrying on the car's hood to answer him, and when Yossi caught sight of what was in the box he was taken aback.

The box was filled with *kippot*.

"What are those for?"

"It's for all of you attending the seminar."

"Rabbi, sorry to break it to you, but I have no intention whatsoever of putting one of those artifacts on my head."

"No problem," the rabbi replied, "I'm just going to put them in the hotel dining room and whoever wants can take one."

That's not going to be me, Yossi thought to himself.

♦ ♦ ♦

Rabbi Wallis often says that for a person to change his life around, it has to come about through a combination of logic and emotion. As Moshe Rabbeinu told the Jews (*Devarim* 4:39), "*Veyadata hayom*—You shall know today"—that is, you shall use your thoughts and logic; "*vahasheivosa el levavecha*—and you shall take to your heart"—you shall engage your emotions. That's how all our decisions are made. Maybe we don't realize it at the time, but that's the way it is. Logic and emotion.

At some point during the weekend, he couldn't listen to the speeches anymore. He needed to decompress. During one of the breaks between speeches, one of the lecturers approached him, a large volume of Talmud in his hand. "Did you ever have the opportunity to study a piece of Gemara in your life?" he asked.

Yossi Wallis (with back to camera), arguing at his very first Arachim seminar

"No," Yossi bluntly replied, "never."

"Well then, get a few guys together and I'll show you what it's all about."

A group of men gathered around a table and for the first time in his life Yossi Wallis saw what the inside of a Gemara looked like. The rabbi began teaching them a piece of Gemara from *Perek Lulav HaGazul* (a stolen lulav) in Tractate *Succah*. Yossi sat, mesmerized. He had never experienced this type of learning in his life. The entire Gemara experience was based on questions and answers. As soon as one thing was taken care of, the Gemara raised another scenario that needed to be dealt with. Back-and-forth, give-and-take, theory raised, theory demolished, and foundation rebuilt from the ground up.

"Don't take anything for granted," the rabbi said to the group of professionals sitting before him. "Ask any question that comes to your minds." He was encouraging them to question and ask and it was so unexpected, since who wants to be challenged by intelligent people?! Wasn't he afraid that someone was going to destroy his arguments? Apparently not.

Yossi had studied physics and mathematics, he'd studied in depth at university, but he'd never encountered a teaching method like this before. He was astounded by the sense of accountability that the Gemara exuded. He'd studied other religions. There, if you dared question, you were labeled heretical. Here, you were being told to question. In fact, he soon came to understand that the more a person questioned and challenged, the greater a scholar he'd become. It was so refreshing and original.

The thought flitted through his brain: *If someone has the truth in his hands, he is not afraid of questions. Nothing scares him. I guess there must be something solid to what these people are saying.*

They were learning the laws of the lulav. How long it should be, what color it should be, what made it unkosher, and Yossi Wallis was struck by a realization:

The Jewish nation has been studying these very same laws for the last few thousand years. Every possible question that can be raised has been raised. Every objection, every contradiction. Look outside the window on Succot and you'll see every religious Jew carrying a lulav in his hand. This means that all the questions have already been answered and every objection has been addressed.

He addressed the rabbi.

"Is there any chance of a person like myself raising a question that hasn't already been scrutinized and debated by countless generations of Torah students?"

"I'm not saying it would be impossible," the rabbi replied, "but statistically speaking, it would be extremely improbable."

"So you're saying, that there is almost zero chance mathematically that I would be able to raise a question that would challenge and possibly eliminate the mitzvah of lulav on Succot—and that if such a question could have been raised, then it would have been raised by the millions of Jews who have argued over these pages?"

The rabbi concurred with the assessment.

Yossi Wallis looked around the conference room and suddenly understood that there was no escaping the facts. Every Jew had to use a lulav on Succot, and there was no way out. It was at that moment that he found himself on board. Logically speaking—and he valued logic tremendously—every mitzvah had been studied, questioned, and analyzed and was found to be unshakable.

It was an earth-shattering revelation for the businessman from Tel Aviv.

But logic alone wasn't sufficient to achieve change of such magnitude. For that a person needs emotion as well. Yossi waited to see what lay in store for him next.

♦ ♦ ♦

Friday night. The hotel was suffused with the glow of Shabbat. Yossi had never seen anything like it in his life. He stood transfixed at the sight of the Shabbat candles flickering on the sideboard. Yossi had never been a person who took his time lingering over meals. Supper was a quick, in-and-out affair that usually lasted about 15 minutes. Why waste time on eating, when there were so many other more important things one could be doing? At least, that had been his philosophy until that evening.

With the staff and speakers interspersed among the tables and the conversation lively and interactive, it took them two hours to get through the meal. For Yossi, two hours for one meal was a lifetime record! He had eaten at many expensive restaurants in his life. Establishments with French waiters. Places where you needed to wear a tie. But—two hours!

Oddly enough, he hardly noticed the time, because of all the singing.

Up until that evening he had never mixed music and eating. When he arrived home from the office to eat supper, that's exactly what he did: he ate supper. Who sang while they ate? Everyone all dressed up, eating and singing. If he wanted to hear singing, he'd go to a concert! He never ate at a concert or sang at a restaurant. But to these people, singing and eating together was the most natural expression in the world.

And they didn't stop there.

All of a sudden, the rabbis on staff were out of their seats, dancing around the table, kicking up their heels to the Shabbat songs he was being introduced to for the first time! The next thing he knew, they were grabbing the men and kids and drawing them into the circle of wildly dancing rabbis with long beards and wonderful smiles. Without knowing how on earth it came about, Yossi Wallis found himself standing between two rabbis he barely knew and hugging them both in an outpouring of rare emotion.

He had never touched a rabbi in his life and now he was hugging two of them!

♦ ♦ ♦

You can't tell a person's heart how or what to feel. Every heart feels things differently. On that Friday night Yossi felt as if he were surrounded by his two grandfathers, one on either side of him, and that he was embracing both of them with all his strength. He was dancing at a Shabbos meal for the first time in his life, singing with all his soul, and the emotion pouring out of him was more genuine than anything he'd felt in years. It was like Yossi Wallis was suddenly touching and connected with authentic

Jewish history—generations and generations of lofty Torah Jews, all smiling as they witnessed their descendant dancing, singing, and cavorting like a *Yid* in a *shtiebel* on Simchas Torah. And he felt as if this was the place he belonged and that he was an integral part of the scene before him and that this was the way it was supposed to be, immutably correct.

It was an absolutely surreal moment for a man who sold weapons and helicopters for a living.

The moment he combined the emotional feeling of utter belonging with the logic of the Gemara, he was a lost cause.

Yossi, he addressed himself, *you are going to return. You are doing teshuvah.*

His decision was made.

◆ ◆ ◆

The magnitude of what had happened to him hit home late Shabbat afternoon as he sat listening to one final speech.

Now what? he asked himself. He hadn't consulted with his wife or family. How were they going to accept his decision? How on earth would he ensure that his newfound desire to keep the Torah remain with him? He'd be facing opposition. His new lifestyle would be fraught with challenges. Who would ensure that he didn't throw it all away the moment his newfound faith began to clash with the things he liked to do? What was going to happen Sunday morning? Yossi knew nothing about how a religious Jew was supposed to live his life! He had no *siddur*, no *tefillin*. The Wallis refrigerator was packed with nonkosher food. This decision on his part had huge ramifications!

He glanced around in desperation, trying to figure out a plan. He felt lost, frightened, and vulnerable, and he needed a way to deal with all these unexpected and unusual feelings that were besieging him from every direction. There was a man sitting to his right. Yossi had met him over the course of the seminar. His name was Benny Feig. He was a building contractor from Rishon LeTzion and they'd hit it off immediately. Benny was affable, down to earth, and easy to talk to. Now Yossi desperately needed a listening ear and Benny was sitting right there.

Leaning over, Yossi gave him a jab with his elbow.

Jolted upright from his somnolent daze, Benny glanced at his neighbor, slightly annoyed. "What do you want?"

"Come outside with me, I want to talk to you for a second."

"Is this really important?"

"It's really important. C'mon, let's get out of here."

They exited the ballroom like two kids running guiltily away from school in the middle of class. Outside in the hallway they found two armchairs face-to-face and sank down into the plushy fabric. Yossi wasn't sure how to begin the conversation, but Benny was waiting impatiently and with no choice he jumped right in.

"Benny, what are you going to do with all the new information that you heard over the weekend?"

"Nothing."

"Nothing? Nothing??!! What do you mean, nothing?! Are these brilliant people talking to the walls? What are you going to do with all the information that you heard here?"

"Nothing."

"Benny, don't you get it? This isn't some university where they teach you information that has no direct bearing on your life. This isn't the type of material you can just choose to distance yourself from! You have entered the school of life!"

His perplexed face staring in bewilderment, Benny retorted, "Fine, let's turn this all around. What are you going to do with everything they've been feeding us?"

"Me?"

Benny nodded.

Yossi Wallis stared straight at Benny Feig.

"I'm going to return."

Understanding began to dawn in Benny's eyes, along with grudging admiration.

"You mean—"

"I'm doing *teshuvah*."

"Wow," Benny breathed, "that's pretty amazing. But why did you call me out of the hall?"

Yossi didn't answer him right away, letting the question hang there for a few seconds. Finally, he replied.

"Because I want you to join me. I want you to do *teshuvah* alongside me!" (His career with Arachim had just begun...)

"What on earth are you talking about! Why would I want to do such a thing? I have a life. I'm not interested in turning it all upside down!"

"You want to know why?"

Benny nodded.

"Because I need a partner, that's why. I won't be able to get on the train by myself. I'll end up crashing. That's why I need you to come along with me."

"Very nice that you need a partner, but why did you have to choose me? There was a lecture room filled with people! Why me?!"

Not happy, Benny, not happy at all.

"I chose you because you were sitting next to me," Yossi replied, as if it were the most obvious reason in the world. "That's the whole truth. Next time, sit next to someone else!"

Feig didn't know what to do with himself.

"Look, Benny, it's happening, so you may as well stop trying to fight the inevitable. I'm doing *teshuvah* and so are you. And we are going to write a contract with each other to make it all official and binding."

"A contract? A contract?!"

"Yes. We will write the following: 'I, Yossi Wallis, am committing to keeping the mitzvot as a commitment to you. And you, Benny Feig, are committing to keeping the mitzvot as a commitment to me.' We are obligating each other to keep Torah and mitzvot. I know myself. I am the kind of person who keeps his word. If I make a deal with someone, I'm going to do my best to keep my end of the partnership."

Yossi walked over to the front desk and asked the receptionist for a piece of paper and a pen. Then he returned to where Benny was sitting.

"Okay, we're both signing this. Then we're shaking hands. Then we say '*mazal u'verachah*' and it's legally binding."

So saying, he laid the piece of paper down on the table and began writing out all the details of the contract. (Ironically, it was still Shabbos; Yossi had a long way to go.)

This is a contract between Mr. Yossi Wallis and Mr. Benny Feig. Due to the fact that Wallis and Feig are both separately interested in undertaking to keep the Torah and mitzvot according to the halachah of the Jewish nation, we are hereby committing to keep Torah and mitzvot as a binding obligation to each other. We will be in touch every week to make sure that both of us kept our side of the deal.

The "contract" then specified how much money each side would forfeit to the other if the terms were breached.

We will hereby shake hands to seal our agreement.

The two of them shook hands. Two businessmen plus a handshake equaled obligation. The obligation to observe the Torah and its mitzvos.

♦ ♦ ♦

Motza'ei Shabbos arrived. There was a grand *Havdalah* extravaganza in the dining room, complete with candles and guitars. Then it was all over. The seminar had come to an end. It was time to go home. They packed up their suitcases, handed their keys in to the front desk, and loaded up the car. Yossi was still wearing a *kippah* on his head. Sandy didn't pay much attention to it, no doubt attributing it to the fact that they were still at the hotel surrounded by rabbis and religious people. Yossi turned the key in the ignition and pulled out of the parking lot, their three boys in the backseat, same as when they arrived. Sandy sat beside him, same as when they arrived. The only difference was the *kippah* still perched on his head. In the semidarkness of the unlit road, his wife didn't notice his unlikely headgear.

As they drove they began to converse.

"Did you enjoy the food?"

"Yes."

"What did you think of the people?"

"Excellent people."

"What about the classes?"

"Blew my mind."

The normal desultory conversation of husband and wife. Suddenly Sandy noticed the *kippah*.

"Yossi, we're on the way home now. You can take that off your head."

No doubt she'd imagined he'd forgotten that he was still wearing it.

"I left it on purposely."

The atmosphere in the car dropped 20 degrees in two seconds.

"Why? There's nobody watching you now, no rabbis in the backseat, you can take it off. The seminar's over."

"I know that it's over."

"So why don't you take it off then?"

"I'm not going to take it off."

"Why are you not taking it off?" (Major edge to the voice.)

"Because I have decided to become religious."

"What do you mean, you're becoming religious?"

He kept his voice silky smooth, belying the immense tension in the air. "I am *dati*."

"But you can't be *dati*!"

"Why not?"

"We're husband and wife; we have to be on the same page! If I'm not *dati*, then you can't be *dati* either!"

"You're right. I really believe that we need to become religious now, and I hope that you will be willing to finding out more about the lifestyle, so we can both be on the same page!"

"Yossi, I didn't sign up for any of this!"

"I know you didn't, but sometimes things change. People change."

"Have you gone crazy? I can't become religious just like that!"

"Why not?"

"We have friends, relatives..."

At that moment, Sandy saw their entire future looming before them, like a deep, dark tunnel. She didn't like what she saw. Not one bit.

"There are many reasons why we can't make this type of life change!"

Three little Wallis boys and Ozzy, the family dog

"Many people change their lives around. All I'm asking is that we give it a shot and see where it leads us."

The three boys in the backseat began exchanging glances with one another, not at all sure where this was all headed.

"Daddy," one of them piped up, "what about us?"

"What about you? We're going to find you a nice religious day school."

"I don't want to change schools," sulked one of his sons. "I like my school. I don't want to move to another school." Suddenly all three of them were on the verge of tears.

Yossi wasn't sure how to handle the situation. This wasn't going the way he'd envisioned it. No one liked his idea. Sandy was upset at the thought of having to change their lives completely and the boys were scared of switching schools. He realized he had gone a few steps too far in his newfound religious zeal. In general Yossi was a genial father and husband, and he wanted to calm down the people closest to him in the world, who had retreated into their own inner dark thoughts, worries, and ruminations.

He turned to Sandy.

"You know what? I just had a great idea."

"Now what, Yossi?"

"Let's stop off at my parents' house in Tel Aviv."

The kids perked up at the thought of a surprise visit to Saba and Savta.

"Why now?" Sandy asked him.

"I need to pick up my *tefillin* for tomorrow morning," he replied. "I haven't worn them since my bar mitzvah. When we got married I gave my parents a bunch of stuff that I didn't need. At that time I thought that I'd never put them on again. Guess I was wrong."

Sandy, who was very close to Yossi's parents, gave her husband a wry look. "Great! This will give me a chance to tell your father about your crazy idea. Maybe he'll be able to convince you to stop talking about changing our lives around completely just because you heard a couple of classes! You're going to mess up the entire family if you take us in such a fanatical direction. I'm going to tell him everything!"

Yossi shrugged his shoulders, because there really wasn't that much to say. He was hoping for the best, but not at all sure where they were headed.

They parked outside his parents' building. It was late, but everyone in the car was wired and wide awake. Yossi knocked and his father opened the door. He saw his son standing on the doorstep with his family, a *kippah* on his head, a big smile stretching across his face. It was clear that he'd made a decision about something and was content with it. His father also saw Sandy standing beside her husband looking like someone who'd had all the happiness squeezed out of her. The kids were jumpy, on edge. And it was after midnight, when everyone should have long since been asleep. All in all, a volatile situation.

Yossi's father wasn't sure what to think.

"What's going on here, Yossi?" he asked bluntly. "And what's with the *kippah*?"

"Yossi decided to become religious over the weekend," Sandy interjected. "He wants to change the entire family. Please, please, talk him out of this!!"

Her plea emanated from somewhere deep within her. Sandy was really afraid for the future.

His father waved his hand in classic Polish fashion.

"Why are you making such a *tzimmes* out of this, Sandy? Give him a few weeks, you'll see, he'll forget all about becoming religious. He got excited. Don't you worry—he'll get over it just as fast."

Yossi met his father's eyes.

"No, Abba," he told him. "This is no two-week phase. This is for life!"

Mr. Wallis looked from Yossi to Sandy and back, as if he couldn't believe what his son was telling him.

"Abba, I need you to give me my *tefillin*, please. I'm putting them on tomorrow. Do you remember where you packed them away?"

His father nodded slowly.

"Sure, Yossi, sure I remember where I put your *tefillin*. I'll go get them."

Yeedle Wallis climbed up a little ladder to the storage closet. He rummaged around for a few minutes, eventually emerging with an old, dusty suitcase, which he opened. There, nestled within, were his son's *tefillin*, still cradled in their velvet pouch. He handed them over to Yossi and suddenly, amazingly, his face was wet with tears.

"What's the matter, Abba?" Yossi asked in alarm. "Why are you crying?"

His father was a tough man, definitely not the type to just burst into tears.

The words came pouring out. "You don't understand what you're doing to me here. You want to begin putting on *tefillin*. Your wife wants me to talk you out of this. Do you know what you're asking of me?! Do you have any idea who your grandfather was? You can't even imagine what a *tzaddik* he was...and you were named after him."

Tears were now streaming down his face. "It looks like you're also going to be a *shtickel tzaddik*, Yossi. Sandy, you want me to talk Yossi out of this. How can I even think of doing such a thing?"

Yossi saw that the last few minutes had thrust his father into a deep, emotional turmoil, one he was finding himself ill equipped to deal with. He stood in the living room watching his strong father falling apart.

"Come," Yeedle said at last. "Sit down. All of you. You too, Sandy. Yes, come sit down right here next to me. There's something I have to tell you. It's the story of my *tefillin*. Yossi, you know parts of the story. Now it's time for all of you to hear it. All together. The whole story."

Everyone sat down on the couch in a living room in Tel Aviv and heard the story that shook the heavens.

♦ ♦ ♦

Then Yeedle Wallis told his son, daughter-in-law, and grandchildren about the day he almost died in Dachau. About the man who threw a pouch containing *tefillin* into his hands. About his dilemma whether to put them on or not and how he was caught by the Nazis and sentenced to death by hanging in front of the entire camp.

"As I stood on the table with a noose around my neck, the Nazi officer offered me a final request before they killed me."

"Did you accept his offer?" Sandy, completely focused on the tale she was hearing for the first time, asked.

Yeedle nodded.

"I did."

"What did you ask for?"

"I asked for one last chance to put on the *tefillin*. I asked to be killed wearing the *tefillin* on my arm and head."

Sandy's eyes were focused on her father-in-law; his words seemed to be processed deep within her soul.

"I wrapped the *tefillin* around my arm and head," Yeedle continued, "and recited the words every Jew says when donning his *tefillin* at morning prayers. '*Ve'eirastich li le'olam*—I will betroth you to Me forever. *Ve'eirastich li betzedek u'vemishpat, u'vechesed u'verachamim*—And I will betroth you to Me with righteousness, justice, kindness, and mercy. *Ve'eirastich li be'emunah, veyadaat es Hashem*—I will betroth you to Me with fidelity, and you shall know Hashem.' As I uttered the ancient words, I felt such a sense of peace washing over me. I was the Jew of old, about to die for my beliefs. I knew that the Germans were going to kick the table out from under me at any second. I was almost dead! But I didn't feel like a victim. Can you understand how it feels to know that this is the absolute final act you are going to do before leaving this world? I didn't feel beaten down, I felt I had won the war all by myself!

"'*Yidden*!' I yelled out at them, 'Why are you crying? Don't you understand that I am the winner here?! Can there be a greater revenge than this?'

"Those were my final words in Dachau."

Sandy was staring at her father-in-law. "What happened then, Abba?" she whispered. "How did you survive that day?"

And Yeedle Wallis told his daughter-in-law how Otto Tybet forced him off the table and about having to hold the heavy rocks in his hands as he was beaten over the head.

"Twenty-five lashes," he told Sandy and his three grandchildren. "Twenty-five lashes, but I didn't drop those rocks. I lived to tell the story."

♦ ♦ ♦

That is what Yeedle Wallis told his family that evening in Tel Aviv. Yossi had heard bits and pieces of the story before, but never in such detail. Yeedle turned to Sandy. Looked at her, his eyes gleaming with emotion.

"Sandy, after hearing such a story, do you really think I could convince my son not to become religious—to talk him out of putting on *tefillin*?"

He paused.

"You know something—Not only am I not going to talk him out of this, I'm going to join him! Yossi, you and I, we're going to keep Shabbos together! You and I will begin putting on *tefillin* together! I'm with you 100 percent."

In that instant, Yeedle Wallis, the man who stood up to the Nazis in Dachau and asked to die with his *tefillin* on, returned to his faith. Yeedle had never meant to leave it; he wasn't one of those Jews who were angry at Hashem for what happened to them. But somehow he had slipped away after the war, like so many whose entire families and support systems had been lost in the camps. He had never meant to lose his faith, nor had he. He had been willing to die for his *tefillin* and now, he suddenly realized, he wanted to live with them as well.

Yossi's mother had been standing quietly off to the side listening to her husband. Now it was her turn to speak. "I'm joining both of you," she said quietly but firmly. "I'm also doing *teshuvah* right now!"

Sandy stared at them. At her husband, with a *kippah* on his head and a look of utter happiness on his face. At her father-in-law, glowing with excitement and fresh resolve. At her mother-in-law, ready to begin life all over again. A stunned silence filled the room. Yossi didn't know what she was going to say. Then something changed in her eyes and she opened her mouth to speak.

"If all of you are committing to living a religious life, I'm not going to be the only one left out. If all of you are in, then so am I."

Sandy's parents had moved to Raanana by then. When they heard what had happened to their daughter and son-in-law, they decided to join them as well. Yossi's brother-in-law, who lived in Los Angeles, heard that everyone had gone crazy while discovering religion. He hurried to catch a plane to try to talk some sense into the family—and then changed his own mind and decided to become religious himself! Yossi's sister, his nephews...everyone in the family was becoming observant.

Yossi Wallis knew that he was going to have to figure out a new role in life. He was already middle aged. He would probably never be a big rabbi or rosh yeshivah because he had never studied Torah. That didn't matter; he didn't need to be a rabbi. He just needed to be religious. And with his wife at his side, there was nothing in the world to hold him back. He looked around the room and knew in his heart that everything was going to be okay.

It wouldn't be easy, but that was fine.

Challenges would abound, but they didn't frighten him.

Together with Sandy, Yossi Wallis knew that they were going to change the world.

When they finally left his parents' home that night, the *kippah* was still perched on Yossi's head. Sandy glanced at it and didn't say a word.

CHAPTER EIGHTEEN

A week had passed since the Wallis family attended the seminar and made the decision to follow the religious way of life. A week after they'd surprised his parents at midnight. A week after Yeedle had shared his story. A week after Rabbi Wallis had signed the contract with Benny Feig. Now it was time to celebrate their first Shabbos as a religious family.

Becoming religious was a huge deal for Yossi and he had his personal set of worries to contend with. Chief among them were all the friends he'd acquired over the years. Possessing an outgoing personality and affable disposition, he made friends easily. At that time, however, all those friends were not religious and he was concerned that they were going to drop him the moment they discovered he had shifted allegiances. He couldn't imagine a life without friends around, and he couldn't depend on religious people to fill the void, since he didn't know any. He was thrilled with his decision, and at the same time he was hoping he hadn't just made the worst mistake of his life.

Years earlier Yossi Wallis had negotiated a deal with the Raanana country club, which allowed his family to use its pool and adjacent facilities as often as they wanted throughout the week. In exchange, he served as the lifeguard at the pool every Saturday for the entire day. Yossi figured he'd be hanging around the pool regardless; he might as well sit up on the lifeguard's platform in exchange for free membership. In addition to his lifeguard duties he changed the filters and made sure there was enough chlorine in the water. He enjoyed every minute at the pool and loved the fact that his family was able to run over for free anytime they wanted.

When he awoke on that Shabbat morning, he was faced with a dilemma.

You can't go sit by the pool all Shabbat, he told himself. *You're religious now and that means that you have to go to beit knesset!*

On the other hand, he couldn't just not show up at the pool. He was the lifeguard and the person with the key. If he didn't show, no one would be able to go swimming—and the residents of Raanana waited all week to use their magnificent pool.

Clearly there were changes to be implemented in his life, but at the moment there was no way he was going to go get busy with filters and chemicals. He was filled with the zeal of the fresh returnee and he wanted to go pray. Knowing that there would be dozens of children already waiting for him to show up, he made up his mind to pass the pool on his way to the *beit knesset*, where he'd inform the children that the pool would not be opening up this Shabbat and that they'd work something else out in the future.

Up until now, Yossi would rise bright and early on Shabbat morning, and leave the house for his four-minute walk to the pool through the peacefully serene Raanana streets, dressed only in his bathing suit, a whistle hanging jauntily around his neck. He saw no reason to put on any additional clothing, knowing that he'd be near the water all day long.

The "bathing suit on Shabbat" look, he told himself when he awoke, *is a thing of the past. Today is Shabbat and you are going to beit knesset. Obviously, you can't walk into beit knesset in a bathing suit.*

Yossi Wallis put on a dress shirt and pants and left his home: destination, the *beit knesset*, with a five-minute stop at the pool to send all the (disappointed) kids home. He made his way through the still deserted streets, the sounds of chirping birds and rushing wind accompanying him as he strolled. He felt good about his decision, felt good about going to the *beit knesset*, and felt good about wearing a shirt and pants instead of his "normal" Shabbat attire. The kids, standing outside the locked gates of the country club, took one look at him and understood that something very strange was happening.

"Hey, Yossi," they yelled, "why are you all dressed up? Where's your bathing suit?!"

"I'm going to the *beit knesset* today."

"But you need to open the pool!"

"I can't do it today, I'm really sorry. We'll work it out for next week—maybe hire another lifeguard—but right now I have to go to the *beit knesset*. All you kids go on home. No reason for you to remain here now because the pool is closed."

They were very disappointed. Yossi felt sorry for them, but he didn't really see any alternative. He had to go to *beit knesset*, didn't he? After all, wasn't praying at the *beit knesset* on Shabbat morning an integral part of being religious? He didn't see that he had any choice in the matter.

♦ ♦ ♦

Prayers commenced at 8 o'clock, but Yossi planned his arrival for a quarter to 8. Being that he knew absolutely nothing about praying—when to sit or stand, what to say, how to say it, or when he was allowed to talk—he figured that he'd better get there before everyone else, so he could find a seat in the back of the room, which would allow him to see and not be seen. Upon entering the *beit knesset* he found himself a seat in the very last row, and settled down to wait for the prayers to begin. Over the next 10 minutes the *beit knesset* began to fill with people and eventually a man approached and tapped him on the shoulder.

"Excuse me?"

"Yes?"

"You're sitting in my seat."

"Would you mind very much if I sat here just for today?"

"You can't sit here. This is my seat. I've been sitting here for years."

Seeing the look of consternation on Yossi's face, the man must have felt he'd been unfriendly to a stranger, and, wanting to make it up to him, he grabbed Yossi by the hand and pulled him through the *beit knesset* up to the very first row.

"You're a guest here with us," he explained, "and guests are usually honored with front-row seats."

So saying, he showed him to a comfortable seat right in the middle of the front row. Yossi was now visible to the entire congregation, who would take one look at him and know that he was completely clueless. Mortified at his ignorance, he found himself a *siddur* and tried to pretend that he knew what he was doing. Hoping to pick up some pointers from his *tallit*-clad neighbors, he glanced at the man on his right, but saw to his chagrin that he was using a different edition of the *siddur* than Yossi was. A look over at the man on his left and he knew that his salvation was not coming from that direction, since the man was using yet a third type of *siddur*. The man on the right was on page 36, the man on his left was on page 72, and Yossi was left in the middle, overwhelmed, ashamed, and vulnerable, not knowing which page to turn to, and just feeling miserable.

The people started to pray and he sat quietly trying to blend in and not make a scene. He did his best to follow the clues left him by his fellow congregants, but managed to misread them time and again. From the corner of his eye he saw one man stand up—he was trying to adjust the *tallit* that had begun to slip off his shoulder—and Yossi jumped up with alacrity, thinking it was a time that everyone stood. It was like a nightmarish game of Simon Says or Monkey See, Monkey Do, and for the first time in his life, Yossi Wallis was the monkey and not liking it even one little bit.

Being a person who respected self-sufficiency and finding himself completely dependent on taking cues from other people, he couldn't deal with his newfound reality. And yet, being resourceful and smart, he would have no doubt eventually figured out how to adapt.

Except for one thing.

He hadn't figured Ozzy into the equation.

♦ ♦ ♦

It happened to be that Raanana was a city where the citizens owned dogs. Almost every family had a dog, generally, the bigger, the better. Shortly after moving into their new home, Yossi was approached by a friend of his who had just retired from the police force. He told Yossi that he had a very well-trained dog named Ozzy, who had worked with him on the force and who needed a new home now that his owner was retiring. Ozzy was a boxer with a scary-looking face and stripes down the sides of his athletic body. He reminded Yossi of a tiger, and after spending a few minutes with him, he knew that Ozzy would be a loyal companion who would protect him with his life if need be.

Being so well trained, Ozzy had developed into a truly intuitive canine. He knew when things were okay and when things were off kilter, and ever since the Wallis family had returned from the Arachim seminar, Ozzy had felt that something momentous was going on. In the past, Yossi would get up on Shabbat mornings and take Ozzy for a walk before heading out to the pool. That Shabbat morning, however, not only did he get dressed in a manner that was unfamiliar to the dog, but he also failed to take him for his customary morning stroll. In Ozzy's mind, something was very wrong, but for the life of him he couldn't figure out what it was.

Ozzy was not allowed to leave the house without permission. Everyone needs rules and dogs are no exception. The Wallis house had a huge backyard and Ozzy had plenty of room to stretch his legs. But he was nervous and agitated by his owner's strange behavior and didn't quite know what to do with himself. Here Yossi was already leaving the house—without a bathing suit and even wearing a shirt and pants. Worst of all, there was no whistle hanging around his neck. Ozzy was very concerned.

How concerned was he?

Concerned enough that he made what for him constituted a huge decision. Disobeying his training for the greater good of canine responsibility, Ozzy took a running leap and jumped the high fence surrounding the Wallis's property. Then he set off behind his man, following him from a distance, remaining sufficiently far back that he wouldn't be seen, but close enough that he could follow along discreetly. This way, he'd be able to protect Yossi in case he was doing something foolish and needed assistance. Though Yossi was his master and Ozzy the dog, Ozzy "knew" that he would be thanked for breaking the rules this one time.

Ozzy had become a spy. Discreet. Staying in the shadows. Padding silently on hunter's feet. Protecting his master from a distance.

Yossi had sometimes taken his dog along with him through the streets of the city. Ozzy knew he was expected to wait outside when his master entered a public building like the post office or a department store. In such cases, Ozzy waited outside. That was the rule and Ozzy followed it. Usually Yossi wasn't inside for more than 10 minutes and Ozzy knew that he was punctual and reliable about not taking too much time. In short, Ozzy didn't have to worry about his master. But that was all when things were normal and his master was acting himself.

Today, however, that was clearly not the case.

When Yossi Wallis entered the *beit knesset* that Shabbat morning, little did he dream that a very big boxer named Ozzy had followed him stealthily through the residential Raanana streets and was even now waiting for his master to exit the building.

Ten minutes passed. Fifteen. Yossi still hadn't come out of the *beit knesset* and Ozzy began to get agitated. Twenty minutes, half an hour. Ozzy began to pace back and forth. Something was wrong. He was sure of it. Why was his master remaining inside this strange building for so long, when he normally never stayed inside any building for longer than 20 minutes! From inside the *beit knesset* Ozzy heard people singing and didn't know what to make of the unfamiliar tunes. Ozzy was growing more and more concerned about his master.

Desperate times call for desperate measures and Ozzy made the decision to flout the rules once again and to enter the *beit knesset* to search for Yossi Wallis.

In the middle of the *tefillah* Yossi suddenly heard a huge commotion behind him. People were jumping out of their seats and yelling, "Dog in *beit knesset*, dog in *beit knesset*!"

Not knowing what was going on, but thinking it was part of the service, he also jumped out of his seat and began to yell, "Dog in *beit knesset*, dog in *beit knesset*!"

Turning around he caught sight of Ozzy the boxer frantically running between the rows of seats, shoving people to the side in his haste to find his master and to ensure that all was fine. He had caught his master's scent and knew he was there and it was only a matter of time until he tracked Yossi down, and then what? This wasn't some cute little poodle who had docilely entered the *beit knesset*. This was a great big dog, one who had scared the living daylights out of half the congregants as he charged through the rows.

Twenty seconds later Ozzy reached the front row and caught sight of his master trying to make himself invisible. No such luck. Ozzy was ecstatic, greeting him with his huge, wet tongue, licking his face, barking for sheer joy. Yossi tried to pretend that he didn't know him and shoved him away with his foot while hissing at him to go away, but Ozzy was having none of that. He'd been very worried about his master and was too overjoyed at having found him in a healthy condition to pay any attention to the fact that his master was not reciprocating the love. It was obvious to one and all that this was Yossi's dog and that it was his fault that the entire *beit knesset* had almost suffered a collective heart attack.

The *gabbai* approached.

"So this is your dog," he said in accusatory tones. "Don't you understand that you are not supposed to bring dogs to the *beit knesset*?"

Yossi hung his head with embarrassment. Ozzy, realizing that he'd done something wrong but not sure what it was, hung his head as well.

"Get your dog out of the *beit knesset*!!"

Ozzy and his master were shown the door and began walking home, tails between their legs (in Yossi's case metaphorically speaking). The walk home seemed to last an eternity as Yossi contemplated the very shameful fact that he'd just been thrown out of a *beit knesset* on his very first attempt to pray with a *minyan*.

"We just made world history for being thrown out of the *beit knesset* faster than anyone else," he told Ozzy.

The dog barked in response.

Sandy was sitting in the garden when they walked through the gate.

"Where did you disappear to so early this morning?"

"I decided to go to the *beit knesset*."

She looked at Ozzy and Yossi. It was obvious that they'd gotten into some kind of trouble.

"And then what happened?" She glanced at her watch. "Is *tefillah* over already?"

"No," he replied shortly, "they threw me out because of Ozzy."

"You think getting thrown out of the *beit knesset* is your big problem right now?"

There was something in her tone that spoke of much bigger issues.

"What do you mean?"

"Do you know that the entire city is out searching for you, for the lifeguard who didn't show up! Do you know that the pool is locked because you didn't open it and the people are steaming mad at you?! Apparently everyone woke up this morning, wanted to go swimming, but couldn't because there was no lifeguard! You want to go to the *beit knesset*? Wonderful. But to close the pool in a city like Raanana because you found religion! What on earth got into you, Yossi?"

"Truthfully? I didn't really think it all the way through."

"Well, you have a problem, because the entire city thinks that you lost your mind!"

"And on top of that, the religious people threw me out of the *beit knesset*."

In one Shabbat he had managed to alienate everyone: both religious and nonreligious. It would take him quite a while to convince everyone he knew that he was still the same Yossi they knew and loved.

So ended the story of their first Shabbat in Raanana.

The Wallis family's journey toward becoming completely religious would be long and filled with twists and turns. Parts of the road would be arduous. Other parts rocky. But one thing was for certain. It would never be boring.

CHAPTER NINETEEN

The Wallis family had begun a brand-new life. Their focus had changed. The things which had once been important to them had become less so.

And what did his wife have to say about that?

"*Baruch Hashem*, I merited to marry a true *eishes chayil*," Rabbi Wallis says unequivocally. "Once Sandy recognized the truth inherent in Torah and mitzvos, she accepted them upon herself and became the motivator for the entire family."

♦ ♦ ♦

For a person or family who decides to make that giant leap into a brand-new world, it is imperative that those who helped bring them to Torah in the first place remain at their sides to guide them as they emerge, blinking like newborn babies coming into the light. Even with all the help they received, it was not easy for the Wallis family to exchange everything they knew for an entirely new way of life, but the ancient Wallis roots stood them in good stead and they didn't waver from their decision.

Yossi began studying with the young religious men he had met through Arachim and they introduced him to the fascinating world of Torah study. Possessing the analytical mind that naturally examines everything through the prism of engineering, Yossi found himself drawn toward Gemara learning and the intellectual honesty contained within its ancient words.

♦ ♦ ♦

Yossi Wallis's decision to become religious meant that he needed a shul near his office. His aviation supply company was located in a three-story residential-turned-office building near King George and Maccabi streets in the heart of Tel Aviv. To his delight, he discovered a little shul on one of the nearby side streets and he began frequenting it for Minchah and Maariv. Though Tel Aviv has a reputation for being an irreligious city, there are many pockets of Judaism scattered throughout; one just has to know where to look. In addition to *minyanim*, the shul boasted a *kollel* as well, and after joining them for davening, Yossi made a habit of remaining behind to learn for half an hour—which over time turned into an hour and then two. Eventually his focus on the business diminished to the point where his partners began taking him to task for ignoring his business responsibilities.

"You're never around," one of them said to him. "And even when you're here, you're not here."

He couldn't even argue with them, because they were right. As much as he enjoyed his business and was even passionate about anything to do with fast machines (choppers, planes, motorcycles, sports cars...), there was a strong inner feeling warring with his natural inclinations. Having become religious later in life, Yossi felt a gaping hole where his years of learning should have been. Whereas other religious people his age had spent their formative years developing their minds in yeshivah, he had spent his time in a gang in the Bronx, in the Israeli army, and selling weapons, aircraft, and their parts to international companies around the globe. He loved the give-and-take of a good business negotiation and the feeling of clinching a deal, but his soul wasn't satisfied; his *neshamah* kept pushing him to learn.

Sometimes at the end of a long day at the office, he'd leave Tel Aviv and drive over to Bnei Brak for more learning at Kollel

Chazon Ish. His circle of religious acquaintances widened until he had come to know quite a few *talmidei chachamim* who were willing to devote time to a middle-age *baal teshuvah* with a burning desire for Torah study.

But he was still straddling both worlds, with a foot on either side, and he was not at all sure where he truly belonged.

♦ ♦ ♦

Being a supplier and purchaser of parts and weaponry, there were times when Yossi's partners relied on him to put in the company's bids to Israel Aircraft Industries, and he just didn't get around to it in time, or didn't follow up afterward, resulting in their company missing some crucial deals. He was still doing his share of the work more or less, but the old passion and love had been redirected toward Torah learning and it showed in the bottom line.

It was especially difficult for him when there were trade shows overseas that his partners expected him to attend: trade shows he was reluctant to visit for religious reasons. There was an annual show for businesses involved in the helicopter industry that took place in Las Vegas. There was no question that he needed to attend, but the fact that the convention was in Las Vegas convinced him that he wasn't the right man for the job. Whereas in the past, he wouldn't have thought twice about hopping on a plane to Vegas for an important business trip, now he thought twice and three times—in the end concluding that he did not want to subject himself to the glittering impurity that awaited him in the golden world of the Vegas casinos. He recalled earlier trips when he'd visited the Strip, with its dozens of neon-lit hotels and casinos, and he shuddered at the memory. Simply put, Yossi Wallis had changed and was not the same person anymore. He gave the matter a lot of thought, but in the end, knowing the Vegas atmosphere, he just couldn't bring himself to go.

And that was bad for business.

On another occasion their firm had a crucial business meeting in Germany which he had been tapped to attend. The meeting was with the German military, one of their major clients, which purchased a significant amount of military equipment, especially airplanes, from their company. The meeting had been arranged before he became religious and Yossi couldn't find any way out, reluctant though he was, as the son and grandson of Holocaust victims, to set foot on the accursed German soil. In the past, he would have suffered emotionally from having to visit Germany, but that would have been his sole area of struggle. Now, however, he couldn't figure out what to do regarding his head covering. Should he travel to Germany with a *kippah* on his head or not? If he would remove his *kippah*, should he do that before he got into the taxi to the airport, or at the airport, or when he boarded the plane, or before they actually landed in Germany?

In the end he decided to remove his *kippah* on the airplane itself, just as they were descending into Germany. Once they landed he left the plane, hand luggage in tow, and made his way through customs and out into the Munich streets, where he waited for his German army contacts to come pick him up. Walking the streets of Munich felt strange to him. Strange and alien. This was Munich, after all—seat of Hitler's failed putsch on November 8, 1923; birthplace of the Nazi party; home to the people who had killed so many of his family members just a few decades earlier. Forty years before and his life would have been in danger just from being seen on the street, and now here he was, in Munich, about to enter into a meeting where he'd be negotiating on equal terms with some of the top officers of the German Air Force!

As a German military officer helped him stow his luggage into the back of a jeep, Yossi Wallis's conscience kept on berating him for having made the decision to remove his head covering.

How could you, he heard the little voice inside his head protesting over and over. *If you're religious, you're religious, and that means wearing a kippah wherever you go, even in the middle of Germany!*

He had no answer for the little voice and was ashamed.

The jeep sped them through the Munich streets, until they arrived at an air force base. The driver flashed his credentials, the bar lifted, and they were permitted entrance. Traversing a Munich military base gave him a surreal feeling, but that was nothing compared to the emotions coursing through him a short while later, when they took their seats around a polished conference table at one of the air force officers' clubs and he glanced upward at the walls, only to find himself staring at a series of portraits containing the faces of the German Air Force's highest-ranking officers all the way back to the Second World War.

Yossi Wallis was forced to conduct his business negotiations under the dourly Teutonic gaze of former Nazi Luftwaffe officers. At least if he would have been wearing his *kippah* it would have evened up the score a little bit. During the dinner that followed, the awkwardness only increased as the waiters served platters of the finest meats and most expensive wines, and as the people around him proceeded to empty bottle after bottle, while he abstained. When the waiter grew concerned and asked him what he could possibly serve the honored guest from their excellent kitchen, Yossi told the man to bring him a plate of iceberg lettuce salad and nothing more.

"And after the lettuce salad, sir?"

"Nothing."

He was served a gigantic plate of salad, and there they sat, the carnivorous officers of the German Air Force with their bratwurst, blood sausage, and lager, and the Jewish "vegetarian" from Raanana, breaking bread around the table as the Nazis on the wall looked on in horror.

Being an honest person, Yossi came to the realization that he wasn't contributing his full part to the business any longer. He decided to sell his share to his partners, who were more than happy to buy him out. For the first time in years, his mind was no longer occupied with the sales of aircraft and weapons, and he was left free to pursue his newly acquired love for Torah study, while still negotiating the occasional business deal on the side.

♦ ♦ ♦

One evening, after they'd concluded their learning for the night, his study partner closed his Gemara and informed Yossi that it was high time that he met some of the local Bnei Brak *gedolim*.

"What do you mean by *gedolim*?"

"*Gedolim* is another way of saying 'great leaders of Klal Yisrael.'"

"Who exactly do you have in mind?" Yossi asked his friend.

"I'm taking you to meet Rav Chaim Greineman," he replied. "I think you will find in him the kind of mentor and confidant that you are searching for."

In truth, Yossi had been told by many that he needed to find a rebbi and it had been weighing on his mind for a while. Consequently, he was more than happy to follow his study partner's advice and meet Rav Chaim, hoping that their initial meeting might blossom into something much deeper.

To his great joy and satisfaction, the relationship that developed between Rav Chaim and his *talmid*, Yossi Wallis, would span the decades until Rav Chaim's passing in 2015.

♦ ♦ ♦

Rabbi Wallis with Rav Chaim Greineman

From the start of their long relationship, Rav Chaim Greineman treated his new student with warmth and kindness.

"As someone who had experienced rigorous university learning of the highest caliber," Rabbi Wallis says, "I found myself extremely impressed with Rav Chaim's intellect and broad grasp of every topic we discussed. I was able to converse with Rav Chaim about any topic under the sun. We discussed finance and the state of world economy, and every time he made a comment I was struck anew by the relevance of his thought processes. During our initial meeting I came to the realization that I wanted Rav Chaim for a rebbi."

Rav Chaim, for his part, instructed his children and *gabbaim* that Yossi Wallis should be let in to see him whenever he came to visit. Rabbi Wallis took full advantage of his rebbi's generosity and began visiting him on a regular basis, and it was Rav Chaim more than anyone else who helped Yossi transform himself from a fresh *baal teshuvah* to a full-fledged member of the *chareidi* community.

Rav Chaim was also the one who guided Yossi toward becoming more and more involved with the world of Arachim. He suggested that Sandy and Yossi hold sessions at their home in Raanana and told him to invite his friends and business acquaintances to hear the world-class lecturers who were coming to speak. With Rav Chaim's constant encouragement, the Wallis home underwent a complete change, becoming a Torah center with classes being given for people on all levels at least four evenings a week. There were classes for beginners and classes for the more advanced. Classes for men, classes for women, and classes for couples. On Shabbos there were *Tehillim* groups for the neighborhood children. Arachim sent their best speakers to the Wallis home and their friends and neighbors were able to ask any questions they had. The gatherings drew Sandy closer to the cause, since she served refreshments for the sessions and was able to listen to as many classes as she was able to handle. Within a very short time, the family's life came to revolve around Torah learning and education, and, says Rabbi Wallis, it was mainly due to Rav Chaim's direct encouragement and guidance.

"I had become religious through Arachim and felt a tremendous amount of gratitude toward the rabbis who devoted their days and nights working for the Jewish nation. Rav Chaim, seeing how devoted I was toward Arachim, persuaded me to become CEO of the fledgling operation. He had become familiar with my approach to all matters of business and suggested that I apply my drive and my past experience in the world of international business to transforming Arachim into a brand name in the *kiruv* world. While I had a vision for what I wanted Arachim to become, Rav Chaim had a vision for what he wanted *me* to become, and he never hesitated to share it with me. In the end, I listened to him and accepted the job, and the responsibility."

◆ ◆ ◆

There were numerous *gedolim* living in Bnei Brak at that time and Rabbi Wallis would end up meeting many of them. Before entering the inner sanctum of Rav Yaakov Yisrael Kanievsky, the Steipler Gaon, his escort turned to him and said, "Yossi, we are about to enter the presence of one of the holiest men of our generation. This is the *Kodesh HaKodashim*, the Holy of Holies, of the Jewish people!" When he stood before the Steipler for the first time, Rabbi Wallis felt as if he had just come face-to-face with a majestic lion. The timbre of the Steipler's voice was very deep and powerful and he possessed an awesomely serious mien that resonated with intense fear of Heaven. Sitting in his tiny, simply furnished Bnei Brak apartment, the Steipler turned his laser-sharp gaze at Rabbi Wallis, shaking him to the core.

During the course of that memorable meeting, the Steipler questioned Rabbi Wallis about the status of his *tefillin*. For his part, Yossi Wallis wasn't quite sure that he understood the *Rav's* question.

"My *tefillin*?" (A little nervous by this line of questioning.)

"Yes, where did you buy them?" (The *Rav's* deep voice rumbling as it shook the room.)

"They are the *tefillin* I received when I turned 13."

"Your bar mitzvah *tefillin*! Most likely, they aren't kosher anymore. You have to change them."

Yossi stood frozen in his place, slightly stunned by the interchange. The whole conversation was puzzling. What was the Steipler talking about? *Tefillin* were *tefillin*, weren't they? His were black and square and there were long straps hanging down...and what else was supposed to be there anyway? Yet here was the Steipler, whom he didn't know at all, telling him that the chances of his tefillin being useable were virtually nil!

Meeting the *baal teshuvah's* confused gaze the Steipler said, "I'm going to give you my *parshiyos*."

Now he was really confused. What on earth was the man talking about?

"What?"

"Yes," said the Steipler, confirming what he'd just said. "I've just changed the *parshiyos* (inner parchments) in my *tefillin* [the Steipler did this periodically] and I want you to have the old ones."

Calling over his assistant, the Steipler instructed him to give Yossi the *parshiyos*, and then he asked Yossi's escort to make sure he replaced the old ones.

Before they left the room, the Steipler rose from his chair and, reaching out his hand in his guest's direction, blessed Yossi with a lengthy *berachah*, of which he understood nothing at the time. He only knew that something momentous had occurred from the reaction of the onlookers, who later explained to him that the Steipler's behavior that day—the fact that he had risen from his seat and the amount of effort that he'd put into the actual *berachah*—was almost unprecedented.

Until this day, Rabbi Yossi Wallis wears the Steipler's *tefillin* every morning. And as he places them on his head and wraps the black straps around his still powerful bicep, he can't help but recall their meeting in those early days, when he was still struggling mightily to find his way.

♦ ♦ ♦

It was the mid-1980's and the Arachim team was heavily involved in building the organization. They were putting in crazy hours and organizing seminars as fast as they could, but the demand was great and they found themselves in the middle of a growth spurt, without the necessary funding to take the organization to the next level. They had the staff, they could bring people in and book hotels, but they lacked the funds to pay for all of their activities.

One evening Rabbi Wallis had invited the Arachim team that dealt with seminars for intellectuals, academics, and people with college degrees over to his house for a meeting. They were all sitting in his living room involved in a brainstorming session, when there was a knock on the door. He went to answer and saw a rabbi with a big, impressive beard and beautifully expressive eyes. The sight of a rabbi whom he didn't recognize standing on his doorstep was not a foreign one (his home was on the route of many a *tzedakah* collector), and he greeted him cordially.

"My name is Rav Shimshon Pincus," the man said by way of introduction. "Can I talk to you for a second?"

Not recognizing his name, Rabbi Wallis replied, "I'd love to talk to you for a lot more than that, but as you can see, I'm in the middle of a meeting right now. You can either return in about an hour, or wait in my study until the meeting comes to an end and we can talk then."

"I'll be happy to wait."

Rabbi Wallis showed Rav Pincus into the study, inviting him to make himself comfortable. He then returned to the meeting, leaving the rabbi to his own devices. Since the door to the study had been left ajar, Rav Pincus was able to hear everything the Arachim team was discussing: future plans, ideas, and strategy. At the meeting's end, the staff went home and Rabbi Wallis entered the study.

"I'm sorry for keeping you waiting," he said. "What was your name again, and what can I do for you?"

"Rav Shimshon Pincus. I'm the *rav* of Ofakim, down south, and the question is what can *I* do for *you*."

"Okay then," Rabbi Wallis replied. "What can you do for me?"

"Before I arrived at your home," he said, "I wanted to help you out."

"Why? How did you even know about us in the first place?"

"I've been keeping tabs on Arachim."

"You have?"

"Yes. Lately I've been running into more and more nonreligious people from down south—some of them even live in Ofakim. One day they're walking around without a *kippah* on their heads, and the next, they've become religious. So I started asking them how they became religious and they told me that they attended one of your seminars. After hearing this enough times, I decided that I have to meet you myself and offer my assistance."

"I see. So you want to get involved with Arachim?"

"That's what I thought when I walked into your home tonight. But now, after listening to one of your meetings and hearing firsthand what Arachim is all about, I've become excited about helping you take your organization up to the next level! You look at doing *kiruv* as if it's your mission, as if all of you sitting here feel a personal sense of responsibility to save the Jewish people! I had no idea of the scope of your plans. All I can say is that hearing all this has made me rethink what I wanted to tell you originally, because your work is absolutely essential! Now I really want to get involved with Arachim, far more than when I first walked into your house!"

"Okay, so what can you do for me?"

"I'm very well connected in the United States and Canada. I want to take you on a whirlwind fund-raising trip across North America, to help you raise the kind of money that Arachim needs to fund itself and realize its ambitions."

Rabbi Wallis looked at the *rav* and wasn't sure what to make of the whole thing. They had never met before, and here he was, offering to take Rabbi Wallis to the States, introduce him to several wealthy people, and sell Arachim to them. They didn't even know each other, yet Rav Pincus was promising him the world.

"I'm ready to go with you," Rabbi Wallis told him. "Just tell me when."

Rav Pincus called the next day. "I purchased the tickets."

Rabbi Wallis was shocked.

"We're leaving in a few days."

Thus was he introduced to Rav Shimshon Pincus.

They flew to America one week later. Rav Pincus rented a car at the airport and drove them to his parents' home in Flatbush. There was no time to rest up from the jet lag. Rav Pincus woke Rabbi Wallis early the next morning, and after davening they set out on the whirlwind fund-raising trip he had been promised.

One thing became obvious very quickly. Rav Pincus hadn't been exaggerating about his connections in the States or his readiness to use them for Arachim. At some point along the way, they arrived in Baltimore and drove to Yeshivas Ner Yisroel, where Rav Pincus introduced Rabbi Wallis to the *menahel* (principal), Rabbi Naftali Neuberger. At their meeting, Rabbi Wallis outlined what Arachim was all about, its future goals, and what had already been accomplished. Rabbi Neuberger, a legendary doer himself, grew excited by what he was proposing.

Meetings led to more meetings, and eventually Rav Pincus secured a meeting for Yossi with Mr. Moshe (Paul) Reichmann in Toronto. Rav Pincus was unable to make it, so Rabbi Wallis flew there alone. Rav Pincus had arranged for him to stay at the home of Mr. David de Ancona. By the time he landed, however, and after crawling through the heavy traffic and even heavier rain, there was no time for him to unpack at his host's home before the meeting with Mr. Reichmann. With no choice, Rabbi Wallis told the taxi driver to take him and his suitcases directly to the Reichmann home.

When they pulled up, he told the driver to wait while he went outside to ring the bell.

A voice came through the intercom. "Who is it?"

"Rabbi Yossi Wallis. I have an appointment with Mr. Reichmann."

"He is in the middle of a meeting now," the disembodied voice said. "Can you please return in 15 minutes?"

Yossi retraced his steps back to the cab. The rain was still pouring down.

"Listen," he told the driver, "the man asked me to wait 15 minutes. Can you do that?"

"I'm sorry, sir, I have to take another fare."

With no choice, Rabbi Wallis paid the driver and lifted his suitcases out of the trunk. The taxi sped off and he was left standing in the middle of the sidewalk in the pouring rain. Coming from Eretz Yisrael, he was unprepared for the Canadian winter, and the freezing rain was hitting him harder than he'd expected. He had to find shelter. After walking around for a few minutes, he found a restaurant. After walking inside, however, he soon realized that the store sold pork and that he couldn't take refuge in such an establishment, so he left. There was nowhere to hide, so he returned to the Reichmann home and waited outside the gate. By then the rain had completely destroyed his hat, and he had turned into one gigantic puddle.

He rang the bell again.

"Who is it?"

"Rabbi Yossi Wallis."

The next thing he knew, he was buzzed inside.

Mr. Reichmann opened the door and Yossi entered his house wheeling his two suitcases. The shape of his hat had been completely obliterated, any resemblance to a normal black hat nothing more than a suggestion. Needless to say, his host was quite taken aback and unsure what to make of his visitor, or if he intended to move in for an extended stay.

"What's going on?" he asked, trying to get a handle of the soaking-wet apparition who had just appeared on his doorstep.

"Don't worry about the suitcases," Rabbi Wallis said by way of explanation. "I had no time to go to my host to unpack, and had the taxi take me here straight from the airport."

"And you are again?"

"Rabbi Yossi Wallis, from Arachim."

He recalled the name.

A short while later, they were sitting upstairs getting to know each other—Rabbi Wallis minus his sopping coat, though still way too wet for comfort.

"Please tell me about yourself."

"Well, I've come here to raise money for my organization."

This led them into a conversation, and Yossi mentioned a name they had in common: his mother's uncle from Vienna, who had been Moshe Reichmann's business partner at one point. That brought his wife into the room and the conversation finally got off the ground. Eventually Mr. Reichmann brought things around to the reason they were all sitting there.

"Can you show me some letters of approbation?"

That simple, straightforward request placed Yossi in a bind. His letters were buried deep inside his suitcase and the last thing he wanted to do was start digging through all his clothing to find them. This visit was not turning out the way he had envisioned. Here he had received a wonderful opportunity, but nothing was working out! He had come into the Reichmanns' beautiful home soaking wet, dripping water all over the spotless floor, and now he was going to have to start digging through all his clothing to find some letters!

But Mr. Reichmann wanted to see some letters; how could Yossi refuse such a logical and obvious request?

Reaching over to his suitcases and ignoring the growing puddle of water that was spreading around him from his dripping clothing, he bent over and began rooting around inside one of the bags, searching for the folder with the letters. But as Murphy's Law would have it, the more he searched, the more they eluded him. Tossing aside neatly folded piles of clothes, he began turning that suitcase upside down in his search.

Suddenly, the events of the day caught up with him and he found that he couldn't do it anymore. The rain, the travel, the discomfort, the sopping pants and shirt, the fact that the long-awaited meeting was slipping away from him... It was all too much.

Turning to his host, he said, "Can I ask you a question?"

"Certainly," he replied.

"How come I have to travel all the way to you to receive funds to help create *baalei teshuvah*? What makes me more responsible for these nonreligious Jews than you? Why don't you travel to come see me? I'll carry on with my business, you take over my organization, and I'll support you! Why do I have to go through this whole fund-raising ordeal when we're both equally responsible for the future of Klal Yisrael?!"

Mr. Moshe Reichmann regarded Rabbi Wallis thoughtfully for a minute.

"You know something," he said at last, "you're absolutely right. There is no reason why you should have to come to me to raise money for such an essential cause."

With those few words, it was as if they were starting everything over again from the beginning—as if they had been reintroduced and Rabbi Wallis hadn't been sopping wet and hadn't dripped water all over the floor and hadn't arrived with two suitcases in tow. Suddenly the two men understood each other with 100 percent clarity. When it was time to leave, Yossi walked out of the house with Moshe Reichmann's personal phone number and his promise to arrange a parlor meeting for him.

The parlor meeting took place at the Reichmann company offices of Olympia and York in New York City a few weeks later. It was very well attended by influential and wealthy people who had been personally invited by Rav Pincus on behalf of Mr. Reichmann—who had become a friend of Rabbi Wallis and with whom he would share a long-term relationship. At the initial parlor meeting, it was Moshe Reichmann who made it his business to personally raise the money from the assembled, proving once again how very responsible he felt for the future of the Jewish people. It was a very successful meeting, with the team of Mr. Reichmann (the host) and Rav Pincus (the organizer who had been involved throughout) raising the astounding sum of $3 million in about one hour!

This incredible episode served as a springboard for Rav Pincus's close involvement with Arachim, in the capacity of lecturer (he was a phenomenal speaker) for its seminar graduates and others who were more advanced and showing interest in further growth. Rabbi Wallis also learned from Rav Pincus what simplicity was all about, how to set goals and stick to them, what determination meant, how to never be content with mediocrity, and how it was possible to raise $3 million in an hour if you trained yourself to aim for the sky and think out of the box.

Gratified though he was by the turn of events, Yossi was not surprised; they were doing Hashem's work. These were Hashem's children they were talking about, and He wants them back home.

♦ ♦ ♦

Becoming involved in such a personal way with Arachim was the best decision Rabbi Wallis ever made, but it meant that he wasn't seeing as much of his children as he would have liked. By the time he arrived home in the evening they were usually already sleeping; he felt that their childhood was passing him by. He therefore did whatever he could to show them his love with certain unspoken gestures that he knew they'd appreciate and intuitively comprehend for what they were: signs of their father's deepest love for them.

On the mornings that Sandy had to leave early and he was left in charge, Rabbi Wallis made them sandwiches just as she did. But instead of just putting two pieces of bread together with some cheese placed between, he made a whole production out of it. He'd cut the sandwiches into cubes, each one a perfect, bite-size shape, just begging to be placed delicately into one's mouth. The kids rejoiced when they saw their father constructing his culinary masterpieces.

Still, he felt that it wasn't enough. He was constantly looking for ways to show them that he was a presence in their lives—involved, despite the fact that they didn't see him as much as they would have liked. He gave the matter lots of thought and finally he began a tradition that lasted for years. Upon arriving home in the evening he'd say hello to Sandy and then go on up into the children's rooms. They'd be lying in bed, blankets all tangled up, faces relaxed in sleep mode.

Rabbi Wallis would gather the blankets together, making everything all neat again. Then he'd encase them in their blankets, while placing his hands on their backs so they'd actively feel his presence. He wanted them to feel a father's touch and know that they were safe and being looked after with love. Sometimes they'd roll over and look at him sleepily for a second before going back to sleep, but usually they just slept through it all. Still, he knew that this was a very important gesture on his part. It allowed them to know he was there. That he wasn't a spectator, but very much an active participant.

Years later the rabbi overheard a conversation between his three grown-up sons on a Shabbos afternoon that filled his heart with joy.

"Remember what Abba used to do when we were kids?" one of them asked.

"Which thing?"

"How he used to come into our rooms—"

"And tuck us in," another brother interrupted.

"Yes, and then he'd place his hands on our backs until we felt the pressure of his arms, strong and powerful, you remember how strong Abba was—"

"Sure I remember," chimed in the third brother. "I used to pretend I was asleep, but the truth is I was really awake watching him and the care he was giving us."

"I didn't know you were also awake," said the first brother.

"I remember it like it happened yesterday."

"Me too. It was really special. I felt all warm and protected, like Abba was always watching us and making sure we were okay."

Rabbi Wallis heard them speaking and didn't disturb them. But inside, he was overjoyed that his boys had felt what he had wanted them to feel and that he had accomplished his goal.

◆ ◆ ◆

Years later he would do something similar on the night before each of his children got married. The tradition began on the evening prior to his oldest son's wedding. Rabbi Wallis entered his room when he was already half-asleep and sat down near his bed. The *chasan*-to-be looked at his father, puzzled, not sure why he was there.

"What is it, Abba?"

"Nothing, sweetheart, go to sleep," he told his son.

"But why are you here?"

"There's something I need to do."

"What?"

Rabbi Wallis didn't reply, merely patted his shoulder.

"Abba, what is it?"

"My son," he replied, "you're moving out of the house tomorrow, about to begin a brand-new life. Sure Ima and I will be a part of it, but it will never be the same. I'm going to miss you so, so much. That's why I plan on sitting here by your bed tonight, on your final evening as a single boy in our home, and I'm going to show you my deepest love. Do you understand?"

He nodded.

"Go to sleep," Rabbi Wallis told him, "Abba's here."

Then he patted his shoulder and eventually his son's eyes closed in peaceful slumber until he fell into a deep, calming sleep. Rabbi Wallis sat there for most of the night, never moving from his son's bedside, until he heard the chirping of the early-morning birds through the window.

"*I love you*," whispered the impossibly busy CEO of Arachim to the sleeping form. Then he left the room to prepare for the big day.

He did this with each of his children, and though they laughed at him and called him sentimental, he wouldn't have missed those experiences for the world—and neither would they. Because his actions told his children what their Abba felt for them. And how much he loved them and always would.

CHAPTER TWENTY

Having chosen to become religious at a later stage in life than the average *baal teshuvah*, Rabbi Wallis soon found himself filled with a burning desire to make up for all the lost time of his youth. He felt as if everyone in the world knew more Torah than he did and that the only way he'd be able to catch up was if he sat himself down in a real yeshivah, with students 20 years his junior, for full-time learning, leaving his work at Arachim and miscellaneous business activities for the night hours. Though his rabbinic advisers—Rav Chaim Greineman chief among them—tried to talk him out of following his dreams, Rabbi Wallis couldn't get the desire out of his heart and head. He wanted to learn. He needed to learn. Not to hear the occasional *shiur*. To really learn. To sit and *shteig*, to completely immerse himself over a Gemara from morning till night.

But Rav Chaim felt that learning a full day would not be good for his student.

"Test me," Rabbi Wallis begged his rebbi. "See if I can stand the pressure."

Realizing that Yossi Wallis wasn't planning on giving up and that he sincerely desired to learn Torah, Rav Chaim eventually gave him permission to become a *yeshivah bachur*. Upon receiving the official okay from Rav Chaim to immerse himself in the depths of Torah, Yossi was so intensely happy that he couldn't control himself. Taking leave of his rebbi, he rushed through the door of Rav Chaim's shul, situated right off Chiddushei HaRim Street, and began dancing in the street, yelling to Rav Aryeh Shechter, who had accompanied him to Rav Chaim, "He said yes, I can learn, I can learn!!!"

Now that he had received permission to learn, Yossi asked Rav Chaim to suggest an appropriate yeshivah for him.

"You should go to Slabodka," Rav Chaim declared. "That's the yeshivah for you."

Yossi gaped at his teacher. "You don't think I should attend a yeshivah for *baalei teshuvah*, Ohr Somayach, Aish HaTorah?"

"No, I want you to go to a regular, mainstream yeshivah."

"But I don't know anything! How can I go to a regular yeshivah?"

"Go to Slabodka, you'll do well there."

If Rav Chaim Greineman felt that way, who was Yossi Wallis to argue?

And so he entered a world of 18-year-olds, though he was already in his mid-40's. He didn't have a choice in the matter. There was no way he was prepared to remain an ignoramus, an *am ha'aretz*, for the rest of his life. He had been presented with a million-dollar opportunity and a once-in-a-lifetime chance, and he intended to take full advantage, with no thought or care of the disparity between the age of the student body and himself.

♦ ♦ ♦

The Slabodka Yeshivah was located on Rabbi Isaac Sher Street—a hilly road branching steeply upward off Rabbi Akiva Street, Bnei Brak's main traffic artery. The yeshivah building towered above passersby with impeccable dignity and an almost royal sense of service to the Creator. The years Rabbi Wallis spent learning at the Slabodka Yeshivah were some of the best, most productive years of his life. He arrived at the yeshivah early enough each day to daven Shacharis with the rest of the student dy, no matter what time he had gone to bed the night before. He learned at the yeshivah for eight sweet, powerful hours every day. He also ate breakfast and lunch in the dining room like any other student. The administration was even gracious enough to provide him with a room and bed if he needed a rest during the day. After a full day at the yeshivah, he'd leave, return home, eat supper, and then devote the next three or four hours to running Arachim.

The time he spent at Slabodka was a far more genuine and accurate introduction to the world of *chareidi* Jewry than anything else Yossi had ever come across. Just being with the students, watching them as they learned, seeing the incredible piety with which they lived their lives, helped the middle-age *baal teshuvah* bridge the gap between his upbringing and the world he had chosen to inhabit. It also provided him with the insight that he'd need when it came to raising his three boys, who were rapidly growing up into first-class products of the *chareidi* education system. The fact that their father had immersed himself in the life of a yeshivah student would help him understand his children and ultimately enhance their relationship.

Rabbi Wallis's schedule left him with almost no personal time. There were times that he had to leave the yeshivah for a few weeks of travel and there were times when he only managed to study there for a few hours a day, but for the next 10 years of his life the Slabodka Yeshivah in Bnei Brak was his second home. He gained so much that today as an employer of religious workers, he requires the male workers on his staff to spend at least part of their day involved in serious learning. This requirement is a prerequisite for working at Arachim, since in his opinion, there is no better way for a person to start his day.

Even after he was already running a national organization, his learning at Slabodka remained his number one priority, with Arachim following closely in second place. Running such a large-scale operation is not without its share of challenges, both political and financial, and there were many times that he'd enter the yeshivah building knowing that he had a seemingly insurmountable problem to resolve and a limited amount of time in which to do so. But the moment that he walked through the doors of Slabodka, he'd force himself to let it all go—to focus exclusively on his learning—and that approach had a way of putting all the challenges that arose on a daily basis into perspective. He was able to remain calm in the most stressful situations because of his realization that Torah learning was the main thing. Until today, it never ceases to fascinate Rabbi Wallis how much smaller even real problems become after a few hours spent learning in the *beis midrash*. A few hours hunched over the Gemara is the equivalent of a healthy dose of spiritual penicillin and does absolute wonders for a person's soul.

Torah study is so vitally important that the guests at Arachim seminars spend time involved in hands-on Gemara classes even before committing to a religious lifestyle. Rabbi Wallis and the entire Arachim staff have learned that it's the greatest game changer there is and its power to reach even the most alienated Jew should never be underestimated.

♦ ♦ ♦

Rabbi Wallis realized very early on that it was imperative for Arachim to remain apolitical, or, in a word, universal. Arachim was returning the Jewish nation to its collective roots and that was a matter of celebration for every single member of Klal Yisrael, no matter with which stream they associated themselves. As the organization grew and he had to hire more and more employees to fill the developing positions, Rabbi Wallis took the time to familiarize himself with his staffers, and to learn which rabbis, Chassidic Rebbes, and teachers they turned to for guidance, and he would then ask his staff to introduce their leaders to him.

If they were Chassidim, he'd drive over to meet their Rebbes. If they belonged to the Lithuanian yeshivah world, he'd request an introduction to their roshei yeshivah. The same went for the Sefardim in their ranks. Arachim was to be affiliated with everyone.

With
Rav Kaduri *zt"l*

With Rav Michel Yehuda Lefkowitz *zt"l*

With the Admor of Seret-Vizhnitz *zt"l*

With the Admor of Kalev

With Rav Chaim Kanievsky

With the Novominsker Rebbe

With Rav Aryeh Malkiel Kotler

With Rav Mattisyahu Salomon

With the Satmar Rebbe

With the Sanzer Rebbe

With the Bobover Rebbe

There's a beautiful video that was filmed during one of Rabbi Wallis's many visits to the home of Rav Ovadia Yosef *zt"l*, with whom he shared a very close relationship.

It was well known that Rav Ovadia greeted visitors with a gentle slap on the face as a sign of affection. Even former Israeli president Shimon Peres was not exempt during his visits to the *gadol hador*. Rav Ovadia must have been extremely fond of Peres, since there were times that he gave him not one or two, but three slaps. (Rav Ovadia was probably the only person in Eretz Yisrael able to slap the president's face without being arrested.)

If Rav Ovadia's slaps were commonplace, his kisses were not. In fact, there are precious few documented cases where Maran, as he was called, gave a kiss to anyone.

Back to the video that was filmed during the visit. It was a busy day at the home of Rav Ovadia Yosef, with many people coming and going. One after the next, they approach the *gadol hador* with submission, and receive a slap on the cheek. Some merit a slap on both sides. This happens multiple times.

Enter Rabbi Yossi Wallis. He approaches Rav Ovadia, greets the undisputed head of Sefardic Jewry worldwide with humility and respect.

Rabbi Wallis with Rav Ovadia

And Rav Ovadia reaches over to Rabbi Wallis, takes a gentle hold of his face, and gives him a kiss on both cheeks.

More than anything, Rav Ovadia's kisses showed in the most genuine way what he felt for Rabbi Wallis and Arachim. Because Arachim, like Rav Ovadia, belonged to the entire nation. And so does Rabbi Yossi Wallis.

♦ ♦ ♦

Over time Rabbi Wallis met with many of the *gedolim*, who warmly welcomed him into their homes, yeshivos, and courts and were supportive of Arachim's mission. He'd eventually come to connect with the Gerrer Rebbe, the Nadvorna Rebbe, and the Sanzer Rebbe. Every time he met one of the leaders of Klal Yisrael, he explained that he wanted them to be kept abreast of what was happening in Arachim, giving them access to the same information that he had, because doing Jewish outreach wasn't just his responsibility, but theirs as well.

The Admor of Belz in particular was a huge inspiration to Rabbi Wallis. The Rebbe's ongoing involvement in *kiruv* showed

Rabbi Wallis and the Belzer Rebbe

a broadness of scope that impressed him greatly. Rabbi Wallis met the Belzer Rebbe for the first time in the early years following his introduction into Arachim, when he'd learned that the Rebbe had been one of the sponsors of the seminar that had made him religious. Fascinated by the idea that the Chassidic master of thousands should be busying himself with a fledgling outreach organization, Rabbi Wallis drove to meet with him in Yerushalayim, where he introduced himself to the Rebbe as a direct beneficiary of his generosity, explaining that he, Yossi Wallis, had become religious through a seminar for which the Rebbe had paid the expense. Setting eyes on a concrete result of his *kiruv* work made the Rebbe's eyes light up with joy.

This initial meeting began a relationship with the Rebbe that has spanned decades and in which Arachim and the Belzer *kiruv* organizations have worked hand in hand to help one another.

When Rabbi Wallis's eldest son, Nadav, turned 13, he drove him to Yerushalayim to meet the Rebbe, where Nadav thanked the Rebbe for his part in changing all of their lives for the better.

♦ ♦ ♦

By the time he had been running Arachim for a few years, Rabbi Wallis had come to meet many of the greatest Torah Jews alive. But he had yet to develop a relationship with the individual whom many considered to be the leader of the Lithuanian world: Rav Elazar Menachem Mann Shach *zt"l*, Rosh Yeshivah of Ponovezh and a man whose every word carried tremendous weight among his fellow *gedolim*. Were Arachim to truly be allowed to spread its wings, he needed to meet with Rav Shach and convince him of the integrity of his cause and their need for his endorsement of Arachim's mission.

Complicating matters, however, was the fact that Arachim was widely acknowledged as operating under the auspices of Rav Chaim Greineman, making the mission slightly more difficult. As everyone knows, a kingdom needs but one king, and Arachim had always been mentored by Rav Chaim. And yet Rabbi Wallis

Rabbi Wallis meets with Rav Shach

wanted a *gadol* of Rav Shach's stature to be involved as well. The question was, in what capacity?

Undaunted by challenges, Rabbi Wallis sallied forth in his quest to welcome the *gadol hador* into the Arachim family. Having had the opportunity to meet some of his right-hand men, Rabbi Wallis contacted one of the most prominent of them, an individual very close to Rav Shach, and explained that he needed to meet with the Rosh Yeshivah as soon as possible.

"Why is it so important for you to meet with the Rosh Yeshivah? You have the backing of Rav Chaim Greineman; that should be sufficient."

"Rav Shach is a world-class Torah leader and his involvement is invaluable."

The man considered Rabbi Wallis's words and couldn't help but agree. However, before recommending that Rav Shach meet with the Arachim CEO, he decided to do some investigating of his own and asked Rabbi Wallis to arrange for him to attend one of their seminars—a request Rabbi Wallis was happy to accede to. At the seminar's conclusion, the *gabbai* found himself favorably impressed and they sat down together to discuss the upcoming meeting.

"I will arrange a meeting between you and Rav Shach," he said, "and I want you to write down a list of questions to discuss with the Rosh Yeshivah."

"But I don't have any questions at present for the Rosh Yeshivah," Rabbi Wallis protested. "All the questions pertaining to Arachim have already been addressed to Rav Chaim Greineman!"

"Nevertheless," the *gabbai* insisted, "a relationship takes time to establish. You must know that by now. Asking the Rosh Yeshivah's advice is an effective way for both you and him to come to know each other. Do me a favor and present me with a list of questions for the Rosh Yeshivah; this will be the foundation on which to build a future relationship."

Having been informed of the protocol, Rabbi Wallis decided to follow the *gabbai*'s advice despite his misgivings, and to present Rav Shach with a list of approved questions.

The meeting was set for a few days later. Rabbi Wallis parked his car on one of the side streets adjacent to Ponovezh, and continued up a wide flight of steps that would lead him toward the nearby apartment building where Rav Shach resided in a world of *sefarim*. He passed the main building with its legendary golden *aron kodesh* and heard the sounds of Torah learning floating out of the open windows. And then Yossi Wallis was entering the lobby of Rav Shach's building—a throwback to the Bnei Brak of decades before. Moments later he was knocking on the door. The *gabbai* welcomed him into the *gadol's* home and he was shown to a seat.

The *gabbai* introduced him.

"Rosh Yeshivah, this is Yossi Wallis. He's a *baal teshuvah* who runs a small *kiruv* organization called Arachim and he has a few questions he wants to ask."

Rav Shach turned encouragingly in Rabbi Wallis's direction and waited for him to speak his mind, but as he stared at Rav

Shach, the rabbi found that he couldn't begin talking. Something was holding him back. A sense of wrongdoing and guilt.

He said to himself, *Yossi, you're sitting at the top of the world right now. In the presence of the person whom many consider the elder of the generation. Yet you're about to ask him questions you've already asked someone else and whose answers you know full well, just because of some form of protocol—because you want to connect with him! Protocol or no protocol, this is wrong and you can't do it. Imagine for a second if you were sitting here a few thousand years ago and instead of Rav Shach, it was Moshe Rabbeinu sitting at the head of the table. Would you fool him too?*

"Rosh Yeshivah," Yossi said, "I have to be honest with you. The truth is that I have no questions that I need to ask you. I came here today for one reason only. I would like to expand the activities of Arachim, both in breadth and scope. There is so much more to do throughout the country and all across the world; our fellow Jews are just waiting for us to enter their lives...but in order for me to drive us where we need to go, I need lots of support from the entire community and countless *avreichim* to volunteer for me. Without the Rosh Yeshivah's support, I will not be able to convince them to assist me. That is why I have come to see the Rosh Yeshivah—because I need his help in turning Arachim into the household name it has the potential to become. That will only happen if the *Gadol HaDor* is willing to become part of Arachim."

A pause.

"To conclude, I am here because I need the Rosh Yeshivah's support to turn the Arachim dream into a reality."

The *gabbai* had grown more and more agitated throughout the course of the visitor's little speech, which had completely deviated from their original agreement, and he gave him a none-too-gentle kick under the table, causing Yossi to jump out of his chair and exclaim out loud in shocked surprise!

Rav Shach witnessed the whole thing. He saw the look on his *gabbai's* face and understood that there was something taking place beneath the table. Grasping the situation in the twinkling of an eye, Rav Shach turned to his devoted *gabbai* and said in

Yiddish, "*Der mensch iz an ehrliche Yid un men darf eim helfen*" (This man is a sincere Jew and we need to help him).

Turning back in the direction of his guest, Rav Shach said, "I want to help Arachim, but I have one question for you. How do I know that you are going to run your organization in a way that I agree with and with *hashkafos* and decisions that I can support? How do I know that you will follow my path and that I won't regret supporting you?"

It was a valid question.

"I have an idea," Rabbi Wallis replied. "Why doesn't the Rosh Yeshivah appoint one of his *gabbaim* to take a seat on our oversight committee? Anytime this individual notices something that he feels raises questions, he will be there to report directly back to the Rosh Yeshivah, who will tell us how to act in that particular case. This will ensure that the Rosh Yeshivah's position will never be compromised."

"Who do you have in mind?"

They discussed a few possibilities and in the end, Rav Shach chose Rav Dov Lederman to be his man on the Arachim team. Rav Shach explained that Rav Lederman was closely affiliated with both him and Rav Chaim Greineman and would therefore be a worthy candidate for the position.

"There's one more thing," Yossi Wallis told Rav Shach.

"And that is?"

"I have to clear our arrangement with Rav Chaim Greineman before I commit."

Rav Shach told him to go ahead and do so. Rabbi Wallis's next stop was Rav Greineman's home, where he filled him in on the background of everything that had transpired since they last spoke and asked his rebbe for permission to bring Rav Lederman onto the team. Permission was granted immediately. And that was how Rav Dov Lederman came to work in a supervisory capacity at Arachim, in a relationship that spanned decades. In fact, after Rav Shach passed away, Rabbi Wallis held a meeting with Rav Lederman where Rabbi Wallis pointed out that Rav Shach had never stamped an expiration date on his involvement with

Rav Aharon Leib Shteinman and Rabbi Wallis

Arachim and that he would be honored for the *gabbai* to remain on the Arachim board for the foreseeable future. Needless to say, Rav Lederman agreed.

From the day of their initial meeting, Rav Shach and Rabbi Wallis developed a close relationship, which inevitably led to his coming in close personal contact with Rav Aharon Leib Shteinman and many other top leaders of the yeshivah world.

These relationships have continued until today and Rabbi Wallis attributes much of Arachim's incredible success through the decades to the precious cadre of *gedolei hador* who have always made themselves available for consultation, and who consider Arachim and its vital mission a top priority for the entire Jewish nation.

CHAPTER TWENTY-ONE

Even after he had become Torah observant, Rabbi Wallis still received a yearly letter calling him up for *miluim*, Israeli reserve duty. The letter ordered him to report to one of the air force bases up north for his annual month of military service. He drove up from Raanana, the soldier at the front gate checked his credentials and raised the bar, and he drove onto the base. Since it was his first day on the base and he had some free time until he'd be assigned to whatever job they needed him for, Rabbi Wallis figured that he'd look around a little bit and become acquainted with the religious services there. Not content to rely on the official air force manual, which boasted that every base had a *mashgiach* (*kashruth* supervisor) and fully equipped shul, he needed to see things for himself up close and personal. Though there were quite a few bases where the kitchen standards were up to par, there were many bases that were not and he needed to know to which category of base he'd been stationed for the next month.

His first stop was the kitchen. Soldiers were busily washing dishes, suds flying in every direction, while the radio blared pop music and the cook slid a tray of chicken out of the oven. The atmosphere was one of nonstop activity, which appealed to Yossi, but he needed to find the *mashgiach* and, try as he might, he was having a very difficult time doing that. Eventually the rabbi tracked him down in the officer's dining room, and he took a seat at his table to get a good look at whom he'd be relying on. It took Rabbi Wallis about one minute to get the impression that this *mashgiach* was doing a superficial job, if he were doing any job at all. Thinking that maybe he was being too hard on the man and expecting too much, he questioned him and asked for details as to how he supervised the food operation on base. The more he questioned him, the more he came to the realization that the man just didn't seem to care. It was not a good feeling. He was stationed on this base for the following 30 days, but there was no *kashruth* supervision and that made him very nervous. How was he supposed to eat food prepared in a kitchen manned by nonreligious soldiers and overseen by a *mashgiach* who just didn't care?

What to do?

Upon exiting the dining room, the rabbi passed the rectangular metal sink in the anteroom, and he was disappointed to see that the army hadn't seen fit to provide a plastic or metal washing cup for the use of the religious officers who needed a utensil to wash their hands for bread. Turning around he reentered the room and retraced his steps over to the "*mashgiach.*"

"There's not even a washing cup in the sink," he said.

The *mashgiach* sighed, not looking forward to having to deal with someone like this newcomer who was clearly intent on making his life miserable with demands.

"So take a plastic cup from the dining room," he replied, turning away and continuing his conversation with one of the other officers.

He really didn't care.

Rabbi Wallis wondered if he was even allowed to eat the food from a kitchen under such lackadaisical supervision. He would have to figure this out, but before he did anything, he needed to daven Minchah. There was a wooden signpost outside the dining room and one of the yellow arrows pointed him toward the base's shul. Following the arrows, he soon discovered the shul and entered the dimly lit room. As a captain, Rabbi Wallis was the highest-ranking officer in the shul; the rest of the congregation were all lesser-ranked soldiers who had been assigned to that base for the duration of their three-year stint.

When the room was reasonably full, he addressed the assembled.

"Tell me something," he asked the soldiers. "How's the religious situation on this base? Does the army provide you with everything you need?"

"No," one of them replied, "this base is terrible from a religious standpoint. It's great for the nonreligious guys, terrible for us."

"What do you mean?"

Another spoke up. "Look, Captain, the base commander is as secular an officer as you can find in the air force. He doesn't care about religion at all. Though, officially, there's not supposed to be any *chillul Shabbat* on any army bases, on this base no one even pretends to enforce the rules. In fact, the brass themselves set an attitude where Shabbat desecration is to be expected."

"How so?" Yossi asked quietly, keeping the edge out of his voice.

"Well, it can get very boring here on the base on Shabbat. Truthfully there isn't much to do and the soldiers take the army jeeps off the base for joyrides through the mountains. Yes it's illegal and against the manual, but the brass condones their behavior and even encourages it tacitly."

"Anything else?"

"Yes. There's a pool on the base for the soldiers' use and a club just adjacent to the pool. Every Friday night, there's a major party at the pool, complete with huge speakers blasting rock music: singing, dancing, and yelling until the middle of the night. Try enjoying a Shabbat meal under such conditions! Try sharing words of Torah while competing with rock music! You can't even go to sleep at a normal hour because the music is so loud that you hear it everywhere on the base—even in the shul, with the door closed and the air conditioner on. But if we try to complain to the commander, there's nobody to talk to. Just the opposite, the base commander encourages the Friday-night parties and throws his weight behind them."

"And there's nothing you can do about this?"

"We've tried talking to the base chaplain, but he's probably afraid of the commander and never does a thing about the situation here on Shabbat. By now, there's a status quo that hasn't been questioned in who knows how long, despite the fact that what goes on here is not only against halachah, but is in blatant violation of military law as well—never mind the fact that we can't even eat in the kitchen because the *mashgiach* doesn't care about *kashrut*!"

"So you guys just gave up the fight?"

"What do you want from us? We're all low-ranking soldiers. There are no officers who care enough to join the fight. Even the chaplain can't be bothered to help us out. What are we supposed to do?"

"Let me tell you what we're going to do," the rabbi said. "But first, bring me the *Sefer Torah* from the *aron kodesh*, the holy ark."

One of the soldiers removed the *Sefer Torah* and brought it over to where Rabbi Wallis stood.

"Do you see what I'm holding in my hands?" he asked the group. "This is a *Sefer Torah*. As religious Jews, we must obey everything written inside this scroll. This *Sefer Torah* is our highest authority and overrules the laws on this base. In addition, you must remember that even military law is on your side here. You have every right to object to the current situation on base. I want every single one of you to approach your superior officers and tell them unequivocally that the way the base is being run right now directly contradicts both your religious way of life and military law—and that you refuse to serve under these conditions."

He paused, taking a moment to scrutinize the group. Many of them appeared frightened by his suggestion, though a minority seemed heartened by the fact that an officer was finally standing up for them.

"If anyone questions you, wanting to know who put these ideas into your heads, feel free to blame it all on Captain Yossi

Wallis. I'm an officer in the Israeli Air Force and I'm telling you that you have every right to protest the behavior on this base."

He then replaced the *Sefer Torah* in the ark, they davened Minchah, and every soldier went his separate way. Yossi didn't know if they were planning on following his advice—it can be very scary to take an opposing stand in the military—but he made his way to the office of his commanding officer, introduced himself, and then explained that he would not be able to remain on the base.

"Why on earth not?" the officer demanded.

"Because of the blatant disrespect to religion that goes on here, which directly contradicts both religious and military law."

"What are you talking about?"

"Don't act so naive," Yossi replied. "The soldiers take the trucks and jeeps out for joyrides every Shabbat and all Friday night, there's music blasting over at the pool, and don't get me started on the state of the *kashrut* supervision in your kitchen! Haven't any of the officers on this base read the official air force rule book, which stresses that Shabbat must be kept in public?"

"It's not as bad as you're making it seem, Captain."

"Really? From what I understand, it's even worse. I'm sorry, you seem like a nice guy and I would have been honored to serve under your command, but there's something rotten happening on this base and the religious soldiers are suffering. Someone should have done something about this a long time ago. At the moment, it will not be possible for me to serve on this base under these conditions."

Turning around, Rabbi Wallis made his way to the parking lot, got into his car, and returned home, knowing that the story was far from finished. He had managed to antagonize the brass on his first day on base and they were not going to take his behavior sitting down. On the other hand, how could he possibly serve on a base where such blatant Shabbos desecration was officially condoned by the commanding officer?

It took him a few hours to drive home. He had eaten supper and was reviewing some business documents when the phone rang.

"Captain Wallis?"

"Yes?"

"This is Private Hoberman calling from the air base up north."

"What can I do for you, Private?"

"You are ordered to return here tomorrow morning for a meeting with the commanding officer of the base at 10 o'clock sharp. The CO will be waiting for you in his office."

Knowing the air force, Rabbi Wallis understood there was a good chance he'd be locked up in a military prison for his insubordination, though that had not been his intention at all. He therefore took Ozzy the dog along with him, knowing that the boxer's presence would make people think twice about arresting him without a fair hearing. Ozzy was more than happy to come along for the ride with his master and settled himself comfortably in the front passenger seat for a nice, long nap. They made good time and reached the base a few hours later, coming to a stop alongside the guardhouse.

"Name," asked the young serviceman.

"Captain Yossi Wallis."

"The commanding officer is waiting for you in his office, drive straight there right away."

The barrier was lifted and Yossi drove onto the base in the direction of the staff offices. Parking outside the two-story brick building, he walked up the staircase to the second story, Ozzy following closely behind. The door to the "inner sanctum" was guarded by the commanding officer's secretary. Approaching the desk the rabbi informed her that he had an appointment with her boss and had been told by the soldier at the front gate to present himself to the officer immediately.

As they entered the commander's office together, the officer looked from Rabbi Wallis to Ozzy and said, "What in the world is that?"

"That," the rabbi replied, "is Ozzy."

"Why did you bring him with you?"

"No special reason," he replied. "I take Ozzy along with me wherever I go."

"Sit down."

Rabbi Wallis took a seat directly across the desk from the CO, while Ozzy waited for his command.

"Ozzy, down."

Ozzy settled on the floor beside Yossi. He was a large dog, and his head ended up very close to the commander's side of the desk. From the commanding officer's perspective this was not an optimum situation, but deciding to pretend there was no dog lying nearby, the officer went on with the attack.

"I have to tell you, Captain Wallis, that what you did here on base yesterday was extremely serious. I heard how you addressed the soldiers and called for action and I want you to know that the dramatic message you delivered while holding a *Sefer Torah* in the shul has reached my ears, both from your commanding officer and from many others. Being that this is your first time serving on my base, I'm sure you can understand that we have our rules and regulations—and I'm a little surprised that you would take such an aggressive approach in trying to change the way we've been operating on this base for many years. Frankly, I've never witnessed such disgraceful behavior in all my years as a base commander!"

Rabbi Wallis looked the commander in the eye.

"Why don't we come straight to the point?" he replied respectfully, but firmly. "I arrived at the base with every intention of serving to the best of my abilities in the air force, as I have always done. Unfortunately, there are serious problems on your base that need to be taken care of. If your intention with this meeting is to inform me that you will be continuing your tradition of Friday-evening parties at the pool, complete with booming loudspeakers that disturb every Shabbat-observing soldier on the base, then I cannot back down, much as I would like to. You have both a military and halachic obligation to keep and honor Shabbat on this base. I meant every word that I said yesterday and won't be convinced that it's okay to desecrate Shabbat in public, no matter what you say."

"Captain, I want you to understand something," the commander replied. "The majority of the soldiers on this base identify themselves as secular. There is nothing for them to do here on

Shabbat. I have to provide them with some form of entertainment so that they don't go out of their minds!"

The commander spoke earnestly, as if he truly couldn't fathom where Rabbi Wallis was coming from.

"What's wrong if the soldiers take a jeep and drive out for some fun? Let them enjoy themselves, they work hard enough during the week and deserve to have a party at the pool!"

"Commander, I know that you are an exceptional pilot and outstanding officer, but I pity you very much for not knowing how to solve this problem—and I'm willing to help you if you want my help. I'd be happy to bring in lecturers and teachers who can give all these intelligent boys access to crucial Torah information that will blow their minds! Trust me, you'll find that in a very short time, you won't have a problem of boredom on this base any longer!"

"Nobody is interested in any of that archaic stuff. I have to provide them with the type of things they like to do, not the kind of things that you like to do!"

"Commander, whether you like it or not, that's the only solution that I can think of. Any other solution in which the Shabbat will continue to be violated in such a blatant fashion is unacceptable to me."

Rabbi Wallis stated his piece without rancor, but in a firm voice that made it extremely clear that his views were not up for sale.

"I do not regret the stand I took yesterday and I have no intention of backing down."

"Captain, do you understand what you are doing?"

Rabbi Wallis nodded. "I do."

"You are instigating a revolt within the base."

"Call it what you want. But the fact remains that you, as the commanding officer of this base, are defying military law on a regular basis."

"I see that I'm not getting anywhere with you."

"That's correct. I stand by my words. If you insist on maintaining your unfortunate attitude toward the religious soldiers on your base, I see no way to bridge the gap between our positions. Until I hear that things have changed or that there is at least an official willingness to take a fresh, new look at the situation, I am leaving here and going home."

"You'll be hearing from me."

"I'm sure I will."

The rabbi rose and left the building, Ozzy the boxer following closely behind.

Early the next morning the phone rang in the Wallis home.

"Captain Wallis?"

"Speaking."

"I am calling from the Kiryah in Tel Aviv. You are hereby ordered to report here tomorrow morning at 10 o'clock for an emergency hearing. The hearing will be presided over by a full colonel, the chief air force military chaplain, the commanding officer of the base, the rabbi of the base, and your commanding officer. You are to be charged with two military misdemeanors: instigating a revolt within the base and threatening the base commander with your dog. These are the charges and I would advise you to take the time to prepare a proper defense."

When Rabbi Wallis hung up the phone, the first thing he did was put in a call to the air force base up north, where he spoke with some of the religious soldiers who had been present when he made his impassioned speech with the *Sefer Torah* in his arms.

"I have been confronted with the possibility of being court-martialed," he told them, "and am facing two serious charges. I'll therefore need your help to serve as witnesses for me tomorrow at the Kiryah."

They promised to arrange leave so they could be outside the courtroom on the morrow in case he needed them to give testimony regarding the accuracy of his complaints against the base commander's ignominious disgrace of Shabbat. Rabbi Wallis had now done all he could to prepare himself for the trial. The fact that the truth and the law, both military and religious, were on his side, helped him feel a certain confidence about the trial's outcome, though being at the mercy of IAF officers was something to which he was not particularly looking forward.

♦ ♦ ♦

The Kiryah, Israel Defense Forces' central headquarters, in Tel Aviv, is located in what began as a Templar settlement founded in the 19th century, and was renamed Camp Rabin sometime after the assassination of Prime Minister Yitzchak Rabin. It is not far from the coastline and one can smell the ocean breeze from within its guarded walls. These days, the base is home to the Matcal Tower and the Marganit Tower and serves as the headquarters of the IDF general staff. The Matcal Tower was completed in 2005 and stands at a respectable 17 stories, serving as an army landmark which can be seen from a great distance, and is connected to the Azrieli Center, another Tel Aviv landmark.

All that construction, however, was yet to come on the morning when Rabbi Yossi Wallis presented himself at the Kiryah for his trial. Wherever one looked the base was teeming with soldiers, but the landscape in general tended not to call too much attention to itself. The low oceanside buildings of the '50's may have given way to taller hotels—progress can't be stopped—but the general atmosphere had resisted change.

Rabbi Wallis parked his car and asked a passing soldier for directions to the office that he needed. Ozzy was not with him on this visit and he missed his watchful presence. It would have been nice to have a friend along for the ride. Leaving his witnesses outside the door, the rabbi entered the courtroom and saluted the five men who were sitting behind the table staring at him.

"You have been charged with two offenses."

It was the colonel speaking. As the highest-ranking officer present, he was running the proceedings.

"You have attempted to instigate a revolt and threatened a senior officer with your dog."

"Why don't we begin by addressing the second charge first?" Rabbi Wallis replied, contesting the charges. "In what way did I threaten the officer?"

"By bringing your dog to his office."

"So what if I did? I certainly didn't tell him to do anything that endangered anyone. He was just lying on the floor minding his own business."

Turning to the base commander he said, "Did the dog do anything to you?"

"You threatened me."

"How?"

"When you walked into my office with your gigantic dog."

"That's correct, and I then commanded him to lie down on the floor, which he did."

The officers around the table couldn't hold back their smiles. Seeing the macho air force base commander so discombobulated by a dog would be cause for some good laughs in the officers' mess hall later on, that was for sure. Besides, every one of them understood the reasoning behind the rabbi's decision to bring Ozzy along with him.

Turning to the officers Rabbi Wallis said, "Gentlemen, do you and me both a favor and drop the threatening-dog charges. There is nothing substantial behind them and you're wasting your time. I took Ozzy with me because I take him everywhere. That's the long and short of the matter."

Bottom line, every officer in the room was smart enough to figure out that he'd brought Ozzy along just in case the commander decided to arrest him and throw him in military lockup before he was given a chance to defend himself, and they were able to identify with his actions.

If Rabbi Wallis had been fairly jocular up until that point, now he grew serious. Looking the base's military chaplain in the eye, he said, "Regarding your first charge against me, this is what I have to say.

"I would like nothing more than to remain on the base for the duration of my service. All I want is to follow my orders and do my job. I am not interested in creating disillusionment in the ranks or discord on the base.

"However, there is a long-established military rule that soldiers are not allowed to have parties and music in public areas on Shabbat within a military base. However, not only were there parties happening on the base, they were occurring with alarming frequency every single Shabbat! If you do not believe me, there are soldiers here right now waiting outside who are prepared to testify to the fact that there were poolside parties on the base every single week, with loudspeakers and live music and singing and dancing. Such behavior is misery to people trying to celebrate a peaceful Friday-night meal. Try competing with the heavy thud of the bass drum and the whine of the guitar. It doesn't work. Yet this is what happened, week after week, with no regard to the religious soldiers on the base. Simply speaking, I have zero intentions of serving on a base where the commanding officers have such blatant disrespect for the rules of the military, their religion, and for the troops under their direct and indirect command."

Here he paused.

"Never mind the Jewish rules, but at least you should be mindful of the army manual.

"All I did—and I want to stress, that everything I said was in my capacity as a loyal officer in the Israeli Air Force—was to tell the soldiers that they shouldn't have to serve under conditions such as these, and that they should make that fact clear to their commanding officers. That is a perfectly legitimate suggestion."

Turning away from the chaplain, Rabbi Wallis met the gaze of all five officers.

"Gentlemen, the matter is a simple one, both legally and morally. The moment this situation is resolved, everyone involved will be happy to do their respective army service in a heartbeat."

"Step outside while we confer," he was told.

Rabbi Wallis stepped outside.

It was clear that the officers were in a bind. The base chaplain had not been able to deny anything Yossi had said, which reflected badly on him, since he'd known about it and hadn't done anything to help the religious soldiers. The well-being of the soldiers had been violated by their senior officers and covered up by the chaplain. The entire case did not reflect well on the air force and it was obvious that the officers understood this and weren't exactly sure how to deal with the allegations.

After conferring among themselves for a while, they summoned the rabbi for their verdict.

"We have decided the following," began the spokesman. "Under the circumstances, you will not be serving in the air force any longer, unless it is in the capacity of a *mashgiach kashrut* or some other job in the air force rabbinate. Barring your acceptance of such a position, your service with the air force is hereby terminated henceforth. We will not be charging you with the original charges, in deference to your defense, but you will no longer go on serving as a regular officer in the IAF."

"Being that I've just been given a personal tour of how the air force rabbinate behaves," the rabbi replied, "I regret to tell you that I really can't see myself serving under such an authority."

"In that case," said the colonel in great tones of authority, "you, Captain Yossi Wallis, are out of the air force."

And so ended his career in the IAF.

After years of endangering his life on many occasions for his country, Rabbi Wallis had been unceremoniously terminated from his official role and would be reassigned to some other job. It mattered not that his complaint had been justified and that the senior officers were wrong. Instead of dealing with the issues that had been laid on the table and actually fixing them, the air force's preferred method of problem solving was to throw the "problem" out, while leaving things status quo, completely ignoring the needs of the religious men on base.

Though he would miss being part of the air force, Yossi did not regret his actions or the fact that he had been forced to take a stand. Shabbos was being shamed on the base, and he was not prepared to turn away and pretend that everything was okay.

Whatever the cost.

CHAPTER TWENTY-TWO

Following the Camp David Accords, Egyptian president Anwar el-Sadat and Israeli prime minister Menachem Begin signed a historic peace treaty on the White House lawn in Washington, DC, on March 26, 1979. The treaty ensured mutual recognition, cessation from the state of war that had existed up until that point, normalization of diplomatic relations, and the complete withdrawal of Israel from the Sinai Peninsula, which had been captured by Israel during the course of the 1967 Six Day War. With the signing of the treaty, Egypt became the first Arab country to make peace with the Jewish State. Sadat's political move was considered to be backstabbing by much of the Arab world, especially the Palestinians, and though Anwar el-Sadat was eventually assassinated, the treaty lives on until today—cold peace though it may be.

In the wake of these political decisions by the higher-ups in both countries, Israel was forced to evacuate the town of Yamit, which caused an absolute furor throughout the land and was accomplished with military force, though the soldiers cried their eyes out as they pulled their civilian countrymen from the doors of their homes.

In the months following Israel's staged withdrawal from a territory three times the size of what they'd previously controlled, both armies drew lines in the sand (literally, it was a desert) and placed an officer and a few soldiers from both armies at close quarters with one another as a sort of border patrol. When one section of desert was returned to Egypt, another line would be drawn in the sand and the officer and his troops would be moved to the next location, where they would sit all day and do absolutely nothing, because there was absolutely nothing to do out there in the middle of the desert.

One day Rabbi Wallis received a letter in the mail, informing him that his next reserve command was as a liaison officer at one of these desert outposts. Officially he had been chosen because he spoke English and they needed officers able to communicate with the UN forces. It was their responsibility to be polite to everyone they met and to make sure that no one crossed the line who was not authorized to do so.

♦ ♦ ♦

The army jeep dropped them off in the middle of the desert.

In the middle of nowhere.

There was nothing to look at, nothing to do, no one to talk to. It was a miserable outpost. The governments on both sides had simply drawn an arbitrary line in the middle of the desert and placed soldiers there to guard the meaningless line. It was horrible, thankless work. There was nothing but sand, as far as the eye could see.

Rabbi Wallis managed to contact his commanding officer.

"Where are we supposed to sleep and eat?"

It was one thing for their Egyptian counterparts. They knew how to live off the desert like Bedouins. The Israelis, on the other hand, were completely clueless when faced with the relentless vastness of Mother Nature. The army swung into action and it wasn't long before a flatbed truck pulled up to the border carrying a metal container, the kind used by people transporting their belongings to another country by ship. This was to be their home for as long as they were stationed on the western frontier. Army metal workers cut into the container to make a door and two windows, and when they finished working, smiled and wished the soldiers well as they drove off into the sunset. The army also delivered a tank of water that was kept on a tripod with an attached hose, and a generator for electricity. Now the troops were all set.

Rabbi Wallis had been used to being housed in the comfortable quarters of the IAF—the most respected section of the IDF, where the officers' every need was met with alacrity. This was a completely different experience. Their new home was a metal box: the sun beat down on it from morning until night, baking the metal container in the powerful desert rays and making it impossible to remain inside. The walls of the container were hot enough to fry on egg on (literally) and they had to take refuge outside in the desert sands. Even once evening arrived and the sun finally began to set, it was still almost impossible to enter the container because with the onset of night, the absorbed heat of the day began to emerge from the metal walls, giving the container the feeling of a furnace. They had a small jeep for patrols, four metal walls for protection against the elements, and they were ordered to get used to their new existence because it was not going to improve. Once in two days a jeep arrived carrying their rations for the next two days. It was so hot that by the time he'd return home four weeks later, the rabbi's skin was black and leathery from constant exposure to the desert sun and elements.

Picture the scene. Rolling sand dunes in every direction. Sun so powerful you'd find yourself squinting every time you opened your eyes. Sunglasses became the most essential article of apparel they owned. Survival became a battle of soldiers against sun. In the morning they'd find seats on the side of the container farthest away from the sun. As the day wore on and the sun kept to its relentless cycle, they'd move their seats to whichever side provided the most protection.

The troops were so bored out there in the middle of nowhere that they became friends with the Egyptian border guards. The Egyptian troops were suffering as much, if not more than they were, and since misery loves company, the two opposing sides were joined in a rare binational bond born in the crucible of the Sinai desert furnace. It wasn't long before they were playing soccer and backgammon against each other and engaging in lengthy conversations; both sides taking turns hosting the opposing team outside their containers. The Egyptian menu consisted of beans and hot water, three meals a day, seven days a week. Feeling bad for them, the Israelis shared their rations with the less-fortunate Egyptian soldiers.

For the next few years Rabbi Wallis spent his month of reserve duty out in the middle of the Sinai, being chased by the sun and playing soccer with Egyptians. The relationships they developed with their dark-skinned friends were long lasting, to the point that both sides wrote letters to one another in the years that followed, sharing life events and milestones amid the recollection of a fiery ball of light in a cloudless sky.

♦ ♦ ♦

Operation Peace for Galilee, later to be known as the First Lebanon War, commenced on June 6, 1982, when the IDF entered Southern Lebanon. With the war lasting longer than anyone anticipated, Rabbi Wallis was reassigned to a new post: this one in the opposite direction, near Israel's northern border with Lebanon. Speaking fluent English, and being part of the liaison corps of the IDF, he was to be sent into the war zone to accompany United Nations representatives and foreign journalists on their forays throughout Lebanon and to provide them with translation and any assistance they might need along the way. Ironically, his newest position was even worse than being stuck in the desert for a month, since it was incredibly dangerous. Foreign press and UN people all sported neon signs that could be seen from a distance, which identified them and kept them safe from being shot by Lebanese snipers. On the other hand, those same signs turned the Israeli officers accompanying the foreign dignitaries into sitting ducks, because it was obvious to the enemy snipers that Israeli officers were serving as their guides. The Israelis had been turned into prime targets.

On the day before they traveled up north, the soldiers were given the next day's itinerary. They would be leaving Tel Aviv by bus for Lebanon—a drive of between four and five hours. Their destination was the Lebanese town of Tzur, where they'd be quartered in the police station for the night. The police station was a heavily fortified brick building, commandeered by the army for the use of its liaison officers. In the morning they were to be dispersed to various locations throughout the military zone, with each officer responsible for a particular section of territory. They were ordered to meet at the Kiryah in Tel Aviv, where they'd be given last-minute instructions and then board the bus for the long trip.

When parting from his colleagues at Arachim, Rabbi Wallis asked one of them, Yehuda Rubin, to please keep in touch with his family, just in case they needed anything while he was away.

♦ ♦ ♦

Morning dawned. A pleasant day, with a refreshing breeze coming off the Tel Aviv coastline. The rabbi took a bus to the Kiryah, enjoying his last free morning prior to his upcoming stint in the reserves, and met up with all the rest of the soldiers traveling to Lebanon outside the Paratroopers Building. A bus stood nearby waiting for them to board, its engine idling gently, the driver reading the daily paper spread across his steering wheel. There was a nice-size lobby in the building and everyone made themselves at home on the floor—soldiers resting their heads on their duffel bags in the classic pose of soldiers at ease, as they waited for the order to board. Rabbi Wallis also found a seat in the corner of the lobby and got busy with his daily learning regimen. Dressed in pressed uniform, freshly showered, and ready to serve, he contemplated idly how different everyone was going to look in three days' time.

The order was given to board. Soldiers rose, grabbed their gear, and began heading in the direction of the bus. A female soldier stood alongside the door, clipboard in one hand, pen in the other, and proceeded to cross off names as more and more soldiers boarded and took their seats. Not in a rush to stuff himself into a narrow seat, Rabbi Wallis decided to wait until everyone boarded. Suddenly an officer appeared out of nowhere and made an announcement.

"It looks like we have too many soldiers for our current needs," he announced. "Fifty-five soldiers were ordered to report here today—50 regular soldiers and five reservists. We sent out orders to more soldiers than we needed," he continued, scratching his chin, "operating under the assumption that some of you were not going to show up. However, to our surprise, every single soldier has presented himself on time, and five of you will be able to temporarily return home until further notice. Whoever feels that they have a valid reason to be one of the five who will leave, please present yourself to me immediately."

Unsurprisingly, there was a massive rush in the officer's general direction, with each soldier attempting to persuade the officer that he was a worthy candidate for a "get out of jail card"—this one had a business, the other one's wife was expecting...

Rabbi Wallis did not rise off the floor when he heard the announcement or attempt to convince anyone of anything, knowing that even were he to succeed in convincing the officer, he'd just be ordered back to the army in a few months' time to do his 30 days. There was no reason to postpone the inevitable. So he stayed right where he was. All of a sudden, the officer walked over and tapped him on the shoulder. Rabbi Wallis looked up at him.

"Yes?"

"How come you didn't come over to me? Don't you want to go home?"

"Of course I want to go home, doesn't everyone?"

The rabbi wasn't going to approach the officer, but if he had decided on his own volition to choose him, then far be it for Rabbi Wallis to look a gift horse in the mouth.

"Then go home right now," the officer said.

"I wasn't released."

"All you have to do is get up off the dirty floor, walk over to the soldier with the pen who is standing beside the door of the bus, and tell her to erase your name from the list. She'll cross your name off and then you'll go home."

Rabbi Wallis stared at the officer for a long minute, trying to figure out if he was playing with him, but the man merely told him to get a move on. The whole thing didn't make any sense. If they would have known each other, fine. But he had never seen this man before in his life, so why was he so intent on helping him escape active service?

After a few seconds more he stopped wondering and just followed the other's advice.

Approaching the soldier at the bus, he said, "You can erase my name; I've just been released."

"Says who?"

He pointed at the officer standing across the room. "He told me to go home." The officer waved his hand at her in an unmistakable "let him go" gesture.

Shrugging her shoulders, the soldier drew a line through his name and told him that he was free to leave. And just like that, Rabbi Yossi Wallis hoisted his duffel bag onto his shoulder, turned around, and left the building and then the Kiryah behind. Standing on the bustling Tel Aviv street five minutes later, he felt utterly bemused, as if he couldn't quite grasp what had just transpired and why. But facts were facts. He'd been released through no action on his part and was free to do whatever he wanted. He could go home, go back to work at his Arachim office, go out to eat, or go learn. The whole thing was almost surreal. He'd gone from sitting on the floor of the Paratroopers Building amid cigarette butts and sunflower shells, about to head up to Lebanon for a month, to standing outside the gates, free to do whatever he wanted.

What was the next move? What to do with all the unexpected freedom?

No-brainer. Rabbi Wallis hailed a passing cab, hopped inside, and said, "Bnei Brak."

It was 10 in the morning. He could spend the day learning at Kollel Chazon Ish, one of his favorite places to learn in the city.

When the taxi pulled up at the *kollel*, the rabbi called Yehuda Rubin from a nearby pay phone.

"Yehuda, remember how I was supposed to be on my way up north right now and how I was planning on spending the night at the police station in Tzur?"

"Yes?"

"Well, I'm actually standing outside Kollel Chazon Ish in Bnei Brak right this second—long story—and I need you to send a *chavrusa* for me to learn with."

"I'm on it."

Rubin was true to his word and 20 minutes later a full-bearded scholar entered the women's section. They proceeded to spend the day productively engaged in learning. At 9 o'clock that evening, Rabbi Wallis left Kollel Chazon Ish and boarded a Raanana-bound bus for the short trip home. When he knocked on the door 40 minutes later, Sandy stood frozen, staring at him.

"Aren't you supposed to be in Lebanon?"

"Yes, but the army let me come home. Wasn't that nice of them?"

"Best surprise ever."

He got out of his uniform and ate a delicious home-cooked meal, then washed up and made an early night, grateful to have been granted this unexpected reprieve.

Morning dawned, thin slates of light filtering through the bedroom window. Always an early riser, Yossi got out of bed and joined Sandy in the kitchen before going out to daven. It being wartime, she'd already turned on the radio and was waiting for the 7 o'clock news.

"*Kol Yisrael MeYerushalayim*… The Voice of Israel from Jerusalem…"

They waited to hear the evening's developments.

"At about 3 o'clock in the morning, a truck carrying a full load of TNT and gas tanks rammed itself through the protective fence surrounding the police station in Tzur, Lebanon, and drove straight into the lobby of the building, before detonating itself in a blaze of fire that decimated the entire structure and everything inside, including a group of liaison officers who had arrived in

Lebanon that day to take up their posts in the military zone and were all sound asleep on the building's first level when the truck exploded. There are no survivors."

At that moment the liaison officers unit ceased to exist by default, since almost the entire unit had been killed. Everyone except for five soldiers released from duty, among them Rabbi Yossi Wallis, sent home to his bed by an officer he had never seen before, who had released him unasked and practically ordered him to leave when he showed little inclination of wanting to get out on his own.

For years afterward, the rabbi tried and tried to identify the officer who saved his life—with no success. Though Rabbi Wallis recognized many of the higher-ranking officers in his section of the military, he had never seen that particular officer before and never saw him again. He had appeared when the rabbi needed him most, picking him out of a group and literally saving his life before disappearing—almost as if he'd been dispatched down to earth like an angel from Heaven.

Eliyahu HaNavi? Sometimes Rabbi Wallis wonders...

CHAPTER TWENTY-THREE

It took time to work out all the details, but eventually Arachim began making inroads among the Israeli public through the seminars they offered at cut-rate prices. People loved the idea of getting away for the weekend, and if they had to participate in a few classes while on a gala vacation, it was a price they were willing to pay.

These days Arachim has a broad array of specially developed and designed courses for the general public. There are courses for couples and courses for singles. Courses for university graduates and courses for members of the academic world. And of course there are courses for the average individual. But 25 years ago things were more simple, with one type of seminar catering to everyone.

Through the years the Arachim staff has met a wide assortment of interesting, sometimes even fascinating people, ranging from widely read and intelligent college professors to actors, doctors, engineers, and restaurant owners. Yet Rabbis Wallis says he has never met anyone quite like Yossi Gevili.

Yossi walked into his life on the first day of a seminar being held in a hotel in Arad. All the guests had checked in and were settling into their rooms when a dangerous-looking man walked into the hotel lobby, escorting an elderly Moroccan woman by the arm. There was a wicked scar etched across half his face and it was obvious by the clothing he wore and the way he surveyed the room and carried himself that here was one man who was no stranger to the streets.

The staffers all had the same thought: What was this man doing at an Arachim seminar?

No one walks into Arachim seminars off the street. Knowing that there were people around Eretz Yisrael who were unhappy with their work and might consider attending a seminar with the intent of sabotaging the atmosphere, Arachim's devoted staff made sure to screen prospective attendees before permitting them to come. Yet here was a man who appeared to have wandered in off the streets of the seediest districts of Tel Aviv. The whole thing was bizarre, like seeing a cherry-red Ferrari parked smack bang in the middle of Meah Shearim.

One of the staff approached the man and the elderly woman and politely asked them what they were doing there.

"We want to join the seminar," the man replied.

"Everyone at the seminar registered before arrival," he was told, "and there's no room at the hotel. Every room is booked."

"No, no," he protested, "it's extremely important that we attend this seminar!"

Seeing the staff member shaking his head, the scarred stranger said, "Look, do me a favor and go find your boss. Tell him there's a man down in the lobby with his mother and that both of them want to attend the seminar more than anything in the world!"

He spoke with such urgency that the staffer went off to find Rabbi Wallis.

"Strangest thing I've ever seen," he told him. "Anyway, he's insisting on seeing the boss. You're on, Boss."

US president Harry Truman had a sign on his desk with the words "the buck stops here" written on it. Fully agreeing with those sentiments, Rabbi Wallis hurried down to the lobby to meet the man who didn't belong. The man and his mother were standing awkwardly in the center of the lobby when Rabbi Wallis approached and introduced himself.

"What's your name, sir?"

"Yossi Gevili. And this," he added, nodding toward the older woman, "is my mother."

"Mr. Gevili, here's the thing. You haven't registered with us and the hotel is completely full. Besides, as a general rule, we require guests to be in touch with us prior to the seminar so we can get to know them."

Yossi Gevili gave the rabbi a look. And in that look Rabbi Yossi Wallis saw a man who had been wounded by life, who was drowning in the ocean and was begging him for a life jacket.

"Listen, Rabbi," he said at last. "I know how I look, the impression I make. That's why I brought my mother with me—so that you'd give me a chance."

The next line he uttered really threw the rabbi for a loop.

"The truth is, I'm a prisoner at one of the prisons near Netanya."

Wonderful, Rabbi Wallis thought. *A prisoner at the seminar*.

"Which prison?"

"Kfar Yonah."

"I've driven past it many times."

"This is only my second furlough in seven years. After what happened the first time I was allowed out for a few days, they were very hesitant to let me out anytime soon."

The inevitable question: "What happened?"

"Oh, fights. Criminal activity. Not pretty. Now they're finally allowing me out again for a few short days."

"And you've chosen to spend your few days of vacation from prison at an Arachim seminar?"

Yossi Gevili looked at the floor, ashamed. "I figured this would be the one place where I wouldn't get into any trouble. I have to tell the warden where I am at all times. I know the warden and I know the system. Nobody can complain about me coming here. No crime to be found at an Arachim seminar. None of my friends from the streets. Only rabbis."

"Yossi," Rabbi Wallis said gently. "Even if I overlook your appearance and the fact that you didn't register and the fact that you are currently a prisoner and aren't normally allowed out on vacation due to your violent tendencies... Even if I ignore all of that—what are you going to do here for four days? People come here to listen to speeches from the top lecturers in the country. Are you the kind of person who enjoys sitting around listening to speeches?"

"Rabbi," Gevili replied, "I know exactly what I'm getting into here and I'm okay with all of it."

"There's one last problem."

"And that is?"

"And that is the fact that we honestly have no available rooms."

"Rabbi, take a good look at me. Do I seem like the kind of guy who needs a king-size bed? Do I look like the kind of guy who needs room service? Don't worry about me. After everyone settles into their rooms for the night, I'll sit myself down on one of the couches here in the lobby and get through the night. Believe me, I've slept in worse places."

"And your mother... Should I put her on another couch?"

"My mother is so happy that we're at an Arachim seminar, you could put her anywhere in the hotel and she'd be thrilled. Why don't you put her in the room with the babysitters? She won't bother anyone or get in the way. She's the exact opposite of me when it comes to getting along with people."

"Having someone sleep in the lobby is not exactly the kind of image that we're trying to achieve here, Yossi."

"I know, Rabbi, I know. Do me a favor and throw me a line here. I promise to wait until everyone is sleeping. When the lobby is completely empty and every single guest and staff member has retired for the night, I will take a seat on a couch and doze until morning. I don't need a pillow or a blanket. I'll be up before anyone even dreams about coming down for breakfast and nobody will ever know. Come on, Rabbi, I'm begging you here."

Yossi Gevili could tell that the rabbi was wavering.

"Also," he said pressing his advantage, "I'll help out with whatever you need. I'll clean up the conference room at night after all the lectures are over. I'll help set up the dining room. Whatever you need, just call my name and I'll be there."

He lowered his voice. "I don't have that much money and I know that the seminar costs a few thousand, but this is all I have."

He removed a few crumpled-up bills from his pants pocket and placed them on a nearby table, a hopeful, hungry expression on his face as he waited for the decision.

Rabbi Wallis just couldn't turn the man away. Here was a man who hadn't exactly been born with the proverbial silver spoon in his mouth, yet he sincerely seemed to want to transform himself, to change for the better. And wasn't that what Arachim was all about?

"Okay, Yossi, you can stay. You'll sleep on one of the lobby couches and we'll find your mother a bed with the babysitters. You're in."

The man's scarred face broke into one of the broadest, most honest smiles Rabbi Wallis had ever seen. His entire body seemed to glow with happiness.

For the next few days Yossi Gevili proved to be an asset for the entire staff. Whenever anyone needed assistance with anything at all, Yossi was there to provide it. He listened to every class, his face focused, his gaze unwavering, taking it all in: a model participant in every way.

Then Friday arrived.

Rabbi Wallis walked into the lobby first thing after davening and there was Yossi sitting on the couch beside his mother, their bags on the floor beside them, looking for all the world as if they already had one foot outside the door.

"Good morning, Yossi, Mrs. Gevili. Are you leaving already?"

Yossi was on his feet. "Yes, Rabbi, unfortunately we have to leave right now."

"Why is that?"

"Because my prison furlough is over. I was only given four days and there's no way in the world I'll be given permission to stay here for Shabbat."

"Let me call the warden and ask him to make an exception for one day."

"Waste of time, Rabbi. It's not up to him. There are prison rules that everyone has to obey. One of them is returning on time, no matter what the excuse."

"Do you care if I call the warden?"

"Call, but I'm telling you it's a waste of time."

Rabbi Wallis called the jail from the hotel office. He was put through to the warden.

"Hello, my name is Rabbi Yossi Wallis and I work for Arachim."

"What can I do for you, Rabbi Wallis?"

"Over the last few days I've had the pleasure of hosting one of your inmates—a man by the name of Yossi Gevili—at my seminar."

"Did he behave himself?"

"He was a perfect gentleman."

"Really?"

"Yes. He helped us throughout the seminar, set up, cleaned up, came with his mother, and was just a truly helpful and positive person to have around."

"I'm happy to hear that it all worked out okay."

"Yes, so here's my question for you. It's Friday morning, and the seminar is continuing over Shabbat. I would respectfully like to request that Mr. Gevili be granted special dispensation to remain here with us for Shabbat. He will return the moment Shabbat is over."

"Out of the question," countered the warden immediately. "Not a chance in the world. Gevili must return to the jail right now. If he doesn't return within the next few hours, he'll be in a heap of trouble."

Rabbi Wallis regretfully hung up the phone.

"Well, I guess you were right, Yossi. The warden won't hear of you remaining here for Shabbat."

"It's not his fault, Rabbi. There are official rules and he has to follow them. Anyway, on behalf of my mother and I, we would like to thank you for allowing us to join your seminar. These were truly some of the greatest days of my life!"

Yossi Gevili and his mother exited the hotel. The CEO of Arachim watched them leave and wished that things could have turned out differently.

♦ ♦ ♦

The seminar was over and the rabbi was on the road. Seeing a road sign for Netanya, his thoughts turned to Yossi Gevili, the surprise star of the recent seminar. Wasn't he incarcerated at Kfar Yonah? On the spur of the moment Rabbi Wallis decided to surprise him with a visit. First, however, he had to call the warden and ask if that was okay. The rabbi still had his number from the previous call and was able to reach him straight away.

"It's Rabbi Wallis from Arachim," he said, introducing himself. "I was in the neighborhood and wondering if—"

"You better come on over," the warden replied, not giving him a chance to finish the sentence. "Things are happening and you'll never believe your eyes."

He needed no second invitation.

Fifteen minutes later he was taking the exit and burning rubber for Kfar Yonah. It wasn't long before the jail's barbed-wire fences came into view. Guard towers surveyed the prison grounds and the coils of razor-sharp metal looked ferocious enough to dissuade anyone foolishly considering an attempt at a breakout. He pulled into the service road leading to the prison and drove until he reached a guardhouse.

"Can I help you, sir?"

"Yes, I'm here to see the warden."

The guard made a call and 10 seconds later Rabbi Wallis was entering the prison proper, where the warden was waiting for him. He was a short Yemenite man, who introduced himself as Shmaya.

"Can I offer you a cup of coffee, Rabbi Wallis?"

"Certainly."

In short course they were sitting in the warden's office sharing a companionable mug of coffee.

"So how's Yossi?" the rabbi asked.

"I have to tell you something. Since his arrival at Kfar Yonah, Gevili has always been one of our worst prisoners. He never got along with anyone, argued aggressively and constantly, was the meanest person you could ever meet, and broke all the rules. We could never let him go home for a visit, because knowing Yossi, there'd be some terrible fight 10 minutes after his arrival in the old neighborhood and then the police would have to come, and who needed the aggravation? But when he returned to the prison on Friday, he was a different person. He was quiet, polite, and even started using a *siddur* for prayer. What on earth did you do to the Yossi we knew so well, because the man who left here last week was not the same person who returned!"

"We didn't really do anything other than what we normally do at a seminar. Yossi sat in on all the lectures, listened carefully, spent some time in a different environment, and met some interesting people. We didn't brainwash him or anything."

"Well, you have to see him now. Come with me."

Rabbi Wallis followed Shmaya through locked doors that opened at his approach and past guards who stared at him with watchful gaze. Eventually they reached a yard on the side of the prison where they could see some prisoners standing in a group involved in what looked like some type of discussion.

"We grow vegetables in this garden and raise some chickens. Prisoners who behave well are rewarded by being able to spend time out here tending to the garden and the animals. Since Yossi was so well behaved these past few days, I sent him out to our farm for a couple of hours' work. Let's go over and say hello. I'm sure he'll be thrilled to see you."

As they drew closer to the prisoners, the rabbi realized that there were about 10 of them in the group. A second later it hit him: they were davening Minchah. Then he realized something even more bizarre: It was Yossi Gevili, standing in front of the assembled, who was leading the prayers! Rabbi Wallis watched in wonder as the worst prisoner of Kfar Yonah began reciting *chazaras hashatz*, the repetition of the *Shemoneh Esrei* prayer, from his *siddur*. Every time Gevili reached the end of a blessing, he'd raise his hand and motion for the rest of the prisoners to answer amen. If the response was lukewarm, he'd turn his head to stare at them in a way that made the recipients of his fierce look raise their voices with loud cries of "amen!"

After taking the three steps back at the end of *Shemoneh Esrei*, Gevili noticed the rabbi standing beside the warden and broke out into a huge smile. Seconds later he was at Rabbi Wallis's side, wrapping his arms around his new spiritual mentor and engulfing him in a gigantic bear hug.

"So Yossi, old buddy, how are things these days?"

"Rabbi Wallis, I decided to change my life around. I'm becoming religious. It's time for me to start getting serious and to do the right thing in life."

"So what's the plan?"

"The plan? I'm going to open a yeshivah here in the prison and start to learn."

Turning to the warden the rabbi said, "And you're okay with all of this?"

The warden nodded. "Yossi will receive everything he needs to learn Torah. If he wants a yeshivah, he'll get a yeshivah. The fact is, he's been a different person since he went away and if he wants to learn, then I will support him 100 percent. And it won't be only him. Yossi Gevili is a born leader. If he starts to learn, then you can be sure others will follow. He has the potential to foment serious change for the better."

"How much more time does he have here in Kfar Yonah?"

Shmaya gave Rabbi Wallis a pensive look. "Another seven years."

Rabbi Wallis took a deep breath when he heard that. Looking the warden in the eye he said, "You see what happened to Gevili after four days? Imagine what would happen to the entire prison if you provided them with the same treatment."

The warden was wary.

"What are you talking about? You know I can't send all my prisoners to your seminars."

"Who said anything about you sending people to us? I was talking about bringing my people to you. Give me the okay, and

I'll set up a five-day seminar at Kfar Yonah, with the best speakers in Israel!"

Shmaya looked at the rabbi scornfully. "You can't have a seminar in a prison!!"

"Why not?"

"It's against the law. We're not allowed to hold an event like that here. And even if I go ahead with this," he went on, "even if I give you permission to bring in speakers, you'll be dealing with men who have the attention span of a gnat. These people aren't capable of sitting and listening to religious classes for five days straight, so what's the point?"

Rabbi Wallis considered his words. "Not a problem," he said. "Instead of planning a huge happening, why don't we begin with something small and simple. One class. I'll bring a speaker, you bring the prisoners to listen to him in the prison dining room; we'll see how they react and take it from there."

The warden was intrigued.

"Here's what I'm going to do," the rabbi continued. "I was on the way to a seminar in Netanya when I decided to stop at Kfar Yonah. I'll just get back into my car and drive over to the seminar. I'll return with one of my best speakers and bring him back with me to the prison. He'll give a class to your boys and we shall see what we shall see."

Though dubious, the warden gave his okay to the wild plan.

Rabbi Wallis left the prison and drove to Netanya. On the way he mentally reviewed the A-list lecturers who were waiting in Netanya to deliver classes, trying to decide who would be the best choice to bring back with him. In the end, he chose Mordechai Arnon, formerly known as "Pupik," a popular comedian and actor turned rabbi and speaker. Pupik had been famous back in the '70's and there wasn't an Israeli alive who didn't know his name. With his easy wit and familiar speaking style, the audience was going to love him. Now he just had to convince Rabbi Arnon to come with him.

Rabbi Wallis ran into Rabbi Arnon in the lobby.

"Mordechai," he said to him, wrapping an arm around his shoulder, "I'm taking you to prison."

"What did I do?"

"You probably did something wrong."

"Seriously, Yossi, what are you talking about?"

"I want you to come with me to speak to the prisoners at Kfar Yonah."

"You're not just kidding around here?"

"No, I'm really taking you to prison with me. Don't worry, I have a good reason for doing this. Get in the car and let's go."

Rabbi Wallis told Rabbi Arnon the entire story on the way.

"So we have permission to get into the prison and—"

"I don't need permission to get into the prison," Rabbi Arnon interjected with classic humor. "I need your help getting us out of there!"

It wasn't long before they were back at Kfar Yonah. Rabbi Wallis introduced the warden to Pupik Arnon.

"Okay," the warden said, "you kept your part of the deal and I'm going to keep mine. I'll bring one section of prisoners into the dining room so we can see how you boys handle yourselves."

Twenty minutes later, the drab, functional room was filled with prisoners staring at the two rabbis like they couldn't for the life of them figure out what they were doing there. Standing up, Rabbi Wallis addressed the crowd.

"Good afternoon, gentlemen. My name is Yossi Wallis and I run an organization called Arachim. We present seminars to people all around the country and I am trying to convince the warden to allow Arachim to present a seminar to you as well. Having a seminar here will entail a few days of morning till evening classes, plus some singing and dancing. You'll have a good time. Just to be clear, however, I am reiterating to you that a seminar means a lot of lectures. Now, the warden doesn't believe that you guys have the ability to sit and listen to anything for more than two minutes. I believe that you do possess this ability. To settle this question, we are going to have a sample lecture right now, delivered by my good friend Rabbi Mordechai Arnon, whom some of you may remember from his movie-star days as 'Pupik.' After the lecture, you'll decide if you want us to hold a seminar and whether you want to commit to sitting and listening to four days of classes.

"If you like what you hear and are ready to commit, we hope to hold a seminar right here at Kfar Yonah. If not, we go away and you forget you ever met us."

Rabbi Arnon spoke for about 45 minutes, and it was evident that the prisoners were enjoying the stimulation immensely. They asked numerous questions and addressed the rabbis respectfully. The whole situation was surreal: a bunch of hardened criminals in a maximum-security prison, who were actually fascinated by the Torah they were hearing.

Speech over, Rabbi Wallis rose.

"Okay, gentlemen, decision time," the rabbi said. "What's it going to be? Seminar or no seminar, commitment or no commitment?"

The prisoners were fiercely united in their desire for a seminar, firmly committing to take it seriously. They had obviously never heard anything like this before and were filled with wonder and excitement at the Torah concepts to which they had just been introduced.

Rabbi Wallis turned to the warden. "Did you see their reaction?"

Shmaya nodded.

"Do we have a deal to hold a seminar here at Kfar Yonah?"

"Yes."

"I want your word."

"You have my word, only do me a favor and keep a low profile."

"In order for us to hold a seminar at the prison, there are a few conditions."

The warden looked startled for a second, then intrigued.

"What kind of conditions?"

"The tables in the dining room are metal. For the seminar, they need to be covered by tablecloths."

The warden smiled.

"What else?"

"The dining-room windows are covered with bars. For the seminar, we're going to need drapes or curtains."

"Anything else?"

"In the evenings after we finish that day's speeches, I'll be bringing in entertainment: singing and dancing. There will be more singing in this prison during the week of the seminar than in all the years this place has been operational."

"You drive a hard bargain."

"There's still one more thing, and this is the big one."

"What now?"

"Since every seminar includes a Shabbat as part of the program, Arachim will be spending Shabbat here at Kfar Yonah. Our staff will be moving in for the weekend. We're going to need glatt-kosher food and decent accommodations, since there's no way in the world that my rabbis will be sleeping in prison cells. If you're capable of fulfilling these conditions, prepare yourselves for an Arachim Shabbaton."

Shmaya the tough-looking warden took a deep breath and said, "Rabbi, you got yourself a deal."

♦ ♦ ♦

It was a different dining room; at least, it looked completely different. Tablecloths and drapes really make a room. With the new ambiance, one could have been forgiven for thinking it was a hostel—not a five-star hotel, but definitely a welcoming place. Close to 100 prisoners were ushered into the dining room and took their seats around the tables. There was a look of shock on many a weather-beaten, hardened face when they caught a glimpse of their dining room transformed. The prison guards made sure everyone was seated in their places and then stood on the perimeter. As time passed and it was clear that everyone in the room was completely involved in the assimilation of Torah information, the guards relaxed to a degree and sat down among the inmates to hear the words of Torah.

Rabbi Wallis couldn't believe his eyes. Shmaya couldn't believe his eyes. The inmates were asking question, the guards were asking questions. It was something out of this world!

In Arachim events the classes of the day are a prelude to the music of the night. A guitar-strumming singer helps release some of the tensions of the day, as a rousing round of song and dance transports those attending to the highest peaks of emotion.

Logic and emotion; it's not enough to have one without the other.

Logic, to break through the boundaries of years of ignorance; emotion, to allow people to rise above the decades of soul neglect and to find the joy and beauty within Torah.

Logic and emotion—an unbelievably powerful one-two punch.

Shabbos arrived at Kfar Yonah. It was the first genuine Shabbos atmosphere in that sad place. When the prisoners entered the dining room that Friday night, they stood in their places as if transfixed. The row of Shabbos candles sending out their warm glow into the coldness of the world pulled at them. They couldn't get over the freshly baked challos on every table, brown, warm, and exuding a love that had been lacking their entire lives. The staff was there for them the entire Shabbos: classes and singing and dancing and speeches and stories. Shmaya watched from the sidelines, keeping his distance, never getting involved.

On *motza'ei Shabbos*, however, Rabbi Wallis asked Shmaya to attend the symposium—the final event of the seminar—at which a portion of the participants are handed the microphone to describe their feelings and how the seminar has impacted on their lives.

Shmaya agreed.

♦ ♦ ♦

The stage was empty. The mike stood waiting in its stand. The first prisoner walked up hesitantly, unsure of himself, unused to baring his soul and emotions.

"How did you enjoy the seminar?" the questioner asked him.

"It changed my life."

"How?"

"I want to be a religious Jew now. I missed out on all the things you people take for granted. I never had any education, nobody ever shared any of this amazing information with me. That's what happens when you're raised in the worst neighborhood in the country. But I feel like everything is going to change now."

He thanked Arachim with tears in his eyes. The next prisoner walked onto the stage. Another person whose life had been dramatically altered forever. He spoke with honest emotion.

"The people who run the prisons claim that they want to rehabilitate us. They bring in criminal psychologists to analyze our behavior and to treat us. They have us meet university students who come to talk with us. They send us out to kibbutzim around the country, so we can feel the land and find our roots. But it's all a waste of time. The criminologists don't have any idea how to successfully communicate with us. These rabbis on the other hand have the secret—and the answers—and they know exactly what to say and how to say it. And it's just a shame that we were only introduced to them now, after we wasted so many unproductive years bouncing around the system.

"There's one more thing I have to say. Though we appreciate this seminar more than you could ever imagine in your wildest dreams, you have no idea what type of opposition is waiting for us when we get home. Our wives have no concept of what it means to be religious, to light Shabbat candles. They've never been introduced to the ideas which have become familiar to us over the last few days. I don't even want to imagine the scene that will greet us when our families discover that we changed so drastically!"

The rest of the prisoners nodded their heads in agreement. The man was making sense. What to do?

"Don't worry, my friends," Rabbi Wallis told them reassuringly, "Arachim will invite your wives and families to seminars that we will organize in their areas. We'll give them special rates and make it worth their while, and once they hear what you have heard, they'll understand you and it won't be so hard.

"Not only that," he continued, "maybe we'll be able to receive special permission on a one-time basis for you to leave prison and join your families for Shabbat at the seminar that we will make for them."

He turned to the warden.

"What do you say to my idea, Shmaya? Do you want to rehabilitate these people, or do you want them to spend the rest of their lives in places like this?"

Shmaya was shaking his head in exasperation.

"It's not that I don't agree with you, Rabbi, but I have a prison system to deal with and it doesn't really encourage the type of work that you do. I could get in real trouble just for allowing you to make this seminar."

Then the tough warden, with the crusty, hardened facade, couldn't hold back his feelings any longer and they could see the tears shining in his dark eyes. He wanted to help his prisoners, wanted to see them living productive lives in the outside world, but he knew how difficult it was to make that dream a reality. Shmaya stood silently for about a minute and when he realized that he wasn't going to be able to get his emotions under control, he exited the room. Every eye followed his broad, capable back—the prisoners exchanging knowing looks with one another, because they knew that their warden was choking up in a most unseemly manner for a warden, but not for a caring human being who wanted the best for the people under his control.

In the end, many of the inmates returned to a life of Torah and mitzvos. Once the Arachim staff saw that they were serious in their newfound desire to change, they began making phone calls to the prisoners' wives and families. Many of them made the decision to attend a seminar, and sometimes they even got permission for the prisoner to join his family for Shabbos. In this way, Arachim was able to achieve a significant breakthrough within the population of Kfar Yonah.

And fascinatingly enough, Yossi Gevili was the cause of all of this.

So impressed was Shmaya the warden with Gevili, that he was willing to facilitate pretty much any change needed to assist him in his quest to reinvent himself as a Torah Jew. Shmaya was even willing to turn a prison cell into a *beis midrash* for the erstwhile bad boy of the prison. He also allowed a daily influx of *avreichim* from Netanya into Kfar Yonah to serve as rebbeim for any inmate who wanted to learn Torah. Within a very short time Yossi Gevili went from being a feared, aggressive bully who controlled much of went on among the prison population to a purveyor of Torah learning and uplifting thought. This in turn was the cause of an indirect shift in the entire atmosphere of his section of the prison, so much so that Arachim was able to secure Gevili's release from Kfar Yonah two years later, citing such reasons as good behavior and his beneficial influence on everyone around him.

"You are asking us to release Gevili," said the spokesman of the parole board, "when he has five years left to the end of his time. While we have verified your claims about Gevili and his apparent change of heart, we still need to know that he will have a worthwhile job outside the prison when he rejoins civilian life."

And so Arachim promised to provide Yossi with a job.

Which they did, taking responsibility to make sure that he wouldn't lapse into old behavioral patterns. He became a driver for Arachim—ferrying rabbis to speaking engagements around the country. This kept him surrounded by eminent *talmidei chachamim* and also provided him with opportunities to listen to countless Torah lectures. After he'd been with the organization for a while, the staff felt that he'd matured into someone capable of getting married and settling down, and it wasn't long before Yossi Gevili met his future wife and the rabbis of Arachim were celebrating at their wedding, and then at the *kiddush* that Yossi made for his first child.

That's *nachas*.

♦ ♦ ♦

One afternoon, there was a surprise visitor at the Arachim offices in Bnei Brak. Rabbi Wallis's secretary knocked at the door.

"Rabbi, Yossi Gevili's mother is here to see you."

"Show her in."

Mrs. Gevili took a seat in one of the leather armchairs surrounding the conference table and the secretary brought her a glass of tea.

"Rabbi Wallis, I just wanted to thank you for everything you did for my son. He has a wife, a home, a job. Honestly, I never dreamed that my Yossi would be able to attain any of those things."

He had to agree with her. Yossi had traveled an impossibly long way from where he'd been when they had first met. Almost as if there were two different people named Yossi Gevili.

"Rabbi Wallis," she continued, "I just wanted to tell you about something that happened to Yossi when he was a child."

Her wrinkled face had the look of a tragic map of the past.

"It happened at his bar mitzvah."

There were fat tears perched on the corners of her eyes poised to emerge.

"When they lifted the *Sefer Torah* at his bar mitzvah, the person who picked it up didn't realize that there was a revolving ceiling fan spinning rapidly not far above the table."

She swallowed.

"The *Sefer Torah* hit the fan. The fan was moving with such speed that it broke off a sharp wooden piece from the Torah's crown, which flew through the air and hit my Yossi right in the face, scarring him for life on what was meant to be the happiest day of his childhood. Instead, we spent his bar mitzvah in the emergency room. They stitched him up, did their best to ease the pain. But they couldn't do anything about the scar. Or the fact that he lost eyesight in one of his eyes."

She sighed heavily and continued her tale of sadness.

"The children in the neighborhood used to laugh at Yossi and tease him about his scar, and after a while he couldn't take it anymore and began to fight back, until not a day passed without him getting into a fight with someone else. This went on and on, with Yossi becoming more and more bitter until it reached a point where he gave up on normal society and found a group of friends that accepted him for who he was. But they weren't good kids. Not at all. Things got really bad after that, and as he grew older, his friends were worse and worse until he had become part of a group of neighborhood criminals. Now it wasn't parents knocking on my door anymore, but the police. And then he was caught doing something bad enough that the judge decided to send him away for a whole bunch of time in prison.

"Rabbi, until we met you, I was sure that he'd be spending the remainder of his life in prison because the first time they let him return home for a short visit, he managed to find trouble almost immediately. The warden didn't trust him and wouldn't allow him any vacations. And now look at him. Married with a child. I have a grandchild. He has a wife and a job with responsibilities. You've made a man out of my son."

♦ ♦ ♦

After the extremely positive prison experience at Kfar Yonah, Arachim came to the realization that the Israeli prisons were fertile ground for outreach and should be made a focus. With this in mind they arranged a meeting with some of the top brass at the Israel Prison Service. The meeting took place in a conference room at the Vizhnitz hotel in Bnei Brak. On the agenda was the possibility of Arachim's future involvement in the rehabilitation of thousands of prisoners.

The IPS refused Arachim's request.

"If we allow you into our prisons," they explained, "you will be taking advantage of the distress of the prisoners and the natural vulnerability inherent in their situation to turn them into *baalei teshuvah*, which is not something we can allow you to do."

Naturally Rabbi Wallis protested their shortsightedness.

"Look at what Arachim managed to achieve in so short a time at Kfar Yonah," he argued. "What the staff accomplished for the prisoners was way more effective than a million meetings with criminologists, students studying for their psychology exams, or sending them to live on kibbutzim! Admit it, the results were impressive."

"We're sorry, but the work Arachim does has been compared to missionary activity. It's not allowed."

"You're comparing introducing Jewish people to their heritage to Christian missionaries?!"

But they wouldn't budge, no matter how Arachim argued the case or explained their position. They maintained that allowing

Arachim to rehabilitate the prisoners was against the law, and no argument made a dent in their way of thinking. In the end, Rabbi Wallis had to comfort himself with the knowledge that at least Arachim had managed to make inroads within the prisoner population at Kfar Yonah. Yes, they could have done so much more, but ultimately, we live in an imperfect world and have to accept that sometimes, there are certain things that we just cannot change.

CHAPTER TWENTY-FOUR

In many situations, when people become *baalei teshuvah*, they choose to give up all the things they used to enjoy before they were religious. That can be a mistake. Being religious does not mean that a person has to undergo a complete personality change. Even if they do want to fit into their new lifestyle, they should consult a rabbi who knows them well and who can guide them as he suggests appropriate stages of change.

The Wallis family might have become religious, but they were still very much their own people who enjoyed many of the same hobbies and activities they had always liked.

Including pets.

One of those pets was a parrot.

A parrot named Pepe.

What Pepe the parrot did and what Pepe the parrot accomplished was far beyond the scope of a normal African gray.

♦ ♦ ♦

The Wallis family enjoyed wildlife. In the backyard of their Raanana home there were birds and a fishpond where you could watch a nice assortment of colorful fish swimming back and forth. For a while they even had two horses and a goat. And of course there was Ozzy, who kept watch over everything and everyone. But the star of the menagerie was a parrot named Pepe, an animated African gray who loved to repeat the things he heard at home. After the family became religious, Pepe's vocabulary increased and took on a whole new sound as he started regularly dropping phrases like "*Baruch Hashem.*"

When Pesach time arrived and the children were learning the "*Mah Nishtanah*" by heart, Pepe could recite it before they could. Pepe's favorite song was the "*Shalom Aleichem*" with which the Wallis family greeted the Shabbos Queen; not being overly picky about dates or times, Pepe sang it anytime he was in the mood, no matter what day of the week it was.

Pepe possessed a wicked sense of humor. During the years that he lived with the family there was an Australian terrier at home as well, and for the most part the two of them got along well. A point of contention, however, was Pepe's enjoyment of dog food. Anytime he was let out of his cage, he'd head straight for the terrier's bowl and begin sampling. Needless to say, this was not looked upon kindly by the dog, who objected vigorously, raising a hue and cry that could not be ignored. Pepe, having caused the commotion, would then nip the dog's nose with his beak, sending the dog into total hysterics and causing him to run back and forth barking frantically, while Pepe would calmly partake of even more of his food.

Pepe knew the terrier's name and wielded that knowledge like a weapon. At times the dog would be outside in the garden and Pepe would call his name.

"Gremlin, Gremlin," he'd squawk in an uncanny replica of one of the children's voices. The dog, hearing his name, would come running into the house, eager to be of service, and find to his dismay that there was no one there and that he'd been the butt of yet another one of Pepe's practical jokes.

On one occasion the Wallis family decided to do some renovations on the top floor of their home. The contractor brought his Arab workers into the house, and while one of them got to work on the top level, the other remained down below, sending tools and materials to his friend up above. Pepe watched the goings-on, his sharp, intelligent eyes taking it all in. It wasn't long before he'd learned the names of the workers and was able to accurately copy their voices. One day, Pepe started calling the name of the worker on the third floor.

"Achmed!"

Achmed heard his name being called and yelled down, "What?"

No one answered because no one had called his name. Achmed, thinking that his fellow worker hadn't heard him, rushed down the stairs to ask him what he wanted, only to learn that no one had called him.

"But I heard you call me!"

"Can't be," insisted the first-floor worker. "I didn't say a word. I wasn't even here!"

Achmed shrugged his shoulders and trudged back up to the third floor. Two minutes later Pepe called him again.

"Yes?"

"I didn't call you!"

"But I heard you calling my name!" Achmed was getting angry now.

"It couldn't have been me. I was outside the entire time mixing cement!" The second worker was getting all worked up now too. "I just came in now!"

Before anyone knew what was happening, a fistfight had broken out between them—grown men rolling on the floor, beating each other up—with Pepe taking it all in from the safety of his cage. In the end, Rabbi Wallis had to move Pepe outside, so they'd be able to work in peace. The story reminded him of what had occurred at the Tower of Babel, and was still another proof of how communication is the key if one wants to achieve results.

During the meal one Friday night, they were sitting round the table, eating, drinking, and enjoying conversation with their guests, when Pepe, who wasn't in the room, began imitating the sound of a ringing phone. After he'd allowed the "ringing" to go on for long enough, Pepe "answered" the phone and said, "Hello, *mah nishma? Baruch Hashem!*" The guests, under the impression that the Wallis family was religious and didn't answer the phone on Shabbos, were taken aback, and the Wallises had a great time explaining exactly who had called and who had answered. Just another example of the spice that Pepe added to their lives.

♦ ♦ ♦

Not everyone knows this, but people who keep parrots as pets have the unenviable job of clipping their wings every so often, to keep the parrots from flying away. Being very busy with Arachim, there were times when the rabbi didn't get around to clipping Pepe's wings when he was supposed to and then, instead of having to deal with the relatively small length of time it would have taken him to clip the wings, he had to spend much more time searching for his beloved parrot when Pepe inevitably took to the sky and couldn't find his way home.

It was a Friday afternoon, and the Wallises were sitting in the garden enjoying the peace and tranquility of a long summer day. Pepe was out of his cage, keeping them company on his perch and regaling one and all with songs and general parrot wisdom. The adults sipped at coffees, the kids drank liquid sugar, and Pepe sang. It was a beautiful day and all was right with the world.

In Eretz Yisrael, most water is heated with a device called a *dud shemesh*. Today, these solar water heaters often lie flat on roofs, but back then the *dud shemesh* stood upright and could be seen from afar. Suddenly, without any warning, the *dud shemesh* started to leak. The stream of water landed directly on Pepe's head, frightening him and causing him to take off into the sky. Having never seen their home from a bird's-eye view, Pepe became disoriented and couldn't find his way back. The family watched as Pepe flew back and forth and then out of sight. The children burst into tears at the sight of his empty perch. Pepe had been a very friendly bird whose presence added much to their home, and the fact that they might never see him again was cause for huge distress.

They recalled him fondly. How he'd perch genially on their shoulders, making funny comments whenever he felt like it. How he would fly across the room on a Friday night to snatch a particularly luscious-looking strand of noodles out of one of the soup bowls, or a leftover chicken bone. It was a terribly sad Shabbos meal they had that night—the sight of Pepe's empty cage bringing some of the children to tears—but there was nothing anyone could do about it. Pepe was gone—disappeared from their lives, and they were just going to have to get used to it.

♦ ♦ ♦

A year passed. Though not having Pepe around had been difficult at first, the family had accepted it, and the sight of his empty cage didn't reduce the kids to tears as it did when he'd first gotten lost.

One morning, Rabbi Wallis was sitting at his desk in the Arachim office when one of the Arachim rabbis came to see him seeking advice.

"Rabbi Wallis, I have a problem."

"What's going on?"

"There's a family living in Kfar Saba named Harari, who recently became *baalei teshuvah*."

"Doesn't sound like a problem to me."

"Wait, I didn't get to the problem part yet."

"Go on."

"Anyway, since they're all fired up about becoming religious, they offered Arachim their home as a place where we could hold *shiurim* for their friends and neighbors."

"Still don't see the problem."

"Getting there."

"Go on."

"The problem is that this family loves animals and they own this big parrot that doesn't seem physically able to shut its mouth. Every time a speaker comes to the house to give a class, the parrot throws in its two cents in the middle of the speech and sends everyone sitting there into hysterics, which is cute and fun, but really kills the classes."

"And you want me to—?"

"To talk to the host and request that they please move the parrot out of the living room during the classes so as not to lose the serious atmosphere needed to impart Torah."

"Can't you just ask the father to move the bird?"

"I asked him, but he wasn't interested, claiming that the parrot is part of the living-room décor and that they never move him. Anyway," the staff member went on, "it wouldn't be a bad idea for you to speak to him regardless of the whole parrot affair, because you like animals yourself and you can give him an introductory course to the numerous laws involving animals: how and when to feed them, Shabbos care, the laws of *muktzeh*, and everything else. And, please convince Avi Harari to get that parrot out of the living room during the classes."

So the rabbi called up Avi Harari.

"Shalom, Avi, my name is Yossi Wallis and I'm calling you from Arachim."

"What can I do for you?"

"I don't know if you know this, but we're practically neighbors."

"Really?"

"Yes, you live in Kfar Saba and I live in Raanana and I'm surprised that we haven't run into each other until now."

"I guess Israel is growing."

"I guess it is. Anyway, I'm calling you because one of my staff mentioned that you're a bunch of animal people, and quite frankly so are we and—"

"You love animals?"

"You better believe it. We have all sorts of them at home. You name it, we have it, and I figured that who better than me to give you a halachic overview about the things you need to know when it comes to animals and living a Torah lifestyle."

"I'd love to find out more," Avi Harari said sincerely.

So began a really interesting conversation. Harari had lots of questions and Rabbi Wallis was able to answer them from the perspective of someone who had been there himself. Their conversation meandered and drifted and at one point, the rabbi began to reminisce about their African gray parrot and how he had flown away about a year before. They had barely begun discussing Pepe the parrot when Harari cut the conversation short.

"Rabbi Wallis," he suddenly said, "I'm sorry, but I have to go now. Maybe we'll talk another time."

Then he hung up. Just like that. It was bizarre, especially since they were really having a wonderful conversation, but the rabbi shrugged his shoulders philosophically and got back to whatever it was he'd been doing before the phone call. He was busy and had no time to worry about why someone had chosen to hang up on him. If he was meant to find out, he would. In the meantime, there was work to be done.

♦ ♦ ♦

Harari called him back the next day.

"Rabbi."

"Yes, Avi?"

"Remember how I cut the conversation short yesterday?"

"Yes."

"Do you want to know why I did that?"

"Yes."

"Okay. It's because I think that the parrot that flew away from your home a year ago is now living in my house in Kfar Saba. Since I love that bird and truthfully have no desire to see it go live somewhere else, I told you that I had to go, and I hung up on you. But my conscience bothered me and wouldn't allow me to just go on living with a parrot that might not belong to me. So I called the rabbi of Kfar Saba to ask him what I'm supposed to do in this situation."

"What did he say?"

"He recommended that I call you back and tell you the truth. He also suggested that you come to my house to try and identify the parrot and that if you were able to do so successfully, then the parrot belongs to you and there is really nothing to do about it, no matter how much I love it."

Rabbi Wallis was very excited by what Avi Harari was telling him and promised to come over to see the parrot (and to hopefully identify it as Pepe) as soon as possible. He drove up to the Harari residence in Kfar Saba and Avi welcomed him into the house. He escorted his guest into the living room, where the contested parrot stood perched on his stand, staring at everyone with beady eyes that showed no sign of recognition.

The problem was this: All African grays look pretty much the same.

Now what?

Avi Harari looked at Rabbi Wallis, who shrugged a little helplessly.

"Look, Avi, this is kind of difficult. Pepe doesn't really have a physical sign, but I have an idea how we can figure this thing out."

Harari was all ears.

"Why don't we take the parrot over to my house? I trained Pepe to say the names of all my kids."

"How did you do that?" he asked, amazed.

"Every time one of the kids passed by Pepe, they'd call out their name," Rabbi Wallis explained, "so that Pepe came to associate the sight of the child with the sound of that name. Pepe was a master of speech by association and the approach worked well. The approach only backfired a little when it came to the names of my wife and I. Pepe heard my wife calling me Yossi and me addressing her as Sandy, which led him to the conclusion (obvious to him) that I was called Sandy and my wife was called Yossi. Every time I'd pass by his cage or perch, he'd greet me with a nice parrot screech and a 'Sandy!' while my wife received the same adoring treatment only with my name. There's a good reason they're called 'birdbrains.'"

Harari agreed that this experiment might be just the thing to determine the identity of the parrot. Bundling the African gray into his cage, they maneuvered him into the car and drove him over to the Wallis home, where his cage was placed in the living room. Then they told all the Wallis kids to pass before him. It was a huge moment for the Wallis and Harari families (Avi had brought his kids along with him for the trial) and all of them waited to see how this thing would be settled. It was as if they had stepped back in time, to the court of Shlomo HaMelech in Yerushalayim thousands of years earlier.

One by one, the kids passed before the parrot's cage. Ruti walked by. Racheli walked by. Shaike walked by. A palpable silence emanated from the cage, almost as if the parrot were punishing them—or teasing them—by not saying a word. Though he kept silent, inside Rabbi Wallis was urging the parrot to open his mouth and say something.

Do me a favor, he silently begged the bird, *and say one of their names! C'mon, you can do it!*

All of a sudden, the bird opened its mouth and squawked, "Shaike! Ruti! Racheli!"

The rabbi turned to Avi and gave him a look.

Avi spread out his arms in surrender and said, "I guess I can't ask for better proof than this."

He then agreed to leave Pepe with his family and Rabbi Wallis gave him some money toward the purchase of another bird, since he could see how disappointed the Harari kids were by losing their beloved parrot.

As they were leaving the house the rabbi turned to Avi. "Before you go," he said, "you have to tell me how Pepe ended up at your house."

"It's a funny story," Harari replied. "The backyard of my house in Kfar Saba lies adjacent to the soccer field of HaPoel Kfar Saba. So close that we actually share a wall. You said that Pepe flew away on a Friday, right?"

Rabbi Wallis nodded.

"That Shabbat, there was a game being played on the soccer field about 12 o'clock in the afternoon. In the middle of the game, a parrot suddenly flew down onto the field. The referee could tell that this was no ordinary bird and blew his whistle for a time-out. He stopped the game, approached the bird, and picked it up to remove it from the field. Knowing that I'm into rare and exotic animals, the referee walked over to the wall separating my yard from the field, saw me sitting in my yard, and told me that he was about to throw a parrot onto my property."

Appreciating the African gray for the special bird that it is, Harari accepted it with thanks and brought it into his house, where it perched in the living room and accepted choice tidbits of food from the family members.

"The parrot was obviously tired and famished, not having received any nourishment since leaving your house, and it partook of the food and water greedily. A few days went by and the parrot began returning to itself, sitting up straight, making eye contact with the children, and eventually opening its mouth and talking to us. But the words that came out of its mouth had never before been heard in our home.

"The first thing he said was '*Baruch Hashem*.' This was followed by '*Shabbat shalom*.' Before we'd gotten over our shock at having adopted a rabbinical parrot, the parrot started to sing '*Shalom Aleichem*'!

"Our children were filled with wonder at the situation.

"'Look, Abba,' one of them pointed out, 'this parrot flew down to our home from Heaven and instead of just saying anything, every word coming out of his mouth has to do with religion. Maybe this is a sign for us?'

"There was no way to ignore the phenomenon. Pepe had a comment for every occasion and the sound of his playful counsel and wise voice filled our home. In the midst of our everyday conversations he'd feel compelled to interject his two cents with a sincere '*Baruch Hashem*' or a heartfelt '*Shabbat shalom*.' It wasn't long before thoughts of religion were on all our minds and eventually we made the collective decision to attend an Arachim seminar where we could learn in depth about all the things the parrot was trying to teach us. We felt that if being religious was obvious even to a parrot, surely we should be willing to give it a real chance. We attended the seminar and decided to become *baalei teshuvah*. Of course you know that we were convinced by what we heard, and so taken were we by our decision that we even opened our hearts and home to Arachim, so the staff could offer home classes for our friends, acquaintances, and neighbors in Kfar Saba and convince them to give Arachim a chance as well."

Now Rabbi Wallis understood the entire story.

The *hashgachah* was beautiful. The speakers hadn't been able to lecture properly with Pepe singing "*Mah Nishtanah*" in the background (though Pepe was clearly just trying to assist the people from Arachim). This had led to Rabbi Wallis being asked to speak with Avi Harari, and had culminated with the Wallis family's reunion with their beloved Pepe, who resumed his previous activities of flying across the room for noodles or a chicken bone and singing all his favorite songs, charming them all as he had in the past.

"You little rascal," the rabbi said to him from time to time. "Look at you. It's obvious that you are an Arachim parrot. I mean, what other parrot would make an entire family religious and convince them to attend a seminar!!"

Pepe would stare at him, eyes not blinking and then without warning call out, "Sandy!"

They knew he was a parrot and didn't understand the results of his actions, but sometimes, it really seemed that Pepe knew exactly what he was doing.

◆ ◆ ◆

You'd think that after Pepe flew away once because the rabbi had forgotten to clip his wings that he'd make sure to clip them "religiously" in the future. And yet there were times that Rabbi Wallis did forget, which brings us to Pepe's escape number two. Once again it all started on a Friday afternoon. Like the last time, they were all sitting on the patio enjoying the sunshine and some coffee. Pepe stood perched in his usual spot giving his opinions on life from time to time. Since he was no youngster (African grays can live up to 100 years of age) everyone listened respectfully.

Taking a sip of coffee, Rabbi Wallis realized that it wasn't sweet enough, and he rose to go to the kitchen for sugar. At that moment, one of the neighborhood cats decided that Pepe had the look of a tempting morsel. Clearly imagining how delicious the giant parrot would be on his plate, the cat made a sudden flying leap toward Pepe and attempted to knock him off his perch. Pepe caught a glimpse of a wild fur ball flinging itself at him and took off into the wild blue, intent on putting as much distance as possible between himself and the attacker. With Shabbos rapidly approaching, there was no time to search for the bird and they were resigned to the fact that they might never see Pepe again.

Come Sunday morning, however, Rabbi Wallis decided to make an attempt at getting him back. Sitting down at the kitchen table he wrote out copy for an ad to be published in one of the local Raanana newsletters. Detailing what happened, he asked fellow Raanana inhabitants to be on the lookout for the parrot. He even offered a reward.

On the way to the newsletter's office he dropped in at the local pet shop.

"Do me a favor," he said to the man behind the counter. "My parrot flew away last Friday. If anyone comes into the store looking to purchase a cage or starts asking you about an African gray, please get his phone number and put us together so I can get my bird back."

The man smiled.

"I have some news for you. Friday afternoon just prior to closing time, a car pulled up right outside my store and honked his horn at me in such a way that I understood that he wanted me to come outside to see him. So I went. I approached the car, while the guy inside lowered the window and motioned me over.

"'What do you want?'

"'I found this bird,' he told me, gesturing at an African gray perched on the backseat, 'and I don't want to leave him alone in the car. Would you be willing to bring a cage for the parrot and some bird food and coax the parrot out of the car and into the cage?'

"So I went into the store and brought out a cage and did exactly as he wanted. Then, after the parrot was safe and sound and the man had everything he needed, I accepted his money and he turned to go. But before he left, I asked him for his phone number.

"'Why do you want my number?' He was suspicious.

"'You found the bird in this area, right?'

"He nodded.

"'Just in case the owner of the bird comes to see me searching for his parrot, I want to be able to point him in the right direction.'

"In the end he gave me his number slightly begrudgingly, clearly hoping that no owner would call. Take down the number, give him a call, and good luck getting your parrot back."

Rabbi Wallis called the number and the man answered the phone.

"Yes?"

"Hello, my name is Yossi Wallis and I received your number from the pet shop owner when I approached him 10 minutes ago asking if he'd seen my parrot."

From his reaction the rabbi could tell that the stranger suspected him and the pet shop owner of having joined forces to defraud him of the expensive and rare bird that he'd found, and that they were only in this for the money.

"I don't believe that this is your parrot. I think you're in cahoots with the pet shop owner."

He delivered this line in the flat tones of a man about to hang up the phone.

"It's really my parrot. His name is Pepe and he's an African gray!"

"If he is your parrot, give me some proof."

"What kind of proof do you have in mind?"

"I'll ask you a question about the parrot's behavior and let's see if you know the right answer."

"You're on."

"Okay, here's the question."

Rabbi Wallis waited tensely.

"What does the parrot do when someone drinks while standing near him?"

The rabbi smiled. It was actually a really good question and if Pepe hadn't been his parrot, he would never have guessed the answer. But he knew Pepe and his eccentric ways.

"He burps," he replied.

The man softened. "I guess it is your parrot."

"I can give you another proof. Bring the bird over to my house and when Pepe catches sight of me, you'll see that he'll call me Sandy and my wife Yossi."

Ten minutes later the man appeared with Pepe and cage in tow.

When Pepe saw the rabbi, he called out, "Sandy!"

"I know when I'm beaten," the finder said, raising his hands in good-natured defeat. "He's all yours."

"Thank you. Now please tell me how and where you found Pepe."

"Okay. I'm a gardener. Last Friday, I was doing some landscaping on the front lawn of one of the neighborhood houses, when the parrot suddenly flew down to the ground nearby. I approached him slowly, trying not to scare him, and Pepe jumped right onto my outstretched arm. Not wanting to lose him, I walked really slowly over to my car and maneuvered him inside so he wouldn't fly away and disappear. You know the rest. I drove to the pet shop, purchased the cage, and gave the owner my phone number when he asked for it. Then you called and proved that he was yours and now here we are."

The friendly gardener had been a good messenger and the least Rabbi Wallis could do was invite him in for breakfast. Over omelets and orange juice, they got into a nice conversation. The rabbi asked him all about his line of work and he described the enjoyment he received from seeing a garden perfectly sculptured.

"And what do you do?"

"Me? I'm the CEO of Arachim. I do *kiruv*. You know, Jewish outreach."

"Really!! That's amazing!"

"Why is that amazing?"

"Because you know how to talk to secular people about religion."

Rabbi Wallis could see that his new friend had something on his mind that he wanted to discuss.

"Do you want to ask me something?"

"Well," he replied, slightly embarrassed and a little at a loss for words, "I've been going out with this girl for a while—"

"And?"

"And she's a Filipino girl. Really nice and sweet and I want to marry her."

The rabbi had heard this story a million times before.

"So you went down to the Rabbanut and you found out that for her to convert was going to be a huge ordeal, right?"

He gave his host a look. "You know the drill, huh?"

"I meet people in your situation every single day."

Now the gardener's face held a hopeful look.

"Can you help me settle this thing? Maybe speak to someone at the Rabbanut who can help speed up the process? I don't want to wait 10 years to marry her!"

"Of course I can help you straighten the whole thing out," Rabbi Wallis replied. "But first, I want you to attend an Arachim seminar so you can also learn what it means to be a Jew. I mean, you're making this non-Jewish girl convert so she can marry you, when you yourself don't know the first thing about what it means to live a Jewish life. That's not exactly fair, is it?"

He considered this for a minute.

"I guess not. What do you propose?"

"Come to Arachim for an extended weekend. Hear some classes about Judaism that will give you a whole new perspective and then you'll have a much better idea what you're talking about."

The man signed up for a seminar a few weeks later. Asked a thousand questions. Heard an answer to every one. And decided to become religious. In the process he found himself another girlfriend—one who was Jewish this time. Last Rabbi Wallis heard, they were happily married and building a beautiful Jewish home.

But the story wasn't finished yet. The pet shop owner had done Rabbi Wallis a good turn and deserved to know the story's outcome. Standing inside the pet store surrounded by frolicking puppies and mewling kittens, slithering snakes and brightly colored fish swimming around well-lit tanks, the CEO of Arachim thanked the owner for his help.

"You see what happened, you took a number, gave it to me, and the result—I got Pepe back. What a mitzvah you did! By the way, this wasn't the first time Pepe got away. It happened once before and when he landed on the soccer field of HaPoel Kfar Saba, it led to an entire family's decision to do *teshuvah*!"

The pet shop owner was properly overwhelmed by the chain of events.

The next morning, one of his pet food suppliers dropped in to deliver his weekly load. The owner, still excited about Pepe (the "rabbinical" bird) and the whole cause-and-effect thing, shared the entire chain of events with the man from the pet food company.

"I can't believe this story," enthused the deliveryman. "I have to meet this man and his unbelievable bird!"

So the pet store owner gave him the rabbi's number. He called up and after introducing himself, told Rabbi Wallis that he'd heard all about the amazing Pepe and that he wanted to see the African gray for himself. The rabbi invited him over to meet Pepe the parrot and sure enough, they found themselves in deep conversation—the outcome of which was his decision to attend an Arachim seminar, so he could see for himself what the excitement was all about. It wasn't long before he too decided to become religious.

In the wake of Pepe's incredible success in the field of outreach, Rabbi Wallis likes to tell people, "If a bird can make people *frum*, why can't you?"

♦ ♦ ♦

Sandy preferred keeping the animals outside the house. With this in mind, her husband began keeping Pepe outside in a cage in the garden. Though the lock mechanism of the cage involved a four-step process to open it, Pepe was smart enough to figure out how to open the door all by himself. One day, Pepe opened the door of the cage, surveyed his domain one last time, spread his wings (once again, in need of a clipping), and flew away—intent, no doubt, on spreading Torah among more and more Jews.

The family has not yet been reunited with their beloved parrot, but Rabbi Wallis hopes to meet yet another person one day who will tell him about a parrot that convinced him and his family to become religious.

And Rabbi Wallis will know that Pepe the parrot is still out there doing the work he does best.

BOOK FOUR

REUNIONS

CHAPTER TWENTY-FIVE

Rabbi Yossi Wallis is not one of the official lecturers for Arachim. He's not one of the rabbis who stands up to prove Hashem's existence to the audience. He's not the one they call upon to prove that the Torah was given on Sinai. That's not his job or field of expertise. Arachim has others who do that amazingly well and he's not needed there. He does something else. He tells the guests at the seminars his story. He usually shares it with them during the second day of the seminar, a time when people are starting to relax and to realize that Torah-observant people aren't so bad after all. That's when he speaks to them: from the heart.

Many times when he speaks, he tells the crowd about an old friend of his from the past.

A friend who helped him when he needed it most.

A friend who had what it took to become successful within the complex hierarchy of the New York families of crime.

A friend named David.

♦ ♦ ♦

David and his old friend the rabbi spoke and visited occasionally, keeping up with each other. Even though the days they'd spent together back in the Bronx had been painful in many ways, and even though there were things the rabbi had been part of that he would have chosen to forgo if he could do it all again, it was also obvious to Rabbi Wallis that he had learned many lessons from those days of challenges. Lessons that had stood him in good stead throughout the years; lessons that taught him to never back down if the mission was important enough.

Yet the contact between the two of them was infrequent. How could it have been otherwise?

David was in the Mob.

His friend Joe was a rabbi.

Two very separate lives with nothing in common and no frame of reference to connect them.

Then something happened during the mid-1990's to cause Rabbi Wallis to remember the power of friendship and to realize anew just how close they still were despite the time that had elapsed.

♦ ♦ ♦

Chaim Kellerman (not his real name) was a longtime supporter and friend of Arachim. Rabbi Wallis met him at the first seminar Arachim held in New York. They hit it off and a close relationship developed. A resident of Monsey, New York, Kellerman owns a thriving jewelry business on 47th Street in the city and contributes financially to Arachim whenever he can. The '90's were the glory years for many Jewish businessmen. The recession was over, the money was coming in faster than it could be printed, and the businesses on 47th Street gave out charity with an open hand. It was during a fund-raising trip to the States that the CEO of Arachim dropped in to see Kellerman in his sparkling store. Entering the establishment he was struck by the beauty and glow that hit him from every angle. Endless mirrors bounced the diamonds' rays in every direction and recessed fixtures kept the store's lighting muted yet welcoming.

The moment he caught sight of his old friend sitting behind a counter, Rabbi Wallis could see that he was downcast and upset about something.

Rabbi Yossi Wallis is not the type of person to beat around the bush.

"What's wrong, Reb Chaim?"

"I was robbed this morning."

"What, when?"

"A few hours ago. Some gangster ripped me off."

"What happened?"

"A guy I never saw before walked into the store. Asked to see some samples of my finest pieces. I unrolled a few trays filled with very expensive goods for him to study."

"But how did he get out of the store with all the jewelry?"

"The safe was opened at the back of the store. I didn't feel comfortable leaving it all exposed like that, so I walked over to close it. It took less than a minute. The second it was locked, I turned around to check on my customer and saw that he had disappeared, and that he'd taken the trays along with him. I ran to the doorway and out to the street, but he was gone; there must have been a getaway car waiting for him. I'm down a couple of hundred thousand dollars now. Insurance will help, but it won't get anywhere near covering the loss. And it takes months, maybe longer, to get the insurance funds."

He spread his hands and looked at Rabbi Wallis, eyes filled with desperation.

"I don't know what to do. Tell me what to do!"

"What about calling the police?"

He gave Rabbi Wallis a look. "You really think the police are going to solve this? They came, took the information, and they'll file it somewhere and forget all about it. This guy was a professional. He knew exactly what he was doing."

"You think organized crime was involved?"

"That's what it seemed like to me."

"Fine. Then give me some information I can use to help you. Something. Anything."

He stared at his friend, incredulity written in his eyes.

"Rabbi Wallis, what kind of ties do you have with the Mob? I mean I know you're well connected, but this is ridiculous!"

"Stop wasting time," the rabbi told him. "Every second is precious. Did you speak to the man about anything at all? Exchange a few words, make a couple of jokes? Give me something to work with here!"

Kellerman closed his eyes and searched his memory.

"The only thing I can tell you—and I don't know how much this is going to help—is that he mentioned the Bronx during the course of our sparse conversation. If I was going out on a limb here, I would assume that the Bronx is his sphere of influence in the city. I know it's not much, but that's all I have."

"Reb Chaim," the rabbi told him, "I'm going to get you your diamonds back."

♦ ♦ ♦

Back when he'd escaped the Mafia, Joe's best friend, David, was just a kid with no particular prominence or importance in the organization's hierarchy. Sure he was tough as nails, but there were a lot of kids his age who were just as tough. David, however, proved to be more resilient than most. He stood firm and powerful, even as many other trees were knocked over by the wind, or chopped down to the ground. He rose through the ranks and by the time he hit his 50's, David was a man of prominence in the organization. Every person has their own personal road to success and for David that road led from the West directly toward the East.

As mentioned earlier, David was Russian born. Whereas Joe had left the organization, David never felt the need to run away. But his real break came with the fall of the Iron Curtain. As the USSR crumbled into a million pieces, David was sent to Russia to make contact with members of Russian organized crime. Being fluent in Russian and knowing how to talk to people, David succeeded in creating a bridge between the two organizations. He was so good at what he did that he found himself the conduit between the two separate worlds, with some "very important people" depending on him on both sides.

Bottom line, David made it. He was powerful and charismatic.

It was only natural that his old friend would turn to him now for help.

♦ ♦ ♦

"David, it's Joe."

"Joe, what can I do for you?"

"Listen, David, my friend was the subject of a hit by someone from the Bronx. The guy stole a couple hundred thousand dollars' worth of merchandise. Please help me get it back."

David was never a big phone conversationalist. His reply was a terse, "Come over."

So Rabbi Wallis did.

David's offices sat within a huge warehouse in the Bronx, from which he directed a multilevel operation. The entire area was one gigantic open space, where people sat and worked at computer stations. From his glass-walled office in the center of the room David kept watch over his empire. Before the rabbi was allowed entrance into the room, the guard at the door spoke to David, who airily waved his friend in.

There was a mahogany conference table seating 20 comfortably, a respectable captain's desk, and a deep leather swivel chair. David sat in his chair and cheerfully surveyed his kingdom. Rabbi Wallis stood out like a sore thumb in his black hat, suit jacket, and beard—the typical religious Jew lost in a sea of Mafia hirelings. David was wearing a nice pair of slacks and a pressed striped shirt. The pure white hat that he constantly wore sat beside him on his desk and he kept a lit Montecristo cigar in his mouth, the ashes of which he kept on flicking into a nearby crystal ashtray.

"Joe," he said by way of greeting, pointing his glowing cigar in his old friend's direction, "you used to be a tough guy, strong—stronger than me. What happened to you?!"

This was his standard opening line every time their paths crossed.

Shifting his short, husky frame in the leather chair, he gazed at Rabbi Wallis with a challenge in his eyes. "Do you think you could still take me down?"

Used to David's unorthodox greetings, the rabbi replied, "I could beat you with two hands tied behind my back."

"I don't think so," David replied, "but I'd sure like to find out. Why don't we begin with an arm wrestle? What do you say, Rabbi, are you up to losing an arm wrestle with your old buddy from the Bronx?"

"Put your arm on the table," said the rabbi, "and get ready to lose."

David did not want to lose the arm wrestle. Neither did Rabbi Wallis. Both of them put their considerable strength into the fight. They struggled against each other, muscles straining with effort, until Rabbi Wallis finally managed to wrestle David's arm down to the table.

David admitted defeat.

"Sit down, Joe," he said, his breath coming quickly from the effort, "and tell me what this is all about."

"It's really very simple."

David raised an eyebrow.

"A friend of mine was robbed."

"Where, when, and how?"

"His jewelry business, 47th Street, today."

"Name?"

"Chaim Kellerman."

David picked up the phone on his desk and asked one of his men to come into the cubicle. When the man entered the room, David introduced him to Rabbi Wallis.

"This is Pete," he said. "Pete's an ex-cop. Used to work for me when he was on the force. Now he's retired from the force and works for me full time."

He turned to Pete. "Put out the word that a Jew named Kellerman was robbed on 47th Street. The hit was a mistake and everything taken must be returned immediately."

The next day Rabbi Wallis got a phone call from Chaim Kellerman.

"Rabbi, something unbelievable happened."

"Go on."

"This morning, the same guy who stole the jewelry reentered my store carrying everything he stole from me the day before and placed the trays down on the counter.

"'It's all here,' he told me. 'Every last piece.'"

"I'm very happy for you," Rabbi Wallis said. "And now there's something you have to do."

"What are you talking about?"

"You have to thank my friend. The one who helped you get your jewelry back. In my friend's world, this is called 'showing respect'; in our lexicon, '*hakaras hatov*.'"

"What's the correct way to show respect to such an individual?"

"I'll set up a meeting with David at his house in Westchester and we'll drive over, and then you'll have the opportunity to thank him in person for his involvement."

"I'm ready to go whenever you set up a meeting. Your friend saved my business, I owe him a tremendous debt of gratitude!"

The rabbi called David.

"Listen, David, I'm sure we'll live to fight again. Maybe you'll even beat me one of these days, though I doubt it. Right now, however, I'm calling about something else."

"And that is—?"

"And that is, that Kellerman wants to come over to your house to thank you for your personal involvement."

"Of course, of course—" David was at his most expansive. "Come on over whenever you want—Tonight, tomorrow—Whenever's good for you."

"We'll come over tonight."

"Wonderful, looking forward. My house is your house. You're my best friend."

His booming voice filled the receiver until the rabbi had to move it away from his ear.

♦ ♦ ♦

They drove over to David's house in Kellerman's car. Reb Chaim wore a long Chassidic-type of jacket and a round-brimmed hat. He sported a full beard and *pei'os*. He looked like a rosh yeshivah and Rabbi Wallis knew that David would get a kick out of meeting another authentic *Yid*. He just hoped that he wouldn't feel the need to challenge him to a wrestling match. The drive out to Westchester gave Rabbi Wallis lots of time to update Reb Chaim on Arachim's latest achievements. Soon enough, the houses went from two-family homes to one-family homes and then, as the streets grew wider, the houses turned into mansions with substantial gaps between properties.

David lived in a residence guaranteed to make your eyes open wide. The house (or what you could see of it from behind the thick wall surrounding the property) made a statement, even surrounded by other impressive mansions. When they pulled into the driveway and stopped by the tall wrought-iron gates, two men emerged from a nearby guardhouse. There was something very serious about their expressions and Rabbi Wallis noticed that their hands were never too far away from their sides.

Reb Chaim slid down the window on the driver's side and one of the bodyguards leaned down and gave them the once-over with a penetrating gaze.

"Can I help you, gentlemen?"

"Yes, please," the rabbi replied. "My name is Joe Wallis and this is Chaim Kellerman. We're here to see my old friend David."

"Wait here."

The guard walked over to an intercom set in the gate, pressed the button, and waited for a response. He must have been told to allow them entrance, because the black iron gates with their elaborate design swung open slowly, and the long driveway lay open before them. Parking the car, they approached the front door, activating the exterior lights that illuminated the front of the rambling home. David was standing in the open front door by the time they had made it to the top of the steps. He welcomed his old friend into the house, then turned to Reb Chaim, with his arm draped over the rabbi's shoulder.

"This is my buddy," he announced grandly. "Whatever I did for you is because of him. I love this man and will do anything he needs. A friend is a friend, and I'd do anything—anything—for a real friend! We used to be in the streets together. Do you have any idea how many times I put my life in danger for this guy and how many times he endangered himself for me?"

After this declaration of brotherly love, David ushered the two men into the living room, ordering them to make themselves comfortable. Turning to Chaim Kellerman he said, "So what do you have to say?"

"Well, I wanted to thank you for your assistance."

"Don't worry about it," David roared, waving his hand in the air. "I'd do anything for Joe. He's my best friend."

David told his wife that the rabbi had come over to visit and she came downstairs to say hello. They were a fascinating couple: she was as gentle as he was rough. He reeked of the streets and the underworld and she radiated culture and genteel charm. She was the sister of one of the original members of the Louie Louies and they had been married for decades. It was a genuine case of opposites attracting each other. After she left the room, David began to gleefully reminisce to Reb Chaim about all the "good deeds" Rabbi Joe had done as a kid, until the rabbi had to remind him that all those stories had taken place in an earlier life. With a twinkle in his eye and a grumble in his voice, David paid him no heed.

"Are you ashamed of your rough-and-tumble past?" he yelled at the rabbi. "Are you ashamed of me, your best friend?"

"If I was ashamed of you, would I have come over to see you with this fine gentleman? You're my best friend and I'm not ashamed of my friends!"

Their visit ended soon afterward and as they drove through the gates and onto the suburban streets, Rabbi Wallis reflected on David and how much he still loved him even though they had traveled so far apart from each other—and how the feelings and friends of one's youth remain with a person for the rest of their life, no matter the roads they may take.

CHAPTER TWENTY-SIX

The next installment between the Mafia chief and the Arachim CEO happened a few years later.

At the story's conclusion, Rabbi Wallis's every preconceived notion would be shattered and he would come to truly understand, once and for all, that no person is beyond salvation and that it is absolutely forbidden to ever give up hope for any Jew.

♦ ♦ ♦

It all began when Rabbi Aderes was arrested on his way out of Russia. A well-known rosh yeshivah, Rabbi Aderes was guilty of a legal mistake and ended up being bundled off to a Russian prison. Of course, pressure was put on high-ranking politicians with Russian connections to try and intervene, but the Russians refused to listen to anyone, preferring to keep Rabbi Aderes incarcerated deep within Mother Russia. Nothing worked. Anyone who tried to make headway in the case was stonewalled and got nowhere.

It was around this time that Rabbi Wallis's son came over to see him. They got to talking and somehow the conversation turned to Rabbi Aderes's plight.

"Didn't you mention to me a few times that you never cut the connection with your old friend David?" Rabbi Wallis's son said.

"That's right."

"Maybe you can pull off a deal, like Rav Aharon Kotler and Irving Bunim did with Joe Bonanno during World War II, when they were trying to save a bunch of *yeshivah bachurim* stuck in Italy."

Now that was a story. A little-known piece of Jewish history, the meeting with then "godfather" Joe Bonanno and the Lakewood Rosh Yeshivah served as living testimony to the lengths Rav Aharon Kotler was willing to go to when it came to helping his nation. As his son spoke, Rabbi Wallis's mind drifted back in time to the streets of Bensonhurst of 60 years before, as he imagined the scene.

♦ ♦ ♦

It was late at night when he heard that the Rosh Yeshivah wanted to see him. When it came to a summons from Rav Aharon Kotler it made no difference what time of the day or night it was, he ran. He had accompanied the Rosh Yeshivah to meetings all over the country and to fund-raising events where the rav had raised substantial amounts of money for the Jews of Europe. They were a familiar sight over on Capitol Hill, where they lobbied in support of their project and where they met with many influential American leaders of the day. Yes, Mr. Irving Bunim was the Rosh Yeshivah's right-hand man.

It was a starry, chilly night as he left his home and got into his car. He started the engine and headed over to meet the Rosh Yeshivah. There was a light burning in one of the back rooms of Rav Aharon's apartment, and that was where the Rosh Yeshivah led him, where they sat across from each other, where Mr. Bunim waited to hear what his mentor had to say. The Rosh Yeshivah's face was luminous in the softly lit room, the whiteness of his beard offset by the creases in his forehead and the seriousness of his expression.

"My dear friend," he greeted Mr. Bunim, "we have a very pressing issue facing us right at this very moment!"

"What seems to be the problem?" inquired Mr. Bunim.

Rav Aharon stared straight into the eyes of his devoted friend and student, at the activist who didn't know the difference between day and night, and explained.

"I have received a report about a group of yeshivah bachurim who found shelter in Italy who have been taken into custody and who are in danger of being deported back to Germany, where they face almost certain deportation to the camps."

Rav Aharon's eyes were on fire as he spoke, as they were anytime there was a mission to be done. "So, Irving," he said again, "what can we do to save them?" And Mr. Bunim thought. And when Mr. Bunim thought, he always came up with an idea.

"The Mafia may be the answer," he told the Rosh Yeshivah.

"What do you mean?" Rav Aharon asked.

"You see, it's like this," explained Mr. Bunim. "The Italian Mafia is extremely powerful and influential here in America. They control businesses all over the country, from strongholds in the Bronx, Bensonhurst, Cleveland, and of course Chicago. They are the winners in every situation they find themselves in and there are never any witnesses to anything they don't want people to see. They have a hand in everything illegal, from gun smuggling to gambling to race fixing. They have thousands of politicians on their payrolls and they are the strongest loan sharks and usurers around. In short, if you are on their team, anything you need taken care of will be."

"If they are based in the United States, how does that help us? We need someone who can take care of things over in Italy."

Mr. Bunim had thought of that. "All these people were originally Italian immigrants and retain strong connections to their homeland until this very day. They speak the language among one another, shop in Italian, sing in Italian, and conduct all their business in Italian. And just as they are the leaders of the underground in this country, so too, their uncles and cousins lead similar businesses back in their homeland."

"Well then," said the Rosh Yeshivah, "let us meet with them."

◆ ◆ ◆

Through business connections that he had in the garment industry, Mr. Bunim was able to put the word out that he was looking to get in touch with the "Boss." It wasn't long before his messenger got back to him with the "Family's" response. Mr. Bunim was to go to the corner grocery store, go into the telephone booth, and wait for a phone call directing him where to go. At 3 o'clock that afternoon Mr. Bunim entered the store and made his unassuming way to the telephone booth. He closed the glass door and sat down on the scratched wooden seat, making himself comfortable as he waited for the phone to ring. At 3:15 on the dot the telephone rang. Mr. Bunim lifted the receiver to his ear and answered, "Hello."

A voice with a heavy Italian accent spoke quickly and Mr. Bunim had to strain to hear every word. "Your meeting with Mr. Bonanno is scheduled for 6 o'clock this evening at the Italian Center on 18th Avenue and 74th Street." The conversation came to a close before he was able to ask any questions. He arose, left the booth, and made his way out of the store.

♦ ♦ ♦

That evening, Rav Aharon and Mr. Bunim drove through the residential streets of Brooklyn, eventually reaching Bensonhurst, with its pizzerias and purveyors of aged cheese. Wizened Italian men sat and smoked on benches, shooting the breeze without an apparent care in the world, while others played serious games of bocce ball. It wasn't long before they reached the Italian Center. From the outside, the building appeared unobtrusive and nonthreatening, blending right in with the houses surrounding it.

They got out of the car and approached the front door.

A small plaque was attached to the wall alongside the door.

"Rubbish Removal Service."

Interesting...

They knocked on the door and a young man with olive skin and dark curly hair looked them over and then let them in. The main room was long and narrow, the floor covered in shiny tiles of black and white. Off in a corner a few men were discussing soccer. Loudly.

They were led through the room and down a gloomy hallway, eventually coming to a halt in front of an unadorned door.

Their guide knocked once, then again.

"Come in," someone said from inside.

The next thing they knew, they were waiting in an anteroom. Waiting to meet the Boss.

♦ ♦ ♦

Mr. Bunim was feeling just a tiny bit uncomfortable, knowing whose place of business they were currently visiting, but the Rosh Yeshivah smiled at him and he felt better. The few men lounging around were impeccably dressed in three-piece suits and fine felt hats. Two of them were heavily involved in a game of backgammon, glancing their way for a moment when they arrived but quickly turning back to their game. After about 10 minutes their escort came back and motioned for them to follow him, halting outside a thick wooden door. He knocked, it swung open, and once again they were scrutinized before they were allowed entrance.

There, sitting regally behind an enormous desk, was the godfather of the Italian Mafia, Joe Bonanno. Mr. Bonanno was smoking a thick cigar, inhaling deeply from time to time, exhaling clouds of smoke toward the ceiling. He was wearing a beautifully tailored gray suit and a tie with gray and burgundy stripes. He looked like a banker. A very well-to-do banker at that.

The godfather told the young Italian to exit the room and he did, leaving behind just one bodyguard at the door. Nobody spoke.

Finally Bonanno looked at Rav Aharon and said in a gravelly voice, "Well, Rabbi, you wanted a meeting and you got one. Now what's on your mind?"

Mr. Bunim translated the gangster's words into Yiddish for the Rosh Yeshivah's benefit, then spoke to Bonanno. "Would it be okay if I would serve as spokesman for the Rabbi?"

"Certainly," Bonanno replied.

Mr. Bunim proceeded to explain the dire situation facing the group of rabbis, who were in deadly danger. Bonanno listened carefully to the whole story, asking a question from time to time, but otherwise taking in every word. When Mr. Bunim finished speaking, the godfather turned penetrating eyes on the Rosh Yeshivah. Then, turning to Mr. Bunim he asked, "Who exactly is this old man sitting next to you?"

"This man," replied Mr. Bunim, "is Rabbi Aharon Kotler, the godfather of the entire Jewish nation. Worldwide."

"All the Jewish people?" asked the Mafia chief in amazement.

"That's correct."

"Tell him that I want a blessing," said the gangster, and Mr. Bunim relayed Bonanno's request to the Rosh Yeshivah. "Er vill a berachah fun der Rosh Yeshivah," he told his rebbe.

Rav Aharon calmly inspected the notorious criminal sitting opposite him and said, "Zog em, 'Er zol shtarben alt un in zein bet.'" Mr. Bunim translated the blessing into English for the godfather's benefit. "The Rabbi blesses you that you should die as an old man in your own bed."

The Mafia chief stopped for a moment, thought about the profound wisdom of the blessing, and began to laugh, visibly pleased with the Rosh Yeshivah's unique and (for him) most appropriate blessing.

"Rabbi," Bonanno said, "for a man like myself, there can be no greater blessing."

He then promised to arrange the students' complete release within the next two weeks. They took their leave with good wishes all around and were escorted back through the center and out to the street. And that would have been the end, except that it wasn't.

♦ ♦ ♦

About 25 years later, a shiny black stretch limo pulled up the drive into the parking lot of the Lakewood Yeshivah. The car came to a halt outside the building and a young man wearing a black leather jacket emerged. He went around the side of the car and opened the back doors for two gentlemen. Both were dressed as if they had just stepped out of Savile Row, in worsted suits and designer shoes. They wore sunglasses, although the day was not sunny. Their hair was gelled and brushed into place and they sported Rolexes on their right arms. They walked into the office and asked to see "the Rabbi."

Five minutes later they were sitting before the Rosh Yeshivah, Rav Shneur Kotler in his simply furnished office. The older of the two came straight to the point.

"We," he began, "that is, my brother and I, are children of Mr. Joe Bonanno of New York City. You may have heard of him." The Rosh Yeshivah nodded to show that indeed he had most certainly heard of the infamous gangster.

"Our father has recently retired from active business," continued the man, "and has handed the reins of the business over to us. Here's the thing"—the man leaned forward as he prepared to make his point—"my father is healthy and well although he approaches old age, something pretty rare for a man in as strenuous and difficult a business as his. My father always attributed his long and healthy life to one factor." Here he paused significantly before saying, "To the blessing that he received from the rabbi of this school many years ago, the man known as the 'godfather of the entire Jewish nation.'"

The Rosh Yeshivah listened in amazement as the brothers related the story of how Rav Aharon and Mr. Bunim had come to see their father so many years before and how Rav Aharon had blessed Bonanno with a long and healthy life.

"Now that we are taking over the family business," they went on, "we feel the need for a blessing for ourselves as well."

The Rosh Yeshivah turned to them and said, "Gentlemen, that was my father who gave your father the blessing. I don't have the power, although I love the story."

He saw them out of the yeshivah, a disappointed look on their faces as they climbed back into the limo. He watched it drive off with a sigh of relief and marveled at the myriad ways that his father, the gaon Rav Aharon, had managed to help Klal Yisrael, and the wisdom and fearlessness with which he did so every time.

◆ ◆ ◆

Rabbi Wallis came back to earth with a thud.

"I'll see what I can do," he promised his anxious son.

"Please, Abba, the Rosh Yeshivah's family is at their wits' end."

"I'll do my best."

"Thank you."

◆ ◆ ◆

"David, it's Joe."

"Joe, what's going on? When am I seeing you again for a wrestling match?"

"Next time I'm in New York. A couple of weeks."

"I'm looking forward."

"I called you about something else."

"What could be more important than sitting down together for a nice, long conversation about the good old days?"

"What could be more important? Getting a rabbi out of the Russian prison cell they threw him in!"

David turned serious. "What are you talking about, Joe?"

The rabbi described the case. The legal ramifications. How there was a prominent rabbi sitting in a Russian hole in the middle of nowhere.

"Did the family try the normal channels?"

"They've been trying that for a week."

"And?"

"And the Russians just stuffed him deeper into Russia."

David was quiet for a bit.

"What do you think?" Rabbi Wallis finally broke the silence.

"The first thing you have to do is tell the family that they have to pull all their lawyers off the case. No doubt the family is making too much noise for the Russians' tastes. Tell them to stand down and I'll get to work making magic."

"Okay. Will do."

The rabbi called the Aderes family and relayed David's message.

"Pull your lawyers off the case."

"Not a chance," they replied.

"This is the only way for you to get anywhere!"

"How do we know this guy has what it takes?"

It was a fair question. Rabbi Wallis called David back.

"They want to know if you really have the ability to pull this off."

"Okay. Tell them that the Russians will allow someone in to see the rabbi tomorrow. A rabbi from some group called Chabad. He will bring the rabbi food. They'll also allow a few other people in to see him."

Everything David promised came true, exactly like he said. The family believed him now. They pulled their lawyers off the case and gave David the freedom to do what he needed. It didn't take him long to arrange for Rabbi Aderes's release from prison.

When Rabbi Aderes walked out of his prison cell, Rabbi Wallis knew that he'd never doubt anything David told him ever again.

♦ ♦ ♦

The two of them met in New York not long afterward. They took seats on two opposite couches in a hotel lobby, a solid glass coffee table between them.

"You know, Joe, I never understood you at all."

"What do you mean?"

"Look, we both started out in the Organization at the same time. We had the same opportunities. But then, just when things were starting to move for us, you bailed out and joined the military. Then you ran off to Israel. You're a religious Jew. You're a rabbi. How can that be? What happened to the guy I knew who wasn't afraid of anything?"

Rabbi Wallis looked him in the eye. "I'm tougher than you are, David."

"I don't think so."

"Trust me. And anyway, didn't we go through this whole ritual last time when I came to see you at the office? If you remember what happened, I won the arm wrestle."

A waiter approached. They ordered drinks. David was in an ebullient mood.

"So if you're the same guy, then how come you decided to leave? Why didn't you stick around? And how did you of all people end up religious? How did you change so drastically? You see what's bothering me?!"

"I see where you're coming from."

Suddenly David snapped his fingers.

"I got it."

"Got what?"

"I'm leaving for a cruise to the Bahamas next week. But after that I'm flying to Israel and I'm going to stay in your home for a week or two so I can find out why you did what you did and made the choices that shaped your life."

"Sounds like fun."

"It'll be great!"

When they parted later that evening, Rabbi Wallis was looking forward to showing his old friend around Israel in general and Arachim in particular. He was excited to finally have an opportunity to show David the truth about Torah and about life—if he was really open to seeing it.

The initiative had come from David. But was he really serious about being open to the possibility of changing his life around?

That remained to be seen.

♦ ♦ ♦

Not long afterward, David's wife called the rabbi.

"Joe?"

She sounded terrible.

"What happened?"

"David was killed!"

"What?"

"We were on our cruise, and it looks like he was poisoned on the boat."

"I can't believe it! The last time we met we were sitting and talking about the future, and now he's gone!"

Rabbi Wallis couldn't get over David's death. He flew to New York that night to be with his old friend's family.

"You know something, Joe," David's wife said to him. "David changed in the last few weeks. He was talking about you all the time. He kept on saying, 'I want to understand why Joe chose the life he did.' He also started sending checks to some of the local synagogues. It was really uncanny. But he never made it to Jerusalem."

Rabbi Wallis nodded sadly, shaking his head, thinking how the *Chovos HaLevavos* writes that if a person intends to repent—really intends to do *teshuvah*—and is stopped by matters out of his control, it is considered by Heaven as if he had actually returned to Hashem.

You were almost there, David, he whispered quietly. *What a shame we didn't get started a little earlier.*

♦ ♦ ♦

David's son knew nothing of Jewish practices, including Kaddish, and the rabbi knew that if he didn't take care of it, it wasn't going to happen. He got in touch with his own son— the one who had convinced him to contact David for Rabbi Aderes's release— and asked him to arrange for someone who lived in Yerushalayim's Old City to say Kaddish at the Kosel every day. Once a month, Rabbi Wallis gave his son $100 to pay the man for reciting Kaddish.

The months passed.

Rabbi Wallis thought of David often and what could have been if he'd only had the chance to explore his heritage. It was a tragic story.

One day, a year after David's passing, Rabbi Wallis drove to Yerushalayim to meet his son and make the final payment for the Kaddish that had been said. Sitting in a parking lot and handing him the money through the open car window, the rabbi caught sight of a familiar face passing by. It was Rabbi Aderes. Talk about coincidence.

He caught his attention and Rabbi Aderes approached the car.

"This is a wonderful opportunity for me to introduce you to the man who gets the real credit for your release," Rabbi Wallis said to him.

"Is that so?"

"Yes, this is my son. It was his idea to ask my friend David to get involved."

"Well then," Rabbi Aderes said, turning in his direction, "I can never thank you enough."

"There's another thing I have to tell you," Rabbi Wallis said slowly.

"What's that?"

"David was killed."

"I'm so sorry to hear that. When did it happen?"

"A year ago. In fact, today is the final day of the year of mourning for David."

"Today is his *yahrtzeit*?"

Rabbi Wallis nodded.

“Today is the anniversary of something else as well.”

“What are you talking about?”

“Today is the anniversary of the day I was released from the Russian prison. Because of David.”

Rabbi Aderes took a deep breath.

“In the end it all came together,” he concluded. “We share an important date. On that day, in a way we were both released from prison—David and I.”

CHAPTER TWENTY-SEVEN

Dr. Shalom Srebrenik is one of the founders of Arachim. He was involved with the initial organization that fathered Arachim and was one of the speakers at the seminar where Yossi Wallis made the fateful decision to become religious. It wasn't long before the two of them had begun working together to develop Arachim into the international organization that it is today. Both Rabbi Wallis and Dr. Srebrenik are *baalei teshuvah* and both are the same age. In additional to his brilliance as a speaker, Dr. Srebrenik is an acclaimed scientist with a Ph.D. in chemistry.

One afternoon while working from home, Rabbi Wallis called Dr. Srebrenik to discuss a particular matter of policy. As everyone knows, there are times that people find themselves disagreeing with their partners over policy and matters both technical and procedural. Since both men were people with a healthy sense of self-esteem and very definite ideas about what needed to be done, they came to a standstill that afternoon. Eventually they hung up the phone, still disagreeing on the points raised.

Rabbi Wallis's mother happened to be visiting them at the time. Turning to her son, she asked, "Who was that?"

"One of my colleagues at work. Don't worry, it's no big deal."

"What's his name?"

"Shalom Srebrenik."

"*What*?" she asked, visibly surprised.

"Shalom Srebrenik," he said again.

"How old is this man?"

"About my age."

His mother continued her unexpected interrogation.

"Where are his parents from?"

"From Europe. Holocaust survivors, same as you and Abba."

"Holocaust survivors... He's your age... Yossi, I have to tell you something."

She steadied her fingers on the tablecloth.

"What?"

"Your father and I were in the same DP camp after the war as the Srebrenik family."

Now it was the rabbi's turn to look shocked. His mother knew Shalom's parents? What a strange coincidence.

"I didn't just know them," she went on. "We were friends. Good friends. We were together on the ship that took your father and me to Israel. At least, Shalom's mother was on board. She was expecting, just like I was. Her husband hadn't received a certificate and apparently wasn't up to smuggling himself aboard ship like someone else we know."

She smiled to herself, recalling her joy at seeing Yeedle Wallis in his splendid white uniform with the gold braid and the peaked cap suddenly showing up below deck, carrying a tray filled with quality chocolates and other luxury items. No, there hadn't been anyone else like her husband, that was for sure.

"You and Shalom were born around the same time, both of you at Beilinson Hospital in Petach Tikvah. Your father couldn't make a living back then because he was constantly on the run avoiding the British and smuggling weapons for the Irgun, so Mrs. Srebrenik and I shared an apartment. She went out to work, to bring home the money we needed, while I looked after both of you."

Rabbi Wallis looked around him, at the kitchen cabinets, at the stainless steel appliances, at the coffeemaker perched on a nearby counter. Everything so normal, while his mother proceeded to heap surprise after surprise on top of him. This story was becoming more and more surreal.

"You slept and played in the same crib and I changed both of you, one after the other. I took you out to play in the garden and fed you mashed bananas from the same glass jar. Our arrangement lasted until both of you were old enough to start preschool. That was when Shalom's father was finally able to enter the newly established State of Israel. After that, our paths separated; the Srebreniks immigrated to Canada, while we moved to the United States."

"Dr. Shalom Srebrenik is a *baal teshuvah*," the rabbi told his mother. "He chose to become religious later on in life, same as me. And today we are both involved in the running of Arachim."

She couldn't get over the turn of events. Neither could her son. He called Dr. Srebrenik on the phone.

"Shalom, are you sitting down?

"Should I be?"

"I have to tell you something that's going to blow your mind."

"What's that?"

"Both of us grew up together. Our mothers crossed the Mediterranean to Haifa together. We slept in the same crib, ate the same food, played the same games. We were like brothers."

Now it was Shalom's turn to call his mother.

"Mommy," Dr. Srebrenik said to her. "You remember telling me about the man who smuggled himself onto the ship that transported us to Israel?"

"Yes?"

"Well I just discovered that he is the father of Yossi Wallis, my partner at Arachim. The woman you shared an apartment with when you first arrived in Israel—the woman who fed and bathed me along with her own son—is Yossi's mother!"

Now it was Mrs. Srebrenik's turn to grow excited.

She called Rabbi Wallis five minutes later.

"Yossi, we need to arrange a reunion immediately!"

He was only too happy to do so.

The reunion took place at Mrs. Srebrenik's apartment in Yerushalayim—Dr. Srebrenik and Rabbi Wallis watching and "kvelling" as their parents shared precious memories of times long past, adventure on the high seas and days of rebuilding their lives.

And as for the two old friends, the partners at Arachim? More than ever, they felt like brothers.

◆ ◆ ◆

The following story did not involve Rabbi Wallis or his family, but it is an extraordinary one that should never be forgotten. It happened to Dr. Srebrenik's father during the darkest days to befall our nation.

Upon entering Auschwitz I today, one passes beneath the infamous metal arch with its slogan of infamy. With those few steps one leaves the world of normalcy behind to enter an alternate universe and reality. Unlike Auschwitz and Birkenau—camps that were spread out over a large area, filled with low, one-story barracks and surrounded by barbed wire that sizzled with electricity at all times to prevent escapes—Auschwitz I had the appearance of a small town. Instead of rows of low barracks, the prisoners were housed in three-story buildings constructed from brick. Today Auschwitz I has taken on the appearance of a museum, with many of the buildings filled with artifacts from those dreadful years. These include a shocking collection of hair, the tresses of thousands of Europe's Jews, a collection so vast that the display case covers the entire width of one of the rooms. There is a display of suitcases and huge piles of shoes and pots and pans and cooking utensils and even dolls forcibly taken from their tiny, doomed owners—the Nazis unwilling to give little children the gift of dying with something to comfort them.

Ironically, when the prisoners left the camp in the morning on the way to a day of brutal labor, they were accompanied by the sounds of some of the finest musicians of Europe, handpicked by the Germans to play classical music. These orchestras were also used by the Germans to brighten their long, dreary Polish evenings. After all, the culture of the "master race" could not be allowed to stagnate while they were carrying out their vital mission of brutal murder. Plays were staged, music was played, and professional magicians performed tricks for an eager audience. The performers were prisoners and the audience was their guards.

♦ ♦ ♦

Why the Germans chose Prisoner Srebrenik to play the violin on that particular day will probably remain a secret until the end of time. But the fact is that he was ordered to report to one of the squares in Auschwitz to provide musical entertainment for the "masters of the world." With no choice in the matter, the prisoner reported to the area where the German officers loitered in anticipation of the upcoming show. He withdrew the violin they'd given him from its case and, running his bow up and down the strings, gave it some preliminary tuning.

"Jew, play a song."

So many possibilities ran through his mind. He could play Beethoven or Bach, Strauss or Mozart. What should it be? One thing he knew clearly: The Germans might be under the impression that he was playing for them, but the truth was that whatever music he would play would be heard and listened to by thousands of Jewish prisoners in the nearby buildings. He went through the treasure trove of melodies that lined the libraries of his brain and tried to choose the perfect precious piece to sanctify the moment and help it transcend the starkly unbearable world they inhabited. Eventually the Germans grew impatient.

"Begin playing, Jew," one said. "What are you waiting for?"

Suddenly Prisoner Srebrenik knew what melody he had to play. Raising the violin to his chin and settling the bow correctly, he closed his eyes and prepared to create magic. Seconds later a velvety sweetness took shape in the stillness of dusk, as the sounds of perfectly formed notes effortlessly transported the listeners to another world. Srebrenik played like the virtuoso he was, his bow flying across the strings as he translated the music into a language all could understand. The German officers sat entranced, eyes closed as they swayed back and forth in time to Srebrenik's playing. The music rose through the putrid air, beauty and death intermingling in the streets of Auschwitz.

Slowly the tune wound its way to the end. The final note lingered in the dusty motes of light, as the daylight began to fade.

"*Wunderbar*," an officer called out, "excellent, perfect."

The audience of officers applauded.

"Play it again!"

Srebrenik stared at the officer in surprise.

"You heard me," the man said. "I want to hear that piece of music another time."

Behind him, the rest of the culture-loving Germans were nodding their heads in unison, agreeing that they too wanted to hear the song again.

Srebrenik raised the instrument to his chin and ran the bow over the strings. The violin responded with a primal purring sound that came from deep within, almost as if it knew what it was supposed to do without being told. The song began. A tiny sound rose from the depths, through the chill, cold, and fear. What began as a low, throaty humming rose gradually higher and higher in pitch, the violin's voice opening up until it became a roar that resounded through the stony roads, past the gallows and the courtyard where people were shot to death. The sound was pure, rich, and filled with a certain elusive majesty that bespoke finer days and happy times.

The Germans were almost dancing with ecstasy, loving every second of it. And if you closed your eyes and listened very carefully you could hear the sounds of murmured conversation going on behind closed doors on every floor and in every room. Srebrenik threw everything he had into the tune. Love. Soul. Emotion. What began with soft feeling escalated into a frenzy of active sound and high velocity: an outpouring of musical genius escaping its owner in a waterfall of sound that astounded all who had the good fortune to hear it. The song reached its climax and died away, the final notes echoing through the gas chambers and houses of burning, until they disappeared completely.

The German officer who'd asked for the encore found himself at a loss.

"I have never heard such a thing," he confessed. "This is talent of another level and variety. The music of another world."

He removed the cap from his head and scratched his carefully shaved scalp.

"Karl," he said, turning to one of his fellow officers, "have you ever heard such wondrous music?"

The other shook his head in the negative, awe in his eyes.

"Music of angels," he murmured, "music of angels."

The fact that a cursed Jew was the source of such heavenly sound didn't seem to bother the "master race," or serve in any way as a matter of contradiction or deterrent. Music was music. Culture was culture. Jews were Jews. One had nothing to do with the other.

The streets of Auschwitz I were by now completely enveloped in a darkness that was only broken by the streetlights' shallow glow. Utter silence filled the void left by the absence of music. The Germans appeared slightly drunk, their reaction to the song unexpected and bizarre by any standard. The order for Srebrenik to return to his barracks did not come. Instead he heard, "Play the song again!"

Srebrenik raised the violin to his chin once more.

Held the bow in his hand like a long-lost friend.

Turned to face his audience. They were eager, lips slightly parted in anticipation. And Srebrenik knew that it wasn't only the Germans who were feeling the magic in the cold Auschwitz night; the Jews confined to their wooden bunks were feeling it to a much-greater degree. He could sense it in the ethereal energy that emanated from every structure. And when he played, he played like a man possessed, like a whirlwind of musical energy, as if he, Srebrenik, had become one with his violin and that it was telling him what to do with his fingers and how to use his instrument to its best advantage.

He was through with small sounds now—and the violin's voice rose and soared, peaking and churning, climbing and falling, wailing one moment and howling plaintively the next. Every emotion coursing through Srebrenik's soul was immediately translated into music and brought to life. The depths of his pain, the degradation, the stripping of self, the inhumanity… But above all of that rose a feeling that outlasted all others, that took control. It was a sense of pride in who he, Srebrenik, was and what he represented, along with the rest of the Jewish people.

The final notes died away, disappearing in the thick Polish mist.

Srebrenik waited for the order. Would they ask him to carry on, or would three times prove sufficient?

"Return to your barracks," said the officer in a hoarse voice.

Srebrenik turned and went to his barracks, making his way through the neat rows of buildings until finally reaching his own, the tune that he'd chosen that evening reverberating through his mind.

He'd never forget what happened that night.

He'd never forget that Yom Kippur night in Auschwitz I. Or the song he'd been requested to play for the Germans and their Jewish prisoners three wondrous times. The song Jews around the world refer to as Kol Nidrei, and chant in utter sincerity three times in a row, just as he'd done that very night.

So it went in Auschwitz on the holiest night of the year.

With a father like this, was it any wonder that Dr. Shalom Srebrenik embarked on his particular course of life, as one of the founding fathers of Arachim?

CHAPTER TWENTY-EIGHT

Though many decades have passed since Rabbi Wallis's days in the air force, the memories are still there, sharp and crystal clear, as if they happened yesterday, instead of 40 years before.

◆ ◆ ◆

Nighttime. Planes were taking off at two-minute intervals from the Ramat David air force base in the Galil, speeding past them at Mach speeds. Destination: Damascus.

Yossi Wallis was in a helicopter, providing a nearby combat jet with radar countermeasures. On this particular mission Wallis and his buddies were serving as protection for a Skyhawk A4 that was filled with bombs meant for the Syrians. The Syrians were shooting missiles from below, trying to take down as many planes as possible. The sky was filled with the streaking light of death-dealing missiles. The helicopter detected incoming missiles aimed at the Skyhawk and tried to countermeasure, but the Syrians were shooting so many missiles that it was almost impossible to avoid being hit. It was like lethal rain that never stopped or slowed down. They could avoid three, four, five, even ten missiles, but there were hundreds of missiles filling the air. It was like a chess game in the sky, with every one of the Israeli countermeasures being answered by a Syrian counter-countermeasure and on and on with no end. The biggest challenge lay in waiting too long before jamming the enemy systems—because if you waited too long they'd latch onto you and blow you up.

♦ ♦ ♦

Noach Hertz was piloting the Skyhawk that night. The air force's first line of offense was the F4 Phantoms—multipurpose jets that could bomb the enemy and just as easily engage in dog-fights. They were first-rate combat planes. The Phantoms were followed by the Skyhawks, with their payload of bombs. Today the air force no longer uses Skyhawks except for training purposes, but back then, they were standard.

Hertz was from Michmoret, a moshav located about nine kilometers north of Netanya. He was a successful pilot, whose mission was to bomb Damascus and its outlying areas. It was Yossi Wallis's job to cover Hertz and protect him from the missiles. Down on the Syrian bases, the Russian military advisers were showing the Syrians how to counter the Israeli countermeasures.

The Russians were good. Too good.

Noach Hertz was hit and managed to eject from his jet over enemy territory. For a pilot to eject from the cockpit is extremely dangerous. The length of time from the moment he pulls the ejection levers until he is thrown out of the jet is almost infinitesimal. If the plane is heading in a downward trajectory, the pilot will normally eject safely, because there is nothing to impede his progress. But if the plane is heading upward when he presses the button, the angles of his seat will work against him, placing him in immediate danger. Hertz was banking upward at the critical moment, in preparation for bombing his target, when the missile slammed into the back of his plane, sending him into a spin and making him lose control. He immediately pulled the levers and was ejected from the plane, a move that saved his life while simultaneously cutting off one of his legs. Not being a small man, Hertz had been unable to straighten out his legs in time. He landed in Syrian territory losing blood and in critical condition.

Caught by the Syrians, Hertz was put in prison where he underwent severe torture, both physical and mental. The Syrians were infamous for willfully ignoring the Geneva Convention's rules when it came to dealing with prisoners of war. Noach Hertz was released eight months later and sent home, having been to Gehinnom and back.

Along with some of the other Israeli POWs, Hertz fought back, trying to gain a crucial psychological edge by connecting to his long-ignored heritage, there, in the darkest of prisons. Using the wax from their ears and pieces of thread from their prison uniforms, the soldiers managed to fashion Shabbos candles which they lit on Friday afternoon to remind themselves of home and of the hope they harbored of returning to Eretz Yisrael.

Upon their triumphant return home, the surge of religious feeling which the soldiers had used to comfort themselves while in captivity was in most cases relegated to their wartime experiences, to be placed inside a drawer, locked, with the key thrown away.

♦ ♦ ♦

The Wallis family became religious in the years following the Yom Kippur war and it wasn't long before they had begun to organize private classes in their home for neighbors, friends, and business acquaintances. Rabbi Wallis doesn't remember who initially invited Noach Hertz, but the pilot showed up at the Wallis home and listened to a lecture with interest. They knew each other slightly from their time together in the air force, but nothing more than that. One lecture led to another and eventually Noach became a *baal teshuvah* as well.

The friendship between Wallis and Hertz deepened, although they never discussed their wartime experiences. The phenomenon of soldiers who had gone into battle together never discussing the nightmares they had faced was very much a part of who they were, and the war barely ever came up in conversation. Sure, Yossi knew that Noach had been forced to eject from the jet after being hit by a missile and that he'd been taken prisoner by the Syrians and tortured for months—and Noach Hertz knew that Rabbi Wallis had been the radar expert who put his life in danger countless times, devising countermeasures to save the Israeli pilots and planes from being hit by enemy missiles, but they never discussed what happened during those fateful months. The closest they'd come to opening up about their wartime experiences was when Hertz pointed jokingly at his prosthetic leg and said, "It's all your fault, Yossi, you should have protected me better." It was gallows humor and didn't mean a thing.

♦ ♦ ♦

The years passed—40 of them.

Arachim had since become an international organization with seminars being held around the world. In 2013, Arachim organized a seminar in Ukraine and flew in first-class Russian-speaking lecturers from Eretz Yisrael. One of the lecturers, a man by the name of Rabbi Shimon Grillias, was a fascinating individual about Rabbi Wallis's age. The people loved him and connected to his lectures and the sheer intelligence with which he framed his answers. Wanting to get to know this man better, Rabbi Wallis found the time to take a walk with him between lectures. As they strolled through the hotel grounds engaged in pleasant conversation, Rabbi Wallis asked his new acquaintance to tell him something of his background.

"How did you become religious?"

Rabbi Grillias's face took on a serious, introspective look.

"I was a refusenik back in Russia—unwilling to compromise with the government, part of the movement that stood up to the Communists. Eventually I was allowed out of Russia and made it to Eretz Yisrael, where I found my way to Judaism."

"That's fascinating, what did you study in university back in Russia?"

"I have a degree in electronic engineering and specialized in missile systems," he replied.

Rabbi Wallis's face lit up. "I specialized in a very similar field in university and used what I studied in the Israeli Air Force," he said. "I assume you had a connection to the Russian military as well, correct?"

The other nodded. "In a very roundabout way."

"What do you mean?"

"I was never actually in the military, which is a miracle considering my educational background and the type of sciences I studied in university. Had I been in the military, even for a short time, I would have never been granted an exit visa from the Soviet Union on grounds of security."

"Meaning?"

"The army would have claimed that I knew too many military secrets and that my being allowed to leave would compromise government security. But since I was never part of the military, I was eventually allowed to leave the country for Eretz Yisrael."

"Were you connected to events during the Yom Kippur War in any way?"

"Like I said, in a roundabout way."

"Roundabout in what way?"

"While in university I was part of a group of Jewish students who were working on extremely sensitive technology—technology that would eventually be used by the Russian government to penetrate the radar systems of enemy armies."

"I know exactly what you're referring to."

Rabbi Grillias nodded again. "If you were flying over Syria during the war, I'm sure you do."

"I remember it like yesterday. The Syrians had help from the Russians just like you said. They were never able to figure out how to use the sophisticated equipment by themselves, so the Russians sent a team of advisers over to Syria to help teach them what to do."

"That's right," Rabbi Grillias replied, "the Soviet team showed the Arab soldiers how to jam the Israeli frequencies and get their missiles through the Israeli radar systems, and it was my fellow students who developed the very technology that the Russian/Syrian team was using to bring down the Israeli planes. In fact, they felt badly about this and blamed themselves for so many Israeli pilots losing their lives."

Rabbi Wallis gave a short laugh. "So basically, you're telling me that I was fighting all those battles against your friends: me fighting for the Israelis/Americans, you guys for the Syrians/Russians."

It was one of those moments when truth is stranger than fiction.

"I have to call Noach Hertz," Rabbi Wallis told him, "and tell him that I just met the man whose friends were responsible for shooting him out of the sky!"

Rabbi Wallis called Hertz when he got home.

"Noach, old buddy," he said, "I have some news for you."

"What's that?"

"Remember how you're always blaming me for the loss of your leg?"

"Yeah?"

"I just found the people really responsible for your leg."

"And they are—?"

"Jewish Russian friends of Rabbi Shimon Grillias—brilliant thinker, Russian *baal teshuvah* and *talmid chacham*, who also happens to moonlight as a lecturer for Arachim from time to time. It was his friends who developed the technology used by the Syrians in jamming our countermeasures during the Yom Kippur War."

They met a few days later at the Arachim offices in Bnei Brak: the Russian scientist, the Israeli pilot, and the countermeasure specialist. *Mishpacha Magazine* sent a reporter to cover the meeting, where they reminisced about days long past and hours spent fighting some truly epic battles. And where they shared their love of the Jewish heritage that all three had somehow discovered, against all odds.

CHAPTER TWENTY-NINE

Ask anyone who runs an organization about their fund-raising stories and no doubt they'll be able to give you enough information to write a book. It's just the way it is. The Hand of Hashem is very evident when it comes to the financial element. In fact, not only does Hashem ensure that organization heads meet the people who will become their partners, in many cases, the donors are the ones who seek out the organization!

So it was with Arachim's biggest donors: Reb Pinchus and Reb Chaim Gross of Boro Park.

When Reb Chaim Gross originally contacted him, Rabbi Wallis had no idea that the New York–based businessmen would end up becoming Arachim's biggest supporters: to the tune of one million dollars a year. At their initial meeting, Reb Chaim said, "I want you to understand something about me."

"What's that?"

"I'm a very careful businessman. Before I make an investment, I scrutinize it from every angle. I never rush into anything, always taking my time to make sure that it is financially sound and stable. And it's the same when it comes to my *tzedakah* investments. I didn't call you out of the blue, Rabbi Wallis. I checked into Arachim and did my own series of investigations until I was satisfied that your organization would grant me a very profitable return on my investment, which is why I want to buy in to what you're doing. I want to be a part of your team."

Reb Chaim looked at the annual donation to Arachim as an investment in a successful business model, and treated their relationship as that of one partner to another. It took time, but over the years the relationship between Rabbi Wallis and the Gross family developed into one of close friendship, the way the best partnerships do.

Reb Chaim was the proud father of quite a few beautiful children and would send his "partner" across the ocean an invitation whenever there was a wedding. The Gross family was located in America and the rabbi lived in Eretz Yisrael, and something always seemed to come up to make it impossible for Rabbi Wallis to attend. When Reb Chaim's youngest daughter got engaged, he called Rabbi Wallis up and personally invited the Arachim CEO to the wedding. Rabbi Wallis understood that it was very important to his generous partner, and he made up his mind to try and make it happen. He had the office staff plan a seminar in New York for the same week as the wedding.

After a successful seminar and a gorgeous wedding, Rabbi Wallis decided to stay a little longer, since Reb Chaim had urged him to join the family for *Shabbos sheva berachos* at the Vizhnitzer hall in Boro Park.

During the festive meal Reb Chaim walked over to his guest, bent down, and said, "Reb Yossi, I would appreciate it very much if you would head over to the podium and say a few words."

"Chaim," Rabbi Wallis replied, "it's not for me." (This story took place in his pre-public speaking days.)

"Yossi, I need you to give a little speech. Not too long. Something."

"Chaim, you just killed my appetite."

"Please, you're my main organization. I give much of my *tzedakah* to Arachim. Please say a few words."

They sparred for a good few minutes, Reb Chaim insisting that the rabbi speak and the rabbi insisting that he didn't want to speak.

"Look, Yossi," he said at last, "let me tell you why it's so important to me that you get up and give a speech."

Rabbi Wallis waited with interest to see where he was going with this.

"Yossi, this is my last big celebration. The wedding of my youngest daughter. My wife and I have reached this incredible milestone in our lives, and I want you to stand up and tell my family what I have given Arachim through the years."

Rabbi Wallis was taken aback.

"I don't quite understand what you want me to do, Reb Chaim."

"Yossi," he replied, "all my children are sitting here right now. I want them to understand what it means to give away their money. I want them to understand what it means to give. Who better to explain this concept than you? More than that, everything I've done and all the money I've given away came about because I was influenced by my father and the way he lives his life and the way he gives charity. I want my children to understand that they too are part of this chain of giving. Who better to explain all this to my family than the person who knows it all firsthand?"

The rabbi sat in silence, finally grasping why his host was so insistent that he speak.

"And while you're sharing all this with my family," Reb Chaim continued, "please tell them how you once stood in line about to buy a whole bunch of pork sandwiches for your family and how you were saved in the merit of your grandfather—the *tzaddik* who refused to capitulate for one moment even if it meant certain death. And how your organization came about through the merit of your roots."

"Okay," the rabbi said at last. "I'll speak."

Sometimes he recalls how nervous he was at that *sheva berachos* and he laughs at himself. These days Rabbi Yossi Wallis addresses audiences of thousands of people without blinking an eye, but back then he was really nervous. He stood at the podium and grasped the top with both hands, trying to find the right words to convey the message he meant to give. He couldn't even bring himself to meet the gaze of the people sitting before him.

Instead he looked up at the ceiling and at the walls, anywhere but at the crowd of people whom he barely knew, but who were all looking at him expectantly, waiting to hear what he had to say.

It was a difficult moment.

Hashem, he pleaded silently, *place the right words into my mouth, because I have nothing to say!*

As he looked around the room, the rabbi noticed that many of the objects in the hall had been donated by key Vizhnitzer supporters. He also noticed plaques with the donors' names, designed to make it obvious what each donor had given.

Suddenly Rabbi Wallis knew exactly what to say.

"Take a second and look around the hall," he told the assembled. "Notice all the plaques. This one donated the tables, that one donated the chairs. Donations made in memory of family members long gone. A beautiful thing to do.

"Our host Reb Chaim has another kind of plaque. He gave money to turn people into *baalei teshuvah*. And since people don't walk around with signs on their backs telling everyone who donated them, nobody knows how many Jews keep the Torah today because of our host."

Then the rabbi related a few amazing stories of people who had become religious through the donations of Reb Chaim Gross—stories about people who should have had signs on their backs with his name on it. He drew his listeners into the world of Arachim—a fascinating world where miraculous moments occur every single day. The audience was spellbound. Finally he turned to address the *chasan* and *kallah*.

"I am sharing all this with you, to help you understand something very important. Your father has been doing this all his life. He's been giving and donating and assisting people. And his actions need to be continued by you, his children. This is his legacy and by following in his path you will make him proud of you. Of course, the reason he chooses to live his life the way he does is due to the influence of his father, sitting up on there on the dais, who inspired him and showed him the right path to take.

"The truth is," the rabbi continued, "I myself am only standing here before you today in the merit of my holy *zeide* who perished at the hands of the Nazis when he refused to eat a piece of pork on the day of liberation."

Then he told them about his grandfather's death and his own moment of truth as he stood on line at The Elephant Steakhouse waiting for a pork sandwich.

"Because it's all about the chain and the tradition: the *mesorah*."

Suddenly someone interrupted him. Rabbi Wallis looked over to his side to see who it was and what he wanted. It was Mr. Rubin, the bridegroom's grandfather, and he had a look of burning intensity on his face.

"Rabbi Wallis, can I ask you a question about your holy *zeide*?"

"Certainly."

"What was your *zeide's* full name?"

"Rav Shraga Feivel Winkler."

"Where was he from?"

"My *zeide* lived for part of his life in the town of Debrecen and for part of his life in a little village called Feldish," he replied, wondering where this was heading.

"What did he do?"

"He was a teacher in the local *cheder*."

Mr. Rubin's voice rang with emotion.

"I want you to know something, Rabbi Wallis. I am a student of your grandfather. I attended his *cheder* in Feldish. The school was located in his house and I remember him well, and I certainly never forgot what a big *tzaddik* he was!"

The entire hall sat quietly. Astonished. Electrified.

"Rabbi Wallis, I know exactly how your grandfather was killed. I know what happened in the camp there that day. How the Nazi offered him his entire life back for a piece of pork and how he turned down the offer and chose to be put to death to sanctify the Name of Hashem. I know this, because many of the people who witnessed what happened that day stemmed from my hometown. When they managed to return after the war, they couldn't stop talking about your *zeide* and the way he died *al kiddush Hashem*.

Every word that you said here today was accurate and I consider myself fortunate to be the *talmid* of such a rebbi."

No one could get over what had just occurred. How a stranger rose to address a Boro Park family at their private celebration and how his words had led to a full-fledged reunion! The rabbi concluded his speech with best wishes to the entire family and especially to his good friends Reb Pinchus and Reb Chaim Gross. Then he left the podium and returned to his seat, his emotions in turmoil by the unexpected encounter with his past.

On the way to his chair he had to pass beside the *mechitzah*, the partition between the men's and women's sections of the hall, where someone was waiting for him.

It was Mrs. Gross, mother of the bride.

"What a story," she said to him, "what a story!"

"And now you know everything about me."

"What incredible *hashgachah*!"

"Tell me," Rabbi Wallis asked her, "are you also from Hungary?"

"No," she replied, "my father grew up in Poland."

"My father grew up in Poland as well. Where was your father born?"

"A little village called Pavenitz."

"My father is from Pavenitz!"

The next thing he knew Mrs. Gross had sent someone over to the head table to ask her father to join them.

Her father looked at the rabbi. The rabbi looked at him.

"Rabbi Wallis, please tell me something. What is your father's name?"

"Yehuda Aryeh Wallis."

"And what's your full name?"

"Chaim Yosef Wallis."

"Who were you named after?"

"My father's father, Chaim Yosef Wallis."

"What did your *zeide* do for a living?"

"He was a teacher."

The old man's eyes filled.

"I was your grandfather's student back in Pavenitz."

Go visit a statistician. Ask him to figure out the mathematical odds for what happened that day. What are the chances that Chaim Gross of Boro Park would seek out Rabbi Yossi Wallis and become his biggest supporter? What are the chances that Rabbi Yossi Wallis, CEO of Arachim, would attend a Gross family *sheva berachos*, stand up to speak, and discover in the hall two people sitting on the dais, not related to each other—one the grandfather of the bride, the other the grandfather of the groom—who were former students of his two grandfathers, one in Poland, the other in Hungary?

Go figure out statistically what the chances are for such a thing to happen.

But that's what happened that day in Boro Park.

CHAPTER THIRTY

One morning the rabbi received a phone call from Rav Peretz, the *rav* of Raanana. Rav Peretz and Rabbi Wallis go way back and share a very cordial and close relationship.

"Reb Yossi, we have a problem."

"What's going on?"

"I just got off the phone with a woman from Kfar Saba. She told me a shocking story and cried for my help, but I have no idea what I can do for her."

"What's the story?"

"She told me that her son, a brilliant boy, left Eretz Yisrael after successfully completing a degree at Tel Aviv University and traveled to Spain to finish his graduate studies at a university in Madrid. He was fascinated by the study of anthropology, with his specific niche being a focus on Christianity. Being that the family originally hailed from Argentina and spoke Spanish at home, pursuing an advanced degree in Spain made sense. Unfortunately he did extremely well in Spain."

"How well? And why unfortunately?"

"Well enough that the Spanish Church offered him an official position in their ranks. That would have been bad enough, but he also decided to get engaged to a Spanish girl that he met—non-Jewish, of course—and, on top of everything else, he—"

"He what?"

"He decided to convert to Christianity."

"It's worse than I thought."

"A few days ago, this young man flew back home to his parents in Kfar Saba and broke the news to them that he plans on converting and marrying his Spanish girlfriend. Though the family is completely secular, their son's decision shattered them. It's one thing to be secular. It's still another thing to marry a non-Jew. But conversion? No one had bargained on that happening and his parents are distraught. He's going to be around for a few days before returning to Spain, but he told his parents that he absolutely refuses to meet with any rabbis or to hear what any religious person has to say about his decisions. He has made up his mind and it's final. Conversion, Catholic girl, and future in the Church."

"So what happened next?"

"The mother called the *rav* of Kfar Saba, who wanted to assist her, but was at a loss how to help, since the son refused to meet with a rabbi. He did however recommend that she give me a call, hoping that perhaps I could come up with some solution."

"Which you couldn't because the boy refuses to meet with a rabbi."

"Correct."

"But if the *rav* of Kfar Saba couldn't think of an approach and you can't come up with any ideas, why do you think I'll be able to help? You just told me that he's refusing to meet or listen to anyone."

"I know, but maybe you'll be the one that Hashem sends to save the day. Please do me a favor and speak to the boy's mother. Can you do that for me?"

Of course the rabbi agreed. How could he refuse?

The mother called Rabbi Wallis a few minutes later. It was one of the most emotionally wrenching conversations he experienced in his life. She was beside herself with grief at the thought of what her son was planning on doing with his life. Rabbi Wallis sympathized with her but short of drugging the son and locking him up in a room with barred windows, he didn't really see any way of changing his mind.

"You're telling me that he's refusing to meet with anyone, correct?"

"Yes, Rabbi, but I'm still not ready to give up hope."

She burst into tears and couldn't catch her breath, and he found that his own eyes were moist as well. Here was a mother suffering the worst pain possible and there was nothing he could do to make things better or to ease the nightmare in any way. It was a terrible feeling, but he was truly at a loss. He couldn't hang up the phone; on the other hand, he had no plan to recommend. Yet though he kept explaining how he couldn't do anything to help, the mother was one stubborn woman who wouldn't back down. Eventually, Rabbi Wallis looked Heavenward and silently begged Hashem to point him in the right direction.

And like many times in his life when he needed it most, Hashem sent him the answer. An idea. A crazy idea, but maybe, just maybe, it could work.

"Send your son to the local supermarket this coming Friday at about 12 o'clock, when it's completely packed, with a long shopping list that will keep him there until I arrive. As soon as he leaves the house give me a call, describe what he's wearing, and I'll track him down for a 'chance' meeting. Then we will see what we will see."

She called the rabbi Friday morning.

"He just left the house with a list the length of the *galus*."

"How will I recognize him?"

"He has blond hair and is wearing a bright-red sweater."

"I'm on my way."

As he prepared to leave the house, the rabbi asked Sandy if there was anything they needed at the store, seeing that he was going anyway. Sandy glanced at him in shocked surprise, knowing his feelings on shopping and trying to recall the last time he'd deigned to set foot in a supermarket.

"It's a matter of saving a Jewish life," the rabbi said, explaining the temporary lapse of his lifetime aversion to supermarkets and shopping of any kind.

Sandy nodded, concerned for the boy but relieved that her husband wasn't experiencing a midlife crisis.

Rabbi Wallis drove through the Friday-afternoon traffic and crossed the invisible border separating Raanana from the township of Kfar Saba. Fifteen minutes later he was pulling into a parking spot outside the supermarket. He locked the car, found a shopping cart, and made his unassuming way into the store, acting the part of the typical shopper. Once inside, he made his way through the numerous aisles ostensibly searching for the items on his shopping list, while in reality searching for a young man in a red sweater. And he found him. His quarry was pushing a shopping cart filled with all manner of goods, and in his hands he held a list no doubt containing a dozen additional items. Apparently, his mother really wanted her son to be there long enough for the rabbi to make contact.

Feeling like a spy or foreign agent on a stakeout, Rabbi Wallis followed the blond-haired kid in the red sweater, pretending that he had no idea who he was and what he was doing there and that the only thing on his mind was carrying out his wife's directives to the letter. It took the kid a while, but he eventually found everything on his mother's list and headed over to the checkout lines to pay. The CEO of Arachim rapidly moved in behind him, making sure there was nobody standing between the two of them. Now, however, with his objective cornered and at his mercy, the rabbi found himself at a loss as to how to proceed. He was not supposed to know who this young man was. The moment he introduced himself to the man in the red sweater, he would be giving it all away.

Or would he?

Rabbi Wallis gave the matter a few more moments of thought before deciding on a course of action. Right now, he needed to find a way past the boy's outer facade and into his inner world so they could begin to talk. And so, the rabbi decided to get him angry, knowing that would probably spark a conversation between them.

"Would you mind watching my cart while I pick up a few more items?"

The rabbi guessed that the boy would be annoyed with this request, something routinely done by many people in Israeli supermarkets. This would especially bother him, coming as he was from Spain, where nobody would dream of making such a request from a fellow shopper. Scowling at him in a way that was meant to accurately convey his feelings on the matter, he acquiesced and Rabbi Wallis walked off, to pick up a jar of peanut butter from the shelf. He returned to his cart, dropped the peanut butter inside, and then headed off in the opposite direction to get a carton of ice cream from the freezer. He did this a few more times before making it clear to a very disgruntled young man that he was done.

Turning to him, the rabbi said, "You know something, I'm thinking that maybe I should take my cart to the back of the line, that maybe my behavior was somewhat immoral. What do you think?"

"Morality is something relative," the other responded, slightly mollified by the man's willingness to admit his wrongs. "It all depends on the society that you're part of."

"I don't know if I agree with you," Rabbi Wallis replied, shaking his head. "Maybe morality is an absolute; maybe we should ascribe to a unified code of behavior applicable in our lives no matter where we live or where we find ourselves?"

This led to a fascinating conversation on the topic of morality and how it should be viewed and what its role should be in an ideal world. The rabbi had been angling their conversation toward the place that he really wanted it to go and it wasn't long before his new friend was spilling the entire story of his engagement to the Spanish girl, his upcoming conversion, the fact that his parents were dead against all these developments, and how he was unwilling to discuss any of this with a rabbi—because he'd made up his mind and there was no point in having to argue it all out with anyone. Rabbi Wallis listened to him silently, never giving away the fact that he had heard the entire story already and that their meeting had not been one of random chance.

At some point they paid for their groceries, and when they were both standing outside in the parking lot near their respective vehicles, Rabbi Wallis made his final move of the day.

"Listen to me. I see that this is weighing you down and that you're not completely sure what to do, but that you don't want to have to defend your position to a rabbi."

The young man nodded.

"I have an idea. I work for an organization called Arachim. Have you ever heard of it?"

He hadn't.

"It's an organization that addresses every single question that people such as you may have. You mentioned to me that you're traveling to Eilat next week to check out a few hotels for your upcoming honeymoon. Why don't you pass through Yerushalayim on the way and stop off at one of Arachim's seminars, where you'll hear the answers to all your questions, with the advantage that you won't have to talk to anyone if you prefer not to? That might be the perfect solution. Just sit there and listen. If you like what they're saying and connect to the lecturers, stay a few days. If you don't, leave for Eilat. Nobody there has to know about your future plans or anything at all."

The young man considered the suggestion.

"You know something," he said at last. "That's a good idea. Maybe I will. This way, I'll be able to get to the bottom of all this once and for all."

♦ ♦ ♦

In the end the young man attended the seminar and liked what he heard so much that he decided to remain for the entire five days. He took a special interest in any speech pertaining to Christianity and argued passionately in favor. None of the staff were certain if they had managed to make a dent in his mindset. On the final evening of the seminar, he requested to address the assembled at the symposium, which was attended by all the seminar's participants. The organizers agreed, curious about what he had in mind. Taking his place on the stage, microphone in hand, the young man addressed the crowd.

"All of you have heard my arguments in favor of Christianity over the last few days," he began. "The truth is that I have lost. I lost my case. I lost and the Torah is right. I want to return and change my life. And because I feel that this is the only true path for a Jew to take, I want to do an external act—something that will force me to retain what I have learned here and what I now know to be genuine and true. That is why I have decided to put on a *kippah* and *tzitzit* right now!"

His declaration was the cause of a spontaneous outbreak of applause, and one of the staff hurried up to the stage with a *kippah* and pair of *tzitzis*, which he helped him slip onto his person. After everyone finished clapping and the uproar died down, the staff waited for him to descend from the stage and make way for the next speaker. But for some reason, it seemed as if he had no intention of getting off the stage.

"Please take a seat," said one of the staff, trying politely to move things along.

He refused. "I can't sit down yet."

"Why not?"

"Because I am engaged to a non-Jewish girl from Spain and if I don't end our relationship right here and now, I don't know if I'll have the strength to do so later on."

"Let me get this straight. You want to break up with your fiancée right now, in the middle of the symposium?"

He nodded earnestly, insisting that he needed a phone right then and that it couldn't wait!

"I have to do it right now and in public."

Someone brought him a phone and in full view of the seminar's participants, the would-be convert called his fiancée. The dramatic scene that followed was simply heartbreaking as he told her with tears streaming down his face that they could never marry since he was a Jew and she was not and that he was never going to convert to Christianity. The Arachim staffers standing next to him could hear her crying through the phone. But he remained resolute and unwavering in his dedication to his newly discovered truth. Finally he hung up, clearly drained by the confrontation. Once again the audience treated him to a loud ovation, while people supported his decisions using adjectives like "tremendous conviction," and "incredible determination"!

Soon everything quieted down and once again they were ready to move on to the next participant. The boy with the red sweater was given a meaningful look from those running the show, but he shook his head and told one and all that he was staying right there on the stage.

"What is it now?"

"I'm not getting off this stage until you arrange for me to go to a yeshivah for *baalei teshuvah*."

"You're preaching to the choir. There is nothing we'd like more than for you to go to a yeshivah, but it's the middle of the night right now and Arachim tries not to disturb people at 12:30 in the morning."

He was resolute and obstinate.

"I'm sorry for causing you all this trouble, but knowing myself, there is no way I can get off this stage until someone agrees to take me to a yeshivah—already tonight—otherwise I might change my mind and then all of this will have been for nothing."

He was adamant and nothing anyone said made a difference. With no choice in the matter the staffers began calling around, trying to find someone willing to come and collect this fresh *baal teshuvah*. Eventually one of the staff of Belz's Torah V'Avodah yeshivah for *baalei teshuvah* agreed to come pick him up, after expressing great surprise at the urgency they were projecting. The stubborn boy remained on the stage until a rebbi from the yeshivah showed up.

"Okay, I'm here," he announced, with a look that spoke volumes. It was clear that he thought the Arachim people were being overly dramatic.

"This isn't us," the staff explained quietly to him. "Do us a favor and get this guy off the stage!"

Together they approached the stage.

"Here's your man," he was told. "He's here to take you to yeshivah. You can get off now. All your conditions have been fulfilled."

"Not just yet," the young man said.

"What now?"

"I'm afraid that if I go home to pick up my clothing, someone will convince me that I've just made the mistake of my life and that I better change my mind about going to yeshivah before I become a fanatic. That's why I need a volunteer to go in my place, with a list of everything I need that I will prepare for them, so that everything we accomplished here over the last few days wasn't for nothing."

"You really think they'll try to stop you?"

"Look, I know that my parents didn't want me to marry a Spanish girl and they certainly didn't want me to convert to Christianity. There's no doubt that they'll be relieved at the changes in me, but on the other hand, they are secular people and they'll be perturbed by my sudden religiosity. I need to go to a yeshivah now. I need to find myself and get on the stove and cook a little. Then I'll be able to face the opposition. But not yet. Not yet."

Two minutes later a volunteer was found and the boy in the red sweater finally, finally descended the stage and left the hall with his rabbinical escort amid a sea of clapping and best wishes for the future on every side.

That was something, Rabbi Wallis said to himself. *You don't see scenes like that every day*. He knew that he would never forget being a witness to the drama of a broken engagement, combined with the fresh resolve of a brand-new life emerging from the heartbreak. It was heady stuff.

Four years later Arachim held a seminar in Mexico City for Spanish speakers. At the end of the seminar, they decided to connect the participants with members of the local Orthodox community, knowing that would provide them with the backup and strength they needed to internalize everything they'd learned over the last few days. An event was organized and members from the local *kollel* were invited to come down and meet the people. As Rabbi Wallis was enjoying cake and coffee, someone tapped him on the shoulder. Turning around, he saw a man with a beard and a black hat.

"Rabbi Wallis, do you know who I am?"

"I'm sorry, I can't recall when we last met."

"I'm the boy that you cornered at the supermarket in Kfar Saba."

"Of course I remember you," he told him, as the memories of that encounter and the seminar that followed came flooding back. "What are you doing here?"

"You sent me to yeshivah and I turned my life completely around. After I'd been religious for a while, I was set up with my wife and we got married. I wanted to learn after the marriage and in the process of searching for the right *kollel*, the idea arose of joining the *kollel* here in Mexico City. I loved the idea, because I figured that this way, I'd get a chance to help make some other Spanish speakers *baalei teshuvah*. When I heard about the event here tonight, I knew that my chance had finally arrived to pay back Hashem for all the kindness He has given me, and to begin working in the field of outreach."

Rabbi Wallis stared at the young man in wonder. Looked at a man who had come so, so close to converting to another religion and to marrying a non-Jew. Looked at a man they had been mere days away from losing—maybe forever.

Were those tears in his eyes?

If they were, would you blame him?

AFTERWORD

Writing a book about anyone involves hours and hours of research and interviews. It's a process like any other and when the process is complete, the writer and subject will have shared a unique journey together.

And so it was with Rabbi Yossi Wallis and me.

At some point in our conversations, I asked Rabbi Wallis to describe his basic operation. How Arachim works, the methodology, the business strategies, a little of the history, and his vision from way back. Or in other words, what Arachim was really all about. Understandably, he had a lot to say on the subject.

He explained that for him to give me a really complete picture of Arachim and its operations, it wouldn't be a book, it would be closer to an encyclopedia. The methods, the lecturers, the changes in style and substance through the years and decades, the dynamics, the training of additional organizations, the adaptation to various populations with their various techniques—like he said, an encyclopedia.

Still, as we talked a picture began to emerge.

We began with the Arachim operation. Rabbi Wallis explained that for Arachim to succeed in changing a person's mindset, the individual must be ready to place himself in a secure, somewhat

Arachim moments

sealed environment for a couple of days, where he will eat only kosher food, stay away from the media, remove himself willingly from his daily routine, and concentrate on deprogramming himself from the misinformation that he's been fed his entire life. And that's just the beginning: the prerequisite for the magic to begin.

He must then be willing to try and incorporate the incredibly vast array of new information that he is being handed, information that will allow the prospective *baal teshuvah* to reach a point where he will be able to genuinely consider making a change in his life.

"You have to understand something," he said to me. "Arachim is first and foremost a process of changing people. We are not a university, it's not about teaching people; it's about helping them change from secular to religious, from being people who don't keep the mitzvos, to becoming people who at least want to keep them.

"Helping a person reach such a stage cannot be done by sitting next to them on an airplane and having a conversation, or by having an argument or by using the media. It has to be a genuine, thought-out process. The person must have the opportunity to question you on every level, and you have to connect with their emotion and intellect. You have to know how to put all the pieces together. There is also the issue of timing, knowing when to present what information. Of course there's also the matter of knowing how to relate to the often unwilling spouse and to the kids, the parents, and the entire extended family—every one of whom has an opinion on the subject. It's a complicated, detailed process."

It was a challenge, and the founders of Arachim channeled all their considerable ingenuity toward the creation of a program that would address all those points.

After giving the matter a lot of thought, the founders decided that the best way to accomplish this goal was via seminars. They would provide babysitters for the children of those attending the seminars, giving the guests the necessary headspace needed to come to a decision about everything they were learning. The guests would be invited to hear several incredible speakers with plenty of time allotted for arguments: time for back-and-forth, time for the staff to challenge them and for them to challenge the staff. At the end of the seminars, the people would find themselves in a much more realistic place to make honest and valid choices.

Arachim's superbly trained staff would assist them as much as possible, even if the decision was not to change their lives around. But one thing was for certain: The seminar attendees would now be in possession of a whole new load of knowledge which they would have to live with and they would inevitably need direction. The Arachim staff would make themselves available to provide whatever support they needed.

♦ ♦ ♦

Okay. We've established that the solution lies within the seminars.

Next question: How is Arachim supposed to get all these people to attend?

The answer lies in marketing, just like in any other business. You have to market and sell the seminars and convince people to put down money and sign over a couple of days of their lives to Arachim—not so easy. In many cases, the prospective clients learn about the organization via home sessions sponsored by their friends, who hold classes in their homes and invite them to attend.

This leads to another round of questions: How much information should people be given at a home session? Should these sessions provide intellectually challenging classes on a high academic level or just whet the appetite of the participants?

Then there's the question of how to deal with the attendees once a seminar is over. They need support and people to follow up with them and ensure that they aren't drowning. It's not so easy for them to make life changes. There are a million details involved in changing things around, and that calls for serious support. What exactly is Arachim's role throughout the transition stage? All this needs systematic planning and oversight.

Every successful business has a research division that develops the product. Arachim is no exception. The Arachim R & D (research and development) team spent years creating lectures and material that would stimulate interest and help people cross the bridge from a home session to a seminar, and other material to help them actively make the transition from irreligious Jews to people who want to keep the Torah. Of course, they also created the material for follow-up to answer the numerous questions that would inevitably arise in the weeks and months following a life-altering seminar.

One of the big topics Arachim has to deal with is whether there is a Creator in the world. This is an obvious question that needs to be answered to the questioner's satisfaction. In truth, this is the most basic, universal question, one that everyone in the world asks at some point or another. Once it has been established that there is indeed a Creator, the next logical question people ask is whether this Creator has a direct relationship with His creations or not. This needs to be discussed and the Arachim staff helps them recognize the impact of Hashem on our lives each and every day. They also address questions like: Is there reward and punishment? Is there an afterlife? What does Hashem want and expect from us?

Who are we?

What makes us Jewish?

What was the process of becoming the Jewish nation?

Why are we different from everyone else in the world?

What exactly happened at Sinai?

Why do we need the Oral Torah?

What is the relationship between the Written Torah and the Oral Torah?

Is what we received at Mount Sinai the same as what we have now?

Why must we follow rabbis?

And how does all of the above fit into the daily life of a practicing religious Jew?

And then there's the question of relationships. The guests need to know the Torah's viewpoint on relationships between a husband and wife, and parents and children. They will have to reexamine all their relationships through the prism of Torah thought. All these topics are covered in the lectures, either at home sessions prior to attending a seminar, at the seminars themselves, or in the follow-up sessions in the months after the seminar, and all of the questions were developed down to the tiniest detail by Arachim's R & D department.

The scientists on staff specialize in addressing questions that have to do with their individual fields of expertise. Arachim's mathematics specialists address issues of statistics. The archeology experts deal with dates and times, relating to the history of the world and the authenticity of the Torah's historical claims. Of course, in order for the many departments to function with seamless precision, there is a need for a training department, to ensure a constant infusion of well-trained and professional staff members to the organization's ranks.

When you combine all this with the logistics and coordination of the seminars and the logistics of sending the follow-up staff everywhere they need to go, you realize how much thought and work it takes to turn Arachim into a well-oiled machine that puts out a quality product on a regular basis.

♦ ♦ ♦

Arachim's original series of lectures were written by Rabbi Zvi Inbal and Dr. Shalom Srebrenik and were developed and perfected over the years by dozens of lecturers and scholars who tweaked and rewrote the material until they arrived at what they considered the perfect formula. Trial and error was always a part of the system. The world today is extremely fluid and dynamic, and the methods and material must be cutting edge and relatable to the people coming to hear the speakers. The attention span of an average person 20 to 30 years ago was between one and a half to two hours. Today it's 40 minutes. In the past, they didn't rely on and didn't need any audiovisual assistance. Today, the audience expects visual aids and "needs" to see movement while you speak.

The Tolna Rebbe at an Arachim event

Rav Yaakov Hillel *shlita* at an Arachim event

In the past, a person who attended a university would inevitably possess a wide range of information on many topics: philosophy, history, sociology... Today, the average university graduate's knowledge is generally limited to the field that he studied, making it that much more difficult to explain new and unfamiliar concepts. When Rabbi Wallis went for a degree in engineering decades ago, he studied history and philosophy, and even vocabulary and public speaking. No more. It's a different world out there and Arachim has to adapt their material and information for the clientele of the 2000's.

◆ ◆ ◆

When Rabbi Wallis first met the staff of what would become Arachim, the operation was fairly small, offering only one seminar a year. When he walked out of that original seminar, Yossi Wallis realized: These people had an absolute knockout product on their hands! But they needed advice on how to take full advantage of their brilliant approach.

At that time Yossi Wallis was running his international business selling weapons and aircraft parts, and his mind automatically examined everything he came across in business terms. He immediately envisioned the Arachim seminar being picked up by agents around the globe; the development of a franchise; huge marketing campaigns. Why be satisfied with a local organization, when it could be just as effective worldwide?! Recognizing Arachim for the tremendous opportunity that it was, Yossi decided to join the team and help them market their product to the best of his considerable abilities. It wasn't long before Rav Chaim Greineman asked him to become CEO of the organization, and he accepted the challenge.

Having instinctively been drawn to more aggressive types of business models, he began to market additional seminars almost immediately.

"We were holding gold in our hands," he said to me, "and we couldn't afford to waste any time."

In the past, Arachim had rented out school dormitories when the students were on vacation for their seminars. Yossi challenged that decision, arguing that they needed to begin holding their seminars in luxury hotels.

Why are we contenting ourselves with holding our seminars in Eretz Yisrael, he asked himself, *when there are so many nonreligious Jews in the United States who'd be perfect candidates for an Arachim seminar!*

After their successful debut in the States (mostly among Israelis living abroad), Rabbi Wallis couldn't help wondering how the seminars would be received across the ocean in the United Kingdom. So he set a date, booked a hotel, and picked up the gauntlet. Canada followed and then more seminars along the East and West Coasts of America. From there it was but a short hop over the border into Mexico, where Spanish-speaking lecturers spoke to packed audiences. Arachim followed its southern initiative with trips to Argentina and Brazil, and then on to South Africa, where thousands of Jews were thirsting to hear Arachim's message.

Then they realized they had forgotten about Europe, so they booked seminars in Italy, Holland, Hungary, and France, meeting thousands of Jews who were hungry for information and ready to make changes in their lives. Being intimately familiar with the thousands of young Israelis just out of the army and heading across the globe to backpack in the wilds of the East, Arachim decided it was time to set up shop there as well and to give some competition to the gurus and Indian monks.

Remembering that decision, Rabbi Wallis smiles. "I said to myself, let's try and catch them while they're trekking through the East, on the prowl for something spiritual."

The opportunity was too good to miss! And so, Arachim began holding successful, sold-out seminars in India and Hong Kong.

Then they realized they had overlooked a very important part of the world. Eastern Europe was filled with thousands of years of Jewish heritage, history, and real, live Jews whom Arachim would be able to reach if they moved quickly and didn't waste time. Russian-speaking Arachim rabbis flew to Moscow and then Ukraine—and held seminars in both places—shocked and slightly overcome by the enthusiastic welcome they were given.

Through the application of that original business model, which has been modified and expanded through the decades, Arachim has moved on and grown, today operating 35 branches on five continents. With incredible *siyatta diShmaya* and with liberal consultation with the *gedolei Yisrael*, Arachim has done its best to reach our brethren, wherever they may be—the outcome of which has been a bountiful estimated 165,000 returnees to Judaism, and countless others who have been touched, affected, and impacted in one way or another, over the course of the last few decades.

♦ ♦ ♦

The social implications and ramifications of an organization like Arachim are immense and end up reaching every corner of Israeli society. For example, there was a company based out of Caesarea that imported smoked meats to distribute all over the country. The owner, being a secular Jew, had no compunction against selling unkosher products and marketed his line of pork products aggressively throughout Eretz Yisrael. When the owner of the factory became a *baal teshuvah* through Arachim, he made a decision to stop selling pork. Of course, anyone determined to buy pork would find a way. But just knowing that *treif* meat was that much less available for a while was satisfying in itself.

Or take the Halber family. The family owned a chain of restaurants across Eretz Yisrael, selling all kinds of food—many of them unkosher—at prime locations on several of the country's busiest intersections. When some family members became *baalei teshuvah* after attending Arachim lectures, one of the restaurants was turned into a completely kosher establishment. But the family members didn't stop there. Having become religious, they wanted to spread the wealth, and did so by providing space in their restaurant for Arachim to give lectures two or three times a week. In an ironic turn of events, a restaurant that had been as proudly nonkosher as a restaurant can be turned into a flagship enterprise for Arachim to spread Torah to Israelis on the road.

♦ ♦ ♦

The Arachim staff crosses paths with an incredibly diverse range of people, spanning all personality types and professions. Many of the people who walk through their doors are there because they are searching and want to find out more, but there are plenty of others who are forced into it for one reason or another. Such was the case with the restaurant owner from Yerushalayim. So deliberately secular was the restaurant owner, that he went so far as to break the city's official bylaws by keeping his restaurant open on Tishah B'Av.

Having met a girl in Holland on vacation, the restaurant owner proposed marriage, but here he ran into challenges because the Israeli rabbinate would not allow them to marry on Israeli soil. With no recourse, the restaurant owner's fiancée commenced a conversion process, and to everyone's great surprise, including her own, found herself genuinely interested in everything that she learned. Once they got to know her well, the rabbis on the *beis din* were not worried about her attitude or whether she was really ready to commit to the Jewish way of life; on the contrary, they were confident that she was ready to take on full Torah observance. Her fiancé, on the other hand, was obviously playing the system and did not inspire any modicum of trust in his assurances.

"There's no way we can allow you to convert and marry such a man," said the judges on the *beis din*. They were emphatic and wouldn't budge. The one thing they hadn't counted on, however, was her sincere desire to become a full-fledged Jewish woman.

"What can I do to change your minds and convince you of my sincerity?"

"You are not the problem," they replied. "It's your husband-to-be that makes us nervous. If someone like you, so new to Jewish practice, marries someone so estranged from Torah, there's no way you can stay religious. If you manage to convince him to attend an Arachim seminar, we promise to place the matter under further consideration. Of course, if he becomes religious, that will be the best outcome."

"I'll do my best," she replied.

Then it was up to her to convince her fiancé to attend a seminar. In the beginning he wouldn't even consider it. However, she didn't let up and after using every ounce of persuasion she possessed, she managed to wear him down.

"I'll attend a seminar," he told her, finally acquiescing, "but I won't enter any of the conferences or listen to a word of the speeches. I'll get a letter from Arachim testifying to the fact that I attended a seminar and everything will be just fine. Nobody said anything about listening to any speeches."

Then she called up Arachim.

"I want to book a place for my fiancé and me," she told the secretary who answered the phone.

"Okay."

"Just to be completely honest with you before we show up," she continued, "my fiancé is insisting that he will not take part in any of the speeches or even step into a lecture room. That's his condition for agreeing to attend the seminar."

Of course Arachim booked the two of them, hoping that somewhere along the line, something was going to change and cause the stubborn restaurateur to open up his mind just a little bit.

They came to the seminar and while she sat in on all the lectures, listening with interest and asking questions, he remained outside, smoking a cigarette, reading the paper, enjoying the fresh air, and taking more naps than he knew what to do with. On the final evening of the symposium, she let it be known that she wanted to say a few words, and her fiancé, curious as to what message she wanted to impart, decided to join the seminar participants for the first time that week. One after the other, participants got up to speak, mostly saying things the Arachim staff had been fortunate to hear countless times before. How what they heard at the seminar had changed their lives and how they were planning on changing everything and becoming religious...

Then the Dutch girl rose. And her speech was not something anyone had heard many times before.

"I chose to attend this seminar because I want to learn as much as possible about what it means to be a religious Jew. I am very sincere about my desire to join the ranks of G-d's chosen nation. But I'm not going to lie to you—I'm currently experiencing a very difficult process. There are numerous obstacles strewn in my path, and for many reasons, I have not been able to achieve what I covet with all my heart: to become a Jew."

Now she looked the assembled right in the eyes and her voice became even more serious.

"But I want to tell you all something."

A pause.

"I don't understand you people. I don't understand you people at all! I'm sitting here in the seminar and I see that all of you are Jewish people. And I also see that all of you are giving a really hard time to the rabbis here who are trying to talk to you and explain all the information which you've grown up lacking. They're doing their best to help you, to share the diamonds they possess with you, but you rebuff them, time after time. To be honest, your attitude doesn't make any sense to me at all. You have such a beautiful Torah, such a magnificent heritage, you have the option of becoming so close to Hashem, and yet you turn it all down and don't cooperate—almost as if you don't even grasp what's lying on your doorstep, just waiting for you to let it into your lives!

"I am not a Jew, yet I so much wish to become a part of your nation—to keep the Torah and mitzvot and to become close to G-d—but I'm not accepted. Can you please explain to me why we have such a difference in our approach toward being Jewish and keeping the Torah?"

The restaurant owner had been listening to every word emanating from his fiancée's mouth. He reacted without thinking, running across the room and up onto the stage.

"Give me the microphone," he said to her, and wordlessly she passed it to him.

"I want you all to know something," he said to the crowd. "For what I've just heard this woman say"—he pointed at his fiancée—"she deserves that every single one of us in this room should be paying homage to her. Why is it that none of us realize the treasure that we possess? She is so, so right and we are so, so wrong!! Hearing what I just heard is sufficient for me to start learning how to become an observant Jew. I have just made the decision this moment, to become religious and to start keeping Torah and mitzvot the way they are supposed to be kept."

And so the restaurant owner who wouldn't enter a lecture for fear that it would have an effect on his soul left the seminar religious. And the Jerusalem rabbinate, when they saw what he had taken upon himself, felt comfortable assisting the Dutch woman along the path she had chosen.

End of the story?

The couple married and the woman—now a Jew—from Holland began working for Arachim, teaching other women about *taharas hamishpachah*, the laws of family purity. As for our favorite restaurateur, he took it upon himself to drive the

Arachim speakers to their destinations every evening, sitting in on every class to make up for all the basic information he had missed in his life.

♦ ♦ ♦

Though Arachim's archives are full of success stories, there are failures too. Or what seem to be failures.

One particular seminar was attended by a doctor who was second-in-command of the orthopedic department in a prestigious hospital. Throughout the seminar, the doctor was actively involved, challenging every statement and making the speakers work hard to provide acceptable proof for everything they asserted. Clearly, here was a person with intelligence and integrity, who wanted to make sure that everything he was hearing was true before signing on the bottom line.

On Friday afternoon, while the guests were in their rooms getting ready for Shabbos, Rabbi Wallis happened to notice the doctor walking through the lobby on the way to his car, suitcase in tow. Though Rabbi Wallis had obviously seen the sight before, there is nothing on this earth that can truly prepare a person for the scene of a Jew walking away from a commitment to Torah and Hashem. Obviously there was nothing personal here, and the doctor was running away for reasons that had nothing to do with him, but seeing the guest making a run for it was something very hard for Rabbi Wallis to accept.

The rabbi followed the doctor out to the parking lot and watched him maneuver the suitcase onto the roof rack.

"Doctor," he said, approaching him, "what happened? Why are you leaving now, so close to Shabbat? Why not stay for Shabbat as well? You were here for the entire seminar and an Arachim Shabbat is really the best, most inspirational part of all."

"I'm going to be honest with you," the doctor replied. "Up until this stage of the seminar, you saw my involvement, you saw the way I argued with the lecturers and speakers. Here's the thing: I came to the conclusion that you are right and that the truth is on your side. This being the case, if I go with what I now know to be true, I will have to take some sort of practical step and maybe become religious."

"And why is that so bad?"

"I'll tell you why. I have a problem with taking such a step at this time of my life and at this point in my career. If I suddenly begin walking around with a *kippah* on my head and *tzitzit* under my shirt, if I suddenly become *shomer Shabbat*, I will be jeopardizing any chance I have of becoming the head of my department: my dream job and what I've been working toward for the last 15 years of my life."

"You mean to tell me that there's no way for a religious individual to make it to the top in your line of work?"

He met the rabbi's gaze with a frank gaze of his own.

"Not in my hospital. I've been part of the staff long enough to have seen the policies and the politics within the system. The staff members who are religious were never privy to the inner workings in the hospital and how decisions are made when it comes to staff promotions. I was always part of the discussions and I know firsthand and without a doubt that for me to show up tomorrow in the garb of a religious person means to actively kill any chances that I have for the number one job. Truthfully, Rabbi Wallis, the job means too much to me to just throw it away without a second thought. I know that if I remain here for Shabbat I won't be able to control myself from taking the big step and since I don't want that to happen, I am making the somewhat cowardly decision to leave now, while I can still escape without any major changes to my lifestyle."

"You're sure about this?"

"Yes, Rabbi, I finished all my arguments. I have nothing left in my arsenal. I have no doubt that staying for Shabbat will be the final nail in the casket and I don't want that to happen."

Rabbi Wallis watched the doctor get into his car and drive out of the parking lot and out of his life. He does not know what happened to him: whether he kept his secular lifestyle or if his conscience gave him no rest and he did what he knew to be right.

A failure? Perhaps. But Rabbi Wallis says he is sure that somewhere down the line, the doctor will live the kind of life that he knows to be right. He was too sincere, earnest, and honest to allow his financial ambitions to get in the way for long. No one can know for certain, but there's a feeling deep within him insisting that all those questions, arguments, and discussions were not for nothing.

Maybe one day they'll find out. Until then, however, he doesn't consider the time the doctor spent with them a "failure." Instead, he chooses to look at him as someone "temporarily under construction."

◆ ◆ ◆

Of course there are questions that arise along the way. At one point, years ago, Arachim began developing a branch of the organization in South Africa. Home to a large, prominent, and active Jewish community, it seemed like a natural place for Arachim. The staff flew in, laid the groundwork, developed and held seminars, and it wasn't long before people started becoming religious. Some of these individuals were men of means and being filled with gratitude for what Arachim had done for them, wanted to help support the organization in its future endeavors. But there was a caveat. A condition.

"There are people in Israel in need of Arachim," they said, "and people around the world in need of Arachim. Both need it. But the people outside of Israel are in imminent danger of assimilation and disappearing off the map completely, as opposed to the Jews living in Israel, where for the most part, that's not really the danger. Therefore, we would like for Arachim to use funds that we will contribute to develop programs and for outreach activities outside Israel."

"You are raising a very important point," Rabbi Wallis told them, "but I cannot be the one to make this judgment call. This is a question for the *gedolei hador*."

Rabbi Wallis was meeting with these potential donors in Yerushalayim, and he suggested that they ask Rav Yosef Shalom Elyashiv for his *psak*.

Rav Elyashiv meets with Rabbi Wallis

Needless to say, they liked that idea.

It took them fifteen minutes to reach Rav Elyashiv's home in Meah Shearim. They filed into his home, the wealthy and influential men drinking in the sight of the simple apartment. There were nine individuals sitting around the table as Rav Elyashiv waited to hear why they had come.

"These men want to support Arachim," Rabbi Wallis explained to the *gadol*. "The question is whether their financial support should be directed toward outreach activities outside Eretz Yisrael—where the danger of assimilation is so strong—or whether the focus should be on *kiruv* work within Eretz Yisrael."

Rav Elyashiv considered the question for a few seconds. Finally he spoke. "Eretz Yisrael takes precedence."

One of the men couldn't control himself. "What about assimilation?"

"The greatest concentration of Jewish people in the world today," explained Rav Elyashiv, "is right here, in Eretz Yisrael. When the Jews living in Eretz Yisrael do not keep Torah and mitzvos, it's a *chillul Hashem*, a desecration of G-d's Name, and when we as a group keep Torah and mitzvos, it's a *kiddush Hashem*, a sanctification of His Name. The issue of making a *kiddush Hashem* takes precedence even over major concerns such as assimilation. Therefore, the focus of doing outreach in Eretz Yisrael must remain your number one priority."

Of course, the rest of the world has not been forgotten, with Arachim having developed branches in 37 countries. But the general policy outside of Eretz Yisrael is to initiate programming and seminars—to get the ball rolling, so to speak—and then to hand things over to people who live locally and who can take what has been done and develop matters even further.

♦ ♦ ♦

It was an ordinary Arachim event: a seminar geared for members of the academic community. There was an army officer in attendance at the seminar. The man held a high post in a select intelligence unit and was articulate, sophisticated, and sincere. Apparently he was also eminently capable of making quick decisions under pressure, because by the time the seminar had come to an end, he let the staff know that he was becoming religious.

He accepted the *kippah* and *tzitzis* offered to all *baalei teshuvah* at the seminar's concluding event, and then sought guidance in how to deal with the upcoming peer pressure that he knew would be coming his way. When a previously nonreligious Israeli enters an office wearing a *kippah*, his friends and coworkers assume that either someone died in the family or that he is coming from a religious ceremony of some kind where he had to cover his head, and he simply forgot to remove the *kippah* afterward.

Before the brilliant analyst left the seminar and returned to his base, the Arachim staff sat him down and had a serious conversation with him.

"There's one thing you absolutely cannot do," he was told.

"What's that?"

"Never argue about religion with the people you know. When they begin interrogating you after your big change, do not attempt to convince them that your path is the correct one."

"Why not?"

"Because you aren't equipped with enough information. It will be a losing battle."

"So what should I do?"

"Tell them that this is what you decided to do because it made sense to you. If they press you for more details, tell them you'll be happy to set up a sample class on the base so that they could see for themselves why you made the decision you did."

This in fact is exactly what occurred. The officer entered his intelligence unit at the army base wearing a *kippah* and everyone had something to say. When he wouldn't rise to their bait and argue with them, they asked him respectfully to explain what happened to him, at which point he offered to set up a class for them so they could see for themselves. And because they were a bunch of brilliant officers with degrees in statistics and mathematics and were eager to disprove anything they considered nonsense, they asked their friend to set up a class for them at the base.

The trouble started when he tried to arrange the meeting and met with a refusal from the higher-ups. The reason: no rabbis were allowed into the base other than rabbis working for the military rabbinate. The military officer then called up Rabbi Wallis and told him about the wall he had run into.

"Here's an idea," said Rabbi Wallis.

"What's that?"

"Ask the officer who refused you if military law allows you to bring a civilian comedian to the base, or if the comedian has to be affiliated with the military as well."

He called back a few minutes later to say that any comedian was fine.

"If that's the case, there's not going to be a problem."

"Why? Which comedian will you bring?"

"None other than Rabbi Uri Zohar."

"You're devious, Rabbi."

"You know it."

Bringing the incomparable Uri Zohar to address a bunch of secular intelligence officers was an inspired move. Though getting on in years, Rabbi Uri Zohar was still famous throughout Eretz Yisrael as the director of several films that had a cult following, despite the fact that they had been produced in the '70's. Zohar was known as the first filmmaker to win the Israel Prize, which he promptly declined due to his disagreement with what the prize represented. When he became religious in the late '70's, many Israelis felt a sense of betrayal and expressed their outrage, perceiving him as a traitor to society and the arts. Though now a *chareidi* rabbi and religious leader, the name Uri Zohar still has strong name recognition and Rabbi Wallis knew that the promise of an upcoming visit to their army base would interest the officers.

"An Evening with Uri Zohar" was scheduled at the base's amphitheater and his arrival was eagerly anticipated by one and all. Permission had been granted. Passes were received allowing Arachim entry to the base. Disaster struck, however, when Uri Zohar called Rabbi Wallis on the morning of the big day.

"Good morning."

"Same to you."

"What's up?"

"I have a problem and it doesn't look as if I'll be able to come with you tonight."

"What happened?"

"My father's in the hospital," explained Rabbi Zohar. "Sudden thing. And I have to go there right now."

Just like that the big plan for the night fell apart. Now what? Rabbi Wallis called up his contact at the base and informed him that Zohar had been forced to cancel.

"What should we do?" asked the man at the base.

"I recommend that we carry on as if everything is normal."

"But the main speaker isn't coming!"

"I know, but since we finally managed to set this up, the last thing we should do is cancel," the rabbi explained. "I'll get on the phone and try to find a replacement. There are a whole bunch of rabbis who were entertainers before deciding to grow beards. I just need one."

But to his great chagrin, despite his intensive efforts, he was not able to find a speaker for the evening who carried the title of both entertainer and rabbi. Everyone he called was either busy or unavailable and in the end Rabbi Wallis found himself sitting at his desk unsure what course of action to take. Finally, knowing that if he canceled the event the chance of it actually happening in the future was small, he made the radical decision of bringing in a rabbi who was not an entertainer and only knew how to teach Gemara. Getting the rabbi onto the base would be difficult—Arachim hadn't been provided with a pass for him—but Rabbi Wallis had learned long before that when it comes to outreach activities, you don't have to see the entire road ahead of you; it's sufficient to take that first step and leave the rest up to Hashem. And that's what he did.

The rabbi's next move was to call Rav Eliyahu Ben Shlomo, a rosh yeshivah whom he knew. Rav Ben Shlomo was most assuredly not a comedian, but they had run out of options. Rabbi Wallis got him on the phone and asked him to accompany Arachim to the army base and to give the speech in place of Uri Zohar.

"Look," replied Rav Ben Shlomo. "I am free to make it this evening. But I'm in no way a replacement for Rabbi Zohar. I'm not an entertainer. All I know how to do is teach Gemara!"

"I know, but this is the situation right now."

"Rabbi Wallis, let me repeat myself. The only thing I will be able to do with those army officers is teach them a page of Gemara."

"Then we are going onto that base and we will entertain those intelligence officers by teaching them a page of Gemara. I have a feeling that it might be the best entertainment they've ever had."

"If you're sure about this," he said, agreeing dubiously to the Arachim CEO's unorthodox proposal.

"What Gemara are you currently teaching at your yeshivah?"

"Tractate *Bava Metzia*."

"Okay, so print up a bunch of copies of the first *daf* of '*Shenayim ochzin betallis*'* and that's what you'll teach."

* Literally translated as "two people holding on to a *tallis*"—the name of the first chapter of *Bava Metzia*.

"How exactly do you want me to teach these people Gemara?"

"Apply the Gemara to the secular world," Rabbi Wallis suggested.

"What do you mean?"

"Take the scenarios presented by the Gemara and apply them to present-day scenarios relatable to nonreligious army officers. Don't even tell them they are learning Gemara. Merely guide them through the various opinions presented by the Gemara and allow them to grasp the different schools of thought. But don't even hand out the actual pages until they're well into the class. That will have to wait until we see their reaction to the learning."

"Okay," the rosh yeshivah said, somewhat enamored by the originality of the approach.

Truthfully Rabbi Wallis wasn't really worried, having seen and experienced firsthand on numerous occasions how potent the power of Gemara is to someone meeting it for the first time. The only question was whether the army would allow them through the door and onto the base, and whether he'd be able to convince the officers to give Rav Ben Shlomo a chance once they realized he wasn't Rabbi Zohar.

No matter, they were setting out on their journey. Their job was to put that first step out. What happens after that was up to the One Above. If He wanted Arachim to succeed in its mission, then they would. End of story.

The base was located in the Sharon region and from the tight security at the gate, Rabbi Wallis knew that getting Rav Ben Shlomo inside was going to be extremely difficult. He was right. When he'd handed over the passes for himself and Uri Zohar, the soldier at the gate explained that Rabbi Wallis could enter the base, but that Rav Ben Shlomo could not, because the pass was not made out in his name. The rabbi explained that Uri Zohar had been unable to attend the event due to a family emergency and that not wanting to cancel he'd gone out of his way to find a replacement. The soldier was sympathetic, but didn't really see a way out. The impasse went on for a while with the question being shunted upward to the brass and eventually, it was decided that an exception would be made and Rav Ben Shlomo would be allowed onto the base for a one-time visit.

The two breathed a deep sigh of relief as the soldier allowed them through the gate. They had survived the first hurdle, but knowing the average Israeli's blunt personality and tendency to call it as they see it, Rabbi Wallis could already foresee their reaction when they realized that Uri Zohar had in fact been replaced by some anonymous rabbi they'd never heard of. His worries were borne out the moment they entered the hall and the assembled grasped that they had been misled—albeit unintentionally. Shouts of "Where's Uri Zohar?" filled the room and it became clear that something better be done quickly before matters got out of hand.

Heading to the front of the room, Rabbi Wallis held up his hand for silence, which was eventually achieved.

"Here's the thing," he began. "Uri Zohar's father is in the hospital and he phoned me this morning, telling me that he would not be able to attend tonight. Not wanting to cancel on all of you, I invited my good friend Rav Ben Shlomo to speak in his stead and he consented to fill in most graciously."

He held up his hands in a "What can you do?" stance, and smiled at them disarmingly.

"Look," he went on, "this is what I propose. Give the rabbi 10 minutes of your time. Ten minutes isn't a big deal, right? In 10 minutes' time, we will have a coffee break at which point you can all choose to leave or return, no hard feelings either way. How does that sound? Ten minutes, okay?"

They grudgingly agreed to the compromise.

"Okay, Rabbi, they're all yours."

Rav Ben Shlomo then threw out the first Talmudical scenario of the evening. Two people walking down the street come across an item of monetary worth lying on the ground. Both grab it at the same time. To whom does the item belong? He opened the floor to questions, comments, and reactions. They had no idea they were actually dissecting a piece of Gemara. To these intelligent people, it was a hypothetical legal situation that needed to be explored. And explore it they did. More and more of the participants spoke up and Rav Ben Shlomo fielded their remarks with expertise and flair. Eventually the room divided itself more or less along two distinct schools of thought, which fascinatingly enough reflected the differing approaches of two major Talmudic commentators, Rashi and *Tosafos*.

Rav Ben Shlomo then moved on to the next scenario and the debate raged on, with the two sides consistently keeping to their previous positions in the debate. He then widened the parameters of the debate, introducing more and more scenarios and variations on the original theme. With two minutes left to the 10-minute deadline, Rav Ben Shlomo divided the assembled into two teams of opposing positions.

"Team one will be called Maccabi Tel Aviv," he said to the first school of thought.

"Team two," he continued, pointing at the second group, "will be called HaPoel Yerushalayim."

Rav Ben Shlomo had just awarded the two sides with the names of Israel's most prominent sports teams and the assembled were satisfied at having been assigned those particular names.

"I want all of you to take a coffee break right now," he concluded. "When you return, it will be with the intention of debating your positions and convincing the opposing team of the righteousness of your opinion. One more thing, when you return, Team Maccabi Tel Aviv should sit on the right side of the room and Team HaPoel Yerushalayim should be seated on the left side."

The group of army officers rose in a noisy mass and left the room to partake of the coffee, tea, and assorted pastries that had been delivered and artfully arranged for them. As they prepared their cups of coffee, both sides were still arguing forcefully with one another, both still involved in the mental gymnastics they'd just been subjected to. They were animated and alive and still completely clueless that they were arguing over *pshat* (correct understanding) in a *sugya* (the topic under discussion). Ten minutes later almost every one of them had returned and taken their seats on either side of the room, ready and eager to defend their position. The discussion resumed as Rav Ben Shlomo guided both sides to explore additional ideas and concepts in addition to those already in play.

"*Chevrah*," he finally interjected, his voice cutting through the excited buzz, "here's a suggestion. How about changing your names from Maccabi and HaPoel to Team Rashi and Team Tosafos? Are you agreeable?"

They were.

If you would have entered the hall on that army base and disregarded the fact that not one attendee was wearing a *kippah* on his head, you could have been forgiven for imagining yourself among yeshivah students of the highest caliber, so intense were their arguments.

Eventually Rabbi Wallis spoke quietly to the rosh yeshivah.

"Maybe hand out the copies of the Gemara now and begin explaining the structure of the page: who's who. Rashi, *Tosafos*. Where they're located on the page. The history of the Talmud. Who wrote the Mishnah, who wrote the Gemara. When were they written and where. Give them a little introduction to the thousands of years of Jewish erudition and knowledge they are holding in their hands."

Rav Ben Shlomo gave them a detailed explanation in what they had been involved with for the last 40 minutes.

"You have all just been studying Gemara," he said, "and now you know what the teenagers study in yeshivos around the country every single day."

"What? This is what they do in yeshivah?!" The officers were taken aback.

"Precisely this."

"All the students? From what age do they start learning all of this? Thirteen? Fifteen? Eighteen?"

"All of the above."

"You mean to say that every single yeshivah student is studying the same books in the yeshivos and age doesn't matter and mental abilities don't matter?"

The rosh yeshivah nodded. "Essentially that's correct."

"How can a 12-year-old in elementary school and an 80-year-old professor study the exact same thing?"

"Obviously there are levels of learning with plenty of room to delve deeper and deeper. You can study the same pages of Gemara in a more complicated, more sophisticated manner, but yes, all of Klal Yisrael are studying the same *sugyot* and everyone finds their niche. Allow me to give you an example of how a Talmudic scholar can take it up to the next level."

Rav Ben Shlomo then proceeded to share some of what the early commentators had to add on the *sugya*, and after he'd dazzled them with five different questions and answers, he quoted a few of the less complex latter-day commentators for them to chew over.

Now they were all mixed up.

"Rabbi," one of the officers said, "can you tell us, on the Talmudical scale from young student to postdoctorate, where we would be ranked?"

Rav Ben Shlomo looked at his coconspirator, a twinkle in his eye.

"What do you think?" Rabbi Wallis whispered to him.

"I don't think they are higher than sixth or seventh graders."

"Don't tell them that." These army officers were the top of the line. Brilliant people. University graduates. Some of them held master's degrees in the fields of statistics and mathematics. The majority sitting in the room held very highly of themselves. To hear the rabbi say that they were on the level of a sixth grader would not go over well.

"Have a little mercy, please," Rabbi Wallis whispered.

He relented.

"You'd be on the level of ninth graders," he told them.

"Impossible," they said. "Do you know who we are and what we've done?!"

"Okay," the Rosh Yeshivah replied, "you boys want to see what a B.A. is for a yeshivah student? What a master's is? No problem."

He then proceeded to raise all sorts of halachic issues that could be derived from what they had discussed. He also quoted a wide range of complex yet practical rules, such as *migo* and *kal vachomer*. To say that the officers were both overwhelmed and impressed would be an understatement. With the hour allocated to the lecture drawing to a close, they were faced with a roomful of officers clamoring to continue the class.

Standing up in front of the group, Rabbi Wallis said, "I doubt we will be able to return to the base for another class. However, if you want to continue this fascinating discussion, all we need is for someone local to volunteer their home for weekly meetings and we're in business."

Almost immediately someone raised his hand and volunteered the rooftop of his nearby home for the coming week.

"To be continued next week at his house, same time. Those of you who want to learn more are more than welcome."

And so it was.

The class became a weekly fixture, developing into something that changed many people's lives and culminating with five or six intelligence officers ending up in *kollel* learning half a day, while furthering their military careers at the same time. Once again, the power of pure Torah learning proved to be a force with the ability to conquer the most powerful opposition.

♦ ♦ ♦

Throughout the decades, there have been any number of celebrities who have become religious through the auspices of Arachim. Some of the best and most popular soccer and basketball players have stepped through Arachim's doors and found fulfillment, as have some of the greatest experts on martial arts and even weight lifting and tennis. If Arachim needed to put together a national soccer team, it could probably do so without a problem.

"I can think of someone who can play every position, from goalkeeper to center fielder..." Rabbi Wallis says. "And every time a 'name' walked into our lives, I asked myself how I could use their presence to touch more lives."

One day, while glancing through the lists of names of those who'd attended Arachim's seminars, he came to a realization.

Arachim was swamped with martial arts experts—black belts, Dan 9, Dan 10—many of them very well known throughout Eretz Yisrael. He asked his secretary to arrange a meeting at his office in Bnei Brak.

Not long afterward, surveying the scene from the head of the conference table, Rabbi Wallis saw a room filled with experts in every branch of martial arts.

"Let me ask you a question," he said to the group. "How many years on average did each of you spend developing your skill set in China, Japan, or Korea, while specializing in tai chi or jujitsu?"

Some of them had been away from home for 10 years, living in some tiny Tibetan village high up in the mountains, devoting all their time and energy toward becoming the absolute masters of their craft. Others had spent nine years away from home, living on rice and seaweed, while studying at the feet of their "masters." Though the actual amounts of time away varied, every one of them had spent endless amounts of time "exiled" from their homes amid the wilderness of the Eastern culture and religions.

"Look here," Rabbi Wallis said to them, "you've spent such a large chunk of your lives away from Israel trying to reach your goals—trying to become the very best martial arts people in the world. And then after working so hard, and devoting the best years of your lives toward actualizing your dreams, you went and became *baalei teshuvah*. So here's a question for you: Why do you think Hashem sent you to study in Japan for 10 years, if at the end of all that time, you ended up studying in yeshivah? Why didn't He just send you to yeshivah right away, instead of having you work so hard to become the best at an art form which you don't even practice anymore?

"Let me throw out a possibility as to why you had to go through all those years of training."

They were intrigued.

"Do you know how many teenagers there are across the country training in clubs—constantly honing their martial arts skills, so that they can become like you? For these kids—and there are thousands of them—you guys are an ideal, as close to perfection as a person can get. You have trained with the best in the world, you have acquired the kind of reputations people can only dream of. I would like to reach these kids—the 16-, 17-, and 18-year-olds. I would like them to come to my seminars, but they are virtually impossible to reach, because nothing interests them other than working out and becoming the best black belts in the world.

"But you will be the ticket.

"We'll use you to draw them in. Arachim will create martial arts retreats, advertising your names as the big draw for the thousands of Israelis who worship at the altar of martial arts. When the kids hear that you will be attending the retreat—and that you will be delivering workshops in every one of your areas of expertise—those same kids, who were so impossible to reach, will come lining up at our doors to put down the entrance fee. Do you see where I'm going with this?"

They nodded, inspired, and even truth be known, happy at receiving an opportunity to teach and discuss martial arts (and Torah) with thousands of eager young men.

"Half the day at the seminar will be devoted to practicing martial arts. We'll have booths set up for karate, for judo, for kickboxing, and for tai chi—each booth manned by one of you, our resident experts, who will serve as the masters at the retreat. The fact that you will serve as the instructors will draw hundreds of people to the seminars, and for half a day, they will get what they want and work on their various skills. But for the second half of the day, there will be Torah classes—with the theme of some of the classes centering around issues of defense and fighting. An example of this might be what is considered in halachah to be self-defense and what is not, or when is a bystander allowed to get involved in a situation where one person is using violence on another. Obviously we will provide all the standard classes we offer at our seminars. But at this seminar, the main focus will be halachic issues that pertain to people interested in the whole concept of defense and war."

They agreed and Arachim went to work developing the idea, which was eventually carried out at various locations around the country—places such as the Eden Inn in Zichron Yaakov, where there are plenty of grassy areas for practice and room to spread out. The formula proved so popular that Arachim was forced to keep on offering the seminars to the wider public who turned up in droves, anxious to meet the celebrities while honing their techniques. Of course along the way, many of the young fighters ended up becoming involved in the ultimate fight—the *milchamta shel Torah*—the war whose victory is defined by deeper and deeper Torah study.

♦ ♦ ♦

Rabbi Wallis has always found himself drawn to the fastest kind of machines. He made his money selling planes and helicopters, and loved the throaty growl of a powerful, souped-up sports car. From the time he was a young teenager, he dreamed of owning his very own Harley-Davidson, the most popular motorcycle in the world. Like many dreams that people have, it eventually came true, and today the rabbi still uses his motorcycle to get around when he needs to reach a particular destina-

Rabbi Wallis on his motorcycle

Rabbi Wallis with Rav Aharon Leib Shteinman.
Rav Dovid Abuchatzeira is standing to the left.

tion very quickly, or when driving somewhere where traffic is a major problem.

Though he tries to avoid using his motorcycle in Bnei Brak, there have been times when he had no choice. On one particular occasion, Rabbi Wallis had to see Rav Aharon Leib Shteinman to discuss an issue of great importance. He was in Raanana at the time, and the *gabbai* told him to come over immediately, since Rav Shteinman would be leaving quite soon. The only way to arrive fast enough was if he went by motorcycle, with all the inevitable attention that a black-suited, bearded man on a motorcycle in Bnei Brak would attract.

Rabbi Wallis asked the *gabbai* to check with Rav Shteinman if he should come.

"It will mean driving down Chazon Ish Street on a motorcycle," he explained sheepishly, "and walking into Rav Shteinman's home with a motorcycle helmet under my arm."

The *gabbai* relayed the question.

"Tell him that he can walk right inside with his helmet," said Rav Shteinman, "and in fact, he should know that I like him with his helmet, more than a lot of other people who only wear black hats."

♦ ♦ ♦

One morning while driving into Elad to visit one of his children, Rabbi Wallis passed another man on a motorcycle. They nodded at one another in passing—two men on Harley-Davidsons—and stopped for a five-minute chat. It turned out that the man was a mechanic and knew the motorcycle world inside out.

"How many Harley-Davidsons are there in Israel?"

"About 300 or 400."

At that moment lightning struck.

Yossi, Rabbi Wallis thought to himself, *what if we were to hold seminars for motorcycle owners?*

He immediately began planning two-day motorcycle seminars/trips—dozens of motorcycles roaring down the deserted roads of the Golan Heights and through the picturesque scenery of the Galil for hours, taking rest breaks for meals and for Torah classes throughout. Wasting no time, Rabbi Wallis pitched the idea to the Harley-Davidson Club of Israel, who loved it and were solidly behind him. It wasn't long before the concept had become very popular with the Harley drivers, who welcomed any opportunity to hit the road for an extended trip. The Harley-Davidson Club helped Arachim map out the routes they wanted to take. As for transporting the Arachim rabbis who came along to address the bikers, Rabbi Wallis merely supplied them with one of his extra helmets and chauffeured them on the back of his own Harley.

Drive for an hour or two, get off the bikes, and hear a *shiur*. Drive for another hour, someone shows up with a guitar for some singing—the atmosphere electric and exciting, with nobody knowing what to expect at any given moment. On one occasion, on Succos, the bikers' seminar stopped at a clearing where a bunch of people were waiting for them with building materials; together, they all built a *succah*. Speeches, shaking lulav and esrog, sharing a meal in the hastily built *succah*, and then back onto their bikes for the rest of an awesome "seminar on the road."

At Arachim's unique "motorcycle seminar"

Bikers the world over are heavy on the tattoos, chrome ornaments on their bikes, leather jackets, and overall feeling of brotherhood, and the entire gathering was like a surreal dream in which nothing made sense and everything made sense—all at the same time. Though some might wonder if bikers are attracted to this kind of thing, the numbers don't lie, and Arachim has already organized 10 of these trips.

And they have organized seminars on health—how to live healthy, satisfying, and productive lives, with classes devoted to topics like proper food and exercise—together with their lectures proving that the Torah was handed down to the Jewish nation at Sinai.

And they held a seminar on a cruise—rented a boat, stopped at numerous exotic locations along the route—with plenty of time to hear fascinating lectures proving the validity of Torah and its relevance to our lives in the ever-evolving world of today.

And they have presented seminars on child raising, and seminars on husband-wife relationships. Seminars on how to run a business in accordance with halachah and seminars on how to achieve peace of mind in a busy world. They even held seminars on employee-employer relationships, with companies requesting that particular seminar for their workers.

The common denominator here is that these seminars are not screaming Judaism. Instead, they are appealing to people from any number of different directions and interests, which Arachim will indulge and satisfy. But at the same time, the Arachim staff will also satisfy and indulge their listeners' unspoken desires for real knowledge and happiness, by providing them with Torah and a true comprehension of what life is really about.

Through the Heavenly assistance that has been granted them so generously by the Master of the World, combined with years of intense efforts on the parts of countless staff members both paid and unpaid, the Arachim organization has witnessed hundreds of thousands of Jews turning their backs on the way they lived their lives in the past, while choosing to become religious or to change their lifestyles in any number of ways.

And that is cause for celebration.

EPILOGUE

In retrospect, my life has been nothing short of an amazing roller-coaster ride, filled with *siyatta diShmaya*. I particularly like looking back at the host of fascinating characters who played roles in my life, some of them in a leading role, others supporting cast or making cameo appearances.

David, my best friend from the Bronx, my partner in the Louie Louies, the New York mafioso who came so close to doing *teshuvah*. The inner-city boys from the ORT school in Ashdod. Noach Hertz, the pilot who was taken prisoner of war by the Syrians, and my fellow IAF officers who accompanied me through missile-infested skies during the Yom Kippur War. Rav Chaim Greineman, who guided me personally and Arachim in general with graciousness and wisdom for decades, and the Steipler Gaon, whose *parshiyos* have remained in my *tefillin* until this very day. Rav Shach, whose wise counsel and insightful advice helped us immeasurably, and the Belzer Rebbe, who sponsored the seminar where I myself became religious.

The incredible staff of Arachim, who work tirelessly at all hours of the day and night to turn our dreams into reality. Dr. Shalom Srebrenik, whose personal journey has been so intertwined with my own. Rabbi Uri Zohar and Rabbi Mordechai (Pupik)

Arnon. Rabbi Aharon Levy and Rabbi Mordechai Neugroschel. Yossi Gevili and Shmaya the warden from Kfar Yonah. Pepe the parrot, who never stopped making people laugh and opened their hearts to their Father in Heaven.

The Yemenite family that lived in our home for months until they were able to stand on their own feet. The rabbis and the philanthropists who are always available to provide assistance when needed. Rav Elyashiv and the *rabbanim* of the Slabodka yeshivah, where I learned what it meant to *shteig* over a piece of Gemara.

◆ ◆ ◆

And what about Benny Feig, my unwilling partner back at that original seminar? Amazingly enough, the two of us are still in touch even after so many years, both of us progressing along our respective chosen paths of life. Benny kept his end of the deal. A few years after becoming religious, he moved his family to Bnei Brak, where a little research helped him discover that his grandfather had been affiliated with the Spinka Chassidus. Benny focused inward and realized that he wanted nothing more than for his entire family to join that very world. He purchased a *shtreimel*, set out to master Yiddish, and enrolled his children in the Spinka education system, where they thrived. If you happen to run into Reb Benny Feig today, you'll meet an authentically garbed Chassid from head to toe, speaking a fluent Yiddish, along with his children and grandchildren.

And then there was Ozzy—loyal dog to his master. As we became more religious, so did Ozzy. We hosted classes in our home on a daily basis and Ozzy attended every single one of them, lying beside the speakers and listening attentively in much the same way that he did in the office of the air force base commander. But as time went on and our home took on a new atmosphere, the fact that we had a giant boxer as a pet stood out more and more. We had become a *chareidi* home, but I couldn't think of one other *chareidi* home that possessed such a dog!

There was a constant stream of people coming and going: people picking up funds for projects, rabbis arriving to meet with me, my *chavrusos* from Slabodka who barely knew what a dog looked like—and Ozzy, galloping through the house…

Ozzy didn't fit in anymore.

But despite the fact that he no longer truly belonged with us, I wasn't prepared to treat him with anything less than he deserved. He'd been a loyal companion for so long and in my mind I knew that as long as he lived with us, we would treat him with love and kindness.

Yes, it was somewhat bizarre seeing the gigantic boxer walking down the street beside a bearded religious man in hat and jacket. Still, I was determined to treat him with affection and respect—just as I'd always done. Sure, this was unusual and different. But you know something? It's healthy for people to know that just because someone becomes religious, it doesn't mean that he has to change everything about himself. As long as you aren't doing anything against halachah, a person should stay loyal to who he is and not be embarrassed to enjoy the activities he always loved.

So we kept Ozzy, but it wasn't easy for us.

And then one day, Ozzy disappeared.

I asked anyone I could think of who might have seen him and came up with a blank. Wherever I turned and whomever I asked, I came up with nothing. It was as if Ozzy had simply disappeared into thin air. He had a collar, but no one called. He was well trained and obedient and should never have left, yet he did. He had been let out without a leash on many occasions, yet always returned home in the past—but not now.

Until today, I never discovered what happened to Ozzy the boxer, though I recall that giant dog with fond memories.

◆ ◆ ◆

I remember all the stories my father Reb Yehuda (Yeedle) Wallis told me about his six years under Nazi rule. How he was forced to bury dead horses and to lay railroad tracks with his bare hands, and how he watched the Germans blowing up bunkers in the Warsaw Ghetto filled with Jews who had refused to surrender.

I will never forget the fact that my father's final request was to don a pair of *tefillin* as the noose was being slipped around his neck—and how 17-year-old Yehudis, the woman who would be my mother, watched her future husband scream at a camp full of Jews that he and not the Nazis was the winner.

Otto Tybet—Chaim Michel Klar—my father's Nazi, who saved my father's life at the last possible second.

Two young survivors, my parents, the first couple married by the Klausenberger Rebbe after the war, with a *kesubah* that the Rebbe wrote from memory.

How my father joined my mother on her trip to Eretz Yisrael against all the odds, first by jumping aboard the truck, then the train, and then by stealing aboard the luxury liner in the guise of a porter. Smuggling weapons for the Irgun. The Atlit jail. Itche Meir Levin. Abba's escape from prison.

I remember all of it. All the stories. Every single detail.

I especially recall—are those tears in my eyes?—how the circle finally came to a close after midnight on a dramatic evening in Tel Aviv, when we showed up at my parents' apartment for my *tefillin*, beginning an entire family's spontaneous decision to make the return journey to Torah and mitzvos.

I cannot be prouder of my parents and their sacrifices for Hashem and His people. It's a special privilege to be their son.

◆ ◆ ◆

Mention must be made of my ancestor Rafael Vallis, who faced the fiery flames rather than betray his Jewish *neshamah*, his eternal soul. I am convinced it was my ancestor's determination and self-sacrifice for Torah that provided me and my family with the spark needed to carry on our *avodas hakodesh*—our holy work.

And of course I will never forget my righteous grandfather Rav Shraga Feivel Winkler, who chose to take a bullet in the head rather than defile his soul with the taste of pork, and whose actions eventually led me to Torah, mitzvos, and my life's goal of returning as many Jews as possible to our Father in Heaven.

◆ ◆ ◆

Through it all, my wonderful children have given me tremendous *nachas*, working with me and providing me with the encouragement needed to further our mutual goals.

And of course my biggest thanks of all goes to my dear wife, Sandy, who stood by my side through everything, supporting me in my quest to change the world and who helped me keep my feet on the ground even while I was soaring to the sky. Thank you for all the amazing years.

Rabbi Yossi Wallis
CEO of Arachim

GLOSSARY

abba (l.c.) — father; (u.c.) Father.
al kiddush Hashem — for the sake of sanctifying G-d.
am ha'aretz — unlearned individual; one not versed in Jewish law.
anusim — Jews who were forced to abandon Judaism during the Spanish Inquisition.
aron kodesh — holy ark in the synagogue, where the Torah Scrolls are kept.
avodas hakodesh — lit., *holy work*; man's service of Hashem by doing His will and observing His mitzvos.
avreich (pl. *avreichim*) — young married scholar.
baal teshuvah (pl. *baalei teshuvah*) — one who has returned to Torah observance.
bachur (pl. *bachurim*) — young man; an unmarried young man, often used to denote a student in a yeshivah.
bar mitzvah — 1. 13-year-old boy, now responsible to do mitzvos. 2. ceremony marking the religious coming of age of a Jewish boy.
Baruch Hashem — lit., *Blessed is Hashem*; colloquially, thank G-d; an expression of appreciation of Hashem's goodness.
becher — cup or goblet, esp. one used to make Kiddush.
beis din — rabbinical court.
Beis HaMikdash — the Holy Temple in Jerusalem.
beis midrash/beit midrash — house of learning or prayer.
beis haknesses/beit knesset — synagogue; house of worship.
berachah — blessing.
bris — circumcision of an infant boy, generally performed on the eighth day after birth.
chamsin — a hot desert wind.
chareidi — strictly religiously observant; a pious, G-d-fearing individual.
chasan — bridegroom.
chavrusa (pl. *chavrusos*) — study partner.
chazaras hashatz — cantor's repetition of the prayer service.
cheder — yeshivah for young children.
chesed — kindness; acts of beneficence; charitable giving.
chevrah — group, esp. a study group; friends; a social circle.
chillul Hashem — desecration of Hashem's Name; behavior that profanes G-d.
chillul Shabbat — desecration of the Sabbath.
Chumash — one of the Five Books of the Torah; the Five Books collectively.
converso — (Spanish) Jew who converted to Catholicism during the Spanish Inquisition.
daf — lit., *page*; one folio of the Gemara.
dati — religious; observant; devout.
daven(ing) — pray(ing).
dayan — rabbinical court judge.
dud shemesh — solar-heated water tank.
ehrliche Yid — (Yiddish) upright, honest Jew.
eishes chayil — 1. woman of valor; worthy wife. 2. verses from *Proverbs* recited before the Friday-night Sabbath meal.
Eretz Yisrael — Land of Israel.
esrog — citron, one of the Four Species

taken in hand during the Succos Festival.

frum — (Yiddish) religious; Torah observant.

gabbai (pl. *gabbaim*) — synagogue sexton; attendant of a Chassidic Rebbe; person responsible for the proper functioning of a synagogue or other communal body.

gadol (pl. *gedolim*) — lit., *great*; great Torah scholar; man of greatness; a term used to refer to a person of great stature; a saintly individual.

gadol hador (pl. *gedolei hador*) — spiritual leader of the generation.

Galil — northern region of Israel.

galus — exile; the Diaspora.

Gehinnom — Hell.

Gemara — (u.c.) the Talmud. (l.c.) tractate of the Talmud.

gingi — (slang) redheaded person.

giyur lechumrah — valid conversion to Judaism performed with rabbinic stringencies.

hakaras hatov — gratitude; expressing gratitude.

halachah — Torah and Rabbinic law.

halachic — pertaining to Jewish law.

Hashem — lit., *the Name*; widely used manner by which to refer to G-d.

hashgachah — Divine intervention; Hashem's involvement in every aspect of existence.

hashkafah (pl. *hashkafos*) — outlook; ideology; worldview; a concept of *emunah;* perspective.

Havdalah — lit., *separation*; prayer recited as the Sabbath or Festival comes to an end.

Ivrit — Hebrew.

Kaddish — prayer recited in memory of the dead.

kal vechomer — logical deduction; an *a fortiori* argument; one of the 13 principles of Biblical hermeneutics.

kallah — bride.

kapote — long black coat worn by certain Orthodox Jewish men.

kashruth — Jewish dietary laws.

kesubah — marriage contract.

kibbutz (pl. *kibbutzim*) — communal settlement.

Kiddush — 1. (l.c.) a reception after Sabbath-morning prayers at which Kiddush is recited and refreshments are served. 2. the blessing over wine recited before the Shabbos and Yom Tov meals.

kiddush Hashem — sanctification of Hashem's holy Name.

kippah (pl. *kippot*) — yarmulke; skullcap worn by religious Jewish males.

kiruv — (lit., *bringing near*) outreach to bring Jews to religious observance.

Klal Yisrael — Jewish people in general; the Jewish nation.

Kodesh HaKodashim — Holy of Holies; the innermost chamber of the Sanctuary.

Kol Nidrei — prayer recited at the onset of Yom Kippur evening services.

kol Torah — the sweet sound of Torah learning.

kollel — academy of advanced Jewish study, usually for married men.

Kosel, Kotel HaMaaravi — the Western Wall, remnant of the *Beis HaMikdash*.

kvell — (Yiddish) to derive satisfaction from (esp. from one's children).

lulav — palm branch, one of the Four Species taken in hand on Succos.

maabarot — refugee absorption camps, specifically in the early years of the State of Israel.

Maariv — evening prayer service.

mah nishma — (colloquial) What's new?

Mah Nishtanah — lit., *why is it different*; usually denotes the Four Questions asked at the Pesach Seder.

Marrano — Jew who ostensibly converted to Catholicism during the Spanish Inquisition but who continued to practice Judaism in secret.

mashgiach — 1. (u.c.) dean of students in a yeshivah who oversees students' spiritual and ethical development. 2. *kashrut* supervisor.

mazal u'verachah — lit., *good luck and blessings* (on you); phrase generally used to conclude a business deal.

mechitzah — partition separating men and women during prayer; partition.

melamed — 1. teacher, esp. of young children. 2. one who teaches; male teacher.

menahel — principal; supervisor.

mesiras nefesh — self-sacrifice; total and unlimited devotion.

mesorah — Jewish heritage; the received tradition.

mezuzah (pl. *mezuzos*) — small parchment scroll in a casing, affixed to a doorpost and containing the first two paragraphs of the *Shema* prayer.

migo — lit., *since*; a rule of procedure. If one makes a claim that on its own merit would be rejected (in court), it nonetheless must be accepted, "since," had he wished to tell an untruth, he would have chosen a more credible claim that is certainly acceptable (to the court).

milchamta shel Torah — lit., *a war of Torah*; an intense striving between study partners to arrive at a clear understanding of Torah.

miluim — required service in the Israeli military; army reserves

Minchah — afternoon prayer service.

minyan (pl. *minyanim*) — quorum of 10 men necessary for conducting a prayer service.

mishnah (pl. *mishnayos*) — paragraph of the Mishnah; (u.c.) teachings of the Tannaim that form the basis of the Talmud, the Oral Torah.

mitzvah (pl. *mitzvos; mitzvot*) — commandment; merit; good deed; a religious obligation; a Biblical or Rabbinic commandment.

moshav — cooperative settlement.

Moshe Rabbeinu — Moses, Our Teacher.

motza'ei Shabbos — Saturday night, following the departure of the Sabbath.

muktzeh — lit., *set apart*; an object that may not be handled on Shabbos.

nachas — satisfaction; pleasure, usually from one's children; spiritual or emotional pleasure.

neshamah — the soul.

oznei Haman — lit, Haman's ears; ear-shaped pastries traditionally eaten on Purim; also called hamantaschen.

parshiyos — parchments inscribed with Torah paragraphs and inserted into *tefillin, mezuzos,* etc.

pei'os — sideburns or side locks.

Pesach — Passover, the festival commemorating the Exodus from Egypt.

pikuach nefesh — mortal danger; a life-and-death situation.

psak — halachic ruling.

pshat — literal meaning; basic explanation.

putsch — (German) a political coup.

rabbanim — rabbis.

Rabbanut — Chief Rabbinate of Israel.

Rashi — acronym for Rabbi Shlomo Yitzchaki, 11th-century scholar who wrote the primary, widely studied commentary on the Bible and Talmud.

rav — rabbi; a spiritual leader.

rebbe (pl. *rebbeim*) — rav; rabbi or teacher.

Ribbono Shel Olam — lit., *Master of the World*; i.e., Hashem.

rosh yeshivah — dean of a yeshivah; senior lecturer in a yeshivah.

Saba — Grandfather.

sandak — person given the honor of holding the baby while the bris is performed.

Savta — Grandmother.

sefer — book, specifically a book on holy subjects or a learned topic.

Sefer Torah — Torah Scroll, written on parchment.

Shacharis — morning prayer service.

Shavuos — festival commemorating the giving of the Torah on Mount Sinai.

Shemoneh Esrei — lit., *18*; the prayer, originally 18 blessings but subsequently 19, that forms the central core of each weekday prayer service.

shlita — acronym for (Hebrew) "May he live a long and good life."

Shlomo HaMelech — King Solomon.

shteig — (Yiddish) advance in learning.

shtender — (Yiddish) a lectern.

shtickel — (Yiddish) piece; segment.

shteibel (pl. *shtieblach*) — (Yiddish) lit., room; a small synagogue, often situated in a house; small synagogue, used mainly by Chassidim.
shtreimel — (Yiddish) fur hat worn by Chassidic Jewish men.
shuckel — (Yiddish) to shake or sway.
shuk — *marketplace.*
shul — (Yiddish) synagogue.
Shulchan Aruch — *Code of Jewish Law*, compiled by R' Yosef Karo (16th century).
siddur — a prayer book.
Simchas Torah — festival honoring the completion of the yearly cycle of the Torah reading.
siyatta d'Shmaya — Heavenly assistance; help from Hashem.
succah — booth in which Jews are commanded to dwell during Succos.
Succos — Festival of Tabernacles; the Festival during which one is required to dwell in a *succah.*
sugya — (pl. *sugyot*) topic in Talmud.
taharas hamishpachah — the laws of family purity.
tallis/tallit — four-cornered prayer shawl with fringes at each corner, worn by a (married) man during morning prayers.
talmid — disciple; student.
talmid chacham (pl. *talmidei chachamim*) — lit., *student of a wise person*; person learned in Torah and Talmud; Torah scholar.
Talmud — the body of Oral Torah.
tefillin — phylacteries, leather boxes containing select Torah verses, worn by men on the arm and on the head.
Tehillim — 1. Book of *Psalms*. 2. (l.c.) psalms.
teshuvah — 1. answer. 2. repentance. 3. rediscovery of Torah Judaism. 4. response to a halachic query.
Tishah B'Av — [the fast of] the Ninth of Av; day of mourning for the destruction of the Holy Temples.
Tosafos — 1. group of medieval Talmudic commentators. 2. critical and explanatory notes on the Talmud by French and German scholars of the 12th - 14th centuries.
treif — colloquial term for nonkosher.
tzaddik — righteous man.
tzedakah — charity.
tzimmes — (colloquial Yiddish) an uproar; a tumult.
tzitzis, tzitzit — fringed garment worn by Jewish males; fringes at the corners of a *tallis.*
yahrtzeit — (Yiddish) the anniversary of a death.
yarmulke — (Yiddish) a skullcap.
Yerushalayim — Jerusalem.
yeshivah (pl. *yeshivos*) — a school of Jewish studies; a Torah academy.
zeide — (Yiddish) grandfather.
z"l — acronym for "*zichrono livrachah,*" lit., *of blessed memory*, appended to the name of a deceased righteous person.
Zohar — fundamental work of mystical Jewish thought.
zt"l — acronym for *zecher tzaddik livrachah, may the righteous person be remembered as a blessing.*

NICE GUY

BERNARD HEARNE

ILLUSTRATIONS
BY MARY PICKETT

SELECTIONS

The guy makes me mad. He asks too many questions.
Which school did I go to? I can answer that.
What jobs have I done? I can answer that, too.

Am I a nice guy? That's a hard question to answer.
I know I don't answer it well.
In the end he doesn't give me the job.

I sit in my car. I'm angry.
Who does he think he is? Mr Big Shot.
Of course I'm a nice guy,
but that's hard to tell someone.
I want to hurt Mr Big Shot.
I make plans to do bad things to him.
He'll be sorry he didn't give me a job.
He won't forget me!
But it's just a daydream. I won't do any of it.
Not for real.
I'm not that kind of guy.
I sit in my car for a long time. It gets late.
I need to get home.

On the way I see a car on the side of the road.
A man is looking at the engine.
He has oil on his hands. I see who it is.
Well, well, well, it's Mr Big Shot.
I stop. "Can I help?" I ask.

“My car broke down,” he says.
“I can give you a lift home,” I say. “Hop in.”
He locks his car and gets in next to me.
He tells me where he lives.

I take him home. He lives in a big house.
We stop outside.
"This is very nice of you," he says. "Thank you for the lift."
"Thank you," I say. I drive away feeling happy.
I'm glad I took him home. I'm glad I could do a nice thing.
I feel better now.